Birnbaum's
Walt Disney World®

STEPHEN BIRNBAUM
FOUNDING EDITOR

TOM PASSAVANT
EDITORIAL DIRECTOR

ALICE GARRARD
EXECUTIVE EDITOR

DEANNA CARON
SENIOR EDITOR

GLENN NAKAHARA
ART DIRECTOR

ELISA GALLARO
MARY MITCHELL
MARK F. SPOONAUER
PAMELA S. WEIERS
CONTRIBUTING EDITORS

TRACY A. SMITH
COPY EDITOR

ALEXANDRA MAYES BIRNBAUM
CONSULTING EDITOR

HYPERION AND HEARST BUSINESS PUBLISHING, INC.

CONTENTS

165 Disney-MGM Studios

Now's your chance to be part of Hollywood in its Golden Years. Everything from the magic of animation to the excitement of daring stunts and special effects is waiting to be enjoyed. There's also an opportunity to be part of classic TV shows and to create sound effects. We've developed some strategies for seeing this tinseltown, guaranteeing the most fun and the least time standing around.

163 Everything Else in the World

Beyond the boundaries of the Magic Kingdom, Epcot, and the Disney-MGM Studios lie 27,000 acres full of the kinds of wonders for which Walt Disney World is famous: state-of-the-art water parks, a night-time entertainment complex, a nature preserve, and a shopping village among them. So if you want to ride down watery slides, dance the night away, shop at elegant boutiques, wander among exotic birds, or "go to school" behind the scenes, this is all you'll need to find your way.

201 Sports

Walt Disney World boasts more tennis courts and golf greens than most posh resorts, and lots of other acreage is devoted to boating, biking, horseback riding, swimming, and fishing. There also are programs to help improve your skills. Here's how to combine the wide world of sporting options with the rest of the fun at WDW.

209 Good Meals, Great Times

Restaurants around the Walt Disney World property run the gamut from simple snack shops to bastions of haute cuisine. The choices are nearly endless, so we've organized them all into alphabetical, area-by-area, and meal-by-meal directories that let you know where each restaurant is located and what specialties it offers. We also tell you about the various dinner shows, where to dine with the Disney characters, where to have Sunday brunch, and where to find the best ice cream.

For Steve, who merely made this all possible.

Other 1996 Birnbaum Travel Guides

Bahamas and Turks & Caicos
Bermuda
Canada
Cancun/Cozumel & Isla Mujeres
Caribbean
Country Inns and Back Roads
Disneyland
Hawaii
Mexico
Miami & Fort Lauderdale
United States
Walt Disney World For Kids, By Kids
Walt Disney World Without Kids

A Word from the Editors

When Steve Birnbaum launched this guide back in 1981, he made it very clear what was expected of anyone who worked on it. The book would be meticulously revised each year, leaving no attraction untested, no snack or meal untasted, no hotel untried. When Steve became curious as to how efficiently the bus system ran at Walt Disney World, he dispatched an editor to spend one whole day riding buses from place to place around the resort and report her findings. (The buses did, by the way, run on schedule.)

It is experiences like these, accumulated over the past 15 years, that make this book the most authoritative guide to the World. That expertise, however, has not been achieved by our being escorted through back doors of attractions or bypassing lines, but rather by standing with all the other visitors in hopes of uncovering strategies that would allow readers to avoid the pitfalls many first-timers encounter. In one typical case, an editor waited more than an hour to take the

Backstage Studio Tour. Standing in line with notebook and tape recorder in hand, she was asked by the man behind her if there was a quiz at the end of the tour. When she explained what she was doing, he expressed surprise to learn that she was waiting with the rest of the hordes. How better, she replied, to help people like you?

For some of us, our first Walt Disney World experience dates back to 1971, the year this new "Disneyland in Florida" made its debut. At that time, there was only one theme park, the Magic Kingdom, and it could be explored easily in a few days. Early visitors will remember, too, that many attractions were still under construction. Nonetheless, for those who came, it usually was love at first sight, and we've returned again and again.

After nearly a quarter century the World— and the number of visitors—has expanded enormously. On some occasions we've encountered sweltering weather and swelling crowds, times when even the happiest of families or best of friends turn into arch-enemies for the day. At times the lines seemed endless and, in a triumph of bad planning, we managed to take in just a few attractions before dinnertime. Had we known then what we know now, we could have spared ourselves some trying experiences.

What we've tried to do in designing this book is keep you and your family from making the same mistakes. This marks the 15th annual edition of this guide, and we've learned a lot about Walt Disney World over the years. More important, we now know that even the most willing vacation planner needs detailed, accurate, and objective information to prepare an intelligent itinerary.

Anyone who takes the time to read even the outlines of the pages that follow will find an emerging pattern that fits his or her special needs and tastes; for those unwilling to exert even that much effort, we've compiled specific day-by-day itineraries for visits of varying lengths in order to protect you from yourself.

This guidebook owes an enormous debt to the special people who manage and run Walt Disney World. Despite the designation "Official Guide," we want to stress that *the Walt Disney World staff members have exercised no veto power whatever over the contents of this book.* What they *have* done is opened their files and explained operations to us in the most generous way, so that we could prepare the comprehensive appraisals, charts, and schedules that are necessary to help visitors understand the very complex workings of a very complex enterprise.

We daresay there have been times when the Disney folks are less than delighted with some of our opinions and conclusions, yet these statements all remain in the guide. Furthermore, we've been flattered again and again by Disney staff who've commented about how much they've learned from the material presented here.

As for our readers, we firmly believe that the combination of our years of experience and independent voice, together with our access to accurate, up-to-date inside information from the Disney staff, makes this book uniquely useful. We even like to think it's indispensable, but we'll let you be the final judge of that a couple of hundred pages from now.

The fact remains that this guide could never be as useful as it is without the extremely forthcoming cooperation of Walt Disney World personnel on every level. Both in the park and behind the scenes, they've been the source of the most critical factual data. We hope we're not omitting any names in specifically thanking

Kim Carlson (Parks), Robin Dickerson (Resorts), Jack Holland (Product Development), Dwight Dorr (Transportation), Greg Albrecht and Dave Herbst (Publicity), and Gene Duncan and Robbie Pallard (Photography). To Tom Elrod, Bo Boyd, Marty Sklar, Charlie Ridgway, Phil Lengyel, Wendy Wolfe, Michael Mendenhall, Laura Simpson, Robert Sias, and Diane Hancock, who do so much to make our job easier (and often possible), more thanks for their extraordinary help.

In the production of this book, we salute Elizabeth Irigoyen and Margaret Casagrande for their typesetting skills, and Laura Vitale for her keen eye in reading the final galleys. A nod especially is due to Shari Hartford, who kept our own cast of characters on schedule, and to Susan Hohl, who knows that every picture has its place, even if it gives us the runaround. We'd also like to thank our favorite off-site Disney expert, Wendy Lefkon, who edited these guides for many years and is still instrumental in their publication as executive editor at Hyperion.

Of course, no list of acknowledgments would be complete without mentioning our founding editor, Steve Birnbaum, whose spirit, wisdom, and humor still infuse these pages, as well as Alexandra Mayes Birnbaum, who continues to be a guiding light—to say nothing of a careful reader of every word.

Finally, it's important to remember that every worthwhile travel guide is a living enterprise; while the book that you hold in your hands may be our best effort at explaining how to enjoy Walt Disney World at this moment, its text is in no way cast in bronze. Walt Disney World is constantly changing and growing, and in each annual revision we expect to refine and expand our material to serve our readers' needs even better. For this year's edition, though, this must be the final word.

Have a great visit.

The Editors

DON'T FORGET TO WRITE

No contribution is of greater value to us in preparing the next edition of this book than your comments on what we have written and on your own experiences at Walt Disney World. Please share your insights with us by writing to: The Editors, Official Disney Guides, 1790 Broadway, Sixth Floor; New York, NY 10019.

GETTING READY TO GO

The key to a successful visit to Walt Disney World is advance planning. This remarkably varied complex is just too vast and diverse to allow a spontaneous visit to be undertaken with notable success—especially when you consider the rapid rate at which it is expanding. That doesn't mean that even the most casual visitors can't have some significant fun, but they may later find a host of opportunities that were missed because of the pressure of time or an absence of information. The primary purpose of this guide is to eliminate that potential frustration.

What follows, then, is intended to provide a sensible scheme for organizing a visit to Walt Disney World, one that will allow the maximum amount of enjoyment and produce the minimum level of frustration and disappointment. One of the very best ways to judge which of the countless activities in the World are most appealing to you is to have a clear idea of all that is available.

(Unless otherwise noted, all phone numbers are in area code 407.)

When to Go

where. And, most importantly, all these extras can be savored at Walt Disney World at one of its least crowded times of the year.

The Magic Kingdom, Epcot, and the Disney-MGM Studios are all decorated to the nines for the holidays, and nightly tree-lighting ceremonies are held in all three parks. Special events during this period (for which separate admission tickets are required) include Mickey's Very Merry Christmas Party, which takes place several days during the first two weeks of December. The party is held in the Magic Kingdom from 8 P.M. to 1 A.M. and features holiday shows around the park, including Mickey's Very Merry Christmas Parade, and a special finale for Fantasy in the Sky fireworks. A complimentary souvenir photograph and button, as well as hot chocolate and Christmas cookies, are included. Select holiday performances from Mickey's Very Merry Christmas Party also are staged in the park during park hours.

Epcot celebrates the season with a special Holiday IllumiNations program and nightly performances of Holidays Around the World, a chorale show complete with a candlelight processional. Special dinner packages are available for selected World Showcase restaurants. The Disney-MGM Studios features several groups that perform holiday music around the park. At the Disney Village Marketplace, a nativity pageant is performed, and the shops are all decorated for the holidays. It's also a great place to shop for last-minute presents.

The best way to take advantage of all there is to see and do at Walt Disney World during this time of year is to book a Jolly Holidays package, available from November 26 through December 21. The packages are available from two to ten nights and include admission to the Jolly Holidays Dinner Show held at the *Contemporary* resort. The show, available only with the packages, features an all-you-can-eat holiday feast with all the trimmings, as a cast of more than 100 singers and dancers, including the Disney characters, perform a festive musical extravaganza.

There are holiday receptions at all of the hotels as well, including a turn-of-the-century Christmas at the *Grand Floridian*, a seaside party at the *Yacht Club* and *Beach Club* resorts, a Southwestern Christmas at the *Contemporary* resort, and a Cajun holiday at *Dixie Landings*. Transportation is provided to each of the receptions as part of the Jolly Holidays packages. Most packages include unlimited admission to the Magic Kingdom, Epcot, the Disney-MGM Studios, and Pleasure Island. For reservations, contact your travel agent or call W-DISNEY (934-7639).

When talk finally turns to the best time to make a trip to Walt Disney World, Christmas and Easter often are mentioned, as well as the weeks that comprise the traditional summer vacation period—especially if there are children in the family. But there also are good reasons to avoid these periods, chief among them is the fact that almost everybody else goes then. And when Walt Disney World is crowded, it can be very crowded indeed. On the busiest days, visitors may wait more than an hour to see some particularly popular attractions—that's at least twice as long as less crowded times of year.

Considering both the weather and crowd patterns described in the charts that follow, optimal times to visit Walt Disney World are late February through early March, late April through early June, September, October, early November, and most of December (except Christmas week).

Note that during some of the less crowded times of the year—particularly during January and February—some attractions are typically closed for renovations. In addition, the water parks are often closed for a few weeks in winter for refurbishment.

The period between the end of the Thanksgiving weekend and the week before Christmas stands out as the best time to visit. This is the most festive time at Walt Disney World, and savvy travelers who make their pilgrimage during this time are rewarded with special events featuring holiday parades and fireworks displays, special stage shows, holiday parties, themed dinners, and some of the most spectacular holiday decorations any-

Holidays & Special Events

Inside Walt Disney World

Special festivities are often staged not only to mark holidays, but also to salute special groups by offering discounted admissions to the Magic Kingdom, Epcot, and the Disney-MGM Studios. Call 824-4321 for information.

JANUARY: Walt Disney World New Year's Eve Celebration (December 31). There are extra-large fireworks displays over the Magic Kingdom, Epcot, and Disney-MGM Studios, which are open until 2 A.M. for the occasion. Pleasure Island hosts a grand special-ticket bash.

Walt Disney World Marathon (January 7). Some 10,000 entrants run through all three parks and several of the resorts during this 26.2-mile race. Call 939-7810 for information.

Sci-Fi Convention (January 20–23). Science-fiction fans and celebrities gather in Tomorrowland in the Magic Kingdom to discuss the latest happenings in the sci-fi world.

Indy 200 at Walt Disney World (January 27). Indy race cars burn rubber in this first-ever event, held on a track just south of the Magic Kingdom parking lot.

APRIL–MAY: Easter Sunday. A nationally televised, promenade-style parade makes this holiday celebration in the Magic Kingdom special. The Magic Kingdom, Epcot, and the Disney-MGM Studios stay open late during the two weeks straddling the Easter holiday. This is an extremely busy time to visit.

Grad Nights (April 26–27, May 3–4). The Magic Kingdom is open from 11 P.M. to 5 A.M. for graduating high school students in this special-ticket event. Top rock entertainers

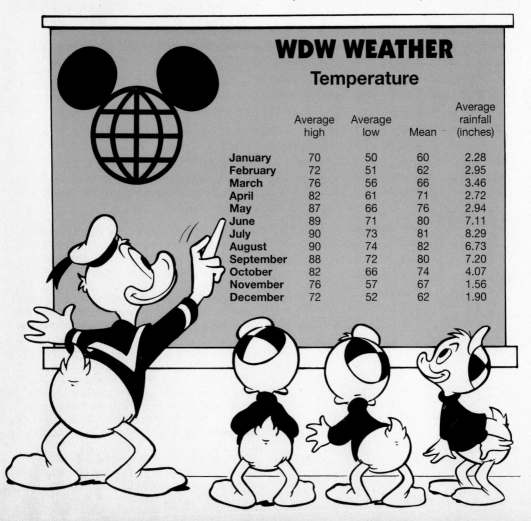

WDW WEATHER
Temperature

	Average high	Average low	Mean	Average rainfall (inches)
January	70	50	60	2.28
February	72	51	62	2.95
March	76	56	66	3.46
April	82	61	71	2.72
May	87	66	76	2.94
June	89	71	80	7.11
July	90	73	81	8.29
August	90	74	82	6.73
September	88	72	80	7.20
October	82	66	74	4.07
November	76	57	67	1.56
December	72	52	62	1.90

perform in the park throughout the night. For details, contact the Grad Night Office; Box 10,000; Lake Buena Vista, FL 32830.

Epcot International Flower and Garden Festival (April 18–June 2). Epcot is blooming with elaborate display gardens, special tours, and gardening workshops during this *Better Homes & Gardens* event.

JULY: Fourth of July Celebration. There are double-size fireworks over the Magic Kingdom, the Disney-MGM Studios presents its spectacular Sorcery in the Sky fireworks show, and Epcot's IllumiNations completes the picture. This is a very busy time to visit.

SEPTEMBER: Disneyana. A veritable heaven for Disney collectors. This year's event will be held here in Florida; some years Disneyland hosts. Packages are available. Call 560-7232.

OCTOBER: Walt Disney World/Oldsmobile Golf Classic (October 5–8). Top PGA Tour players compete alongside amateurs in this big tourney.
Disney Village Marketplace Boat Show. Central Florida's largest boat show displays the newest watercraft.
Pleasure Island Jazz Fest. The greatest jazz from today and yesterday is performed live throughout the island.

WDW'S SILVER ANNIVERSARY

Walt Disney World marks its 25th year on October 1, 1996. The occasion kicks off a year-long celebration, including a slew of special events, new shows and attractions, and resort packages. Call 824-4321 for up-to-the-minute details on celebratory events trumpeting the World's first quarter century.

NOVEMBER–DECEMBER: Festival of the Masters at Disney Village Marketplace (November). One of the South's best art shows draws top exhibitors.
Disney's Magical Holidays (November 26–December 21). Decorations and special festivities abound in WDW's parks and resorts. A variety of packages include admission to special-ticket holiday shows and parties. The Magic Kingdom hosts Mickey's Very Merry Christmas Party several nights during the first two weeks of December. Epcot's nightly Holidays Around the World Show features a special edition of IllumiNations, a candlelight processional, and a chorale concert. The Jolly Holidays Dinner Show at the *Contemporary* resort includes a feast and a musical extravaganza. For information on these events and the two- to ten-day Jolly Holidays packages offered during this period, call W-DISNEY.

Outside Walt Disney World

Several major events in the Central Florida communities around Walt Disney World also are worth a visit.

JANUARY: Orlando; Citrus Bowl. Two leading college football teams square off in this post-season game, held January 2. Citrus Bowl; One Citrus Place; Orlando, FL 32805; 423-2476.
Orlando; Scottish Highland Games. The sizable Scottish population of the area turns out in force for Highland dancing and bagpipe competitions. Scottish American Society of Central Florida; Box 699; Goldenrod, FL 33733; 422-8226.
Eatonville; Zora Neale Hurston Festival. One of the area's premier cultural events, it celebrates the works of this acclaimed writer. Zora Neale Hurston Festival; Box 2586; Eatonville, FL 32751; 647-3307.

FEBRUARY: Daytona; Speed Weeks. Top names in stock-car racing are on hand for a week of competition, culminating in the Daytona 500. Daytona International Speedway; Box 2801; Daytona Beach, FL 32120; 904-253-7223.

Kissimmee; Silver Spurs Rodeo. This three-day event draws professional cowboys from all over the United States to compete in bull and bronco riding, steer-wrestling, and barrel racing. Kissimmee-St. Cloud Convention and Visitors Bureau; Box 422,007; Kissimmee, FL 34742; 677-6336.

MARCH: Orlando; Bay Hill Invitational. Held annually in mid-March; Arnold Palmer hosts this major PGA Tour event, one of five in Florida, at Arnold Palmer's Bay Hill Club. Tournament Office; Bay Hill Club; 9000 Bay Hill Blvd.; Orlando, FL 32819; 876-2888.

Winter Park; Winter Park Sidewalk Art Festival. On the third weekend of the month, more than 250 artists take over a small park in this tony community with displays of photography, pottery, sculpture, and more. Adding to the appeal are concerts and the town's brood of chic boutiques and first-rate restaurants. Winter Park Sidewalk Art Festival; Box 597; Winter Park, FL 32790; 623-3234.

Davenport; Kansas City Royals Spring Training. Baseball enthusiasts can watch the Royals train. Baseball City Complex; 300 Stadium Way; Davenport, FL 33837;813-424-2500.

Kissimmee; Kissimmee Bluegrass Festival. Crafts, food, and children's activities complement live bluegrass and gospel music performances. Kissimmee Bluegrass Festival; Box 456; Kissimmee, FL 32808; 800-472-7773.

APRIL: Orlando; Orlando Cubs baseball season. The summer season for this Chicago Cubs AA farm team begins at Tinker Field in April, and runs through the beginning of September. Tinker Field; 287 Tampa Ave. South; Orlando, FL 32805; 872-7593.

OCTOBER: Orlando Magic Basketball. One of the NBA's top franchises plays 41 home games from October through April at the Orlando Arena. Orlando Arena; One Magic Place; Orlando, FL 32801; 896-2442.

Orlando; Orlando Shakespeare Festival. The month-long event features two Shakespearean productions. Orlando Shakespeare Festival; 30 S. Magnolia Ave., Suite 250; Orlando, FL 32801; 841-9787.

Lakeland; Sun 'N Fun Fly In. Aircraft exhibits and aerial acrobatic demonstrations highlight one of the country's largest air shows. Sun 'N Fun Fly In; Box 7650; Lakeland, FL 33807; 813-644-2431.

DECEMBER: Sanford; Florida Citrus Sailfest. This weekender at Lake Monroe is among the country's largest inland sailing regattas. Florida Citrus Sailfest; 200 S. Orange Ave., Suite 2220; Orlando, FL 32801; 425-0585.

Operating Hours

Hours of operation at the Magic Kingdom, Epcot, and the Disney-MGM Studios vary from season to season. This fact should figure strongly in decisions on when to visit.

For about a third of the year—in May, September, October, parts of November and December, and all of January—the Magic Kingdom is usually open from about 9 A.M. to 7 P.M. During these periods, Epcot is generally open from 9 A.M. to 9 P.M. Note that Future World hours are 9 A.M. to 7 P.M., while World Showcase hours are 11 A.M. to 9 P.M. Normal hours for the Disney-MGM Studios are 9 A.M. to 7 P.M.

Hours for all three parks are extended to 10 P.M. during Presidents' week and during spring school breaks; and to midnight for summer and certain holiday periods (Thanksgiving weekend, Christmas, and the two weeks straddling Easter). On New Year's Eve, additional hours are added to the nighttime schedule, keeping the parks open until about 2 A.M.

Each day, WDW resort guests can enter one of the three theme parks 1½ hours before the official opening time. Information on the exact days this policy is in effect for each park can be found in your hotel room or by asking someone at your resort's Guest Services desk. Note that only some of the pavilions and attractions open early.

Since hours often fluctuate, especially during busy periods, we recommend that you call 824-4321 for up-to-the-minute details.

HOW BIG ARE THE CROWDS?

Most visitors to Walt Disney World routinely assume that weekends are by far the busiest days on the property. But Sunday morning is perhaps the most peaceful time to visit the parks. With the exception of certain holiday periods, Mondays, Tuesdays, and Wednesdays are the most crowded days at the Magic Kingdom. Thursdays and Saturdays are more crowded at Epcot, and at the Disney-MGM Studios, Wednesdays and Sundays tend to be crowded. The chart below offers general information on the density of the crowds during different times of the year. It's very hard to generalize, however, in a property as vast and diverse as Walt Disney World—a crowded day at the Magic Kingdom does not necessarily mean long lines at the Studios—but the chart below does highlight historic trends. Least crowded means that there may be some lines, but by and large most attractions can be visited without much waiting; average attendance refers to those times when there are lots of people around but the lines are still manageable; and most crowded reflects those times when the lines at the most popular attractions can mean a wait of an hour or more.

LEAST CROWDED	AVERAGE ATTENDANCE	MOST CROWDED
	1st week of January	
2nd week of January through 1st week of February		
	2nd week of February until Presidents' week	
		Presidents' week
	End of February through 2nd week of March	
		3rd week of March through 3rd week of April
	Last week of April through 1st week of June	
		2nd week of June through 3rd week of August
	Last week of August through Labor Day	
Week after Labor Day until Thanksgiving		
	Thanksgiving week	
Week after Thanksgiving through week before Christmas		
		Christmas through New Year's Day

Planning Ahead

Organizing a trip properly takes time, but most travelers find that the increased enjoyment is well worth the effort. The fact is, planning can become the most pleasant sort of "armchair" exercise, and kids will enjoy their visit to Walt Disney World all the more if they, too, are involved in the planning process. To aid in that effort, we immodestly recommend our guide, *Birnbaum's Walt Disney World For Kids, By Kids* ($9.95), a comprehensive look at the World from a young person's perspective, written for kids ages 7 to 15. For adults traveling sans children, our newest guide, *Birnbaum's Walt Disney World Without Kids* ($10.95), is the definitive source.

Sample Schedules

It's no exaggeration to say that a visitor could spend three weeks in Central Florida and still not have time to see everything there that's worthwhile. Walt Disney World alone requires every bit of four days just to cover the major attractions, and even that doesn't really allow enough time to take in everything. Just the basic inventory of attractions—the Magic Kingdom, Epcot, the Disney-MGM Studios, Typhoon Lagoon, Blizzard Beach, Pleasure Island, River Country, Discovery Island, *Fort Wilderness,* the Disney Village Marketplace— only begins to suggest the nearly endless and irresistible entertainment opportunities, and we haven't even mentioned the five fine 18- hole golf courses, the beaches, and all the other tempting sports facilities.

The schedules that we suggest here should help put you on the right track—and maybe even keep you there. Deviations from the programs we describe should be based on our "Hot Tips" (pages 122, 162, and 178). In general, good sense and normal human stamina dictate that a first-time visitor should count on spending at least two days at the Magic Kingdom, two days at Epcot, and one full day at the Disney-MGM Studios. That allows time for shopping, the inevitable lines at certain attractions, and unhurried meals. **Note:** The schedules suggested here are for periods when extended park hours are in effect.

Remember, too, that it's crucial to begin days in the theme parks promptly at park opening. It's also wise to recognize that Epcot and the Disney-MGM Studios frequently open a half-hour or more before the officially posted time. For guests staying at WDW resorts, a special program allows admission to parts of the parks on alternating days 1½ hours before they open to the public. Check at Guest Services upon arrival for the exact days that this program is in effect in each park.

ONE-DAY VISIT: There's so much to see and do at WDW that we don't really recommend a visit this frustratingly brief. But if that's all the time you've got, first decide which of the three prime areas (the Magic Kingdom, Epcot, or the Disney-MGM Studios) you want to see, and then study all available material in advance so that you're as familiar as possible with your destination's layout and offerings. Be sure to arrive on the property early and move quickly while you're there. For optimal results, follow our schedules to the letter. **Note:** Because one-day tickets permit visitors to enter *only* one of the three theme parks, visitors must concentrate on that park for the day. Also, if you're lodging at a WDW resort, you might consider taking advantage of early bird admission to get an early crack at selected attractions in the designated park. (Keep in mind that others are apt to have the same idea.)

● If you choose to tour the Magic Kingdom, be in the parking lot at least 45 minutes before the scheduled park opening, so as to be at the Central Plaza end of Main Street at the official opening time. From the Central Plaza, move rapidly and purposefully from one attraction to the next—first to Space Mountain and Alien Encounter, then to Big Thunder Mountain Railroad, Splash Mountain, the Haunted Mansion, Pirates of the Caribbean, and the Jungle Cruise. Plan on lunching at 11 A.M. to avoid mealtime lines. If time remains after the Jungle Cruise, see Tom Sawyer Island and the Swiss Family Treehouse before eating; otherwise go to those attractions after lunch. Then begin making a second trip around the area, stopping at The Timekeeper, Legend of The Lion King, It's A Small World, Peter Pan's Flight, The Hall of Presidents, the shops and entertainment en route, and anything else that catches your eye. (If you're traveling with very young children, your best bet for the morning is to take the Walt Disney World Railroad directly to Mickey's Starland and then visit the

Fantasyland attractions.) Then, having made reservations before leaving home, leave the Magic Kingdom about 4 P.M. for the Hoop-Dee-Doo Musical Revue at *Fort Wilderness*. (These reservations can be *very* hard to come by. Even when you call early, there may not be any seats available.)

During busy seasons, when all WDW attractions are open late, it may be possible to follow this dinner show with another visit to the Magic Kingdom, where fireworks and the late installment of SpectroMagic combine to make an evening especially memorable.

During other months (if you could not get reservations for the Hoop-Dee-Doo Musical Revue), have dinner at *Planet Hollywood* or another Pleasure Island restaurant, and spend the evening exploring Pleasure Island's clubs or the shops at the Disney Village Marketplace next door.

● If you choose to spend the day in Epcot, arrive about a half hour before the park's official opening. If you were unable to get reservations before leaving home, go immediately to Guest Relations to make a dinner reservation for one of the special international restaurants in World Showcase (pick up an entertainment schedule while there). Next, see as much as you can of Wonders of Life and The Land in Future World. When World Showcase opens, head there and see *O Canada!* in the Canada pavilion and *Impressions de France* in the France pavilion. Pausing to grab a bite at one of the international fast-food spots, travel from country to country, making sure to catch the show at The American Adventure and the boat ride in Norway. Check out the street entertainment and any shops that catch your eye. Try to return to Future World by mid- to late-afternoon. See Journey Into Imagination and Spaceship Earth first. Then spend time at Innoventions before heading back to World Showcase for dinner. Keep an eye on the time so that you can secure a good spot around World Showcase Lagoon (we recommend the little island between Italy and The American Adventure) to watch the evening's performance of IllumiNations.

● If you opt for the Disney-MGM Studios, arrive at the park 45 minutes to an hour before the scheduled opening time. Note that some attractions there open later in the morning; pick up an entertainment schedule, and consult it for exact times. If you'd like to try one of the sit-down restaurants for lunch and/or dinner and you were unable to get reservations before leaving home, stop at the corner of Hollywood and Sunset boulevards and make reservations. Try the *50's Prime Time Café* for some old-time television nostalgia, the *Sci-Fi Dine-In* for some wonderful drive-in theater atmosphere, the *Brown Derby* for a touch more elegance, or *Mama Melrose's* for Italian fare. If you're up for a 13-story drop, head directly to the Tower of Terror. Then see Voyage of the Little Mermaid or The Spirit of Pocahontas Stage Show. Afterwards, head for Muppet*Vision 3-D and Star Tours since these attractions are very crowded later in the day. See The Magic of Disney Animation and The Great Movie Ride. Then slot in times to see Indiana Jones Epic Stunt Spectacular, SuperStar Television, and the Monster Sound Show (be sure to volunteer to participate). If small children are along, spend some time at the Honey, I Shrunk the Kids Movie Set Adventure. Browse through the shops along Hollywood Boulevard and Sunset Boulevard, taking time to notice all the Studios' small details. At about 5 P.M., head for the Backstage Studio Tour and the Special Effects and Production Tour. After dinner, catch the Beauty and the Beast show (it's particularly wonderful at night), The Spirit of Pocahontas show if you haven't yet seen it, and any nighttime entertainment.

Note: The following multi-day schedules are predicated on a late-afternoon arrival at Walt Disney World.

FOUR-DAY VISIT: This plan is recommended for only the highly energetic, since all the new attractions at Walt Disney World make it barely possible to see even the high points in such a time frame. During peak seasons, nothing less than four full days will do the trick. Be sure to check (the night before) on required transportation for early morning hours, and allot plenty of extra time for potential delays. Walt Disney World resort guests can take advantage of the early-bird opening hours by planning to visit each park on the day it opens early. On each day, the idea is to make a quick tour of the premises, visiting the major attractions during the least crowded hours of the early morning, then repeating the circuit of the park once again later in the day.

● Before leaving home, try to make reservations for the 5 P.M. seating at the Hoop-Dee-Doo Musical Revue for the evening of the first *full* day of your stay. Then, on the first evening of your arrival at Walt Disney World, go directly to Epcot (try to arrive before 5 P.M.). Purchase a Four-Day Value Pass (or a Four-Day Park Hopper Pass if you plan to visit more than one park in the same day). For admission information, see pages 92, 127, and 166. Grab a quick bite at the *Sunshine Season Food Fair* in The Land, and then see as much of The Land and Wonders of Life as possible before most of Future World closes at 7 P.M. Then visit Spaceship Earth and spend the next hour or so exploring Innoventions. Be sure to stick around the World Showcase Lagoon for the evening's presentation of IllumiNations, a spectacular outdoor sound, light, laser, and water show.

● On your first full day, have breakfast as early as possible in order to arrive at the Magic Kingdom turnstiles half an hour before scheduled opening—and to be at the Central Plaza end of Main Street at the official opening time. Follow our outline for a one-day visit to the Magic Kingdom. Then, having reserved in advance, leave the Magic Kingdom at about 4 P.M. to head for the Hoop-Dee-Doo Musical Revue at *Fort Wilderness*. During busy seasons it's possible to follow dinner with a couple of additional hours at the Magic Kingdom to see the fireworks and the late installment of SpectroMagic. This also is a good time to see many of the more popular attractions with little waiting. During other months (or in the event that Hoop-Dee-Doo Musical Revue reservations were unavailable), head either for Pleasure Island to take in one or more of the unique clubs and restaurants there, or for dinner at the Disney Village Marketplace.

● On your second full day, arrive at Epcot about half an hour before the park's official opening, and wait at the gate until the turnstiles are unlocked. Then, if you were unable to get reservations before leaving home, go directly to Guest Relations to make a 1:30 P.M. lunch reservation at one of the World Showcase restaurants and an 8:45 P.M. dinner reservation (when the park is open late) at another. (See *Good Meals, Great Times* for details about the reservation procedure and our dining suggestions). That done, take in any major attractions in Future World that you missed on your first evening, including those at The Living Seas and the Journey Into Imagination pavilions.

Then head for World Showcase and see the film at the Canada pavilion, the film at the France pavilion, the show at The American Adventure pavilion, and the film at the China pavilion. Save shopping for later in the day when the attractions are more crowded and the shops are not. Check your entertainment schedule for the best times to enjoy the entertainment along World Showcase Promenade. The hours between 6 P.M. and your dinner reservation time should be spent seeing any attractions that were missed on your two previous circuits, including the boat ride at the Norway pavilion. Skip dessert at your dinner restaurant and instead head for the *Boulangerie Pâtisserie* in the France pavilion for pastry and espresso. If you couldn't get a reservation in the Epcot restaurant of your choice, or if a change of pace is desired, head for Pleasure Island, the Disney Village Marketplace, or the Disney Village Hotel Plaza, where there are many restaurants from which to choose (see *Good Meals, Great Times*).

● On the third full day of your visit, arrive at the Disney-MGM Studios 45 minutes to an hour before the scheduled opening. Then follow the schedule outlined in our one-day visit to the Disney-MGM Studios.

FIVE-DAY VISIT: A stay of this length, while not exactly leisurely, is still the shortest time that can be conscientiously recommended for families with young children, older visitors, or anyone else who wants to visit all the best of Walt Disney World at less than breakneck pace.

Before visiting, read as much as possible about the WDW attractions and their locations. This is a must because although the pace of this five-day program is slower than that required during a four-day visit, it is still necessary not to waste time in order to cover all the high points. Remember, too, that the first order of business (before leaving home) is to try to make a 5 P.M. reservation for the Hoop-Dee-Doo Musical Revue for the fourth full day of your visit.

● On the evening of the day of your arrival, visit Epcot and purchase a Five-Day World Hopper Pass. For admission information, see pages 92, 127, and 166. Grab a quick bite at the *Sunshine Season Food Fair* in The Land and then proceed as for the first evening of the four-day visit described on page 15.

● On the first full day of your visit, arrive at the Magic Kingdom 45 minutes before the official park opening. *Tony's Town Square* restaurant and the *Crystal Palace* cafeteria on Main Street begin serving early, so have breakfast at one of these eateries and be at the Central Plaza end of Main Street at the park's official opening time. Then begin circumnavigating the park, taking in just the major attractions described for the first morning of a one-day visit.

At about noon, leave the park and head for River Country, Discovery Island, Typhoon Lagoon, or Blizzard Beach. Have lunch and participate in the varied activities offered. Golfers may want to reserve ahead to sample one of the World's first-rate golf courses instead. Return to the Magic Kingdom at about 5 P.M. and grab a quick bite at the *Cosmic Ray's Starlight Café*. Then take another ride on Space Mountain and Splash Mountain. By 8 P.M. head for Main Street to stake a claim to a segment of curb for the 9 P.M. showing of SpectroMagic. Watch the Fantasy in the Sky fireworks after the parade.

● Devote the second day of your visit to Epcot. Arrive about a half hour before the official park opening. If you were unable to get dinner reservations before leaving home, go to Guest Relations to make an early (around 5 P.M.) reservation. Then visit the Future World attractions you missed on your first evening, including those at The Living Seas and the Journey Into Imagination pavilions.

Next, head for World Showcase as close to its 11 A.M. opening time as possible. First go to Canada to see the film there and to France

for its film. See the show at The American Adventure before heading to Mexico for lunch at the pleasant *Cantina de San Angel*. Afterward, reverse the direction of your route around World Showcase, and stop at the pavilions you missed the first time around, making sure to catch the boat ride in Norway and the movie in China. Even if you hate shopping, look into Germany's arts-and-crafts and toy shops and Morocco's brass and jewelry bazaars. Also be sure to look in on the entertainers who perform daily on the promenade. For a mid-afternoon snack, stop at the U.K. Pavilion's Tea Caddy, buy a box of crackers or cookies, and then head for the *Refreshment Port* for a cold drink. If there's time, go back to Future World and explore more of Innoventions, where you can spend quite a bit of time. Remember to allot a full 20 minutes to walk to your dining spot. Skip dessert at your dinner restaurant and instead head for the *Boulangerie Pâtisserie* in the France pavilion for pastry and espresso. The uncrowded hours after dinner should be spent visiting any attractions missed on previous circuits.

● On the third full day of your visit, head for the Disney-MGM Studios and follow the schedule outlined in the one-day visit. In the evening, head to Pleasure Island for the shows and/or an evening of dancing. If tired feet prohibit such activity, take in a movie at Pleasure Island's multiplex cinema.

● On the fourth full day of your visit, try one of the character breakfasts (described in *Good Meals, Great Times*). Then head over to the Magic Kingdom and spend the rest of the day following our guidelines for the afternoon of a one-day visit, taking time for any other attractions that catch your eye. At about 4 P.M. head over to *Fort Wilderness* for the 5 P.M. Hoop-Dee-Doo Musical Revue. Then go to Pleasure Island for some dancing, comedy, or music, or maybe take in a movie at the multiplex cinema next door.

LONGER VISITS: In addition to our program for a five-day visit, an even longer stay allows a chance to sample some of the World's other offerings. Spend another day in the one park you most enjoyed. Lounge by the pool, play tennis or golf, or bike. Visit the shops at the Disney Village Marketplace. Have lunch at a resort and try a special dinner at *Victoria & Albert's* at the *Grand Floridian* or *Portobello Yacht Club* at Pleasure Island. Check out the clubs at Pleasure Island. Take golf or tennis lessons. Participate in a behind-the-scenes program. Tour Discovery Island. And if you have a few days to spare, enroll for a stay at The Disney Institute. For more ideas, see our *Sports*, *Everything Else in the World*, and *Good Meals, Great Times* chapters.

DISNEY'S WILDEST ATTRACTION YET

Guests who like to plan their vacations to WDW far in advance will be interested to know that its newest and largest theme park, Disney's Wild Animal Kingdom, is due to open in spring 1998. As home to thousands of wild creatures, this live-action adventure park will cover 500 acres on the western edge of the WDW property, making it five times the size of the Magic Kingdom. The park's centerpiece will be the giant Tree of Life, 14 stories tall, with a 50-foot-wide trunk. It will be hand-carved by Disney artists with an intricate tapestry of animal forms to represent the diversity of animal life on Earth. There will be a show inside the tree.

The park will be separated into three major sections:

- **The Real:** Guests will participate in a thrilling safari featuring exotic landscapes and great herds of wild animals.
- **The Mythical:** Guests can expect face-to-face encounters with make-believe animals from legends and fairy-tales, including unicorns, dragons, and other creatures that have a powerful hold on our imaginations.
- **The Extinct:** Disney's most advanced Audio-Animatronics will bring the giants of the Cretaceous period to life in a thrill attraction, as guests are whisked back 65 million years to witness the end of the dinosaur era. Another attraction will lead guests into a primeval forest and allow them to experience prehistoric life on Earth.

In addition, the park's Conservation Station will serve as headquarters for conservation and species survival activities. Information on worldwide conservation organizations will help guests connect back to their own communities.

More Planning Tips

DO YOU NEED A CAR? If you plan to spend all of your time at Walt Disney World, you don't need to rent a car. Within the World, WDW's exhaustive network of bus, monorail, and boat transportation efficiently brings guests from point to point. The bus system is the most extensive form of WDW transportation. Clearly marked buses make finding your way around fairly simple. Bus routing information also is available at Guest Services desks in the hotels.

Also, visitors lodging outside the World can usually get to and from Walt Disney World via their own hotels' bus services. Cabs also are available. But a car is a must for taking in Orlando-area restaurants and any attractions outside Walt Disney World.

From the airport: It's also possible to get to WDW resorts from Orlando Airport without a car. Mears Motor Shuttles operate about every 15 to 20 minutes around the clock, serving on-property hotels, as well as Disney Village Hotel Plaza accommodations and Orlando-area hotels. The cost to most hotels is $13 one way, $23 round-trip per adult; $10 one way, $17 round-trip per child age 4 to 11; free for children under three. (Call for reservations: 423-5566.)

INFORMATION SOURCES: For information about Walt Disney World, call WDW Information at 824-4321 or write to the Walt Disney World Co.; Box 10,000; Lake Buena Vista, FL 32830. For details about other things to see and do in Central Florida, contact the Florida Department of Commerce Division of Tourism; 107 West Gaines St.; Tallahassee, FL 32399-2000; 904-487-1462. To find out about the area directly around Orlando, contact the Orlando/Orange County Convention and Visitors Bureau; 7208 Sand Lake Rd., Suite 300; Orlando, FL 32819; 363-5800.

WDW online: America Online subscribers and Internet users can now tap into WDW updates to take inventory of the World's latest offerings. To access the Disney dispatches and communicate with fellow travelers via a Disney bulletin board, American Online subscribers need only use the keyword "disney." Internet users can simply enter *http://www.disneyworld.com/vacation.html* to gain access to the Disney updates.

Disney/AAA Travel Center: The best time to make or confirm hotel reservations is *before* you're actually standing at the hotel's front desk. Nobody likes unpleasant surprises on a vacation, so it's wise to have an assured reservation. Those driving to Walt Disney World can arrange that assurance easily because there is a full-service information facility in Ocala, Florida, at the intersection of Interstate 75 and State Route 200, about 90 miles north of Orlando. Like a welcome center, the facility will help WDW-bound vacationers plan their time, purchase tickets for the Magic Kingdom, Epcot, the Disney-MGM Studios, and other attractions, and make hotel reservations (or confirm them). And for those departing guests who didn't buy enough pairs of mouse ears, the center also offers plenty of Disney character merchandise.

On-site resources: Upon arrival at Walt Disney World, a variety of other information sources is available. First, tune into the WDW radio stations after entering the grounds—1030 on the AM dial inbound to the Magic Kingdom and 810 approaching Epcot. (Helpful information is broadcast to guests departing from the Magic Kingdom and Epcot on 900.)

Guests at WDW resorts—that is, the *Contemporary*, *Polynesian*, *Grand Floridian*, *Wilderness Lodge*, *Caribbean Beach*, *Swan*, *Dolphin*, *Yacht Club*, *Beach Club*, *Port Orleans*, *Dixie Landings*, *Fort Wilderness*, *All-Star Sports*, *All-Star Music*, *Disney Vacation Club,* and *The Villas at The Disney Institute*—can tune into Channel 5 on their hotel-room television sets to see a filmed overview of all WDW attractions. This programming, broadcast continuously, provides a complete orientation tour of the property, so it is essential viewing for all first-time visitors. Guests at Disney Village Hotel Plaza establishments will see a similar program on Channel 7. (The latter gives somewhat more emphasis to the dining rooms and lounges at these lodging places, which, though located on WDW property, are neither Disney-owned nor Disney-operated.) Guests at WDW properties can watch the daily program "Disney Nights," on Channel 10 to glean information about all the nighttime activities available and other helpful vacation hints. (This program is not shown outside WDW lodging places.) *Fort Wilderness* campers are advised to stop at the Pioneer Hall Information and Ticket Window, call extension 2788, or touch "11" from the phones at the comfort stations located at the center of each campground loop area. And all WDW resort guests should consider the Guest Services desk at their hotel a primary source of WDW information.

Some hotels off the property—but not all of them—show their own version of the WDW resorts' Channel 5 orientation film; this attempts to give visitors an overview of all Central Florida attractions rather than concentrating solely on Walt Disney World.

For day visitors: All day visitors—that is, those staying off the property, as well as those living in the Orlando area—receive a handout at the Auto Plazas detailing admission prices and other useful information. When purchasing one-day admission media at the Transportation and Ticket Center, at Epcot, or at the Disney-MGM Studios, guests receive a copy of the Magic Kingdom guide, the Epcot guide, or the Disney-MGM Studios guide, depending upon which park they have chosen to visit. Guests who purchase multi-day admission media may receive all three park guides upon request. City Hall (in the Magic Kingdom), Guest Relations (in Epcot), and Guest Relations (at the Disney-MGM Studios) distribute extra copies of these guides at no charge.

WHAT TO PACK: Walt Disney World is not so casual that all you need to bring is a bathing suit, but with only a few exceptions, comfortable clothing is the rule. Jackets are required for men for dinner at *Victoria & Albert's* at the *Grand Floridian* resort. Everywhere else the dress is quite casual. T-shirts and shorts are acceptable during the day. For evening, slacks, jeans, and Bermuda shorts are appropriate. This also is true at the full-service restaurants that are found in the World Showcase pavilions at Epcot. Bathing suits are a must, and a spare one is useful, as are the right togs for any other sport you might want to pursue. On the tennis courts, tennis whites are appropriate, though not required. Guests should bring lightweight sweaters even in summer—to wear indoors when the air conditioning gets too frigid. From November through March, warmer clothing is a must in the evening. Always pack something to keep you comfortable should the weather turn unseasonably warm or cool. Especially in summer, lightweight raingear and a folding umbrella come in handy. Be sure to pack plenty of sunscreen, since even the winter Orlando sun can be brutal.

The most important item of clothing of all? Comfortable, well broken-in walking shoes.

WDW WEDDINGS & HONEYMOONS

Walt Disney World is the most popular honeymoon destination in the country. Since honeymooners have been flocking to the WDW resorts for many years, a variety of packages are available that cater specifically to newly married couples. The resorts at Walt Disney World offer romantic stretches of white-sand beaches for evening strolls, fine restaurants for candlelight dinners, and a host of activities to rival any Caribbean or Hawaiian destination. Add to that the Magic Kingdom, Epcot, the Disney-MGM Studios, Pleasure Island, the Disney Village Marketplace, Typhoon Lagoon, Blizzard Beach, River Country, and Discovery Island and it's not hard to see why WDW is number one with honeymooners.

For many years, the folks at Walt Disney World received hundreds of requests from couples who wanted to get married at Walt Disney World. Today, couples can tie the knot in evening ceremonies at all three theme parks. The new Wedding Pavilion near the *Grand Floridian* offers a Victorian-style setting with a prime view of Cinderella Castle. The *Yacht Club*, *Beach Club*, *Polynesian*, *Wilderness Lodge*, and *Contemporary* resorts also do their share of weddings, with *The Villas at The Disney Institute* providing couples with a rustic option.

Weddings at WDW range from elegant affairs without a hint of Disneyana, to ceremonies in which the bride and groom arrive in Cinderella's coach and Mickey and Minnie are among the guests. The WDW wedding coordinators work with couples to tailor each individual wedding. Among the services offered are wedding-gown design, formal-wear rentals, invitations, photographers, hairstyling, manicures, massage, floral arrangements, and musical entertainment.

Wedding specialists also help to arrange accommodations for guests, rehearsal dinners, bachelor parties, and just about any other activities you might require. For additional information about a WDW wedding, call 363-6333. For information about honeymoon packages call 934-7639.

Reservations

Walt Disney World vacations go more smoothly when details are planned ahead of time. Procrastinators may find no room at the inn, or no space left for a show that they wanted to see. Golf starting times, tennis courts, dining reservations, and other special affairs also should be reserved in advance.

Central Reservations Operations: Many arrangements are handled by Central Reservations Operations (CRO); the phone number is W-DISNEY (934-7639). The office is open Mondays through Fridays from 8 A.M. to 10 P.M.; Saturdays and Sundays from 9 A.M. to 6 P.M. Most calls are answered within one minute. Have pen and paper close at hand (and your credit card) when calling, to jot down dates and the number of your reservation.

Room reservations: It is important to book accommodations in advance to get your first choice, although most requests can be satisfied. Popular summer and holiday periods must be booked well in advance. Parties needing ten or more rooms should call 828-3318.

Packages: A great option for the convenience of having all vacation arrangements made with one phone call. For Walt Disney Travel Company package information, call 800-828-0228. For details on Delta Air Lines packages, call 800-872-7786. America Express Vacation Travel also offers packages that can be booked via the same number.

Reservations for meal seatings, dinner shows, and sporting activities: Most meal reservations are handled by one phone number—WDW-DINE (939-3463), while sporting activities are handled by the individual sporting centers. It's always wise to make your plans and reserve your place as far in advance as WDW policy will allow. (See chart below.)

RESERVATION GUIDE

ACTIVITY	Phone for reservations (area code 407)	Advisability of reservations	*How far in advance can reservations be made?*
Sports			
Golf starting times— all courses	824-2270	Necessary from January through April; a good idea at other times	30 days for guests staying at WDW resorts or Hotel Plaza properties 7 days for day guests from May through December, 4 days during peak seasons
Golf lessons, Palm and Magnolia courses	824-2270	Necessary	............................1 year ....
Tennis, *Contemporary*	824-3578	Suggested	............................14 days............................
Grand Floridian	824-2433	Necessary	............................30 days............................
Swan and *Dolphin*	934-4396	Suggested	............................no limit............................
Tennis lessons, *Contemporary*	824-3578	Necessary	............................1 year ....
Trail rides, *Fort Wilderness*	824-2621	Suggested	............................5 days............................
Fishing trips, *Fort Wilderness*	824-2621	Necessary	............................14 days............................
Dixie Landings	934-5409	Necessary	............................14 days............................
Disney Village Marketplace	828-2204	Necessary	............................30 days............................
Waterskiing	824-2621	Necessary	............................14 days............................
Parasailing	824-1000, ext. 3586	Necessary	............................no limit............................

ACTIVITY	Phone for reservations (area code 407)	Advisability of reservations	*How far in advance can reservations be made?*
Good Meals Chef Mickey's, Disney Village Marketplace	WDW-DINE	Suggested	..........................60 days..............................
'Ohana, Tangaroa Terrace, Polynesian resort	WDW-DINE	Suggested Accepted	..........................60 days..............................
Victoria & Albert's, Grand Floridian resort	WDW-DINE	Necessary	..........................60 days..............................
Narcoossee's, Flagler's, 1900 Park Fare, Grand Floridian resort	WDW-DINE	Suggested	..........................60 days..............................
California Grill, Concourse Steak House, Contemporary Café, Contemporary resort	WDW-DINE	Suggested Accepted Accepted	..........................60 days..............................
Artist Point, Wilderness Lodge resort	WDW-DINE	Suggested	..........................60 days..............................
Ariel's, Cape May Café, Beach Club resort	WDW-DINE	Suggested Accepted	..........................60 days..............................
Yachtsman Steakhouse, Yacht Club Galley, Yacht Club resort	WDW-DINE	Suggested Accepted	..........................60 days..............................
Palio, Swan resort	934-1609	Suggested	..........................60 days..............................
Sum Chows, Harry's Safari Bar & Grille, Juan & Only's Cantina, Dolphin resort	934-4025	Suggested	..........................60 days..............................
In the Magic Kingdom	WDW-DINE	Suggested	..........................60 days..............................
In Epcot	WDW-DINE	Necessary	..........................60 days..............................
In Disney-MGM Studios	WDW-DINE	Varies	..........................60 days..............................
Great Times Hoop-Dee-Doo Musical Revue, Fort Wilderness	WDW-DINE	Necessary	..........................2 years ....
Polynesian Luau, Polynesian resort	WDW-DINE	Necessary	..........................2 years ....
Mickey's Tropical Luau, Polynesian resort	WDW-DINE	Necessary	..........................2 years ....
Breakfast à la Disney, Chef Mickey's	WDW-DINE	Necessary	..........................60 days..............................
WDW Character Meals, Resorts and theme parks (see page 241 for locations)	WDW-DINE	Necessary	..........................60 days..............................
Character Brunch, Dolphin resort	934-4025	Suggested	..........................no limit ....
Character Dinner, Swan Resort	934-1609	Suggested	..........................no limit ....

How to Get There

By Car

Here are some suggested routes to WDW from the downtown sections of several metropolitan areas.

Figure on driving 350 to 400 miles a day—a reasonable distance that won't wear you down so much that you can't enjoy your stay.

Atlanta: I-75 south, I-475 south around Macon, I-75 south, Florida's Turnpike south, U.S. 27 south, U.S. 192 east to entrance. Total mileage: 428 miles.

Baltimore: I-95 south, I-495 east and south around Washington, I-95 south, I-295 around Jacksonville, I-95 south, I-4 west, U.S. 192 west to entrance. Total mileage: 914 miles.

Boston: I-90 west, I-84 west, I-91 south, I-95 south, I-287 west, Garden State Parkway south, New Jersey Turnpike south to

Delaware Memorial Bridge, I-95 south (through Fort McHenry Tunnel in Baltimore), I-495 west and south around Washington, D.C., I-95 south, I-295 around Jacksonville, I-95 south, I-4 west, U.S. 192 west to entrance. Total mileage: 1,338 miles.

Buffalo: I-90 west, I-79 south, U.S. 19 south, West Virginia Turnpike south, I-77 south, I-20 west around Columbia (SC), I-26 east, I-95 south, I-295 around Jacksonville, I-95 south, I-4 west, U.S. 192 west to entrance. Total mileage: 1,211 miles.

Chicago: I-94 south, I-80 east, I-65 south, I-465 south, I-65 south to Nashville, I-24 east to Chattanooga, I-75 south, I-285 west and south around Atlanta, I-75 south, I-475 south around Macon, I-75 south, Florida's Turnpike south, U.S. 27 south, U.S. 192 east to entrance. Total mileage: 1,172 miles.

Cincinnati: I-75 south, I-285 west and south around Atlanta, I-475 south around Macon, I-75 south, Florida's Turnpike south, U.S. 27 south, U.S. 192 east to entrance. Total mileage: 810 miles.

Cleveland: I-77 south, West Virginia Turnpike south, I-77 south, I-20 west around Columbia (SC), I-26 east, I-95 south, I-295 around Jacksonville, I-95 south, I-4 west, U.S. 192 west to entrance. Total mileage: 1,059 miles.

Dallas: I-20 east to Shreveport, I-49 south, S.R. 1 south, I-49 south, U.S. 167 east, I-10 east, I-12 east around New Orleans, I-10 east, I-75 south, Florida's Turnpike south, U.S. 27 south, U.S. 192 east to entrance. Total mileage: 1,174 miles.

FROM THE AIRPORT

For the least congested route, take the Central Florida Greeneway, Route 417. Then follow Route 417 to Route 536, which leads directly to Walt Disney World. You can also take Route 528 (known as the Beeline Expressway) west (toward Tampa), to I-4 west until you reach the appropriate Walt Disney World exit. The distance is 22 miles. Tolls on the first route described total $2; tolls on the second route cost $1.25.

Detroit: I-75 south, I-285 west and south around Atlanta, I-75 south, I-475 south around Macon, I-75 south, Florida's Turnpike south, U.S. 27 south, U.S. 192 east to entrance. Total mileage: 1,158 miles.

Indianapolis: I-65 south to Nashville, I-24 east to Chattanooga, I-75 south, I-285 west and south around Atlanta, I-75 south, I-475 south around Macon, I-75 south, Florida's Turnpike south, U.S. 27 south, U.S. 192 east to entrance. Total mileage: 977 miles.

Louisville: I-65 south to Nashville, I-24 east to Chattanooga, I-75 south, I-285 west and south around Atlanta, I-75 south, I-475 south around Macon, I-75 south, Florida's Turnpike south, U.S. 27 south, U.S. 192 east to entrance. Total mileage: 877 miles.

Minneapolis: I-94 east to Madison (WI), I-90 east, I-294 south around Chicago, I-90 east, I-65 south, 465 south, I-65 south to Nashville, I-24 east to Chattanooga, I-75 south, I-285 west and south around Atlanta, I-75 south, Florida's Turnpike south, U.S. 27 south, U.S. 192 east to entrance. Total mileage: 1,581 miles.

New York City: Lincoln Tunnel west, New Jersey Turnpike south to Delaware Memorial Bridge, I-95 south (through Fort McHenry Tunnel in Baltimore), I-495 west and south around Washington, D.C., I-95 south, I-295 around Jacksonville, I-95 south, I-4 west, U.S. 192 west to entrance. Total mileage: 1,117 miles.

Philadelphia: I-95 south (through Fort McHenry Tunnel in Baltimore), I-495 east and south around Washington, D.C., I-95 south, I-295 around Jacksonville, I-95 south, I-4 west, U.S. 192 west to entrance. Total mileage: 1,015 miles.

Pittsburgh: I-279 south, I-79 south, U.S. 19 south, West Virginia Turnpike south, I-77 south, I-20 west around Columbia (SC), I-26 east, I-95 south, I-295 around Jacksonville, I-95 south, I-4 west, U.S. 192 west to entrance. Total mileage: 1,002 miles.

Richmond: I-95 south, I-295 around Jacksonville, I-95 south, I-4 west, U.S. 192 west to entrance. Total mileage: 757 miles.

Toronto: Queen Elizabeth Way south, I-190 east, I-90 west, I-79 south, U.S. 19 south, West Virginia Turnpike south, I-77 south, I-20 west around Columbia (SC), I-26 east, I-95 south, I-295 around Jacksonville, I-95 south, I-4 west, U.S. 192 west to entrance. Total mileage: 1,307 miles.

By Bus

Relatively few vacationers come to Walt Disney World by bus. But it makes sense to consider this means of transportation if you're traveling just a short distance or have plenty of time, if there are only two or three in your party, or if cost is a major consideration. Bus travel is usually extremely economical.

Greyhound provides frequent direct service into Kissimmee and Orlando. Buses drop arriving passengers off at either 16 North Orlando Avenue in Kissimmee or at 545 North MacGruder Boulevard in Orlando. From each of the stops, it's possible to hire a taxi on your own or take one provided by the many area hotels and motels in the area. Check in advance to see if your lodging place offers taxi service. For further information phone Greyhound at 800-231-2222.

Sample Travel Times

Jacksonville, Florida	about 4 hours
Tallahassee, Florida	about 7 hours
Atlanta, Georgia	about 12 hours

AUTOMOBILE CLUBS

Reputable national automobile clubs can offer help with breakdowns en route; insurance that covers personal injury, accidents, arrest, bail bond, and lawyers' fees for defense of contested traffic cases; and travel-planning services—not only advice, but also free maps and route mapping. Programs vary from one club to the next; fees range from about $24 to $75 a year.

Among the leading clubs:

Allstate Motor Club; 1500 West Shure Dr.; Arlington Heights, IL 60004; 800-347-8880

American Automobile Association; 1000 AAA Drive; Heathrow, FL 32746; 800-222-4357

Amoco Motor Club; Box 9046; Des Moines, IA 50368; 800-334-3300

Ford Auto Club; Box 224688; Dallas, TX 75222; 800-348-5220

Gulf Motor Club; 6001 North Clark St.; Chicago, IL 60660; 800-633-3224

Montgomery Ward Auto Club; 200 North Martingale Rd.; Schaumburg, IL 60173; 800-621-5151

Motor Club of America; 484 Central Ave.; Newark, NJ 07107; 800-833-3207

United States Auto Club Motoring Division; Box 660460; Dallas, TX 75266; 800-348-5058

OTHER MAPS: Those who don't belong to a club can get free maps from state tourist boards. Another excellent source is the *Rand McNally Road Atlas* ($9.95 in bookstores).

By Train

Amtrak serves the Orlando area twice daily from New York City. The trip takes about 22 hours and costs anywhere from $138 to $310 round-trip (book early for lower fares). The train stops along the way to pick up additional passengers in Philadelphia and Washington, D.C., as well as various cities in Virginia, North Carolina, South Carolina, and Georgia. (Special discounts are often available; check when booking.)

Amtrak also offers Auto Train service daily in both directions from Lorton, Virginia, 17 miles south of Washington, D.C., direct to Sanford, Florida, just 25 miles northeast of Orlando. Round-trip fares begin at $325 per car, $115 per adult, and $60 for children ages 2 to 15. The fare includes two meals and some entertainment. Special off-peak fares are often offered, so be sure to inquire when you call to make your reservations.

For reservations and current schedule information on these and other routes, send a self-addressed, stamped envelope to Amtrak Distribution Center; 1549 West Glenlake Ave.; Box 7717; Itasca, IL 60143; or call 800-USA-RAIL (800-872-7245).

BY SHIP

Both Premier and Carnival cruise lines offer combination cruise-Walt Disney World vacation packages. Most ships depart from Port Canaveral; Carnival also offers cruises from Tampa and Miami. For details, call your travel agent. For specifics on the Premier Cruise Lines packages, you can also call 800-327-7113.

In 1998, Disney will launch its own cruise ships. Guests will be able to book one-week vacations consisting of three- or four-day cruises combined with three or four days at Walt Disney World. Ports of call will include a Disney private island, where guests can enjoy a day-long excursion. The 2,400-passenger vessels will feature Disney characters on board, and the itineraries will cater to families. Accommodations will include luxury staterooms, family suites, and traditional staterooms.

By Air

The sleek, multi-million-dollar Orlando International Airport is continually upgrading in an effort to keep up with the millions of visitors who flock to Central Florida each year. Shuttle trains transport passengers to and from the central terminal. There's a well-stocked shop where arriving and departing travelers can buy T-shirts and other Disney merchandise.

There are more than a dozen airlines that offer nonstop flights to Orlando. Delta Air Lines alone—the "Official Airline of Walt Disney World"—carries more than three million passengers into Orlando annually. Delta's Orlando service includes nonstop flights from about 30 cities. The airline also offers the special Fantastic Flyer program for kids.

Discovering the Lowest Airfare

If there's a trick to finding the cheapest plane fare, it's this: Shop around. Some tips for bargain hunters follow.

● Find out the names of all the airlines from your point of departure to your destination, then call them all—more than once if your route is complex. Or call your travel agent. The more flexible you can be in your dates and duration of stay, the more money you're likely to save. Fares are usually lowest on competitive, heavily traveled routes.

● Watch the newspapers for ads announcing new short-term promotional fares.

● When it's necessary to change planes en route, it is best to stick with one airline; the airline agent will know his or her own company's routing—and its discounted fares—better than those offered by other carriers.

● Fly when most other people don't—at night; on weekends on routes that usually serve business travelers; or midweek to and from vacation destinations.

● Plan ahead. Most carriers guarantee their fares—which means that you won't have to pay extra to use a valid ticket even if fares go up. Remember too, that most of the least expensive airfares now carry a penalty if you want to revise your flight schedules, and that certain discount fare tickets are nonrefundable. Be sure to ask about restrictions.

WHICH AIRLINE FLIES FROM YOUR CITY?

You can fly nonstop to Orlando from about 50 different U.S. cities, on more than a dozen airlines. Schedules change often, and flights may be dropped or new ones added. This was the operative nonstop service at press time:

Atlanta, GA ....DL, J7, KP
Atlantic City, NJ ....NK
Baltimore, MD.......................................US
Birmingham, AL ....DL*
Boston, MA ....DL, US, TZ
Charlotte, NC ....US
Chicago, IL ....DL, AA, KP, TZ, UA
Cincinnati, OH ....DL, FL
Cleveland, OH ....CO
Columbus, OH ....US, HP
Dallas/Ft. Worth, TX......................DL, AA
Daytona Beach, FL......3M, UA*, DL*, US*
Denver, CO ....UA
Detroit, MI ....SY, NK, NW
Ft. Lauderdale, FL ....DL, DL*, UA, CO, TZ, 3M
Ft. Myers, FL.............................US*, PL*
Freeport, Bahamas ....DL*
Gainesville, FL.....................................DL*
Greensboro/Winston-Salem, NC.........CO
Hartford, CT/
   Springfield, MA...............FL, TZ, DL, US
Houston, TX...CO
Indianapolis, IN..............................US, TZ
Jacksonville, FL ....DL*, US*
Kansas City, MO...................................US
Key West, FL..DL*
Knoxville, TN..FL
Long Island Macarthur, NY ....US, KW
Los Angeles, CA..........................DL, UA
Marathon, FL ....US*
Melbourne, FL............................DL*, US*
Memphis, TN ....NW
Mexico City, Mexico............................DL
Miami, FL.....................DL, DL*, UA, UA*, AA, US, US*, 3M, AA*

Milwaukee, WI ....TZ
Minneapolis/St. Paul, MN ....NW, US
Montego Bay, Jamaica........................JM
Naples, FL....................................DL*, US*
Nashville, TN ....FL, AA
Nassau, Bahamas ....DL, DL*, UP
Newburgh, NY ....FL
New Orleans, LA ....DL, DL*, CO, NW
New York, NY/Newark, NJ ....DL, CO, UA, US, TW, KP, TZ, US*
Pensacola, FL ....DL*, US*
Philadelphia, PA ....DL, US, NK
Phoenix, AZ ....HP
Pittsburgh, PA...........................DL*, US
Providence, RI ....FL
Raleigh/Durham, NC ....JI
St. Louis, MO ....TZ, TW
Salt Lake City, UT ....DL
San Francisco, CA......................TZ, UA
San Juan, Puerto Rico................DL, AA
Sarasota/Bradenton, FL ....DL*, US*
Seattle/Tacoma, WA............................TZ
Syracuse, NY ....FL
Tallahassee, FL..........................DL*, US*
Tampa/St. Petersburg, FL...........DL*, HP US*, TZ
Washington, DC ....US*, DL, US, UA, J7
West Palm Beach, FL ....DL, DL*, US*, TZ

ABBREVIATIONS—AA: American. CO: Continental. CS: Florida Air. DL: Delta. DL*: Comair—The Delta Connection. FL: Airtran Airways. HP: America West. J7: Valujet Airlines. JI: Midway Airlines. JM: Air Jamaica Limited. KP: Kiwi. KL: KLM. KW: Carnival. L8: Leisure Air. NK: Spirit Airlines. NW: Northwest. RL: UltrAir. SY: Sun Country Airlines. 3M: Gulfstream International Airlines, Inc. TW: Trans World. TZ: American Trans Air. UA: United. UA*: United Express. UP: Bahamasair. US: USAir. US*: USAir Express.

SHOULD YOU BUY A PACKAGE?

The sheer number of diverse packages offering vacations in Central Florida is enough to bewilder even the savviest traveler. Still, these packages offer significant advantages. Among them is the opportunity to purchase a vacation that's completely organized in advance, and that will generally cost less than the same transportation, accommodations, and admission elements if they were purchased separately. (A complete Delta Dream Vacation can cost less than just the round-trip economy airfare from certain cities, though the package also may include a hotel room, a rental car with unlimited mileage for a week, and admission to the Magic Kingdom, Epcot, and the Disney-MGM Studios.)

The main difference among the various package offerings—aside from cost—is the matter of lodging in on-site hotels versus off-property accommodations. Delta Air Lines and American Express Vacation Travel packages offer lodgings in Walt Disney World's own on-site hotels; and Walt Disney World itself, along with the Walt Disney Travel Company, offers on-site Grand Plan, Deluxe Plan, Classic Plan, Golf Getaway, Jolly Holidays, Honeymoon Escape, Honeymoon Enchantment, Grand Honeymoon, Romantic Escape, Fall Fantasy, and Sunshine Getaway packages. Many of the Walt Disney World vacation plans are perfect for "top-of-the-line" visitors who

don't mind spending a little extra money to obtain a package that includes virtually everything. Some of the packages are designed with a moderate budget in mind. In 1996, Disney will offer packages that include airfare. For Walt Disney Travel Company package information call 800-828-0228.

Delta Air Lines packages include the added attraction of low-cost air transportation—plus accommodations at the *Contemporary*, the *Polynesian*, the *Grand Floridian*, *The Villas at The Disney Institute*, *Fort Wilderness*, *Caribbean Beach*, *Yacht Club*, *Beach Club*, *Port Orleans*, or *Dixie Landings*. For Delta Air Lines package information, call 800-872-7786. American Express Vacation Travel options can be booked via the same number.

Other major operators offering Walt Disney World tours include Adventure Tours, Kingdom Tours, Go Go Tours, Funway Holidays Funjet, Travel Impressions, Carnival Cruise Lines, and Premier Cruise Lines.

Appraising the value of any package depends entirely on your specific needs. The various sections of this book describe the activities and attractions available at Walt Disney World, and once you've determined which of these are most appealing, call Walt Disney World, the airlines that fly between your city and Orlando, or a qualified travel agent to find a package that comes closest to your specific needs. Don't pick a package that includes elements you don't want or won't use; chances are that you'll be paying for them. And remember that while extras such as welcoming cocktails sound attractive, their cash value is negligible. Also note that some packages announce as selling points certain services that are available to *every* Walt Disney World guest.

On the other hand, there's real value in some elements, such as transportation to the Walt Disney World property from the airport and discounts on meals. Some of the packages also include meals with the Disney characters, tennis lessons, golf greens fees, tennis court fees or boat rentals, and the like.

HOW TO CUT TRAVEL COSTS

Although vacations are not getting any less expensive, scrapping periodic getaways is no answer. If financial considerations are a primary concern, it's far better simply to prune the vacation budget in three main areas:

Food: Eat hot meals in cafeterias instead of waitress-service restaurants. Visit fancier establishments (if you must) at lunchtime rather than dinner. (The same entrées usually cost less then.) Carry sandwich fixings and have lunches alfresco when possible. Look for lodging places with kitchen facilities: The savings on food, especially for families at breakfast time, may be more than the extra accommodations expense.

Lodging: The chief rule of thumb here is not to pay for more than you need. Budget chains such as Days Inns and Days Lodges, Susse Chalet Motor Lodges and Inns, Imperial 400 Motor Inns, Passport Inns and Downtowners, Red Roof Inns, Family Inns of America, and Motel 6s can prove economical, though they may not offer many frills. (The best single guide to their whereabouts from coast to coast is the *National Directory of Budget Motels*, revised annually and available for $6.95 including postage from Pilot Books; 103 Cooper St.; Babylon, NY 11702; 516-422-2225.)

If swimming pools and other amenities matter, consider the non-budget chain establishments that have them—but remember that cutoff ages (above which there is a charge for children sharing their parents' room) do vary. Check with the individual hotel for their policy.

The *All-Star Sports* and *All-Star Music* resorts offer the least expensive rooms on the WDW property. Rooms at the *Caribbean Beach* resort, *Dixie Landings*, and *Port Orleans* are slightly higher priced. See our *Transportation & Accommodations* chapter for details.

Depending on the number of people in your party, guesthouses and tourist homes may or may not be a good buy. Since these establishments usually levy substantial extra charges for more than two people, regardless of their ages, rooms that are inexpensive for two can prove costly for a family. Consult *The Complete Guide to Bed & Breakfasts, Inns & Guesthouses* published by Ten Speed Press ($16.95) for locations and prices. Also look into A&A Bed and Breakfast of Florida (Box 1316; Winter Park, FL 32790; 628-3233). This organization handles reservations for B&Bs in the WDW area.

Consider sharing accommodations with family or friends. It's often possible to rent a resort condominium or a house large enough to accommodate two families for less than twice what each would pay for one conventional hotel room.

Transportation: Comparative shopping is vital. Consider transportation needs at your destination, then figure the total transportation cost. Calculate the cost of driving based on your car's mileage, current gasoline prices, the distance you expect to cover, and the cost of accommodations and food en route, then figure what you'll pay by bus, plane, or train. Don't fail to calculate the cost of getting to and from the airport or terminal, and the cost of renting a car (if necessary) in Orlando.

Magic Kingdom Club: Members can receive discounts on special Disney vacation packages, park admission, accommodations, select flights on Delta Air Lines, select merchandise in The Disney Stores and The Disney Catalog, car rentals, and more. Your company may offer free membership as an employee benefit. Inquire at your human resources department. The Magic Kingdom Club Gold Card provides the same benefits, plus more. The cost is $65 for a two-year membership. Seniors age 55 and over may join the Magic Years Club. The cost is $35 for a five-year membership. For more information or to join either club, call 714-520-2500. Keep in mind that it takes at least two weeks to receive membership materials.

How to Get the Best Photos

There are so many wonderful images all over the World that just about any camera in good working order can capture them for you. Here are some useful hints:

- Don't shoot from closer than 4 feet from your subject, and don't try for a flash picture more than 60 feet away.
- Fill the frame with as much of the prime subject as possible. When shooting people, remember that the larger the subject appears in the picture, the more interesting it will be.
- Don't shoot into the sun. Instead, position yourself so that light is falling directly on your subject—coming from behind you or from the side.
- Flash photography is not permitted inside any WDW attractions.
- Check the camera's batteries and battery contacts regularly.
- Use fresh film. When purchasing film, check the expiration date stamped on the bottom of the box. Keep film cool.
- Keep the camera clean. Blow dust off the lens and then wipe it with a soft tissue.
- When taking movies or using videotape cameras, note that they'll be more effective if you pick a theme such as "A Walk Down Main Street," "A Stroll Through France," or the like. Pan slowly and smoothly.
- If you suspect that your camera isn't functioning correctly, visit the Camera Center on the east side of Main Street near Town Square in the Magic Kingdom; the Camera Center near Spaceship Earth or Cameras and Film at Journey Into Imagination at Epcot; or The Darkroom at the Disney-MGM Studios.

Rental cameras: Video cameras are available for rent at the Camera Center in the Magic Kingdom; at the Camera Center in Epcot near Spaceship Earth and Cameras and Film at Journey Into Imagination; and at The Darkroom at the Disney-MGM Studios. The rental cameras cost $25 per day with a $300 refundable deposit that can be charged to American Express, Visa, or MasterCard. Rental cameras also are available at Magicam at the *Buena Vista Palace* hotel. While no 35mm cameras are available for rent, single-use cameras may be purchased at the above-listed shops.

Film processing: Two-hour processing is available at the Magic Kingdom, Epcot, the Disney-MGM Studios, at the resorts, and the Disney Village Marketplace wherever there is a Photo Express sign. Film is processed right on the premises.

WHERE TO BUY FILM

MAGIC KINGDOM

Main Street—Camera Center; Emporium
Frontierland—Frontier Trading Post
Liberty Square—Heritage House
Fantasyland—Seven Dwarfs Mining Co.;
 Kodak Kiosk
Tomorrowland—Mickey's Star Traders

EPCOT

Future World—All merchandise locations
 (best stock at the Camera Center)
World Showcase—At least one shop
 in each pavilion (film is often stashed
 under the counter)

DISNEY-MGM STUDIOS

The Darkroom
Crossroads of the World
Movieland Memorabilia

HOTELS

Contemporary resort—Concourse
 Sundries & Spirits; Bayview Gifts
Polynesian resort—News from
 Civilization
Grand Floridian—Sandy Cove; M. Mouse
 Mercantile
Wilderness Lodge—Wilderness Lodge
 Mercantile
Caribbean Beach—Calypso Trading Post
Yacht Club—Fittings and Farings
Beach Club—Atlantic Wear Gifts
Port Orleans—Jackson Square Gifts
Dixie Landings—Fulton's General Store
Disney Vacation Club—Conch Flats
 General Store
All-Star Sports—Sport Goofy's Gifts
 and Sundries
All-Star Music—Maestro Mickey's

FORT WILDERNESS

Settlement and Meadow trading posts

PLEASURE ISLAND

Music Legends

DISNEY VILLAGE MARKETPLACE

Guest Services, just outside You & Me Kid

Hints on Traveling with Children

Tell youngsters that a Walt Disney World vacation is in the works and the response is apt to be nothing less than overwhelming—and the journey to the park is likely to be fraught with "Are-we-there-yets?" recurring like a stuck record. Before leaving home be sure to pick up a copy of our guide, *Birnbaum's Walt Disney World For Kids, By Kids* ($9.95). It's filled with information about Walt Disney World from a kid's perspective, written for kids ages 7 to 15.

En route: Certain ploys can quiet this refrain a bit. Get older children involved in planning every leg of the trip, and set up a series of intermediate goals to which they can look forward. Younger children can anticipate discovering the contents of a pint-size suitcase packed with familiar games and toys, plus a few surprises.

In addition, it's smart to take along snacks to keep things peaceful when stomachs start rumbling and food is miles away. Above all, and especially if the trip is by car, take it easy, and allow time for plenty of breaks en route.

Those who fly should schedule travel during off-peak hours, when the chances are better that empty seats will be available. When the plane is taking off and landing, babies should be given bottles, pacifiers, or even thumbs to promote swallowing and clear ears. Newborn babies should not be taken aloft, since their lungs may not be able to adjust easily to the altitude. For finicky young eaters, request special meals when reserving seats. As the "Official Airline For Kids," Delta features the Fantastic Flyer program for children ages 2 to 12. On every Delta flight, kids receive a complimentary Mickey Mouse visor with an enrollment card and a copy of the *Fantastic Flyer* magazine featuring games, puzzles, and prizes. Ask the flight attendant for details.

Budget watchers should pay careful attention to motel rate structures (see page 27 for ideas) when reserving accommodations. Also, some motels charge for cots, while others might bring them in at no charge. Note that some hostelries outside the World *seem* a lot less expensive than the WDW resorts—until the actual costs for everything for a whole family are computed. Sometimes airfares that sound inexpensive actually cost more for a family; air packages might cut costs. The key is to check carefully.

At Walt Disney World: This vacationland ranks among the easiest spots on earth for traveling families with children. Older youngsters don't need to be driven around, and the general supervision is such that kids are hard pressed to get into trouble. All the resorts, plus *Fort Wilderness* and the Villa Recreation Center at The Villas at The Disney Institute, have at least a small room full of pinball machines and video games, much to the satisfaction of kids of all ages; the ones at the *All-Star* resorts are positively vast. And all the hotels have playgrounds; the ones at the *All-Star* resorts, the *Polynesian* resort, *Dixie Landings*, and *Caribbean Beach* get high marks from children.

The *Polynesian, Grand Floridian, Contemporary, Wilderness Lodge, Yacht Club, Beach Club, Swan,* and *Dolphin* have child-care facilities. In-room child care can be summoned to all resort locations; contact the Guest Services desk. And there also is a center known as KinderCare, which accepts kids ages one to four. For details and availability, phone 827-5444.

Strollers are available for rent for a nominal fee (small deposit required) at Strollers—Wheelchairs on the east side of Main Street at the entrance to the Magic Kingdom; in Epcot at the Stroller and Wheelchair Rentals Shop on the east side of the Entrance Plaza and at the International Gateway; and at Oscar's at the Disney-MGM Studios. Be sure to hold on to your receipt. If your stroller disappears while you're inside an attraction, a replacement may be obtained at Merchant of Venus in Tomorrowland; at the Frontier Trading Post in Frontierland; at Tinker Bell's Treasures in Fantasyland; at the World Traveler Shop at Epcot's International Gateway and the Germany pavilion in World Showcase; and at

Oscar's at the Disney-MGM Studios. Present your receipt when you return the stroller and you'll get a Disney Dollar back. Stroller renters should also be aware that guests only have to pay once a day for a stroller. If you rent one in the Magic Kingdom in the morning and plan to spend the afternoon in Epcot, just present the receipt for a free stroller at Epcot.

Baby Services at the Magic Kingdom, Epcot, and the Disney-MGM Studios can be helpful in many ways to parents with young children. There are low-lighted rooms with comfortable rocking chairs and love seats for nursing mothers, and cheerful feeding rooms. Highchairs, bibs, and plastic spoons also are available. The baby centers have facilities for changing infants, preparing formulas, and warming bottles. Disposable diapers and nurser bags, pull-on rubber pants, baby bottles with nipples, formula (Similac, Isomil, and Enfamil), teethers, pacifiers, prepared cereal, juices, and strained and junior baby food in a limited selection are available for sale on the spot at a nominal cost. The decor is soothing; the atmosphere is such that it seems a million miles away from the parks. A stop for diaper changing makes a good break for child and parent alike. Changing areas are available in most women's and some men's restrooms as well. Hours at the baby centers vary; check at City Hall or Guest Relations.

A variety of other baby-care supplies can be purchased at Strollers—Wheelchairs on Main Street, Baby Services in Epcot, and Oscar's Super Service at the Disney-MGM Studios. Disposable diapers are sold, though not displayed, in the Emporium on Main Street in the Magic Kingdom, at Baby Services near the Odyssey Center at Epcot, and at Baby Services in Guest Relations at the Disney-MGM Studios.

There is not any cause for excessive hand-holding inside the Magic Kingdom, Epcot, or the Disney-MGM Studios; with older youngsters, it's enough to establish a specific meeting place and time (allowing a little latitude, just in case). If there are younger children along, it's not a bad idea to stop at City Hall or the Baby Center next to the *Crystal Palace* to pick up a special name tag to facilitate a reunion in case the family gets separated. Name tags also are available at Guest Relations and the Baby Services at Epcot, and at Guest Relations at the Disney-MGM Studios.

Families traveling with small children also should know about the "kid switch" policy at all three theme parks. At attractions with age and/or height restrictions, a parent who waits with a young child while the other parent rides the attraction can go right on when the first parent comes off. If lines are long this can save a lot of time, so be sure to ask the attendant.

Although kids are usually enchanted by all of Walt Disney World, there are some attractions that hold their interest more than others. If you're traveling with very young children, your best bet is the Magic Kingdom. Visit Mickey's Starland first and then spend time in Fantasyland, keeping in mind that some of the attractions here frighten kids who are afraid of the dark. For older kids, thrill rides get the highest rating. Be sure not to miss Space Mountain, Alien Encounter, Splash Mountain, and Big Thunder Mountain Railroad in the Magic Kingdom, and Tower of Terror at the Disney-MGM Studios. Other favorites include The Haunted Mansion, Legend of The Lion King, Pirates of the Caribbean, and Peter Pan's Flight in the Magic Kingdom; Wonders of Life, Journey Into Imagination, and Norway in Epcot; and Muppet*Vision 3-D, Star Tours, the Indiana Jones Epic Stunt Spectacular, and the Monster Sound Show in the Studios.

Aunt Polly's on Tom Sawyer Island in the Magic Kingdom is a good bet for a snack; while adults are sipping lemonade, the kids can bounce across the Barrel Bridge and explore every nook and cranny on the island. *Lumière's Kitchen* in Fantasyland and *Tony's Town Square* on Main Street are good spots for lunch. At Epcot, kids prefer the *Sunshine Season Food Fair* in The Land and the *Liberty Inn* at The American Adventure. The *Sci-Fi Dine-In*, the *50's Prime Time Café,* and the *Soundstage* food court at the Studios are good choices as well. Another favorite is *Chef Mickey's* in the Disney Village Marketplace.

Lost children: The security forces inside the Magic Kingdom, Epcot, and the Disney-MGM Studios are far more careful than the happy appearance of things indicates. This is a welcome thought to those rare instances when a child suddenly disappears or fails to show up on schedule. If this happens to you, check the lost children's logbooks at Baby Services or City Hall in the Magic Kingdom; at Guest Relations or Baby Services (behind the Odyssey Center) in Epcot; or at Guest Relations at the Disney-MGM Studios. Every Disney employee knows where these logbooks are—and what to do if a lost-looking child suddenly starts to call for his or her mommy. There are no paging systems in the parks, but in serious emergencies an all-points bulletin can be put out among employees. The staff at the Guest Relations windows at the entrances to Epcot, the Magic Kingdom, and the Disney-MGM Studios can also assist with lost children.

Helpful Hints

Hints for Older Travelers

Walt Disney World can overwhelm an elderly traveler not accustomed to unfamiliar places; Epcot encompasses significant distances, and the Magic Kingdom and the Disney-MGM Studios can be disorienting because of the profusion of sights and sounds, nooks and crannies. And the heat, particularly in summer, can be hard to take. But with the proper planning and precautions, all of WDW can be just as delightful for older visitors as for kids. Here are a few suggestions:

• Join a tour. Surprisingly enough, not many companies offer tours to WDW specifically designed for older travelers. However, the following firms offer private guides to take guests through the parks: Eventures Unlimited Inc. (7648 Southland Blvd., Suite 101; Orlando, FL; 826-0055 or 800-356-7891) has private guides and charges $20 per hour (four-hour minimum, plus admission for the guide). Suncoast Destination Management (6149 Chancellor Dr., Suite 700; Orlando, FL 32809; 407-859-0027 or 800-827-0028) can provide uniformed guides for either $20 per hour (four-hour minimum plus admission for the guide) or $200 for the entire day (including admission).

• Schedule visits for off-peak seasons and hours when the crowds will not be overwhelming and discouraging. Also, note that special values are available to Florida residents during Resident Salute Days on selected non-peak dates, usually in January and May. Call 824-4321 for details.

• Read all Walt Disney World literature carefully before arrival so that things are familiar.

• In the parks, don't be timid about asking for directions or advice. Disney employees are always happy to help out.

• Eat early or late to avoid mealtime crowds. In the Magic Kingdom, stop in more sedate restaurants such as the *Crystal Palace*, *Tony's Town Square* restaurant, or *King Stefan's Banquet Hall* in Cinderella Castle. Or take the monorail to the still calmer *Polynesian* resort, the *Contemporary* resort, or the *Grand Floridian*, to lunch in one of the full-service restaurants there. In Epcot, the *Coral Reef* restaurant in Future World is an especially restful spot for lunch. At the Disney-MGM Studios, the *Hollywood Brown Derby* offers a relaxing sit-down meal.

• Don't try to save money by scrimping on food. Traveling takes energy, and only a good meal can provide it.

• Protect yourself from the sun. Always wear a hat, and don't stint on the sunscreen. (And remember to cover your legs, which are easily sunburned by light rays reflected from pavements.)

• Don't become overheated. Take frequent rest stops in the shade, and get out of the mid-afternoon heat by stopping for a snack in an air-conditioned restaurant. Avoid standing in line at Frontierland's Big Thunder Mountain Railroad in mid-afternoon; the queue is not wholly protected from the sun and can be very hot. In Epcot, spend the hot mid-afternoon hours in Innoventions, Wonders of Life, or the Sea Base Alpha exhibit at The Living Seas in Future World and avoid the uncovered outdoor queues at all the Future World pavilions and at World Showcase attractions such as *O Canada!*, *Impressions de France*, and *El Rió del Tiempo*. Don't underestimate the distances at Epcot; you may need to walk as much as two miles in the course of a day. If taken slowly and in short increments, this is not too onerous. But if you are not strong enough to cover that distance, be sure to rent a wheelchair at the outset of your visit. The buses that circumnavigate World Showcase Lagoon and the

HINTS FOR SINGLE TRAVELERS

Walt Disney World does not exactly attract the young swinging singles crowd, so those on the lookout for romantic encounters probably would do better elsewhere. But those who travel alone for the freedom and the fun of it can have as enjoyable a time at Walt Disney World as they would anywhere else.

WDW employees are generally a friendly and entertaining lot; chatting with a painter about the perpetual repainting of Main Street woodwork, talking to the animal keepers on Discovery Island, or discussing life abroad with one of the young World Showcase employees born and educated in the country the pavilion represents, a single traveler usually learns more about the ways of the World than any group member. Other visitors who might be encountered in the course of a day are away from their own home base as well, and are apt to be just that much less standoffish.

Pleasure Island has clubs, bars, restaurants, and shows that can prove to be fertile meeting places. In addition to the other Walt Disney World guests, lots of folks from the Orlando area also patronize the Pleasure Island establishments. This is especially true on weekends.

Single women traveling alone will find the bars and lounges at Walt Disney World hotels welcoming. The same relaxed atmosphere prevails in the *Rose & Crown Pub* in the United Kingdom pavilion and the *Matsu No Ma* lounge in Japan, both in the World Showcase area of Epcot. The *Biergarten* in World Showcase's Germany pavilion and the *Teppanyaki Dining Rooms* in Japan's *Mitsukoshi* restaurant are especially convivial since several parties are seated together at one large table. Another good way to meet people is to sign up for one of the tours of the Magic Kingdom or Epcot. River Country, Blizzard Beach, Typhoon Lagoon, and the hotel swimming pools and beaches also are good places for meeting people.

A note for budget watchers: Keep in mind that rates at all WDW resorts and hotels at Disney Village Hotel Plaza, and at some others in the Orlando area, are the same whether one or two persons occupy a room.

launches that make regular crossings can help you cover the distances—but only when there are no long queues. It is better to walk between pavilions, resting frequently en route, than to wait 15 or 20 minutes for a ride in a bus or boat.

● Above all, don't push yourself. Half the fun of Walt Disney World—the part that younger travelers often miss—is just sitting under a tree on a park bench, watching the people go by.

Lost Adults

Occasionally, traveling companions do get separated in the press of the crowds, or someone may fail to show up at an appointed meeting spot. When this happens, it's good to know that messages can be left for fellow travelers at Guest Relations at City Hall in the Magic Kingdom, or at the Guest Relations buildings in Epcot and the Disney-MGM Studios.

Hints for Travelers with Disabilities

Walt Disney World gets high marks among travelers with disabilities because of the attention that has been paid to their special needs. Special parking is available for guests visiting the Magic Kingdom, Epcot, and the Disney-MGM Studios; get directions at the Auto Plazas upon entering. From the Transportation and Ticket Center (TTC), the Magic Kingdom is accessible either by ferry or by monorail (though the former is preferable, since the slant of the ramp to the monorails makes holding a wheelchair a bit taxing when there are any waiting lines at all). All WDW monorail stations are accessible to wheelchairs except the one at the *Contemporary* resort, which can be reached only by escalator. Special vans, with motorized platforms that lift wheelchairs inside, are available too. To request one, day guests should inquire at the Guest Relations window at the TTC, at Epcot Entrance Plaza, in City Hall in the Magic Kingdom, Guest Relations in Epcot, or Guest Relations at the Disney-MGM Studios. Resort guests should contact Guest Services in their hotel. Count on at least 20 minutes between the request and pick-up.

Wheelchairs are available for rent in each of the theme parks and cost $5 per day, with a $1 deposit. In the Magic Kingdom, wheelchairs are rented at Strollers—Wheelchairs on the right-hand side of the souvenir area, just inside the turnstiles. In Epcot, the rental area is just inside the turnstiles on the left. Oscar's Super Service rents wheelchairs at the Disney-MGM Studios. Electronic Convenience Vehicles (ECVs) also are available in each of the parks. The price to rent an ECV is $30 plus a $20 deposit, per park per day. There is a limited number available, and they usually sell out within the first couple of hours that the parks are open.

The *Walt Disney World Guidebook for Guests with Disabilities,* which describes the accessibility of all WDW attractions, will prove beneficial throughout your visit. The guidebook may be obtained at wheelchair rental locations, City Hall in the Magic Kingdom, and Guest Relations in both Epcot and the Disney-MGM Studios. It also is available by mail. Write to Walt Disney World Guest Letters; Box 10,000; Lake Buena Vista, FL 32830.

Most restrooms in the parks have extra-wide cubicles with wall bars for people in wheelchairs and most attractions are accessible to guests who can be lifted to and from their chairs with the assistance from a member of their party, and many can accommodate guests who must remain in their wheelchairs at all times. Guests traveling in wheelchairs and members of their party need only check in with the attendant to bypass the line at attractions requiring ramp access.

The three theme parks and all WDW resort hotels are easily explored by wheelchair. All the WDW resorts have accommodations for guests with disabilities. At the villas some two-bedroom units are accessible to wheelchairs and some are not; the best bets are the planned-for-the-purpose units facing the Lake Buena Vista golf course. In River Country and Typhoon Lagoon, life jackets are available for travelers with disabilities.

For guests who are sight impaired, a tape recorder and cassette that describes the Magic Kingdom, Epcot, and the Disney-MGM Studios in terms of smells and sounds is available. A refundable deposit ($25) is required for recorder use. Service dogs are permitted in the parks.

Devices that amplify attraction sound tracks for guests who are hearing impaired are available at City Hall in the Magic Kingdom, and at Guest Relations in both Epcot and the Disney-MGM Studios. A $25 refundable deposit is required. Guests also are required to present a major credit card when renting. Guests who use telecommunications devices for the deaf (TDDs) can call 827-5141 for WDW information. TDDs are available for guest use at City Hall in the Magic Kingdom, Guest Relations in Epcot and at the Disney-MGM Studios, Guest Services at the Disney Village Marketplace, and at all the resorts. There is no charge for use of the TDDs. Also, written scripts are available at each show and attraction for guests with hearing impairments.

Tours: The Society for the Advancement of Travel for the Handicapped (347 Fifth Ave., Suite 610; New York, NY 10016; 212-447-7284) has a number of member travel agents who are knowledgeable about tours for travelers with disabilities and experienced in arranging both individual and group tours. Send a self-addressed stamped envelope and $3 to receive a copy of their listings. Among the organizations that sponsor trips for travelers with disabilities and offer tours to Walt Disney

World is Flying Wheels Travel (Box 382; Owatonna, MN 55060; 800-535-6790), which also can arrange trips for individuals.

Local Assistance: Friends of the Family (Box 69,081; Orlando, FL 32819; 856-7676 or 800-945-2045) is a valuable resource for travelers with disabilities visiting Central Florida in that it provides free referrals on everything from barrier-free hotels and medical care to hourly helpers.

Traveling by car: Hertz, Avis, National, and Thrifty all have a limited quantity of hand-control cars for rent in the Orlando area; it's a good idea to call well in advance to reserve them.

Traveling by plane: Airlines are more helpful today in dealing with travelers with disabilities. Occasionally, vacationers can go into the aircraft in their own chair—provided the chair is narrow and the plane's aisles are wide; more often, travelers transfer to a narrower airline chair at the door of the aircraft, while their own chair is sent down to the luggage compartment. Passengers in wheelchairs are usually pre-boarded and then deplaned after other passengers. If you're not taking your own wheelchair along and have a tight connection to make, be sure to advise the airline's attendants well in advance. If a passenger wishes to use an airline's wheelchair at a connecting point or destination, this wheelchair service should be ordered at the time that flight reservations are being made.

Allow plenty of time to make all your arrangements, and don't fail to alert all airline personnel to your special needs.

Policies on motorized wheelchairs vary, depending on the airline and the type of chair; check with carriers in advance. Service dogs are always allowed aboard aircraft (though some carriers may require them to be muzzled), but arrangements should be made at the time reservations are made so that a bulkhead seat may be requested.

Traveling by train: Whether riding with or without reservations, it's smart to phone in advance to arrange for one of the special seats that Amtrak maintains for travelers with disabilities. Wheelchairs are available at major Amtrak stations, about 500 in all, including Orlando. Cars have special seats and specially equipped bathrooms and sleeping compartments; older equipment also has been refurbished to accommodate travelers with disabilities. Passengers who are visually impaired or have other disabilities get a 25 percent discount on one-way tickets, though companions must pay full fare. Service dogs may ride with passengers at no extra charge.

Battery-powered, standard-size wheelchairs are permitted in coaches. Fuel-powered and oversize chairs must be stored in the baggage car for the duration of the trip. Always be sure to phone the train stations and reservations center well before your departure date to arrange for any special facilities or services you may need.

Traveling by bus: Greyhound has implemented plans that allow vacationers with disabilities and their companion (for help with boarding and disembarking) to travel together on a single adult ticket. Greyhound carries nonmotorized folding wheelchairs at no additional charge. Some motorized wheelchairs are accepted.

And remember to plan in advance. Allow extra time, and at each portion of the trip, inform air, bus, train, and hotel personnel of your special needs.

Other Information

BARBERS AND SALONS: The most amusing place to get a haircut is the old-fashioned Harmony Barber Shop (824-6550), tucked away at the end of the flower-filled cul-de-sac just off the west side of Main Street in the Magic Kingdom; the Disney books on hand are terrific, and the "Dapper Dans," the park's own barbershop quartet, can often be heard here. Children can get special souvenir Mouseketeer hats, and moustache cups and other nostalgic shaving items are for sale.

Haircuts, shampoos, sets, coloring, waving, manicures, and pedicures are available at the following resort salons: the one on the third floor of the *Contemporary* resort (824-3413), the Periwig Salon at the *Yacht Club* and *Beach Club* (934-3260), Ivy Trellis at the *Grand Floridian* (824-1000, ext. 2581), and the Niki Bryan shop at the *Dolphin* (934-4250).

CAR CARE: Auto- and travel-club members should call their local club-sponsored towing service in the event of problems. The Exxon Tiger Mart on Floridian Way near the Magic Kingdom Auto Plaza is open seven days a week from 7 A.M. to 1½ hours after the Magic Kingdom closes. A second Exxon Tiger Mart opened recently on Buena Vista Drive across from Pleasure Island. It's also reassuring to know that WDW breakdowns don't mean disaster. All WDW roads are patrolled constantly by security vehicles equipped with radios that can be used to call for help.

DISNEY DOLLARS: Greenbacks bearing Mickey's image are available in one-, five-, and ten-dollar denominations. Disney Dollars are accepted at all Magic Kingdom, Epcot, and Disney-MGM Studios restaurants, snack stands, and shops, as well as all WDW resorts.

DRINKING LAWS: In Florida, drinking is legal at the age of 21. There are many bars and lounges all over Walt Disney World; minors are permitted to accompany their parents, but are prohibited from sitting or standing at the bar. There's no drinking in the Magic Kingdom (where even the piña coladas are nonalcoholic), but alcoholic beverages are available at restaurants in Epcot, the Disney-MGM Studios, Pleasure Island, and the Disney Village Marketplace.

By the bottle: Liquor is sold in mini-bottles at Gourmet Pantry at the Disney Village Marketplace, at Trader Jack's in the *Polynesian* resort, at Concourse Sundries & Spirits in the *Contemporary* resort, at Calypso Trading Post at the *Caribbean Beach* resort, at the Conch Flats General Store at the *Disney Vacation Club*, at Wilderness Lodge Mercantile at the *Wilderness Lodge*, and at the Settlement Trading Post and Meadow Trading Post at *Fort Wilderness*. Liquor also may be purchased from room service at the *Polynesian* resort, the *Contemporary* resort, the *Grand Floridian* resort, the *Yacht Club*, the *Beach Club,* the *Dolphin*, and the *Swan*.

LOCKERS: There are coin-operated lockers underneath the Main Street Railroad Station in the Magic Kingdom and at two locations at the Transportation and Ticket Center—next to the Lost and Found on the west end and beside the bus parking lot on the east side. Lockers also are available at several Epcot locations: at the Bus Information Center in the bus parking lot, in an area to the right of Earth Station as you face World Showcase Lagoon, and at International Gateway in World Showcase. At the Disney-MGM Studios, lockers can be found next to Oscar's near the main entrance. Cost is 50¢ per use for the regular size, 75¢ for the larger ones. Items too big to fit into the latter can be checked at the Guest Relations windows at the TTC, at City Hall inside the Magic Kingdom, in the package pickup area or in the storage area in Epcot, and at Guest Relations at the Disney-MGM Studios. Be aware that lockers are available for use at your own risk. It is not recommended that valuable items be stored in lockers.

LOST AND FOUND: The extensive indexing system maintained by Walt Disney World's Lost and Found department is impressive, especially when a prize possession turns up missing, whether it's false teeth or a camera. (Both have been lost in the past; the dentures were never claimed.) If you lose (or find) something, report it on the proper forms at City Hall, at the Guest Relations window on the east end of the Transportation and Ticket Center, at the Epcot Entrance Plaza, Guest Relations, or the Guest Relations desks at the Disney-MGM Studios, in the first floor lobby at the *Contemporary* resort, or the main lobbies at the *Polynesian* resort, the *Grand Floridian*, the *Caribbean Beach*, *Yacht Club*, *Beach Club*, *Port Orleans*, *Dixie Landings, Wilderness Lodge*, *All-Star Sports*, *All-Star Music*, *The Villas at The Disney Institute*, and the *Disney Vacation Club*; at *Fort Wilderness*, phone ext. 7-2726 from a comfort station telephone; from outside the campground, phone 824-2726; and from the Disney Village Marketplace, phone 828-3058.

MAIL

Postcards are for sale at many spots in the resorts. Postage stamps can be purchased at all the Walt Disney World resorts; they also are sold at City Hall in the Magic Kingdom; near the lockers in both Epcot and the Disney-MGM Studios; and at Guest Services in the Disney Village Marketplace.

The old-fashioned, olive-drab mailboxes that punctuate the thoroughfares in the three theme parks are no longer official U.S. post boxes, but letters can be mailed there for pickup by Disney employees and subsequent transportation to the Lake Buena Vista post office. Postmarks read "Lake Buena Vista," *not* "Walt Disney World." All window services are available at the Lake Buena Vista post office, including postal money order and stamp sale, registry, and certification. The post office is located at the Crossroads of Lake Buena Vista shopping center.

Mail may be addressed to guests c/o their hotel at Walt Disney World; Box 10,000; Lake Buena Vista, FL 32830.

Don't forget to arrange for mail at home to be held by the post office.

MEDICAL MATTERS

For travelers with chronic health problems, it's a good idea to carry copies of all prescriptions and to get names of local doctors from hometown physicians. However, Walt Disney World is equipped to deal with many types of medical emergencies. In the Magic Kingdom, next to the Crystal Palace, there's a First Aid Center staffed by a registered nurse; there is another at Epcot, located in the Odyssey Center complex. At the Disney-MGM Studios, the First Aid Center is in the Guest Relations building at the main entrance, accessible from both inside and outside the park.

For Walt Disney World resort guests, as well as those staying at other area hotels, the HouseMed health service can provide non-emergency medical care. Call 396-1195 to have a HouseMed physician dispatched directly to a guest's room. The service is available 24 hours a day. HouseMed also operates the MediClinic, located at the intersection of U.S. 192 and I-4. It's open daily from 8 A.M. to 9 P.M., and transportation is available from all WDW First Aid Centers and resorts, as well as area hotels. Serious emergencies can be reported to the nearby Sandlake Hospital (351-8550).

The most common malady? Not sensitive stomachs upset by rides, but simple *sunburn*. So be forewarned. Wear a hat, and slather on sufficient sunblock or sunscreen, especially during the spring and summer.

For diabetics: Walt Disney World resorts provide refrigeration services for insulin; the villas and the *Fort Wilderness* homes have their own refrigerators.

Prescriptions: The Buena Vista Walk-In Medical Center (828-3434) offers shuttle service from the First Aid Center and Epcot and all WDW resorts. The clinic is open daily from 8 A.M. to 8 P.M. (The shuttle stops at 6 P.M.) for diagnosis and treatment of non-critical injuries and illnesses. A pharmacy, Turner Drugs (828-8125), is located next door to the clinic and is open from 8 A.M. to 8 P.M. daily. Delivery to any WDW resort can be arranged. The Gooding's supermarket at the Crossroads shopping center also has a pharmacy.

Items lost in the Magic Kingdom can be claimed on the day of the loss at City Hall, and thereafter at the main Lost and Found station at the Transportation and Ticket Center. Articles found at Epcot remain at the Epcot Lost and Found for one day before being delivered to the main Lost and Found. At the Disney-MGM Studios, claim or report lost items at the Guest Relations building on the day of your visit. To report lost items after your visit, call 824-4245.

Articles not claimed by the owner may be claimed by the finder—providing an added incentive for visitors to turn over valuable items to Lost and Found.

POCKET PAGERS: Two types of devices are available to WDW resort guests to signal a telephone call or message. They can be rented at all WDW hotels.

RELIGIOUS SERVICES: A variety of religious services are held around Walt Disney World and in the surrounding area.

Protestant: 9 A.M. on Sundays at Luau Cove at the *Polynesian* resort.

Catholic: 8 A.M. and 10:15 A.M. on Sundays at Luau Cove at the *Polynesian* resort. Call Mary, Queen of the Universe Shrine (239-6600 or 876-2211) for specifics, or check with Guest Services at any WDW hotel. The closest Catholic church off the property is Mary, Queen of the Universe Shrine, 2 1/2 miles north of Lake Buena Vista on the I-4 service road. This enormous church seats 3,000 people, and has beautiful gardens and fountains. Call 239-6600 or 876-2211 for mass times.

For more information on nearby Catholic and Protestant services, call the Christian Service Center at 425-2523.

Jewish: Conservative services are at 7:30 P.M. on Fridays and 9:30 A.M. on Saturdays at Temple Ohalei Rivka (11200 Apopka Vineland Rd.; 239-5444) located about three miles from the Disney Village Marketplace. Reform services are at 10:30 A.M. on Saturdays at the Congregation of Liberal Judaism (928 Malone Drive; 645-0444).

MONEY

Cash, traveler's checks, personal checks, American Express (the official credit card of Walt Disney World), MasterCard, Visa, and The Disney Credit Card are accepted as payment for all admission media. Checks must bear your name and address, be drawn on a U.S. bank, and be accompanied by the proper identification—a valid driver's license and a major credit card such as American Express, Visa, MasterCard, The Disney Credit Card, Diners Club, or Carte Blanche. Fast-food restaurants in the Magic Kingdom, Epcot, and the Disney-MGM Studios accept only cash.

For charges at sit-down restaurants and shops inside the theme parks, however, and for all other charges throughout Walt Disney World, American Express, Visa, MasterCard, and The Disney Credit Card are accepted. WDW resort guests may use the WDW resort IDs that each member of a party receives upon check-in to cover purchases in shops, lounge and restaurant charges, and recreational fees incurred inside WDW when a major credit card has been used for their room charges. At the Magic Kingdom, Epcot, and the Disney-MGM Studios, guests can use IDs to charge meals at table-service restaurants. These cards are not valid for charges made past check-out time on the last day of the guest's stay.

Automated Teller Machines: ATMs are located on Main Street in the Magic Kingdom and in Tomorrowland, at the entrances to the Disney-MGM Studios and Epcot, at Pleasure Island, at the Disney Village Marketplace, at the *All-Star Sports* resort, and at the Crossroads shopping center.

Sun Bank: This institution (which has an old-fashioned branch on Main Street inside the Magic Kingdom and one across from the Disney Village Marketplace) can:

• Give cash advances on MasterCard and Visa credit cards, with a $25 minimum in amounts as large as a guest's credit limit will permit.

• Cash and sell traveler's checks and provide refunds for lost American Express and Bank of America traveler's checks.

• Cash personal checks of up to $1,000 for American Express cardholders upon presentation of their cards (part payable in cash and the rest in American Express traveler's checks).

• Cash personal checks for up to $25 upon presentation of a driver's license and a major credit card such as American Express, MasterCard, or Visa.

• Help with wire transfers of money from a guest's own bank to the Sun Bank branch.

The Sun Bank branch in the Magic Kingdom is open from 9 A.M. to 4 P.M. daily; phone 828-6102 for further information. The Sun Bank across from the Disney Village Marketplace is open from 9 A.M. to 4 P.M. on weekdays (until 6 P.M. on Thursdays); drive-in teller windows are open from 8 A.M. to 6 P.M. on weekdays; phone 828-6106.

Traveler's checks: Even the most careful of vacationers occasionally loses a wallet, and traveler's checks can take the sting out of that loss. In deciding which type to buy, travelers should focus on price differences since all the major traveler's check offerers can come through with emergency funds in a pinch, particularly at Walt Disney World. It's a good idea, therefore, to look for special promotions by banks at home in the months preceding a vacation, and check to see which of the five major brands—American Express, MasterCard, Visa, Citicorp, and Bank of America—are available free.

Don't fail to sign checks in the proper place as soon as they are purchased. And stash the receipt bearing the check numbers in a separate place from the checks themselves, along with one piece of identification such as a duplicate driver's license or a spare credit card. These will speed the refund process should your checks get lost.

Foreign currency exchange: This can be done from 9 A.M. to 4 P.M. daily at the Guest Relations windows in all three parks, at City Hall or at the Sun Bank in Town Square inside the Magic Kingdom, and at Guest Relations in Epcot. Currency can be exchanged at WDW resorts at other times. The Sun Bank across from the Disney Village Marketplace also exchanges foreign currency.

In Epcot, sundries are available in at least one shop in each of the World Showcase pavilions and at all the retail outlets in Future World (except the Kodak camera sales kiosk at Journey Into Imagination).

At the Disney-MGM Studios, sundries are available at the Crossroads of the World and Movieland Memorabilia shops.

Gooding's supermarket, at the Crossroads of Lake Buena Vista Shopping Center near Hotel Plaza, has a large pharmacy department.

Reading matter: Newspapers, magazines, bestsellers, and paperbacks are available in a limited selection at Concourse Sundries & Spirits in the *Contemporary* resort, at News from Civilization in the *Polynesian* resort, Sandy Cove at the *Grand Floridian*, Calypso Trading Post at the *Caribbean Beach* resort, Fittings and Fairings at the *Yacht Club*, Atlantic Wear and Wardrobe at the *Beach Club*, the Meadow Trading Post and Settlement Trading Post at *Fort Wilderness*, Jackson Square Gifts and Desires at *Port Orleans*, Fulton's General Store at *Dixie Landings*, Conch Flats General Store at the *Disney Vacation Club*, Wilderness Lodge Mercantile at *Wilderness Lodge*, Maestro Mickey's at the *All-Star Music* resort, Sport Goofy's Gifts and Sundries at the *All-Star Sports* resort, Daisy's Garden at the *Dolphin*, Disney Cabana at the *Swan*, and at 2R's Reading and Riting at the Disney Village Marketplace. Most carry the daily papers from Orlando and Miami, *The Wall Street Journal*, and, on Sundays, *The New York Times* and *The Chicago Tribune*.

The Emporium in the Magic Kingdom has children's books. Epcot offers an interesting selection as well. Books related to the themes of Future World pavilions are available in the Centorium and at the Discovery Center in Innoventions. In World Showcase, the United Kingdom's Toy Soldier and Der Bücherwurm in Germany stock children's books.

Comic books and magazines are available at Lakeside News at the Disney-MGM Studios. Books on the subject of animation are on sale at the Animation Gallery.

SHOPPING FOR NECESSITIES: Almost all everyday needs can be satisfied right on the property. Concourse Sundries & Spirits in the *Contemporary* resort, the Grog Hut on the second floor of the *Polynesian* resort, Sandy Cove at the *Grand Floridian*, Calypso Trading Post at the *Caribbean Beach* resort, Fittings and Fairings at the *Yacht Club*, Atlantic Wear and Wardrobe at the *Beach Club*, Jackson Square Gifts and Desires at *Port Orleans*, Fulton's General Store at *Dixie Landings*, Conch Flats General Store at the *Disney Vacation Club*, Wilderness Lodge Mercantile at *Wilderness Lodge*, Maestro Mickey's at the *All-Star Music* resort, Sport Goofy's Gifts and Sundries at the *All-Star Sports* resort, Daisy's Garden at the *Dolphin*, Disney Cabana at the *Swan*, and the Meadow and Settlement Trading Posts at *Fort Wilderness* all stock a limited number of brands of a wide variety of toiletries; a broader selection is available at the Disney Village Marketplace at the Gourmet Pantry.

In addition, a number of over-the-counter health aids, plus many other useful items, can be purchased in the Books and Records section of the Emporium on Main Street in the Magic Kingdom; they're kept behind the counter, so it's necessary to ask for the supplies you want. Aspirin and suntan lotion also are available at Mickey's Star Traders in Tomorrowland.

TELEPHONE: The folks at home can reach Walt Disney World resort guests at the following phone numbers (all are in area code 407):

All-Star Music:	939-6000
All-Star Sports:	939-5000
Beach Club:	934-8000
Caribbean Beach:	934-3400
Contemporary:	824-1000
Disney Vacation Club:	827-7700
Disney's BoardWalk:	939-5100
Dixie Landings:	934-6000
Dolphin:	934-4000
Fort Wilderness:	824-2900
Grand Floridian:	824-3000
Polynesian:	824-2000
Port Orleans:	934-5000
Swan:	934-3000
Villas at The Disney Institute:	827-1100
Wilderness Lodge:	824-3200
Yacht Club:	934-7000

TIME AND WEATHER PHONE: In the Orlando area, the number is 646-3131.

TIPPING: Walt Disney World is not one of those places where bellmen stick out their hands even before they put down your luggage. Instead, they seem genuinely glad to help out. Oddly enough, this pleasant attitude seems to discourage tipping at the same time that it arouses the sentiments that make most travelers want to reach for their wallets.

Tips are no less valued at WDW resorts than they would be at any other good hotel—the standard 75 cents to $1 per bag is appropriate for lugging luggage. Gratuities of 15 percent to 18 percent are also customary at full-service restaurants all over Walt Disney World.

Gratuities are not required in fast-food restaurants or at the attractions, but in the beauty shops, it's usual to leave a tip of about 15 percent of the total bill.

Cabdrivers in the Orlando area expect a 15 percent tip. Baggage handlers at bus and train stations and at the airport expect at least 75 cents per bag.

PETS

No pets (other than service dogs) are allowed in the Magic Kingdom, Epcot, the Disney-MGM Studios, or at the WDW resorts, except certain campsites at *Fort Wilderness* (request a pet site for $3 extra per day). Travelers who bring pets along can lodge them in one of four attractive air-conditioned Pet Care Kennels: near the Transportation and Ticket Center; to the left of the Epcot Entrance Plaza; at the Disney-MGM Studios entrance; and at the *Fort Wilderness* campground entrance, next to a huge field where pet owners can take their animals out for a run. During busy seasons, it's best to arrive before the 9 A.M. to 10 A.M. morning rush hour. Be sure to note that the kennels close an hour after the Magic Kingdom, Epcot, and the Disney-MGM Studios.

Bears, cougars, and ocelots have all been accommodated by the WDW kennels, and exotic pets may be accepted— if a bit reluctantly. However, owners themselves must put the more unusual animals into the kennel's cages; and snakes, rabbits, birds, turtles, hamsters, and other animals unsuited (because of size) to cat- and dog-size cages must be accompanied by their own escape-proof accommodations.

Guests may board their pets overnight in any WDW kennel. Cost is $11 for overnight stays, including dry food ($9 per night for WDW resort guests); $6 for a day stay, with one feeding. Guests who board pets overnight are encouraged to stop by to walk them at least twice a day, as the animals are not otherwise let out of their cages. Pets will be fed special food, if provided.

Be sure to bring along your pet's certificate of vaccination, since Florida law requires proof of immunization for animals involved in biting incidents. And never leave pets in your car. It is against the law in Florida.

For information and reservations (accepted, not required), call 824-6568.

Outside Walt Disney World: A number of hotels in the Orlando and Kissimmee area permit pets. For further information, phone the Orlando/Orange County Convention and Visitors Bureau (363-5871).

TRANSPORTATION & ACCOMMODATIONS

The popularity of Walt Disney World has made the region around Orlando one of the world's major tourism and commercial centers, and everything from a state-of-the-art airport to an efficient network of highways brings visitors to the area by the millions.

There's no doubt, however, that confusion about getting to and around the Walt Disney World region is pervasive and may be exceeded only by the dilemma of which specific sort of accommodation is right for your family's needs.

The accommodations operated by Walt Disney World itself range from futuristic high-rise towers to treehouses buried deep in piney woods. In between are resorts that evoke striking images of the South Pacific, old Florida, the Pacific Northwest, the Caribbean, New England, Louisiana, and the sports world, plus efficient trailer-type facilities in a sprawling, beautifully maintained campground. And that doesn't include the many villas that provide extraordinary space and luxury at surprisingly affordable prices, or the studios and one-, two-, and three-bedroom homes that can be purchased through a unique vacation ownership system. What follows should help travelers sort out all the lodging options on Walt Disney World property, as well as shed light on the broad range of possibilities that exist outside the WDW gates.

(Unless otherwise noted, all telephone numbers are in area code 407.)

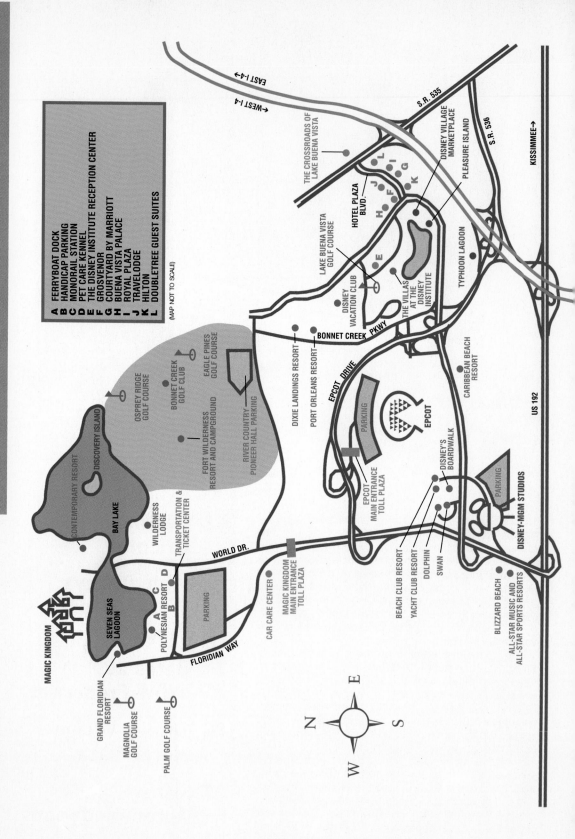

A FERRYBOAT DOCK
B HANDICAP PARKING
C MONORAIL STATION
D PET CARE KENNEL
E THE DISNEY INSTITUTE RECEPTION CENTER
F GROSVENOR
G COURTYARD BY MARRIOTT
H BUENA VISTA PALACE
I ROYAL PLAZA
J TRAVELODGE
K HILTON
L DOUBLETREE GUEST SUITES

(MAP NOT TO SCALE)

Getting Oriented

Orlando, the Central Florida city of more than 165,000 residents, is the municipality with which Walt Disney World is most closely associated. Walt Disney World, however, is actually in a far smaller community called Lake Buena Vista. Many hotels and restaurants are located here, though there are far more in Orlando proper, to the north. Among the more compelling areas are adjacent communities like Winter Park (on Orlando's northeastern extremity), Maitland (just northwest of Winter Park), and Altamonte Springs (north of Maitland).

ORLANDO-AREA HIGHWAYS: The most important Orlando traffic artery is I-4, which runs diagonally through the area from southwest to northeast, cutting through the southern half of Walt Disney World. It then angles on toward Orlando and Winter Park, ending near Daytona Beach at I-95, which runs north and south along the coast.

All the city's other important highways intersect I-4. From south to north, these include U.S. 192 (aka Irlo Bronson Memorial Highway), which takes an east-west course that crosses the WDW entrance road and leads into downtown Kissimmee on the east; S.R. 528 (aka the Beeline Expressway), which shoots eastward from I-4; S.R. 435, also known as Kirkman Road, which runs north and south and intersects International Drive, where many motels catering to WDW visitors are located; U.S. 17-92-441 (aka Orange Blossom Trail), which runs due north and south, paralleling Kirkman Road on the east; and S.R. 50 (aka Colonial Drive), which runs due east and west.

WALT DISNEY WORLD ROADS: The 45-square-mile tract that is Walt Disney World is roughly rectangular. I-4 runs through its southern half from southwest to northeast. There are three highway exits leading to WDW. The first Disney exit (number 27) is marked "S.R. 535/Lake Buena Vista" and should be used by guests heading for Pleasure Island, the Disney Village Hotel Plaza, *The Villas at The Disney Institute*, the Disney Village Marketplace, and the Crossroads shopping center. The second exit (number 26B), marked "Epcot/Disney Village," should be taken by guests going to Epcot, Typhoon Lagoon, the *BoardWalk*, the *Caribbean Beach* resort, the *Swan, Dolphin, Yacht Club* and *Beach Club* resorts, *Port Orleans, Dixie Landings,* and *Disney Vacation Club*. It also is a good alternate route to the Disney Village Marketplace and the Disney-MGM Studios. The third exit (number 25) is marked "192/Magic Kingdom" and leads to the Magic Kingdom, the Disney-MGM Studios,

GETTING AROUND WDW

The internal transportation system at Walt Disney World is quite extensive, and is always being revised to serve the ever-increasing number of attractions and accommodations. All bus stops are clearly marked, and guests staying at WDW hotels receive detailed information about transportation options upon checking in. The system's central link is a hub called the Transportation and Ticket Center (TTC), located near the Magic Kingdom. Day visitors must park here before taking a monorail or ferry to the Magic Kingdom. WDW resort guests can bypass the TTC via direct buses. The TTC also is important as the transfer point between Epcot and Magic Kingdom monorails.

All-Star Music and All-Star Sports resorts, Blizzard Beach, the Contemporary, the Polynesian, the Grand Floridian, Wilderness Lodge, Fort Wilderness, and River Country.

There also are a number of roads inside the World. In some cases, it is possible to drive from place to place on them. Bus transportation also is provided between most points, and is available without charge to most guests. At the northernmost end of Walt Disney World, an elevated monorail train operates along a circular route, making stops at the Polynesian resort, the Grand Floridian resort, the Contemporary resort, and the Magic Kingdom and the TTC; a separate extension of the monorail system also goes to Epcot. Motor launches and cruisers from the Contemporary resort and the Magic Kingdom call at Fort Wilderness, the Wilderness Lodge, and Discovery Island.

TRANSPORTATION ID REQUIREMENTS

Several types of identification and/or admission media are required for use of the various forms of transportation within WDW. This list explains what sort of card, ticket, or pass permits the use of each:

- WDW resort identification cards allow guests unlimited use of any part of the WDW transportation system (including buses, monorails, and watercraft).
- Valid one-day theme park tickets permit guests to use all monorails and the ferries running between the TTC and the Magic Kingdom entrance. These tickets do not allow use of WDW buses.

- Four-Day Value Passes, Four-Day Park Hopper Passes, Five-Day World Hopper Passes, Length of Stay Passes, and Annual Passes allow guests use of the WDW transportation system.
- River Country, Discovery Island, and Pioneer Hall tickets allow guests the use of buses from the TTC, watercraft from the Contemporary resort, and watercraft from the Magic Kingdom to and from River Country, Discovery Island, and Pioneer Hall.
- For up-to-the-minute information about all available transportation routes, call 824-4321.

Accommodations

Orlando and its environs have tens of thousands of hotel and motel rooms. Few of these, however, whether inside or outside the World, are of a design much beyond the predictable Anywhere, USA, motel-modern decor, usually with two standard double beds, plush carpeting, simulated-wood paneling, a color television set, and a private bathroom.

The biggest differences among accommodations seem to be in the dimensions of the rooms and bathrooms, the attention to decor, the level of service, the variety of dining options, the recreational facilities, the landscaping of the surrounding grounds, and the location.

Basically, Walt Disney World area accommodations fall into two main categories: those located within the boundaries of Walt Disney World and those outside the property. Rates are generally higher at WDW addresses than at most other motels in the area with the exception of the new *All-Star Sports* and *All-Star Music* resorts, but the convenience is so much greater that the extra expense is not at all unreasonable. There also are additional benefits available to on-property guests such as guaranteed park admission even when parks are full, use of WDW transportation, closed-circuit TV announcing WDW events, early admission to the three theme parks on designated days, free delivery of purchases back to your resort, and the best possible access to Guest Services personnel. Resort guests also can reserve tee-off times on the golf courses up to 30 days in advance. Considering all of the advantages, you should be wary of anyone who encourages you to stay elsewhere for reasons other than a major difference in price.

It's helpful to think of accommodations on the WDW grounds in terms of their location. Therefore, this chapter is divided into several sections, describing the Magic Kingdom Resorts, Epcot Resorts, All-Star Resorts, Village Resorts, *Fort Wilderness*, and Disney Village Hotel Plaza hostelries.

Locations of the off-site properties are quite scattered. Those closest to WDW are located on S.R. 535 in Lake Buena Vista. Others are located in Kissimmee, along U.S. 192 (which runs east and west) intersecting the WDW entrance road, and along International Drive (off S.R. 435 at the Orlando city limits). The U.S. 192 establishments are closer to the WDW main entrance—usually only a few miles away, depending on the individual hostelry. International Drive, some ten miles from the WDW main gates, has an extensive array of accommodations, restaurants, and other attractions. Its proximity to still more of the same in Orlando, just a few miles farther north, constitutes an additional lure. Off-property options are described in the latter part of the chapter.

In choosing a place to stay, first decide just how much you want to spend. If your budget permits, try to get a reservation at one of the on-site properties. (Remember that there are Disney accommodations in varying price ranges.) If not, select accommodations outside the World based on your budget and on the guidelines given in this section.

Remember, when examining rate sheets for the best buy for your family, check the cutoff age at which children accompanying you (and staying in the same room) will be billed as extra adults. Those with large families should note that the Disney villa-type accommodations and Wilderness Homes, which may seem more expensive at first glance, actually can prove less costly in the long run—by eliminating the necessity of securing an additional hotel room and providing cooking facilities that can mean big savings on meals.

Walt Disney World Resort Properties

With the addition of moderately priced rooms at *Caribbean Beach*, *Port Orleans*, and *Dixie Landings*, and the even more economical rooms at the *All-Star Sports* and *All-Star Music* resorts, we find it difficult to recommend staying off the property. And reservations are generally easy to obtain, even on short notice, since there are now more than 20,000 rooms on the property.

In general, rooms at the *Contemporary* resort, the *Polynesian* resort, the *Grand Floridian* resort, the *Yacht Club* and *Beach Club*, the new *BoardWalk Inn* (opening mid-year), and the *Swan* and *Dolphin* are quite large and can accommodate up to five guests in a single room without difficulty. Rooms at *Wilderness Lodge*, the *Caribbean Beach*, *Port Orleans*, *Dixie Landings*, *All-Star Sports*, and *All-Star Music* resorts accommodate up to four people. Many rooms have patios or balconies. And

considering the incredibly high occupancy rate, it's astonishing that things look so fresh. Even the rooms without views have views, if only across the gardens.

The Villas at The Disney Institute, which can accommodate larger groups, makes particularly good sense for families, especially those who want to cook some of their own meals "at home." The vacation homes at the *Disney Vacation Club* also are good for families. Unsold accommodations at the *Disney Vacation Club* are available as hotel rooms. At *Fort Wilderness* resort there are both campsites and fully equipped Wilderness Homes set on 700 acres of quiet woods. With the mid-year opening of the *BoardWalk Villas*, larger groups will have 532 new vacation cottages from which to choose.

The WDW hotels in this section are broken into five groups: Magic Kingdom Resorts, Village Resorts, Epcot Resorts, All-Star Resorts, and *Fort Wilderness*. The hotels, rooms, and facilities are described in detail. All WDW resorts offer laundry facilities and feature voice mail messaging service. Restaurants are mentioned here but are described at length in the *Good Meals, Great Times* chapter. Note that all restaurants at WDW resorts are non-smoking, as are all public spaces with the exception of lounges.

DISNEY RATES THE RESORTS

The new Walt Disney World rating system helps you choose the resort, hotel, villa, or campsite that best suits your needs. Here's a breakdown of the amenities, standard room rates, and resorts in each category. For specific pricing, see the chart on pages 74 and 75.

DELUXE ($159 to $375)
Full-service restaurants
Room service
Bellman luggage service, valet parking
Swimming pools, beach access
On-site recreation such as boat rental
Most rooms sleep five
On-site child-care programs
Monorail, boat, or bus transportation to all
  theme parks

Resorts
Beach Club (page 57)
BoardWalk Inn (page 61)
Contemporary (page 48)
Dolphin (page 60)
Grand Floridian (page 52)
Polynesian (page 50)
Swan (page 59)
Wilderness Lodge (page 54)
Yacht Club (page 57)

HOME AWAY FROM HOME ($185 to $1,150)
Kitchen facilities, pizza delivery, grocery service
Bellman luggage service
Swimming pools
Front-door parking for your vehicle
Flexible room arrangements accommodating
  4 to 12 guests
Privacy; wooded or golf course environment
Bus transportation to all theme parks

Resorts
BoardWalk Villas (page 61)
Disney Vacation Club (page 67)
Fort Wilderness Homes (page 70)
The Villas at The Disney Institute (page 64)

MODERATE ($95 to $129)
Full-service restaurants, food courts, pizza
  delivery
Bellman luggage service
Swimming pools with slides
On-site recreation such as playgrounds and
  bike rental
Rooms sleep four
Bus transportation to all theme parks

Resorts
Caribbean Beach (page 55)
Dixie Landings (page 63)
Port Orleans (page 62)

VALUE ($69 to $79)
Food courts, pizza delivery
Hourly luggage service
Swimming pools
Bus transportation to all theme parks

Resorts
All-Star Music (page 68)
All-Star Sports (page 68)

CAMPGROUND ($35 TO $58)
The only public campground in the U.S. earning
  a perfect score from Woodall

Fort Wilderness Campground (page 70)

Magic Kingdom Resorts

CONTEMPORARY

Watching the monorail trains disappear into this hotel's enormous 15-story, A-frame tower never fails to amaze first-timers. The sleek trains look like long spaceships docking as they slide inside, or the sight may bring to mind the story of Jonah being swallowed by the whale. (Note that guests who use a wheelchair cannot board the monorail here, but they can board at the *Polynesian* resort or at the *Grand Floridian* resort.)

Passengers, for their part, are impressed by the cavernous lobby, with its tiers of balconies and, at its center, designer Mary Blair's huge 90-foot-high, floor-to-ceiling tile mural depicting Indian children, stylized flowers, birds, trees, and other scenes from the Southwest. (Look carefully and you may be able to spot the five-legged goat.)

This imposing establishment has 1,041 rooms in its Tower and the two Garden Wings that flank it on either side. There are seven shops, three restaurants, two snack bars, two lounges, a large convention center, a marina, a beach, a health club, and more. The larger of the hotel's pair of swimming pools measures a generous 20 by 25 meters. And the lively *Food and Fun Center*—a vast room containing pinball and electronic games, along with a snack bar—is open until midnight.

A concierge package is available for guests who choose to stay in the hotel's 14th-floor suites. Services include special check-in and check-out service, complimentary continental breakfast in the morning and wine, beer, and hors d'oeuvres at night, and nightly turn-down service. The telephone number for the *Contemporary* resort is 824-1000.

ROOMS: Guestrooms are almost evenly apportioned among the Tower and two Garden Wings. Rooms in the Tower boast views of Bay Lake or the Magic Kingdom. Most rooms can accommodate five guests (plus one additional child under three). Typical units have two queen-size beds and a daybed; some rooms have a king-size bed. Adjoining and/or connecting rooms may be requested, though they can't be guaranteed. Rooms equipped for guests with disabilities and nonsmoking rooms also are available. Bathrooms in the *Contemporary* resort are large and well laid out. A variety of elegant suites can accommodate 7 to 12 people.

MEETING AND CONVENTION SPACE: A large convention center is located in a separate building attached by an enclosed walkway to additional space on the second floor of the tower. The external building space features 90,000 square feet of meeting space, including the 42,300-square-foot Fantasia Ballroom and 15 breakout rooms. The 11,968-square-foot Ballroom of the Americas, at the north end of the Tower's second floor, accommodates about 1,400 seated theater-style, or about 1,000 for a banquet. It can be divided into two smaller rooms, each with a capacity of about half the above numbers. The 8,777-square-foot Grand Republic Ballroom holds slightly fewer people; it can be split into three rooms ranging in size from 1,024 to 4,290 square feet. In addition, there are five other rooms nearby of 800 to 1,160 square feet each; and on the 15th floor there are two others measuring 697 square feet and 1,247 square feet. Both these rooms have wonderful panoramic views of the Magic Kingdom. Six hospitality suites are in the Garden Wings.

WHERE TO EAT: Two of the hotel's restaurants are located on the Grand Canyon Concourse on the fourth floor; the third is on the 15th floor overlooking the Magic Kingdom. There are snack spots beside the marina and in the first-floor *Food and Fun Center*.

California Grill: On the 15th floor, it specializes in California fare, including pizza baked in wood-burning ovens, grilled meats, seafood, and market vegetables. An added treat: the spectacular view of the Magic Kingdom, fireworks, and sensational sunsets.

Contemporary Café: On the Grand Canyon Concourse. Features a character breakfast buffet daily and a bountiful, all-you-can-eat international buffet dinner every evening; one of the World's best buys.

Concourse Steak House: On the Grand Canyon Concourse. A full breakfast; burgers, salads, and sandwiches for lunch; and steaks and fresh seafood for dinner are offered on the menu here.

Food and Fun Center: On the first floor; serves light fare from 6 A.M. to midnight.

WHERE TO DRINK: The no-alcohol policy in the Magic Kingdom doesn't trickle over to its nearest neighbor.

California Grill Lounge: On the 15th floor adjoining the *California Grill*. Prime views provide a backdrop for sampling California wines and other drinks. Open from 5 P.M. to midnight.

Outer Rim Cocktail Lounge: On the Grand Canyon Concourse, overlooking Bay Lake. Serves appetizers, cocktails, and specialty drinks. Open from noon to 1 A.M.

ROOM SERVICE: A wide range of offerings can be ordered 24 hours a day. It's a good idea to pre-order breakfast the night before, using the card hanging from the doorknob. For other meals, count on phoning in an order 30 to 45 minutes before you want to be served. When the food arrives, it comes with a smile and, in the morning, with a newspaper.

WHAT TO DO: All by itself, the *Contemporary* resort boasts more activities and recreational facilities than many large resorts.

Boat rentals: Sailboats (including catamarans), pontoon and canopy boats, as well as the zippy little motorcraft known as Water Sprites, are all available for rent at the *Contemporary* resort marina, near the beach. Waterskiing, fishing, and parasailing excursions also are available (see *Sports* for details).

Tennis: This is the spot to find Disney's Racquet Club, WDW's premier tennis center. Recently renovated, it now features six state-of-the-art hydrogrid clay courts. Private lessons are available.

Swimming: There are two main pools here. In addition to a round splash pool that's deep in the center and shallow at the edges, there's a 20- by 25-meter pool that's being transformed into a themed swimming area with slides. A toddler's pool is located near the North Garden Wing, and swimming is permitted in the roped-off area of Bay Lake beside the beach. The bottom is delightfully sandy.

Fitness: The Olympiad Health Club has Nautilus equipment, stair climbers, rowing machines, bicycles, sauna, lockers, and massage (by appointment).

Volleyball: Nets are set up on the beach.

Children's program: The Mouseketeer Clubhouse is open from 4:30 P.M. to midnight for children 4 to 12 years of age. The cost is $4 per hour per child. There is a four-hour maximum stay. Reservations are necessary; call 824-3892. A playground is located near the North Garden Wing.

Gameroom: On the first floor of the hotel, the *Food and Fun Center* is one of the World's great indoor recreational facilities, boasting everything from Skee-Ball to air hockey, and all the favorites of the pinball-and-electronic-games-playing set.

Shopping: The fourth-floor Grand Canyon Concourse is home to several first-class shops. The Fantasia Shop sells kids' stuff and an array of Disney character merchandise that extends from stuffed animals and T-shirts to china figurines of Mickey, Pluto, the Mad Hatter, and company. Concourse Sundries and Spirits, next door, has a selection of newspapers, magazines, books, snack foods, and liquor—just what's needed for a cocktail party on your terrace. On the opposite side of the Concourse, the Contemporary Woman offers a range of good-quality women's clothing (and plenty of bathing suits) in all price ranges, and the adjoining Contemporary Man stocks casual clothes and beachwear.

The adjacent Kingdom Jewels Ltd. specializes in men's and women's jewelry from around the globe. Bayview Gifts carries souvenirs, gifts, and fresh flowers.

Disney's Racquet Club, near the North Garden Wing, has tennis equipment, men's and women's tennis fashions, and tennis shoes. Racquet restringing also is available here.

TRANSPORTATION: The *Contemporary* resort is connected to the Transportation and Ticket Center (TTC) and the Magic Kingdom by monorail trains. Board just above the Grand Canyon Concourse, inside the atrium area of the Tower. From the TTC, Epcot can be reached by bus or by another monorail, and the Disney-MGM Studios, Pleasure Island, Typhoon Lagoon, and Blizzard Beach can be reached by bus. Watercraft also travel regularly from the marina to *Fort Wilderness* and *Discovery Island*.

POLYNESIAN

The *Polynesian* resort is as close an approximation to the real thing as Walt Disney World's designers could create. The vegetation is as lush as anywhere in the World and the architecture summons the tropics.

The mood is set by a three-story-high garden that occupies most of the lobby. To call the construction at the center a fountain is to do it a grave injustice; it's more like a waterfall. The water cascades over craggy volcanic rocks. Coconut palms tower over 75 different species of tropical and subtropical plants—anthuriums, banana trees, ferns, gardenias, orchids, and other greens. The climatic conditions are nearly perfect, so that everything blooms year-round.

The structure that contains this mass of greenery, the so-called Great Ceremonial House, is the central building in the *Polynesian* resort complex. The front desk, the shops, and most of the restaurants are located here. Flanking the Great Ceremonial House on either side are 11 two- and three-story "longhouses" named for various Pacific islands. These structures house the resort's 853 rooms. The monorail stops at this resort, making it an especially convenient place to stay; in fact, it's just a few minutes' ride to the Magic Kingdom. But because the accommodations are scattered around the property, and because the hotel is not quite as large as the *Contemporary* resort, things seldom feel as hectic, and the *Polynesian* resort has a loyal following among returning Walt Disney World visitors.

The *Polynesian* resort also offers a concierge service called King Kamehameha. The amenities are similar to those on the "suite" floor at the *Contemporary* resort: free valet parking, express check-in and check-out, continental breakfast each morning, and soft drinks and hors d'oeuvres every afternoon. A concierge is on duty from 7 A.M. to 11 P.M. The special *Polynesian* resort rooms are located in the Tonga and Bali Hai (exclusively suites) longhouses, and are the most expensive rooms in the hotel. The telephone number for the *Polynesian* resort is 824-2000.

ROOMS: Many rooms have balconies, and most have a view of the gardens, the Seven Seas Lagoon, or one of the resort's swimming pools; those in the Oahu, Moorea, and Pago Pago longhouses are the largest. All have two queen-size beds and a daybed, and all can accommodate five guests (plus a sixth under age three). Connecting or adjoining rooms may be requested. (The Oahu and Pago Pago longhouses have rooms specially equipped for guests with disabilities.) There are nonsmoking rooms available.

Suites are all located in the Bali Hai longhouse, and accommodate four to six guests. Some have a king-size bed in the bedroom and two queen-size beds in the parlor.

WHERE TO EAT: Some of the more interesting Walt Disney World eating spots are located at the *Polynesian* resort.

'Ohana: On the second floor of the Great Ceremonial House, *'Ohana* serves family-style dinners roasted in the World's largest fire pit. Minnie's Menehune character breakfast is held daily. The room is large and open, and offers fine views across the Seven Seas Lagoon all the way to Cinderella Castle. Reservations are requested for breakfast and dinner; phone WDW-DINE (939-3463).

Coral Isle Café: On the second floor of the Great Ceremonial House, around the corner from 'Ohana. This standard coffee shop (with South Seas decor) serves the usual assortment of breakfast items, plus a WDW specialty, banana-stuffed french toast, each morning, and does a booming business at lunch and dinner. A good bet when you want a no-fuss meal.

Tangaroa Terrace: This restaurant serves breakfast buffet-style or à la carte, featuring Mickey-shaped Belgium waffles with hot toppings and banana-stuffed French toast, as well as more usual breakfast fare. Dinner also is available à la carte or buffet-style.

Captain Cook's Snack and Ice Cream Company: Located on the lobby level of the Great Ceremonial House, this is a good spot for continental breakfast. Sandwiches, snacks, and (of course) ice cream are available 24 hours a day.

WHERE TO DRINK: The resort's Polynesian theme has inspired a whole raft of deceptively potent potables such as Seven Seas (fruit juice, grenadine, orange curaçao, and rum), Chi Chis (a standard piña colada made with vodka instead of rum), and WDW piña coladas (which include orange juice in addition to rum, pineapple, and coconut cream). There's even a special Polynesian resort nonalcoholic treat—the pink Lei-Lani, a delicious orange juice and strawberry mixture.

Barefoot Bar: Adjoining the Swimming Pool Lagoon.

Tambu Lounge: Cozy and clublike, this lounge adjoins 'Ohana. A good spot for quiet conversation, it serves appetizers and specialty drinks, and the bartenders do tricks.

ROOM SERVICE: A variety of specialties is available from 6:30 A.M. to midnight. For breakfast, fill out the card on the doorknob outside your room before going to sleep.

WHAT TO DO: A wide range of activities is available at the Polynesian resort.

Boat rentals: Several types of sailboats (including catamarans), speedy little Water Sprites, pedal boats, and pontoon boats are available for rent at the Polynesian resort marina. Waterskiing and fishing excursions also can be arranged.

Swimming: There are two main pools here, the elliptical East Pool, in the shadow of the Oahu, Tonga, Hawaii, Bora Bora, and Maori longhouses, and the larger free-form Swimming Pool Lagoon, closer to the marina and the main beach. This pool is framed by a large cluster of boulders that forms a water slide much beloved by youngsters; to get to the ladder that takes you to the top, you must duck underneath a waterfall. Toddlers have their own shallow areas in both Polynesian resort pools. Swimming also is permitted in the roped-off areas of the Seven Seas Lagoon (when there's a lifeguard on duty).

Children's program: The Neverland Club is a supervised evening activity program for children ages 4 to 12. The program operates between 5 P.M. and midnight, with a kids' buffet from 6 P.M. to 8 P.M. The cost is $8 per hour and there is a three-hour minimum. Required reservations can be made by calling 824-2170 or 939-3463. The Polynesian playground features an assortment of apparatuses for climbing, swinging, and sliding.

Gameroom: Moana Mickey's Arcade has a small assortment of the latest video games and is located alongside the Snack Isle.

Shopping: News from Civilization, on the first floor of the Great Ceremonial House, is where you can buy items with the hotel and Florida logos, as well as daily newspapers, magazines, film, sun-care products, and gifts. Robinson Crusoe, Esq., nearby, sells casual sportswear and swimwear for men, while the Polynesian Princess stocks an assortment of brightly colored resort fashions, bathing suits, and hot-weather accessories for women. Upstairs, Trader Jack's sells souvenirs, toys, fashions, and miscellaneous items; The Grog Hut has food, liquor, wine, beer, soda, and other fixings for an impromptu party.

TRANSPORTATION: The Polynesian resort is right on a monorail line; the entrance is on the second floor of the Great Ceremonial House. Monorails travel to the Magic Kingdom and the TTC. From the TTC, Epcot is accessible by monorail or by bus, and the Disney-MGM Studios, Typhoon Lagoon, Blizzard Beach, the Marketplace, and Pleasure Island can be reached by bus. Launches leave from the Polynesian dock for the Magic Kingdom and the Grand Floridian.

GRAND FLORIDIAN

At the turn of the century, Standard Oil magnate Henry M. Flagler saw the realization of his dream: The railroad he had built to "civilize" Florida had spawned along its right-of-way an empire of grand hotels, lavish estates, prominent families, and opulent lifestyles. High society blossomed in winter, as the likes of John D. Rockefeller and Teddy Roosevelt checked into the *Royal Poinciana* in Palm Beach, enjoying the sea breezes from the ocean-side suites.

The hotel later burned to the ground, and Florida's golden era faded with the Depression. But nearly a century after Flagler first made Florida a fashionable resort destination, Walt Disney World opened a grand hotel—a 900-room Victorian structure with gabled roofs and carved moldings—on 40 acres of Seven Seas Lagoon shorefront, between the Magic Kingdom and the *Polynesian* resort.

Like its late 19th-century predecessors, the *Grand Floridian* boasts abundant verandas, ceiling fans, intricate latticework and balustrades, turrets, towers, and red-shingle roofs. White-sand beaches hold the promise of clambakes. And yet, it has all the advantages of 21st-century living—air conditioning and monorail service. With five restaurants, two lounges, one snack bar, four shops, an arcade, a child-care facility, a swimming pool, a children's activity area, a health club, and a marina, the *Grand Floridian* is not only a grand hotel but a complete resort.

The main building houses a 14,800-square-foot Grand Lobby, a palatial space soaring five stories to a ceiling of stained-glass domes and glittering chandeliers. Potted palms and an aviary decorate the sitting area; an open-cage elevator carries guests to the shops and restaurants on the second floor. The turn-of-the-century theme is apparent everywhere, from the Edwardian costumes worn by the staff to the shop displays, from the restaurants to the room decor. The telephone number for the *Grand Floridian* resort is 824-3000.

ROOMS: The accommodations are quite luxurious, with rooms decorated as they might have been a century ago—in soft colors, with printed wall coverings, armoires and lightwood furnishings, marble-topped sinks, ceiling fans, and Victorian woodwork. The main building houses 65 concierge rooms and 11 suites; five lodge buildings, each four and five stories high, contain 623 standard rooms, 161 slightly smaller "attic" chambers, and 10 suites. Most rooms are about 400 square feet and include two queen-size beds, plus a daybed, to accommodate five people. Many rooms have terraces. Suites include a parlor, plus one, two, or three bedrooms; there are king-size beds in the bedrooms, plus one or two daybeds. Most of the 15 honeymoon rooms, located on the second, third, fourth, and fifth floors, enjoy wonderful views. In the main building, access to the upper three concierge/suite levels is restricted by private elevator to guests occupying rooms on those floors only. On the third floor, the concierge desks offer such personalized services as reservations and information. The fourth floor features a quiet seating area where continental breakfast and evening refreshments are served. Rooms equipped for guests with disabilities and nonsmoking rooms are available.

MEETING AND CONVENTION SPACE:
A convention center with 40,000 square feet of meeting space is available at the *Grand Floridian*. The Grand Ballroom measures 18,216 square feet and there are eight breakout rooms with a total of 8,821 square feet. The Business Center offers clerical assistance, including typing and photocopying.

WHERE TO EAT: Most of the restaurants and lounges are on the first two floors of the main building.

Gasparilla Grill and Games: This snack bar on the Windsor Level (first floor) offers light items for breakfast, lunch, and dinner, plus video games.

Grand Floridian Café: Its peaches-and-cream color scheme and verandalike feel make this the best place to get a quick, sit-down breakfast. Lunch and dinner also are available. Located on the first floor.

1900 Park Fare: A buffet restaurant on the first floor, festively decorated with carousel horses, plenty of plants, and Big Bertha—the carnival organ. Breakfast and dinner with the characters are served.

Flagler's: The largest of the hotel's restaurants, seating 285, features Italian cuisine complete with strolling musicians. Open for dinner. Alcazar Level (second floor).

Victoria & Albert's: Also on the second floor, but much smaller than *Flagler's*, is the hotel's finest dining establishment, named after the former queen and prince consort of England. Elegant meals are served to no more than 90 guests; service is refined and diligent. Jackets are required for men and reservations are a must.

Narcoossee's: Octagon-shaped and open-beamed, this restaurant and bar has a romantic shoreline location. Steaks, fresh seafood, and chicken cooked in an open kitchen characterize the menu. Beer is served by the yard. Open for lunch and dinner.

WHERE TO DRINK: While guests staying on the concierge floors or in suites all have their own wet bars, other guests will find lounges on the first and second floors of the main building.

Garden View Lounge: Windsor Level, with a view of the hotel's lush, landscaped pool and garden area. Afternoon tea is served at this pleasant spot.

Mizner's Lounge: Named after the eccentric, wildly prolific architect who defined much of the flavor of Palm Beach County, this bar is on the Alcazar Level.

Summerhouse: The only bar serving the pool and beach, this spot features a variety of snacks and beverages.

ROOM SERVICE: A wide assortment of items is available 24 hours a day. For the best breakfast service, fill out the card on your doorknob before going to sleep.

WHAT TO DO: The *Grand Floridian* offers all the recreational facilities of a typical beachside resort—and much more.

Tennis: There are two clay courts available for play. Reservations are required; phone 824-2433.

Volleyball and croquet: Equipment for these activities is available at the St. John's Health Club.

Boat rentals: Sailboats (including catamarans), canopy boats, pedal boats, and Water Sprites—are available for rent at the Captain's Shipyard marina. Waterskiing and fishing excursions also can be arranged.

Swimming: In addition to the 275,000-gallon swimming pool outside the main building, the hotel has its own white-sand beach along the Seven Seas Lagoon.

Children's program: The Mousekeeter Club is a supervised children's program for kids 4 to 12 years of age. It's open from 4:30 P.M. to midnight. The cost is $8 per hour for each child. There is a four-hour maximum. Reservations are required; phone 824-2985.

Fitness: St. John's Health Club, open to *Grand Floridian* guests only, offers Nautilus and cardiovascular machines, sauna, locker facilities, and massage. For massage reservations call 824-2433.

Gameroom: The *Gasparilla Grill and Games* on the first floor of the main building features a video arcade.

Shopping: On the first floor (Windsor Level) of the main lodge is Summer Lace, a women's apparel shop, and Sandy Cove, where guests may purchase gifts and sundries. One floor up at the Alcazar Level is Commander Porter's, a men's shop; M. Mouse Mercantile is the character shop.

TRANSPORTATION: The *Grand Floridian* is connected to the Transportation and Ticket Center and the Magic Kingdom by monorail. The monorail entrance is located outside the hotel under an awning on the second floor. From the TTC, Epcot is accessible by WDW's other monorail, or via bus. The Disney-MGM Studios, Typhon Lagoon, Blizzard Beach, Pleasure Island, and the Disney Village Marketplace can be reached by bus. Launches leave from the dock for the Magic Kingdom and the *Polynesian* resort.

WILDERNESS LODGE

This resort recalls both the spirit of the early American West and the feeling of the National Park Service lodges built in the early 1900s. These grand structures architecturally unified the elements of the unspoiled wilderness parks, kept harmony with nature, and incorporated the culture of Native Americans. The *Wilderness Lodge* artfully recaptures this rustic charm.

The resort is situated between the *Contemporary* resort and *Fort Wilderness*. Guests arrive along a winding road shaded by pines. The lobby is in an eight-story, log-structured building. Massive bundled log columns support a series of trusses. Four large chandeliers with torch-cut iron bands featuring silhouettes of Indians and buffalo are topped with glowing tepees. Two authentic Pacific Northwest totem poles soar 55 feet on each side of the lobby. There also is a stone fireplace and an intricately detailed, multi-colored floor that recall Northwest Indian designs. Four levels of corridors surround the lobby providing access to guestrooms, sitting and reading areas, and porches. There are 38 rooms equipped for guests with disabilities, and nonsmoking rooms are available. The telephone number for the *Wilderness Lodge* is 824-3200.

ROOMS: The 728 guestrooms are located in a U-shaped building. Most rooms have two queen-size beds, a table and chairs, and a balcony. Some rooms have one queen-size bed and a bunk bed. The bathroom is a comfortable size with a separate vanity area with double sinks; the fixtures resemble pewter. The cream-colored wallpaper has a Native American–motif border and the curtains are a traditional plaid. Images of wildlife add to the decor and complete the theme.

WHERE TO EAT: The American West theme is carried out with flair in the hotel's eateries.

Artist Point: Decorated with artwork representing the painters who first chronicled the northwest landscape, this fine dining spot features steaks, seafood, and wines from the Pacific Northwest. The Character Stampede breakfast takes place here daily.

Whispering Canyon Café: A family-style coffee shop with all-day dining. The cowboy silhouette cutouts are great for picture taking.

Roaring Forks: Light snacks are available here, in the hotel's arcade.

Lobby Coffee Bar: Continental breakfast is served here, and evenings bring coffee and hot chocolate to this fireside spot.

WHERE TO DRINK: Two spots are available for a relaxing break.

Territory Lounge: Located between the *Whispering Canyon Café* and *Artist Point*, this spot honors the survey parties who led the move westward. Specialty drinks, micro-brewed beer, and espresso are served, in addition to light appetizers.

Trout Pass: The poolside bar features a variety of specialty drinks and snacks.

ROOM SERVICE: Dinner selections are available from 4 P.M. to midnight.

WHAT TO DO: A resort unto itself, there are many activities to pursue.

Swimming: The themed pool actually begins as a hot spring in the lobby. From there, water flows out of the building into Silver Creek, a quiet setting in the upper courtyard. The creek widens as it develops first into a roaring waterfall and then into a swimming area that looks as if it were carved from rockscape. A beach, a kiddie pool, hot and cold whirlpools, and an Old Faithful–style geyser complete the design.

Boat rentals: A variety of watercraft, including Water Sprites, canopy boats, sailboats, and pontoon boats, can be rented for a trip around Bay Lake. Waterskiing excursions also may be arranged.

Bicycling: Bicycles can be rented for a ride around the resort. A ¾-mile path leads to *Fort Wilderness* and River Country.

Children's program: The Cubs Den is a supervised program for kids ages 4 to 12; call 939-3463.

Gameroom: The Roaring Forks Arcade features about 30 of the latest games to keep kids occupied for hours.

Shopping: Necessities and sundries as well as a line of clothing with the *Wilderness Lodge* logo are available at Wilderness Lodge Mercantile. A selection of Disney character merchandise is featured as well.

TRANSPORTATION: Boats go to the Magic Kingdom from the dock behind the hotel. Buses make the trip to all other parts of the World, including Epcot, the Disney-MGM Studios, Typhoon Lagoon, Blizzard Beach, and the Disney Village Marketplace. It's also possible to ride a bicycle to *Fort Wilderness* and River Country.

Epcot Resorts

CARIBBEAN BEACH

This colorful hotel is set on 200 acres southeast of Epcot and near the Disney-MGM Studios. It is composed of five brightly colored "villages" surrounding a 45-acre lake. Each village is identified with a different Caribbean island—Martinique, Barbados, Trinidad, Aruba, and Jamaica—and features cool pastel walls, white railings, and vividly colored metal roofs. There are 2,112 rooms in all, making the *Caribbean Beach* resort one of the largest hotels in the United States.

The villages consist of a cluster of two-story buildings, a swimming pool, a guest laundry, and a lakefront stretch of white-sand beach. Guests check in at the Custom House, a reception building that immediately projects the feeling of a tropical resort. Decor, furnishings, and staff costumes all reflect the Caribbean theme. Old Port Royale, a complex located near the center of the property, evokes images of an island market. Stone walls, pirates' cannons, and tropical birds and flowers add to the atmosphere. The area houses the resort's food court with six counter-service restaurants, two shops, a gameroom, and a lounge. The port opens onto a lakeside recreation area that includes a pool with waterfalls and slides; the main beach; the Barefoot Bay Bike Works and Boat Yard, where boats and bicycles can be rented; a 1.4-mile promenade around the lake that's perfect for biking, walking, or jogging; and Parrot Cay Island, an area with a playground and a wildlife walk. The telephone number for the *Caribbean Beach* resort is 934-3400.

ROOMS: Rooms are located in two-story buildings in each island village. A typical 340-square-foot room has two double beds and can sleep up to four. The rooms here are a bit larger than the standard rooms at Disney's *Port Orleans*, *Dixie Landings*, and *All-Star Sports* and *All-Star Music* resorts, and the bathrooms are amply sized. The rooms are decorated in softer tones than the colors found on the exterior, with furniture made of white oak. Each room has a mini-bar and a coffeemaker. Rooms equipped for travelers with disabilities and nonsmoking rooms are available.

One note for the budget-conscious: all the rooms here are identical in terms of size and comfort, and the only difference between the most and least expensive is the view.

SHADES OF GREEN

The *Disney Inn*, now known as *Shades of Green*, is a recreational retreat for active and retired military personnel and their families, members of the reserves and the National Guard, and Department of Defense employees. The 288-room resort features two tennis courts, two pools, a small health club, a restaurant, a bar and lounge, a gift shop, a gameroom, laundry facilities, and free transportation all around Walt Disney World. Very attractive room rates based on military or civilian grade range from $49 to $92 per day. Discounted Length of Stay Passes also are available. The property's three golf courses—the Palm, the Magnolia, and Oak Trail—are open to all Walt Disney World guests. See *Sports* for details. All of the other activities at *Shades of Green* are for hotel guests and their families only. The telephone number for *Shades of Green* is 824-3400.

WHERE TO EAT: A full-service eatery and a food court with six counter-service restaurants are located in Old Port Royale.

Captain's Tavern: Prime ribs, baked chicken, and crab legs are on the menu at this 200-seat restaurant at Old Port Royale. Tropical drinks, wine, beer, and traditional cocktails also are served.

Cinnamon Bay Bakery: Freshly baked rolls, croissants, and pastries are available in addition to ice cream and other treats.

Port Royale Hamburger Shop: Hot sandwiches and burgers are on the menu.

Kingston Pasta Shop: A variety of pasta dishes is served.

Montego's Deli: Soups, salads, and cold sandwiches are offered.

Bridgetown Broiler: Split-roasted chicken and home-style meals are menu highlights.

Royale Pizza Shop: Very good pizza by the slice or the pie along with a variety of hot and cold pasta dishes is available.

WHERE TO DRINK: The tropical, Caribbean theme is carried out in the specialty drinks found here.

Banana Cabana: Drinks and snacks are available at this poolside spot.

WHAT TO DO: There are many recreational opportunities.

Boat rentals: Sailboats, Water Sprites, canopy boats, canoes, and pedal boats are available for rent at the Barefoot Bay Bike Works and Boat Yard for use on the resort's 45-acre lake.

Swimming: Each village has its own pool, and the main pool features waterfalls and slides in a Caribbean-themed setting.

Children's playground: A lovely playground is on Parrot Cay Island, across the footbridge from the Barefoot Bay Bike Works and Boat Yard. Playgrounds also are located on the Barbados, Martinique, Jamaica, and Trinidad beaches.

Jogging: The 1.4-mile promenade around the lake is perfect for a morning jog.

Gameroom: Goombay Games features a selection of electronic games at Old Port Royale.

Shopping: Calypso Trading Post, at Old Port Royale, stocks a large selection of character merchandise and sundries. The Calypso Straw Market features items with the *Caribbean Beach* resort logo and a variety of island-themed goods.

Bicycling: Bikes can be rented at the Barefoot Bay Bike Works and Boat Yard.

Nature walks: Walks are conducted at Parrot Cay Island.

TRANSPORTATION: The *Caribbean Beach* resort is served by the Walt Disney World bus system. Buses go directly to the Magic Kingdom, Epcot, and the Disney-MGM Studios. Other routes lead to the Disney Village Marketplace, Pleasure Island, Typhoon Lagoon, and Blizzard Beach.

SPECIAL ROOM REQUESTS

Central Reservations Operations accepts requests for a particular view or location, but although CRO agents will try to accommodate requests, they cannot guarantee that they will be able to fulfill every wish. Call (W-DISNEY—934-7639)

YACHT CLUB AND BEACH CLUB

The New England seaside exists at Walt Disney World in the form of the *Yacht Club* and its sister, the *Beach Club,* next door. Situated just west of Epcot, the hotels, designed by noted architect Robert A. M. Stern, are set around a 25-acre lake. (The rooms and restaurants in each hotel differ—and we describe them separately—but since the two adjacent properties share most activities, meeting spaces, and transportation options, we've combined the "What to Do," "Meeting and Convention Space," and "Transportation" sections.)

YACHT CLUB

The *Yacht Club's* design evokes images of the New England seashore hotels of the 1880s. Guests enter the five-story, oyster-gray clapboard building along a wooden-planked bridge. Hardwood floors, millwork, and brass enhance the nautical theme. A lighthouse on the pier serves as a beacon to welcome guests back to the hotel from WDW attractions. The telephone number for the *Yacht Club* resort is 934-7000.

ROOMS: The 630 rooms are spacious and decorated in a nautical motif. The furniture is white, and the headboards on the one king-size bed or two queen-size beds were designed to incorporate small ship's wheels. Some rooms also have daybeds. Most of the suites have king-size beds in the bedroom and two sleeper sofas. The carpeting is blue, and the drapes and bedspreads are blue and dusty rose. The bathrooms are large, with double sinks outside. Mirrors are silver

trimmed with brass. Each room has a color TV set, a ceiling fan, a mini-bar, a table (complete with checkerboard top), and two chairs. Chess and checker sets are provided. There are rooms equipped for guests with disabilities, and non-smoking rooms are available.

WHERE TO EAT: The yachting theme also dominates the hotel's restaurants.

Yachtsman Steakhouse: Select cuts of aged beef are the specialty of the house. Fresh seafood and poultry also are available.

Yacht Club Galley: The buffet breakfast is bountiful. Breakfast, lunch, and dinner are available from an à la carte menu.

WHERE TO DRINK: The lounges here offer a variety of specialty drinks in settings with a nautical feel.

Crew's Cup Lounge: The place to try assorted beers shipped in from the world's seaports. Located next to the *Yachtsman Steakhouse.*

Ale and Compass Lounge: This lobby lounge features specialty coffees and drinks until 11 P.M. to help welcome guests back from a long day in the parks.

ROOM SERVICE: A wide variety of menu items is available 24 hours. For best breakfast service, put the order card on your doorknob before turning in for the night.

BEACH CLUB

Beach is the operative word at the *Beach Club,* which is approached along an entrance drive flanked by palm trees. A patterned walkway leads past a croquet court to beachside cabanas on the white-sand shore. Guests are met by hosts and hostesses dressed in colorful beach resort costumes of the 1870s. The telephone number for the *Beach Club* resort is 934-8000.

ROOMS: The 583 rooms are spacious and reflect a beach motif. The wallpaper is seafoam green, and the curtains and bedspreads are white and seafoam green with a border of mauve beach umbrellas. The room layouts are similar to those at the *Yacht Club*, and each room features a ceiling fan, two queen-size beds (some rooms have a king-size bed and a daybed), double sinks, and a wall-mounted makeup mirror. There are rooms equipped for guests with disabilities, and nonsmoking rooms are available.

WHERE TO EAT: The sea plays an important role in the restaurants here.

Ariel's: Named for the heroine of *The Little Mermaid*, this restaurant serves fresh contemporary American seafood, along with dishes for landlubbers.

Cape May Café: An indoor clambake is held here each night. The varied buffet features several types of clams and mussels, plus pasta and chicken. Lobster is available for an extra charge. A character breakfast is served daily.

WHERE TO DRINK: The two lounges provide a relaxing respite.

Martha's Vineyard Lounge: Selections from American and international vineyards are served in sample sizes and by the glass or bottle at this lounge adjacent to *Ariel's*.

Rip Tide Lounge: The lobby lounge features a variety of California wines, wine coolers, and other frosty concoctions. The bar is open until 11 P.M.

ROOM SERVICE: A large variety of options is available from room service. For the quickest breakfast service, place the order card on your doorknob before going to bed.

AT THE YACHT CLUB AND BEACH CLUB

WHERE TO EAT: These two spots are shared by the *Yacht Club* and *Beach Club* resorts.

Hurricane Hanna's Grill: Burgers, hot dogs, sausages, and other snacks are served at this spot at Stormalong Bay. A full bar also is located here, and poolside beverage service is available.

Beaches & Cream Soda Shop: A classic American soda fountain where shakes, malts, and oversize sundaes are the prime lures. The other specialty is the Fenway Park Burger, served as a single, double, triple, or home run.

MEETING AND CONVENTION SPACE: A mid-size meeting facility is shared by the two resorts and complements the design of the *Yacht Club*. A separate entrance has a porte cochere with a gambrel roof evoking the feel of a coach house. The interior of the meeting space is reminiscent of a grand, turn-of-the-century New England town meeting hall. The Grand Harbour Ballroom is 36,004 square feet and can accommodate 2,800 guests. There also is the Asbury Hall (8,228 square feet) and

other adjacent meeting and function rooms. All the audiovisual equipment is state of the art, and a business center is located in the pre-function area. As with all WDW resorts, meeting planners have all the Disney resources on hand to help arrange parties, banquets, and events.

WHAT TO DO: There is enough to do right at this resort to fill an entire vacation.

Boat rentals: Pedal boats, canopy boats, sailboats, and Water Sprites are available for rent at the Bayside Marina.

Swimming: Between the marina and the beach is the centerpiece of the dual resort—Stormalong Bay, a 750,000-gallon pool that's really a mini water park. There is a lagoon expressly for relaxed bathing, and another "active" lagoon with whirlpools, jets, and sand-bottomed areas. Adjacent to the main pool is a shipwreck where guests can enjoy a variety of unique water slides. There also is a quiet pool and a whirlpool at the far end of each hotel. Note that the pools are open to hotel guests only.

Fitness: The Ship Shape Health Club is located in the area between the two resorts, and features Nautilus and cardiovascular machines, sauna, spa, steamroom, personal trainers, and massage (by appointment). The health club is open to *Yacht Club* and *Beach Club* guests only, and you must be over 13 to use the facilities.

Tennis: There are two lighted tennis courts on the *Beach Club* side of the property. Rental equipment is available at the Ship Shape Health Club.

Gameroom: Lafferty Place Arcade, located in the central area, has about 60 video games and pinball machines.

Children's program: The Sandcastle Club, for children 4 to 12, is available from 4:30 P.M. to midnight. Cost is $4 per hour for each child. Reservations are required; call 934-8000. A variety of toys, children's videos, games, and Apple computers are on hand to keep children entertained. Milk and snacks also are served.

Volleyball and croquet: A sand volleyball court and a grass croquet court may be found on the *Beach Club* side of the property. Equipment for both pursuits is available at no cost at the Ship Shape Health Club.

Beauty/barber shop: The Periwig salon for men and women is located in the central area.

Shopping: At the *Yacht Club*, Fittings and Fairings Clothes and Notions is an all-purpose shop offering nautical fashions, character merchandise, and sundries. At the *Beach Club*, Atlantic Wear and Wardrobe Emporium features a similar selection of goods (albeit with a beach theme).

TRANSPORTATION: *Yacht Club* and *Beach Club* guests ride boats or walk to the nearby Epcot entrance (beside the France pavilion). Buses and watercraft go to the Disney-MGM Studios. Buses also go to the Magic Kingdom, Pleasure Island, the Disney Village Marketplace, Typhoon Lagoon, Blizzard Beach, and the Transportation and Ticket Center. From the Transportation and Ticket Center, transfer to other buses that go to River Country and *Fort Wilderness*.

SWAN

The exterior of this 758-room waterfront hotel, operated by Westin, is painted a sun-washed coral beneath rolling waves of turquoise. The guestrooms are encased in a striking 12-story main building and two 7-story wings. And just in case the shape and color of the buildings weren't distinctive enough, two 46-foot swan statues, each weighing about 56,000 pounds, sit atop the resort at either end of the main building. (The *Swan* faces its sister property, the *Dolphin*, across Crescent Lake. Both hotels were designed by noted architect Michael Graves as prime examples of what has come to be known as "entertainment architecture.") The telephone number for the *Swan* is 934-3000. Room reservations can be made by calling 800-248-7926.

ROOMS: The corridors outside the guestrooms feature patterned carpets and murals on the walls that extend the wave theme from the exterior design. Inside, the rooms are decorated in corals and turquoises, and feature such whimsical touches as lamps in the shapes of birds and pineapples painted on the dressers. They have one king-size or two queen-size beds, and in-room safes, clock radios, voice mail telemessaging, mini-bars, and daily newspaper delivery are among the amenities. There also are 45 concierge rooms on the 11th and 12th floors, and 64 suites. Rooms equipped for guests with disabilities and nonsmoking rooms are available.

MEETING AND CONVENTION SPACE: The *Swan* and its sister hotel, the *Dolphin*, make up the Southeast's largest convention-resort complex. At the *Swan*, there are 54,300 square feet of meeting space, including the 23,064-square-foot Swan Ballroom. A total of 31 meeting and breakout rooms also are available, as are seven hospitality suites and a spacious and elegant boardroom. The hotel can provide all necessary audiovisual equipment, and convention planners have access to all the areas and attractions at WDW.

WHERE TO EAT: An Italian restaurant and a seafood spot are among the eateries.

Palio: A pleasant Italian bistro featuring veal specialities, homemade pasta, and brick-oven pizza. There are tasty daily specials and live entertainment.

Garden Grove Café: This 24-hour eatery features a greenhouse atmosphere, and serves a variety of fresh seafood and steaks daily at lunch and dinner. A buffet breakfast with the characters is held twice weekly, while a character dinner is held three nights a week. Breakfast is served every day. A glassed-in pastry kitchen allows guests to witness the creation of some of the delicious baked goods.

Kimono's: The Oriental decor helps make this spot a pleasant place for sushi and other Japanese specialties.

Splash Grill: A poolside café serving breakfast, lunch, dinner, and snacks. A full-service bar also is located here.

WHERE TO DRINK: The lobby offers a pleasant respite from the hubbub.

Lobby Lounge: Enjoy gourmet coffees with fresh pastries in the morning and wine and other specialty drinks at night in a European-style bistro setting.

ROOM SERVICE: Available 24 hours a day, featuring an extensive all-day dining menu.

WHAT TO DO: Many activities are available at the *Swan*.

Boat rentals: Pedal boats, as well as SunKats and CraigCats (motorized lounge chairs), are available for rent on the white-sand beach between the *Swan* and *Dolphin*.

Swimming: A large rectangular pool, ideal for lap swimming, is located on the shore of Crescent Lake. There also is a themed grotto pool and several whirlpools nearby.

Fitness: A small health club with basic exercise equipment is located near the pool.

Tennis: Eight hard-surface courts, lighted for night play, are open 24 hours a day; the courts are located behind the pool area of the *Dolphin* but are shared with *Swan* guests.

Children's program: Camp Swan, open to children ages 3 to 12, offers supervised activities from 4 P.M. to midnight. The cost is $5 per hour for the first child and $3 per hour for each additional child. Dinner, ordered through room service, is extra.

Gameroom: A small gameroom is located near the pool.

Shopping: Disney Cabanas features men's and women's fashions, character merchandise, and sundries. Located in the lobby.

TRANSPORTATION: *Swan* guests ride boats or walk to Epcot's entrance near the France pavilion. Watercraft make the trip to the Disney-MGM Studios. Buses go to the Magic Kingdom, Pleasure Island, the Disney Village Marketplace, Typhoon Lagoon, and the TTC. From the TTC, other buses run to River Country, Blizzard Beach, and *Fort Wilderness*.

DOLPHIN

The hotel's 27-story turquoise triangular tower was honored by *Progressive Architecture* magazine. It is flanked by four coral-colored guestroom wings, nine stories each, that stretch out to the shores of Crescent Lake. The exterior of the *Dolphin* complements the *Swan* in color scheme, though its exterior walls feature a mural of banana leaves. And not to be outdone by its neighbor, it is topped by two 56-foot-tall dolphin statues. A lush, tropical setting has been created, and a lovely waterfall cascades down the face of the triangle into a series of seashells, then into a large shell-shaped pool supported by smaller dolphin statues. The telephone number for the *Dolphin* is 934-4000. Reservations can be made by calling 800-227-1500.

ROOMS: The 1,510 rooms, including 140 suites, are decorated in a lighthearted fashion, with lamps in the shape of palm trees and colorful bedspreads and curtains. All feature two double beds or a king-size bed, as well as a clock radio, a mini-bar, voice mail telemessaging, a vanity dressing area, an iron and ironing board, a coffeemaker, and daily newspaper delivery. Concierge rooms are located in the main building. There are rooms equipped for guests with disabilities, and non-smoking rooms are available.

MEETING AND CONVENTION SPACE: The *Dolphin's* enormous conference center has its own entrance, and also is accessible from the hotel lobby. There is a total of 202,295 square feet of meeting space. The 55,903-square-foot Hemisphere Ballroom is the largest hotel ballroom in Florida and the second-largest hotel ballroom in the country. There also are 28 meeting rooms, a boardroom, a 51,275-square-foot exhibit hall, and other smaller conference spaces available. The hotel staff can provide all necessary audiovisual equipment and access to the entire Walt Disney World attraction and entertainment inventory.

WHERE TO EAT: There are several restaurants from which to choose.

Harry's Safari Bar & Grille: Grilled beef, poultry, and seafood are served here; a character brunch takes place on Sundays.

Sum Chows: A blend of Asian dishes is served in an elegant atmosphere (usually closed Tuesdays and Wednesdays).

Juan & Only's Cantina: This festive restaurant features authentic Mexican food amid an atmosphere of the warm hues and rich fabrics of old Mexico. There also is a Sunday character brunch buffet.

Coral Café: Bountiful buffets at breakfast and dinner, as well as à la carte selections for breakfast, lunch, and dinner.

Tubbi Checkers Buffeteria: A cafeteria with a little flair. The checkerboard design makes this a pleasant place for a quick meal. The convenience store here sells snacks and baby-care items and is open 24-hours.

Dolphin Fountain: Homemade ice cream in some unusual flavors is the specialty here. Huge sundaes, waffle cones, and an assortment of cakes and pies also are offered, as well as burgers and sandwiches.

Cabana Bar & Grill: This poolside spot serves burgers, sandwiches, yogurt, and fruit for a nice break from the sun. There also is a full bar with specialty drinks.

WHERE TO DRINK: It's not too tough to find an interesting spot for a drink here.

Copa Banana: The tabletops are shaped like slices of fruit, and a variety of hors d'oeuvres make this a pleasant place for a drink. Deejay music is featured nightly.

Harry's Safari Bar: Pull up a stool and enjoy the tropical atmosphere and drinks.

Only's Bar: Patrons at the bar at *Juan & Only's Cantina* can enjoy the warm atmosphere here while sampling rare tequilas and beers from every region of Mexico.

ROOM SERVICE: Available 24 hours a day. For prompt breakfast service, program your selections on the special television channel.

WHAT TO DO: There are many activities at this resort.

Boat rentals: Pedal boats and electric-powered SunKats and CraigCats (motorized lounge chairs) are available for rent on the beach, just past the grotto pool.

Swimming: There's an enormous rectangular pool perfect for laps. A themed grotto pool with slide lies just beyond, and a smaller pool and a few whirlpools are nearby.

Fitness: A branch of Body by Jake (run by television fitness guru Jake Steinfeld) is near the pool. State-of-the-art equipment is available, as are personal trainers. There are aerobics classes (including water aerobics), a sauna, a steamroom, and massage.

Tennis: Eight hard-surface courts, lighted for night play, are open 24 hours a day; the courts are shared with *Swan* guests.

Children's program: Camp Dolphin offers two programs, one for kids ages 3 to 5 and another for kids ages 6 to 12. A lifetime membership in Camp Dolphin costs $40, with a ten percent discount for additional family members. Hourly rates are $3.25 per child for members and $6.50 for nonmembers. The program for three- to five-year-olds runs from 3 P.M. to 5 P.M. A dinner club from 5 P.M. to 8 P.M. is

$15.90 for members and $21.20 for nonmembers. The program for the 6-to-12 age group runs from 2 P.M. to 6 P.M. The dinner club operates from 6 P.M. to 10 P.M., and costs $21.20 for members and $26.50 for nonmembers.

Gameroom: A gameroom is located near *Tubbi Checkers Buffeteria*.

Shopping: Daisy's Garden is the place to find character merchandise and sundries. At Brittany Jewels, a large selection of Cartier and other name-brand jewels is available. Indulgences allows chocolate lovers a chance to sample some tasty concoctions. Statements of Fashion offers resortwear for men and women.

TRANSPORTATION: *Dolphin* guests may take a boat or walk to Epcot's entrance near the France pavilion. Watercraft make the trip to the Disney-MGM Studios. Buses go to the Magic Kingdom, Pleasure Island, the Disney Village Marketplace, Typhoon Lagoon, Blizzard Beach, and the Transportation and Ticket Center. At the TTC, it's possible to catch other buses to River Country and *Fort Wilderness.*

DISNEY'S BOARDWALK

The enchantment of a bygone era is recaptured in *Disney's BoardWalk,* a new vacation escape scheduled to open in July 1996. The *BoardWalk* combines entertainment, dining, recreation, shopping, deluxe hotel accommodations, conference facilities, and vacation villas. It's all designed to recall the boardwalks of yesteryear, where a stroll along the boards was the ticket to excitement, day or night. At the heart of Walt Disney World, the *Board-Walk* is adjacent to Epcot's International Gateway and is slated to become the first WDW area connected to Disney-MGM Studios via a walkway. The boardwalk ambience begins at the entry drive, where colorful roadside billboards beckon travelers, and it continues throughout, with intricately detailed architecture featuring bright facades, deep colonnades, striped awnings, and flagged turrets, reminiscent of the turn of the century. The telephone number for the *BoardWalk* is 939-5100.

ROOMS: Accommodations evoke the charm of early eastern seaboard inns, and include 532 vacation cottages collectively called the *BoardWalk Villas.* The *BoardWalk Inn* has 378 deluxe hotel rooms. Guestrooms at the *Inn* sleep up to five, and feature two queen-size beds (or one king-size bed) and a daybed; all rooms have private balconies. The *Inn* also has concierge rooms, as well as two-story suites that sleep six. The suites feature a king-size bed in the master bedroom and two queen-size beds in the second bedroom, and the romantic two-story cottage suites each

Village Resorts

PORT ORLEANS

This 1,008-room resort invites comparisons to the historic French Quarter of New Orleans. Starting at the entrance gate, with its wrought-iron portal and overgrown landscape, the appeal of the Delta City surrounds arriving guests. The entry drive leads to the heart of the city, which is Port Orleans Square. The central building, The Mint, was based on an original turn-of-the-century mint where farmers would go to trade their harvest for "dixes." A dix was a ten-dollar bill, and when the farmers said they were going to get their dixes, they probably didn't know they had coined a phrase. The Mint houses the hotel's check-in facilities, the Guest Services desk, a shop, the food court, an arcade, and the restaurant. It has a vaulted ceiling, and the check-in desks are designed as old-fashioned bank-teller windows. The mural behind the check-in counter, featuring a Mardi Gras street scene, was painted by an artist in three parts, each shipped to Orlando separately. The musical notes in the mural are the notes to "When the Saints Come Marching In." The telephone number for *Port Orleans* is 934-5000.

have a private New England garden enclosed by a white picket fence. At the *Villas*, studios feature a queen-size bed and a double sleeper sofa; a kitchenette with microwave, coffeemaker, sink, and small refrigerator; and a spacious bathroom. Larger units (one-, two-, and three-bedroom cottages sleeping 4 to 12) feature a dining room, a fully equipped kitchen, laundry facilities, a master bath with whirlpool tub, and a VCR. They also include a king-size bed in the master bedroom, a living room with queen sleeper sofa, and two queen-size beds or a queen-size bed and a double sleeper sofa in any additional bedrooms.

WHERE TO EAT: Four eateries line the *BoardWalk* promenade. At the bakery, the day starts with the aroma of fresh-baked buns. Ice cream, espresso, and baked goods all are available at the soda fountain. For more substantial fare, guests can try either a casual Mediterranean-style restaurant or a dining room featuring fresh grilled seafood.

WHERE TO DRINK: Nighttime entertainment includes "dueling pianos" at the piano bar and ballroom dancing accompanied by a ten-piece band. At the ESPN sports club, video monitors showcase popular sporting events, along with up-to-the-minute scores and highlights. There also is a 220-seat arena with a state-of-the-art television and radio broadcast facility, restaurant service, and an arcade featuring virtual-reality games.

WHAT TO DO: An enormous free-form pool has a towering water slide in the shape of a classic wooden roller coaster. Additional pools and whirlpools are located in private landscaped settings to provide a retreat from the activity of the main pool area. Other outdoor facilities include tennis courts, a croquet lawn, and (for a more vigorous workout) a health club with cardiovascular and weight machines.

TRANSPORTATION: *BoardWalk* guests get to Epcot and the Disney-MGM Studios via boats or walkways. Buses go to the Magic Kingdom, Typhoon Lagoon, Blizzard Beach, Pleasure Island, and the Disney Village Marketplace.

ROOMS: The guestrooms are located in seven 3-story buildings (with elevators), and each can accommodate four people. Each room has two double beds and some king-size beds are available. The rooms are a bit smaller than the standard rooms at the more expensive Disney hotels, but they are comfortable for a family of four. The photographs on the walls were donated by Disney cast members, and the captions explain their history. The buildings are painted cream, pink, blue, purple, and yellow, and feature wrought-iron railings of varying designs. About half the rooms have doors connecting to a neighboring room. Connecting rooms can be requested, but they cannot be guaranteed. The rates are based on the room's view. The least expensive rooms overlook parking areas, the mid-range overlook gardens, and the most expensive offer water views. Rooms equipped for guests with disabilities and nonsmoking rooms are available.

WHERE TO EAT: There is one sit-down restaurant with waitress service and a food court with counter-service restaurants.

Bonfamilles Café: The name of this waitress-service eatery comes from the Disney movie *The Aristocats*. Steaks, seafood, and Creole cooking highlight the dinner menu. Breakfast also is served.

Sassagoula Floatworks & Food Factory: This food court has a 300-seat dining area with one central checkout. A variety of foods is available, including pizza, spit-roasted chicken with red beans and rice and other traditional Creole dishes, a variety of burgers, Louisiana-style fried chicken, ice cream, frozen yogurt, and fresh beignets, and other baked goods.

Sassagoula Pizza Express: Hand-tossed pizza, salads, desserts, and soft drinks can be delivered directly to guestrooms.

WHERE TO DRINK: The New Orleans theme is carried through in the hotel's watering holes.

Scat Cat's Club: A traditional bar featuring a light menu of hors d'oeuvres and nightly entertainment.

Mardi Grogs: The poolside bar serves specialty drinks, popcorn, hot dogs, and ice cream during pool hours.

WHAT TO DO: A special pool is the highlight of the recreational opportunities here.

Bike rentals: Bicycles are available for rent at the Port Orleans Landing.

Boat rentals: Pedal boats, canoes, rowboats, canopy boats, and pontoon boats are available for rent at the Port Orleans Landing.

Croquet: Complimentary equipment is available from Port Orleans Landing for use on resort lawns.

Swimming: Doubloon Lagoon is a pool built around a sea serpent that, as the legend goes, is still lingering underground. His tail can be seen jutting up in spots along the walkways, and the water slide is actually the serpent's tongue. The shower at the pool has an alligator's head, and there is a large clam shell where an alligator band serves as the centerpiece of a fountain. A whirlpool is located nearby. *Port Orleans* guests also may swim at *Dixie Landings*' Ol' Man Island.

Gameroom: South Quarter Games is located at Port Orleans Square. It features state-of-the-art video and arcade games.

Shopping: Jackson Square Gifts and Desires, located at Port Orleans Square, features Disney character merchandise, clothing featuring the *Port Orleans* logo, and sundries.

TRANSPORTATION: Buses go to Epcot, the Magic Kingdom, the TTC, the Disney-MGM Studios, Typhoon Lagoon, Blizzard Beach, Pleasure Island, and the Disney Village Marketplace. Water launches also make the trip to *Dixie Landings*, Pleasure Island, and the Disney Village Marketplace.

DIXIE LANDINGS

The city feel of *Port Orleans* gives way to the rural South upriver at *Dixie Landings*. The resort is divided into "parishes." Closest to the "city," guestrooms are found in Mansion homes; further upriver are the Bayou rooms with a more rustic feel. The guest registration area, "Dixie Landings," is located in a building designed to resemble a steamship. When guests check in, they are booking passage on the steamboat. The food court, restaurant, lounge, and Fultons General Store are all located in the same building. The telephone number for *Dixie Landings* is 934-6000.

ROOMS: The 2,048 Mansion and Bayou guestrooms are the same size, and each room features two double beds (some king-size beds are available); 963 of the Bayou rooms have trundle beds as well. The Magnolia Bend Mansion rooms are situated in sprawling, elegant manor homes with stately columns and grand staircases. The Alligator Bayou rooms are in rustic, weathered-wood buildings with tin roofs that are tucked among trees and bushes native to the area. These rooms surround Ol' Man Island, a 3½-acre recreational area with a pool, a playground, and a fishing hole. Decorative touches in the rooms include wood and tin armoires and pedestal sinks with brass fittings. The beds have hickory bedposts. The rooms are a bit smaller than the standard rooms at the more expensive Disney hotels, but they are comfortable for a family of four. Rooms equipped for guests with disabilities and nonsmoking rooms are available.

WHERE TO EAT: Colonel's Cotton Mill is designed to resemble an old-fashioned cotton mill with a 30-foot working water wheel that powers a real cotton press inside. Here you'll find a food court and a full-service restaurant.

Boatwright's Dining Hall: This 200-seat, waitress-service eatery in Colonel's Cotton Mill serves Cajun specialties from the rural South and traditional American specialties. The restaurant is modeled after a boatmaking warehouse. Breakfast also is served.

Acadian Pizza 'n' Pasta: Fresh pizza with a variety of toppings, pasta dishes, and calzones are on the menu at this food-court location.

Bleu Bayou Burgers and Chicken: Fried and grilled chicken and an interesting assortment of burgers are the offerings here.

Cajun Broiler: Spit-roasted chicken and barbecued ribs are available.

Riverside Market and Deli: This convenience store stocks snack foods, soda, salads, sandwiches, beer, and wine.

Southern Trace Bakery: Pastries, freshly baked pies, and sticky buns are the specialties.

Sassagoula Pizza Express: Hand-tossed pizza, salads, desserts, and soft drinks can be delivered right to guestrooms.

WHERE TO DRINK: The two lounges each possess a certain degree of charm.

Cotton Co-Op: Situated in a room designed as a cotton exchange, this lounge features specialty drinks, some light hors d'oeuvres, and live entertainment.

Muddy Rivers: The poolside bar serves specialty and traditional drinks plus hot dogs, popcorn, and ice cream during pool hours.

WHAT TO DO: A wide variety of activities awaits visitors here.

Swimming: There are five pools set among the parishes of the resort. In addition, Ol' Man Island is a 3½-acre recreation center featuring a themed pool, a whirlpool, a children's wading pool, a playground, and a fishing hole

stocked with a variety of fish for catch and return. *Dixie Landings* guests also may swim at *Port Orleans'* Doubloon Lagoon.

Boat Rentals: Pedal boats, canoes, rowboats, canopy boats, and pontoon boats are available for rent at Dixie Levee.

Fishing: Two-hour guided fishing excursions, are available, and guests may fish on their own at the Ol' Fishin' Hole.

Gameroom: The Medicine Show Arcade is located in the *Dixie Landings* building and features a small selection of video games.

Bicycling: Bicycles of all types can be rented at the Dixie Levee.

Shopping: Fulton's General Store also is in the *Dixie Landings* building and stocks Disney character merchandise, clothing with the *Dixie Landings* logo, and sundries.

TRANSPORTATION: Buses go to the Magic Kingdom, Epcot, the TTC, the Disney-MGM Studios, Typhoon Lagoon, Blizzard Beach, Pleasure Island, and the Disney Village Marketplace. *Port Orleans*, the Disney Village Marketplace, and Pleasure Island also can be reached aboard the Sassagoula River Cruise.

THE VILLAS AT THE DISNEY INSTITUTE

The area near the Disney Village Marketplace is dotted with exceptionally attractive villa-type accommodations (formerly known as *Disney's Village Resort*), many fitted out with fully equipped kitchens and other extras and amenities. Some may cost more than individual guestrooms at the conventional Disney hotels, but they accommodate more people as well. For families of more than five (who might otherwise need to rent an extra hotel room), this is the most economical way to stay hereabouts. Smaller families generally can come out at least even by cooking some of their own meals (especially breakfast) in their villa. Accommodations for guests with disabilities are available in the Fairway Villas. Nonsmoking accommodations are available in the Bungalows and selected villas.

The resort will serve as headquarters for The Disney Institute (slated to open in February 1996), and guests participating in the Institute's enrichment programs are housed in the Bungalows and Town Houses. Recreational facilities are available to all guests when not in use for Institute programming.

Aside from the delights of having lots more space, the villas are exceptionally quiet and secluded; the pace is more relaxed and the atmosphere is low-key (except in the villas near Pleasure Island, which can be lively until late in the evening). They are conveniently located with respect to Epcot, the Disney-MGM Studios, Disney Village Marketplace, Pleasure Island, and Typhoon Lagoon. The telephone number for the villas is 827-1100.

WALT DISNEY WORLD VISITOR
OFFICIAL SURVEY

In order to better understand their guests' needs, Disney has designed the following short survey for readers of this guide. Your help is greatly appreciated.

1. Mr./Mrs./Ms. _____

　　　　　　　First name　　　Middle initial　　Last Name

_____

　　　　　　　Street address　　　　　　　　　　Apt. #

_____

　　　　　　　City　　　　　　　　　State　　　Zip+4

　　　　　　　Area code and phone number

2. Please check here if you prefer <u>not</u> to receive special communications from The Walt Disney World Resort:_____

3. Please provide your age and the number of children in your household: Your age _____ How many children in your household are 13 and under?_____ Ages 14-17?_____

4. Have you ever been to The Walt Disney World Resort in Florida?　Yes___　No___

5. If yes, how many trips have you taken since it opened in 1971?　One___ Two___ Three___ Four or more___

6. What was the year of your most recent trip? 19___

7. On a scale of 1 to 10, with 10 meaning "very interested" and 1 meaning "not interested at all," how interested are you in visiting The Walt Disney World Resort <u>with</u> children?

　1　2　3　4　5　6　7　8　9　10

8. Using the same scale, how intersted are you in visiting The Walt Disney World Resort <u>without</u> children?

　1　2　3　4　5　6　7　8　9　10

Thank you!　　　　　　　　　　　　　　　　　　　B001

WALT DISNEY WORLD VISITOR

OFFICIAL SURVEY

PO BOX 4136

SCHAUMBURG IL 60168-4136

TYPES OF VILLAS: There are five major types of villas. All have either full kitchens or wet bars with small refrigerators. Check-in and check-out for all guests takes place at the Reception Center near the Town Houses.

One-bedroom Bungalows: These are located slightly northeast of the Town Houses. There are 316 Bungalows. The smallest one-bedroom units are roughly L-shaped, with a special sitting area (equipped with a daybed, a refrigerator, a microwave, a coffeemaker, and a wet bar) that's sufficiently removed from the sleeping area (with its two queen-size beds) that business travelers who invite their colleagues in for a nightcap don't feel as if they're entertaining in the bedroom. While the layout was drawn up with special attention to the needs of those attending conferences, it works equally well in providing families with a bit more space and privacy than they would get in the standard rooms at the WDW resort hotels. (The single disadvantage for families is the size of the bathrooms: small.)

The Club Suite Villa Center offers a pool, a spa, and a fitness center.

One- and two-bedroom Town Houses: These accommodations are located about a five minutes' walk from the Reception Center and the Disney Village Marketplace. They are pleasantly straightforward in feeling and decor, and have cathedral-height living room ceilings. One-bedroom units can accommodate four; there's a king-size bed in the bedroom and a sleeper sofa in the living room. Two-bedroom units, which can accommodate six, have a king-size bed in the loft bedroom, a king- or queen-size bed in the second bedroom, and a double sleeper sofa in the living room.

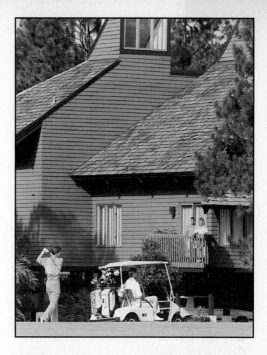

Fairway Villas: These cedar-sided, slant-roofed units, located near the first, second, eighth, and ninth fairways of the Lake Buena Vista Golf Course, are among the World's most spacious and attractive accommodations, with cathedral ceilings, rough-hewn walls, large windows, contemporary-styled furniture, and an overall feeling that there's lots of elbow room. There is a queen-size bed in one bedroom, two double beds in the other, and a double sleeper sofa in the living room. They can sleep eight, plus there's room for a crib.

Treehouse Villas: Guests who lodge in one of these octagonal houses-on-stilts, scattered along a barbell-shaped roadway at the western edge of the resort, go to sleep to a cacophony of crickets and wake up to a chorus of birds. You're literally in the woods, alongside some of the winding WDW canals, and you feel a million miles from the rest of the WDW property and all its hubbub. Upstairs is the small (but modern) kitchen, the living room (where the televison set is located), two bedrooms (each with a queen-size bed), and two bathrooms; the whole floor is surrounded by a deck where you can eat or just sit and look out into the trees. Downstairs, there's a bedroom with a double bed and a utility room equipped with a washer and dryer. The canals offer some of the World's best fishing, mainly for bass, and the roadways—shady, flat, and untrafficked as they are—are terrific for jogging. The nearest swimming pool is the one in the Treehouse area.

Grand Vista Homes: Four ultra-luxurious homes with two or three bedrooms are available for rent. Each features a master bedroom with a king-size bed, and most of the other bedrooms have two queen-size beds (some have two twins). Bed-turndown service and daily newspaper delivery are provided,

refrigerators are stocked with staples when you arrive, and the furnishings are all first class. Use of golf carts and bicycles is included in the price of the suites. (For complete price information, see the chart "Rates at Walt Disney World Properties" on page 74.)

WHERE TO EAT: The new *Seasons* restaurant features four dining rooms, each themed to a season; and it is open for breakfast, lunch, and dinner. Nearest off-site breakfast options include the Gourmet Pantry (which opens at 9:30 A.M.) or *Chef Mickey's Village Restaurant*, where characters put in appearances. Both are at the Disney Village Marketplace. There also are abundant breakfast facilities at the nearby hotels in Disney Village Hotel Plaza. For lunch and dinner, the selections are even broader. (See *Good Meals, Great Times* for more details.)

Groceries: The Gourmet Pantry stocks staples of all sorts, as well as delicacies from around the globe, and good meat, poultry, and fresh vegetables. Purchases can be delivered to your villa; if you won't be home to receive them, arrangements may be made for the delivery person to be let in so that perishables

can be stashed in the refrigerator. It's also possible to order by phone. Touch "Gourmet Pantry" on your room telephone (before 1 P.M.), or dial 828-3886 when calling from someplace other than your villa. There also is a Gooding's supermarket located at the Crossroads of Lake Buena Vista shopping center.

WHERE TO DRINK: For liquid refreshment, head for the Disney Village Marketplace, where you'll find *Cap'n Jack's Oyster Bar* and the *Village Lounge*. Or try Pleasure Island's clubs: *Mannequins*, *Neon Armadillo*, *Rock & Roll Beach Club*, *8TRAX*, *Comedy Warehouse*, *Pleasure Island Jazz Company*, or *Adventurers Club*. (For details about these, see *Everything Else in the World*.)

WHAT TO DO: In addition to boating, fishing, and shopping at the Disney Village Marketplace, and shopping at Pleasure Island (discussed in more detail in *Sports* and *Everything Else in the World*), you also can enjoy a variety of activities in and around the villas themselves.

Bicycling: The rustic pathways and meandering, relatively untrafficked roads around the villas can make for an enjoyable hour or two of pedaling. Two-wheelers are available for rent. (See *Sports* for fees.)

Fitness: A large new health and fitness center, complimentary to Disney Institute guests, features aerobics, a gymnasium, and Cybex equipment. A full-service spa is located within the center.

Gameroom: A small arcade with electronic games and pinball machines is located at the Villa Center.

Golf: Fairways of the par-72 Lake Buena Vista course nudge right up to the Fairway and Treehouse Villas. Once the Institute opens, this course will frequently be given over to Institute programming. Practice greens and a driving range are available, along with top-quality rental clubs and shoes. (For fees and starting information, see *Sports*.)

Playgrounds and volleyball: Two playgrounds and two sand volleyball courts are on the premises.

Swimming: There are six pools around the villas, and several whirlpools are scattered about the grounds.

Tennis: There are two new clay courts, both lighted for night play. Courts are available to all guests when not being used for Institute programming.

TRANSPORTATION: Buses go to Epcot, the Disney Village Marketplace, the Disney-MGM Studios, and the Magic Kingdom. These circulate through the villa areas, making pickups at bus stops located at regular intervals along the roadways.

Another option: Transport yourself to the Disney Village Marketplace via an electric golf cart or bike. Both are available for rent.

DISNEY VACATION CLUB

The *Disney Vacation Club* offers the opportunity to own a real estate interest in a Disney resort. For a one-time purchase price and annual dues, members receive an allotment of vacation points to use for stays at the resort, which features studios, and one-, two-, and three-bedroom units on the Disney property overlooking the Lake Buena Vista Golf Course.

Members also can exchange points for stays at more than 200 premium resorts worldwide, including other Walt Disney World, Disneyland, and Euro Disney properties. Vacation homes not occupied by members are available for nightly rental.

The homes are designed in a Key West theme with color schemes of seafoam green and mauve. The *Vacation Club* has the feel of a resort community and all the amenities that go with resort life.

Membership in the *Disney Vacation Club* is valid until the year 2042. From now until the end of 1999, any members booking a vacation home also get passes to the Magic Kingdom, Epcot, and the Disney-MGM Studios for the duration of their stay. The number of passes varies with the size of the accommodations and the number of people in each party. There also are discount golfing and dining programs available, as well as other exclusive benefits.

Disney has some expansion plans in the works. In the fall of 1995, the first phase of a new beachfront resort opened in Vero Beach, about 1½ hours from Walt Disney World. The location is nearby, making it simple to tack on a beach vacation to a WDW visit. A future phase calls for a resort on Hilton Head Island, South Carolina.

A presentation describing all the details of club membership is offered at the Commodore House. The telephone number for the *Disney Vacation Club* is 827-7700.

HOMES: There are studios and one-, two-, and three-bedroom units available. The studios consist of a large bedroom with two queen-size beds, a table and chairs, and a kitchenette with a small refrigerator, a microwave oven, a coffeemaker, and a sink. The bathrooms are spacious. The one-bedroom units have a king-size bed in the master bedroom and a queen-size sleeper sofa in the living room. The two-bedroom units feature a king-size bed in the master bedroom, two queen-size beds in the other bedroom, a large living room with a queen-size sleeper sofa, a dining room with a table and chairs, and a full-size kitchen equipped with everything one could imagine from dishes, glasses, silverware, napkins, and towels to pots and pans, cooking utensils, and even napkin rings. There's a full-size refrigerator, a dishwasher, a coffeemaker, and a toaster. A VCR is hooked up to the living room television set. The master bathroom has two separate rooms with an extra-large whirlpool tub and a sink in one room and an oversize shower, a sink and vanity, and a toilet in the other. There's a terrace off the living room and bedroom, and there are ceiling fans in each room. The three-bedroom Grand Villas have a similar configuration to the two-bedroom units, but with a third bedroom that has two double beds. Studios and one-bedroom units sleep 4 people, two-bedroom units sleep 8, and three-bedroom homes accommodate 12. Some *Disney Vacation Club* homes are equipped for guests with disabilities. Nonsmoking homes also are available.

WHERE TO EAT: *Olivia's* serves an assortment of Key West favorites plus some more traditional items for breakfast, lunch, and dinner. There is a Winnie the Pooh character breakfast Wednesdays and Sundays. *Good's Foods to Go* offers snacks. There also are grills and picnic tables available. Guests also can make a short boat journey to the Disney Village Marketplace. Pizza delivery is available from *Dixie Landings* from 5 P.M. to midnight.

WHERE TO DRINK: The *Gurgling Suitcase* near the main pool serves specialty drinks, cocktails, wine, beer, and soft drinks.

WHAT TO DO: An activities director is on hand to schedule events for guests and members alike.

Basketball, shuffleboard, and volleyball: Courts are scattered throughout the resort, and equipment is available from Hank's Rent 'N Return.

Bicycling: A variety of bikes may be rented from Hank's.

Tennis: There are two lighted courts located near the main pool. A third court, located in a more removed area, is not equipped for night play.

Swimming: The sprawling main pool is located behind the Hospitality House. A children's pool and play area resembles a giant sand castle. There is a large whirlpool nearby. Additional pools are found around the resort.

Boat rentals: Pedal boats, rowboats, and pontoon boats are available at Hank's.

Fitness: The R.E.S.T. health club features Nautilus and cardiovascular machines, a sauna, and massage (by appointment).

Shopping: Conch Flats General Store stocks groceries, books, magazines, sun-care products, and Disney character merchandise.

Gameroom: The Electric Eel Arcade is located in the Hospitality House.

Conch Flats Community Hall: Table tennis, board games, playing cards, a large-screen television set, complimentary video rentals, nightly movies, and planned activities are all on hand at the Community Hall.

TRANSPORTATION: Buses go to Epcot, the Magic Kingdom, the TTC, the Disney-MGM Studios, Typhoon Lagoon, Blizzard Beach, Pleasure Island, and the Disney Village Marketplace. Water launches also make the trip to Pleasure Island and the Marketplace.

All-Star Resorts

ALL-STAR SPORTS & ALL-STAR MUSIC

The first Disney entries into the value-priced hotel market, the *All-Star Sports* and *All-Star Music* resorts are the most startlingly themed at Walt Disney World. Each resort has 1,920 rooms housed in ten buildings, devoted to five sports or five types of music.

Sports fans will find themselves in a world of baseball, football, tennis, surfing, or basketball at the *All-Star Sports* resort. Brightly colored, larger-than-life football helmets, surfboards, tennis balls, basketball hoops, and baseball bats adorn the buildings. Stairwells in the shape of three-story soda cups, lifeguard shacks, and tennis ball cans lead guests to the second and third floors.

At the *All-Star Music* resort, Broadway, country, jazz, rock, and calypso are the five themes. A walk-through, neon-lit jukebox, a three-story pair of cowboy boots, and a Broadway theater marquee are among the giant icons.

Guests check in at Stadium Hall or Melody Hall, the central buildings that each house a food court, a large arcade, a retail shop, and Guest Services. The telephone number for the *All-Star Sports* resort is 939-5000; the telephone number for the *All-Star Music* resort is 939-6000.

ROOMS: The guestrooms, measuring 260 square feet, are rather small compared with the rooms at *Port Orleans* and *Dixie Landings*, which are 314 square feet. Each room has two

ALL-STAR TRIVIA

● It would take all the water at Typhoon Lagoon's wave pool to fill one of the Coca-Cola cups at the baseball-themed *Home Run* hotel.

● It would take 9,474,609 tennis balls to fill one of Centre Court's tennis ball cans.

● The tennis racquet at Centre Court would almost cover an entire regulation tennis court.

● The gold star in front of Melody Hall, one of 727 stars there, is ¼ the size of Epcot's Spaceship Earth.

● The jukeboxes at Rock Inn could hold 4,000 compact discs, enough to supply music for 135 days straight.

● The boots doing the two-step at Country Fair would fit a size 270 foot.

double beds (with the exception of rooms designed for travelers with disabilities, which have one king-size bed), a vanity area with a single sink, a separate bathroom, a closet bar and shelf, an armoire, and a small table with two chairs. Nonsmoking rooms are available.

WHERE TO EAT: The *End Zone* food court in Stadium Hall and the *Intermission* food court in Melody Hall each feature a bakery, a convenience market, and several stands including barbecue, pizza and pasta, and hamburgers. Each food court has a common seating area with a central beverage bar. The *End Zone* offers interactive trivia and special sporting

events daily from 11 A.M. to midnight. Both *All-Star Sports* and *All-Star Music* offer delivery of pizzas, salads, subs, and desserts to guestrooms from 5 P.M. to midnight.

WHERE TO DRINK: There are no lounges at the *All-Star* resorts; however, the *Team Spirits Pool Bar* and the *Singing Spirits Pool Bar* serve drinks throughout the day and evening. These bars are located at the main pool areas.

WHAT TO DO: Swimming takes first priority at these resorts.
  Swimming: Each hotel has two pools and one kiddie pool. At the *All-Star Sports* resort, Surfboard Bay looks like an ocean. The smaller Grand Slam Pool is shaped like a baseball diamond. At the *All-Star Music* resort, the Calypso Pool is in the form of a giant guitar, while the Piano Pool is designed to look like—you guessed it.
  Children's playground: A playground is located at each hotel's courtyard area.
  Gameroom: The Game Point Arcade in Stadium Hall features 100 games, and Note'able Games in Melody Hall has 90 games.
  Shopping: Sport Goofy Gifts and Sundries in Stadium Hall and Maestro Mickey's in Melody Hall feature magazines, books, sun-care products, character merchandise, and sundries.

TRANSPORTATION: Buses make pickups at Stadium Hall and Melody Hall for trips to the Magic Kingdom, Epcot, the Disney-MGM Studios, Typhoon Lagoon, Blizzard Beach, and the Disney Village Marketplace.

Fort Wilderness Resort & Campground

The very existence of this canal-crossed expanse—more than 700 acres of cypress and pine laced by pleasant blacktop roadways—always surprises visitors who come to Walt Disney World expecting to find the theme parks and nothing more. If they've heard about *Fort Wilderness* at all, they often confuse it with the Magic Kingdom's Frontierland section.

But the *Fort Wilderness* atmosphere is relaxed and not at all frenetic. In one corner, a group of kids may be battling it out at tetherball, and on the playing fields there are often a couple of energetic touch football games in progress. In the morning, the campground smells sweetly of dew-dampened pines, then of frying bacon. In the evening, the warmth and stillness of the afternoon give way to dinnertime bustle, and fish and steaks are thrown onto grills as next-door neighbors organize get-togethers. Later on, groups of kids gather alongside the trading posts or at Pioneer Hall, where the *Fort Wilderness* electronic-games-and-pinball arcade is located. *Fort Wilderness* also has a marina and a beach, a nature trail, and a number of waterways where fishing, canoeing, and pedal boating are popular; these and other recreational possibilities make *Fort Wilderness* one of the livelier places to be at WDW. An expansion project added the Meadow Recreation Complex, located in the area behind the Meadow Trading Post. It features two lighted tennis courts, a swimming pool, an arcade, and a snack bar.

You can enjoy the *Fort Wilderness* experience even if you don't have your own camping gear. Among the 1,192 campsites there are 408 air-conditioned Wilderness Homes available for rent, complete with kitchen utensils, dishes, linens, a color television wired for cable, daily maid service, and enough other amenities that the woods all around are the only reminders of the fact that you're camping out. The cost is comparable to that of some of the more expensive rooms at the resort hotels. (But those don't have kitchens and so don't offer the money-saving option of cooking some of your vacation meals "at home.") The telephone number for the *Fort Wilderness* resort is 824-2900.

CAMPSITES: *Fort Wilderness* has 784 campsites, ranging in length from 25 to 65 feet, spaced throughout 20 camping loops. All types of camping can be accommodated— RV, travel trailer, and tent. Preferred campsites feature cable-TV connections as well as hookups for electricity (100 volt–20 amp, 110 volt–30 amp, or 200 volt–50 amp), water, and sanitary disposal. Partial-hookup campsites supply electricity and water hookups only. All campsites are bordered by lush wilderness and feature a paved driveway pad, a picnic table, and a charcoal grill. All loops have at least one air-conditioned comfort station equipped with restrooms, private showers, an ice machine, telephones, and a laundry room. The per-site fee allows for occupancy by up to ten people. Each site has room for parking one car (in addition to the camping vehicle). Additional cars can be parked in the campground's main parking lot.

The various campground areas are designated by numbers. The 100, 200, 300, 400, and 500 loops are closest to the beach, the Settlement Trading Post, and Pioneer Hall. The 1500, 1600, 1700, 1800, 1900, and 2000 loops are farthest away from the beach and many other *Fort Wilderness* activities, but they are quieter and more private. Pets are welcome at certain campsites for an additional nightly charge of $3.

WILDERNESS HOMES: The 408 Wilderness Homes here provide all the advantages of villa accommodations—with woodsy surroundings to boot. There are two types of homes. One model sleeps four adults and two children; it has a bedroom with a double bed, a bunk bed, plus a separate vanity area, and a spacious living room with a pull-down double bed and a ceiling fan. The other trailers sleep four, with a double bed in the bedroom and a pull-down double bed in the living room. Both types come equipped with pots and pans, dishes, and all the basic kitchen equipment, plus a color TV set and a complete bathroom. The bathroom is not the sort of makeshift setup you might expect; in fact, it's comparable to a bathroom in a standard hotel room. There are Wilderness Homes equipped for travelers with disabilities, and nonsmoking trailers are available. **Note:** No extra camping equipment is allowed on the site; all guests must be accommodated in the Wilderness Home. (For complete price information, see the chart "Rates at WDW Properties" on page 74.)

WHERE TO EAT: Most people cook their own meals. Groceries and supplies are available at the Meadow Trading Post and the Settlement Trading Post (open from 8 A.M. to 10 P.M. in winter, to 11 P.M. in summer). Sandwiches, fruit, ice cream, and chips are available there for takeout; you can eat them at your own site, on the beach, or at tables just outside River Country. A Gooding's supermarket is located at the Crossroads of Lake Buena Vista shopping center across from the Disney Village Hotel Plaza.

When you want to go out, there's the *Trail's End Buffet*, an informal, log-walled, beam-ceilinged cafeteria inside Pioneer Hall, where home-style fare for breakfast, lunch, and dinner is served. Beer and sangría also are available. *Crockett's Tavern*, also inside Pioneer Hall, serves cocktails, unique appetizers, steaks, ribs, and chicken in the evening. A children's menu is available.

Snacks: Snack foods are available at the Meadow Trading Post and the Settlement Trading Post.

Pizza: Served from 9:30 P.M. to 11 P.M. nightly, along with soft drinks and beer, at the *Trail's End Buffet* in Pioneer Hall.

WHERE TO DRINK: Full meals, beer, wine, and cocktails are served at *Crockett's Tavern* in Pioneer Hall. It's also a short ride to Pleasure Island and its many clubs, or to *Cap'n Jack's* or the *Village Lounge* at the Disney Village Marketplace.

FAMILY ENTERTAINMENT AFTER DARK: The Hoop-Dee-Doo Musical Revue is presented three times nightly at 5 P.M., 7:15 P.M., and 9:30 P.M.; reservations are required and are so hard to come by that they need to be made well in advance by calling WDW-DINE—939-3463. Cancellations do occur, however. WDW resort guests who can't get a reservation can go to the Pioneer Hall Ticket Window 45 minutes before showtime and place their names on the waiting list.

There's also a nightly campfire program held at the center of the campground, near the Meadow Trading Post. A sing-along (featuring Chip 'n' Dale) and free screenings of Disney movies and cartoons are the main goings-on. At 9:45 P.M., you can see the Electrical Water Pageant—a procession of waterborne floats, during which an assortment of

guided trail outings), horseshoes, tetherball, volleyball, and waterskiing also are available. Or you can just go out for a stroll along the ¾-mile trail leading to the *Wilderness Lodge*. All of these activities are described in detail in *Everything Else in the World* and *Sports*. There are two gamerooms: Davy Crockett's Arcade in Pioneer Hall and Daniel Boone's Arcade at the Meadow Trading Post.

River Country, a major attraction in its own right, with a separate admission charge, also is located at *Fort Wilderness*. The features of this watery playground—a WDW must, right along with the Magic Kingdom, Epcot, and the Disney-MGM Studios—are discussed in detail in *Everything Else in the World*.

sea creatures is outlined in a galaxy of tiny colored lights. This can be viewed from the *Fort Wilderness* beach; don't miss it. (For more details, see *Everything Else in the World* and *Good Meals, Great Times*.)

WHAT TO DO: There are more on-site activities at *Fort Wilderness* than at almost any other area in the World. There are two tennis courts in the campground, and the Osprey Ridge and Eagle Pines golf courses play from the nearby Bonnet Creek Golf Club.

There are two heated swimming pools and an ample beach for swimming in Bay Lake. You can rent tandems and other two-wheelers at the Bike Barn for afternoon bicycle excursions or as reliable transportation around the campground. Visits to the Petting Farm and the horse barn near *Fort Wilderness* are amusing. Boating is popular; rentals are available at the marina. Canoes and pedal boats can be hired at the Bike Barn. Pony rides are available from 9 A.M. to 5 P.M. Basketball, checkers, electric-cart rentals, fishing (on your own in the canals or on organized morning or afternoon angling excursions), horseback riding (on

TRANSPORTATION: Buses circulating at 20-minute intervals provide transportation within the campground, while buses and watercraft connect *Fort Wilderness* to the rest of the World. The Magic Kingdom, the *Contemporary* resort, and Discovery Island are most efficiently reached via watercraft that depart regularly from the *Fort Wilderness* marina. To reach these places when boats are not operating and to get to other WDW points, take a bus from the *Fort Wilderness* bus stop near the Settlement Trading Post and Pioneer Hall to the Transportation and Ticket Center. Here, change to another bus for the Disney Village Marketplace or the Disney-MGM Studios, or take a monorail train to Epcot, the *Contemporary* resort, the *Polynesian* resort, or the *Grand Floridian* resort.

Practical Matters

The Walt Disney World hotels and villas have some important operating procedures that first-time guests don't always take seriously—much to their later dismay.

Deposit requirements: Deposits equal to one night's lodging (or campsite rental) are required within 21 days of the time that a reservation is made. Personal checks, traveler's checks, cashier's checks, and money orders are acceptable forms of payment. To have deposit charges billed to an American Express, Visa, MasterCard, or Disney Credit Card account, you'll need to provide the reservation agent with your credit card number and its expiration date. Deposits will be fully refunded if you cancel your reservation at least 48 hours before your scheduled arrival. Reservations are canceled if deposits are not received by the 21-day deadline. (Reservations booked less than 30 days prior to arrival will receive special instructions for deposits.)

Check-in and check-out times: While not unique to the Orlando area, the early check-out time (11 A.M. at all WDW lodging places) and the late check-in times (1 P.M. at the campsites, 3 P.M. in the resort hotels, 4 P.M. in the villas) often surprise. They needn't be an inconvenience, however. When checking in, guests should pre-register, purchase passes, and head for the parks. Luggage can be stored at the resorts.

Payment methods: Hotel bills may be paid with credit cards (American Express, Visa, MasterCard, or The Disney Credit Card), traveler's checks, cash, or personal checks. Checks must bear the guest's name and address, be drawn on a U.S. bank, and be accompanied by proper identification—that is, a valid driver's license or a government-issued passport.

Additional per-person charges: In addition to the rates listed on the following pages, charges apply when more than two adults (over 17 years of age) occupy a standard room. Guests at *Fort Wilderness* homes pay $5 per extra adult per day; *All-Star* resort guests pay $8 per extra adult, per day; *Port Orleans*, *Dixie Landings*, and *Caribbean Beach* guests pay $12 per extra adult, per day; and guests at all other WDW resorts pay $15 per extra adult per day.

WDW ID cards: Issued on arrival at WDW-owned resorts, these cards are among resort guests' most valuable possessions while in Walt Disney World. They entitle you to:

● Theme park admission if you've purchased a Length of Stay Pass.

● Unlimited transportation by bus, monorail, and watercraft.

● Use of many of the roadways within Walt Disney World.

● Charge privileges: If you've left a credit card imprint with your hotel, the ID cards may be used (up to certain account limits) to cover purchases in shops, lounges and restaurants, and recreational fees incurred anywhere in WDW. At the Magic Kingdom, Epcot, and the Disney-MGM Studios, guests may use their IDs to charge meals at full-service restaurants and in shops but not at fast-food outlets or food carts.

Note: ID cards are valid for use of the transportation facilities through the end of the last day of your stay, but are not valid for charging past your check-out time. Also note that guests at the *Swan* and *Dolphin* hotels may not charge meals at restaurants outside their hotel to their rooms. Other restrictions may apply. Read the information on the cards carefully when checking in.

Rates at Walt Disney

CALL W-DISNEY (934-7639)

	Charge for single or double occupancy		Maximum room capacity
	Season	Off-season	
DELUXE			
BoardWalk Inn			
Rooms–Standard	$240–$305	$225–$285	5
Rooms–Concierge	$400–$480	$380–$460	5
Suites	Call 934-7639 for prices		6
Contemporary Resort			
Rooms–Garden Wings	$215–$270	$195–$250	5
Rooms–Tower	$290	$270	
Suites	Call 934-7639 for prices		7 to 12
Dolphin			
Rooms–Standard	$255–$335	$220–$280	5
Rooms–Concierge	$365	$310	5
Suites	$525–$2,400	$450–$2,400	5 to 10
Grand Floridian Resort			
Rooms–Standard	$290–$375	$265–$340	5
Rooms–Concierge	$470	$465	5
Suites	Call 934-7639 for prices		4 to 10
Polynesian Resort			
Rooms–Standard	$215–$305	$200–$285	5
Rooms–Concierge	$325–$380	$305–$360	5
Suites	Call 934-7639 for prices		4 to 6
Swan			
Rooms–Standard	$275–$305	$245–$270	5
Rooms–Concierge	$350	$335	5
Suites	$350–$1,650	$325–$1,650	5 to 10
Wilderness Lodge			
Rooms	$174–$290	$159–$270	4
Suites	Call 934-7639 for prices		4
Yacht Club and Beach Club Resorts			
Rooms–Standard	$240–$305	$225–$285	5
Rooms–Concierge**	$390–$405	$370–$385	5
Suites	Call 934-7639 for prices		5 to 10
**Yacht Club only			
HOME AWAY FROM HOME			
BoardWalk Villas			
Studios	$225–$250	$210–$235	4
One-bedroom villas	$310	$285	4
Two-bedroom villas	$406	$385	8
Grand Villas	$780	$780	12
Disney Vacation Club			
Studios	$215	$195	4
One-bedroom units	$290	$265	4
Two-bedroom units	$385	$365	8
Grand Villas	$780	$780	12

World Properties

FOR RESERVATIONS

	Charge for single or double occupancy		Maximum room capacity
	Season	Off-season	
Fort Wilderness Homes	$215	$185	6
The Villas at The Disney Institute			
Bungalows	$215	$195	4
One-bedroom Town Houses	$305	$285	4
Two-bedroom Town Houses	$340	$320	6
Treehouses	$375	$355	6
Fairway Villas	$400	$375	8
Grand Vista Homes	$975–$1,150	$975–$1,150	6 to 8

MODERATE

	Season	Off-season	
Caribbean Beach Resort Rooms	$99–$129	$95–$124	4
Dixie Landings Rooms	$99–$129	$95–$124	4
Port Orleans Rooms	$99–$129	$95–$124	4

VALUE

	Season	Off-season	
All-Star Sports and All-Star Music Resorts Rooms	$69–$79	$69–$79	4

CAMPGROUND

Fort Wilderness Campsites: Preferred loops with full hookups include water, electricity, sanitary disposal, and cable TV ($58 per night; $49 off-season); all other loops with full hookups do not include cable TV ($52 per night; $43 off-season). Sites with partial hookups (electric and water) are $44; $35 off-season. Check-out is at 11 A.M., check-in at 1 P.M.

Check-in time: 3 P.M. except at *The Villas at The Disney Institute* and the *Disney Vacation Club*, where check-in time is 4 P.M. **Check-out time:** 11 A.M. for all hotels.

Season refers to: December 17, 1995 through December 31, 1995; February 11, 1996 through April 20, 1996; and June 9, 1996 through August 17, 1996, except at *Caribbean Beach, Port Orleans*, and *Dixie Landings*, where season dates are December 17, 1995 through December 31, 1995 and February 11, 1996 through August 17, 1996. All other dates are considered off-season, except at the *Swan* and the *Dolphin*, where the summer months of June, July, and August also are considered off-season. These designations in no way reflect park attendance.

Note: The prices listed here were correct at press time, but the rates do change, so be sure to double check with the hotels before finally setting your vacation budget.

Room capacity: All sleeping configurations are based on existing beds. Cots and cribs may be requested in most resorts.

Disney Village

The seven hotels here—the *Hilton*, the *Buena Vista Palace*, the *Travelodge*, the *Grosvenor*, the *Doubletree Guest Suites*, the *Royal Plaza*, and the *Courtyard by Marriott*—occupy a unique position among non-Disney-owned Orlando-area accommodations. They are located inside the boundaries of Walt Disney World, within walking distance of the Disney Village Marketplace, Pleasure Island, and *Planet Hollywood*. Guests here are entitled to preferred access to the five Disney golf courses, guaranteed admission to the theme parks during busy seasons, and priority seating at *Planet Hollywood* before 5 P.M. WDW Central Reservations (W-DISNEY—934-7639) can take your bookings for Disney Village Hotel Plaza properties, and they're included in several Walt Disney Travel Co. packages.

The hotels are served by an independent bus service; buses make regular stops at each hotel and drop guests at the Transportation and Ticket Center, Epcot, and the Disney-MGM Studios. Limited service also is available to other locations around Walt Disney World. The *Hilton*, *Buena Vista Palace*, and *Grosvenor* hotels are closest to the Disney Village Marketplace, which is directly across the street and an easy walk away. The other properties are slightly farther back on Hotel Plaza Boulevard.

Note: The following hotel listings are arranged according to standard room rates, from highest to lowest starting price.

HILTON: This hotel is a good choice for its enviable proximity to the Disney Village Marketplace and for its laid-back poolside ambience. The 814 renovated rooms on this 23-acre property are tastefully decorated. Each has a mini-bar and a high-tech digital telephone system with voice messaging service and computer hookups.

The hotel features seven restaurants and lounges. *Finn's Grill* offers dinners of seafood and steaks in an old Key West atmosphere; *County Fair* serves breakfast (with characters in attendance on Sundays), lunch, and dinner; and the *Rum Largo Pool Bar & Café* offers hamburgers, salads, sandwiches, and tropical drinks. The *County Fair Terrace* features outdoor dining. The *Old-Fashioned Soda Shoppe and Arcade* has everything from ice cream to pizza. A branch of the *Benihana* Japanese steak houses also is on the premises. For drinks, drop by *John T's Plantation Bar* in the lobby.

Recreational facilities include two lighted tennis courts, two heated swimming pools, a children's pool with a fountain at the center, and a spa. Guests traveling with children will appreciate the Vacation Station Kid's Hotel, a hotel-within-a-hotel that has been designed for children 4 to 12 years of age. There is a video room and play area, as well as scheduled recreational activities supervised by a trained staff. The cost is $4 for the first child and $1 discount for each additional child. The *Hilton* also provides a separate entrance for convention and meeting guests. Rates range from $190 to $250. There are rooms for travelers with disabilities. Nonsmoking rooms are available. *Hilton* at Walt Disney World Village; 1751 Hotel Plaza Blvd.; Lake Buena Vista, FL 32830; 827-4000 (800-782-4414).

Hotel Plaza

BUENA VISTA PALACE: The largest of the Disney Village Hotel Plaza properties (and a good choice for its nightlife) is actually a cluster of towers (one of them 27 stories) boasting mirrored, multifaceted facades and a contemporary interior. The lobby area has several nooks with overstuffed chairs and couches. Many of the 1,028 rooms (including suites) have private patios or balconies; each has a ceiling fan, air conditioning, and a remote-control color TV. The concierge rooms have special services and amenities. Many rooms and suites provide a view of Epcot's Spaceship Earth. All rooms have two telephones—one with voice mail at bedside and one in the bathroom. Four guestrooms have whirlpools. There are two swimming pools, a kiddie pool, a health spa, a whirlpool, three lighted tennis courts, and a huge arcade. Kid Stuff is an organized recreational program for children ages 4 to 12 that is available year-round. There also is a play area for children.

The hotel also features 24-hour room service, Disney-run gift and sundry shops, a guest laundry, and the Family Calling Center—a large booth with a speakerphone. Eating spots include the *Watercress Café & Bake Shop*, for counter-service baked goods and deli items, as well as a Sunday character breakfast buffet; *Arthur's 27*, an award-winning rooftop dining room with an international menu (jackets required); *Arthur's Wine Cellar in the Sky*, a private dining room in *Arthur's 27* that stocks 800 bottles (reservations essential); and the *Outback* restaurant, which serves fresh seafood and Black Angus steaks.

The adjacent *Laughing Kookaburra Good Time Bar*, nicknamed "The Kook," offers live bands, dancing, and 99 brands of beer from around the world. Unfortunately, noise from the restaurants tends to flow through the atriums and penetrate the solid oak doors, so if serenity and silence matter to you, choose accommodations in either the 5-story tower or the 27-story tower, neither of which has an atrium. For the perfect perch to view IllumiNations and sip fine wines by the glass, head up to the *Top of the Palace* lounge and piano bar. Extensive convention facilities are available. Rooms range from $145 to $250 per night (no charge for children under 18). There are 12 rooms equipped for guests with disabilities. Nonsmoking rooms are available. *Buena Vista Palace*; 1900 Buena Vista Dr.; Lake Buena Vista, FL 32830; 827-2727 (800-327-2990).

TRAVELODGE: This tri-arc hotel-tower across from the Crossroads of Lake Buena Vista shopping center has 325 spacious rooms and suites. All rooms have either one king-size or two queen-size beds, color TV, phones with voice mail, coffeemakers, safes, hair dryers, and private balconies offering pretty views of Walt Disney World Village areas. The gameroom, pool, and playground are appreciated by youngsters. A coin-operated laundry is on site. *Traders* restaurant serves breakfast and dinner. The *Parakeet Café* serves light entrées for breakfast, lunch, and dinner, as well as snacks. *Toppers* nightclub on the 18th floor is a prime viewing spot for Epcot's IllumiNations; it also has late-night entertainment until 2 A.M. The four suites on the 18th floor have cathedral windows that offer a superb view of Disney Village Hotel Plaza and the fireworks at the theme parks. Rates range from $119 to $169 for guestrooms; $199 to $299 for suites. There are two rooms for travelers with disabilities. Nonsmoking rooms are available. *Travelodge*; 2000 Hotel Plaza Blvd.; Box 22205; Lake Buena Vista, FL 32830; 828-2424 (800-348-3765).

GROSVENOR: The 629 rooms are located in a mauve 19-story tower and two wings. The decor is British colonial, with pale greens, peaches, and pinks evoking the Caribbean. Each room has a VCR, a mini-bar, and a coffeemaker. Current movies are available for rent at *Crumpets Café*. *Baskervilles*, the hotel's main restaurant, incorporates a Sherlock Holmes museum, and serves breakfast and dinner buffets; characters show up for breakfast Tuesdays, Thursdays, and Saturdays, and for dinner on Wednesdays. *Baskervilles* also is the scene, during dinner on Saturdays, for the Murder Watch Mystery Theatre. There's seasonal entertainment at *Crickets* lounge, and continental breakfasts, snacks, and lighter fare are available at *Crumpets Café* 24 hours a day. A new fitness center, two lighted tennis courts, handball and shuffleboard courts, a basketball court, a volleyball court, two heated pools, a children's pool, a large play area, and a gameroom also are available. The *Grosvenor* (pronounced "grove-nor") is affiliated with *Best Western*; it can accommodate meetings and conventions.

Rates range from $115 to $160 for two, year-round ($10 for cots). There are several rooms accessible to guests with disabilities. Non-smoking rooms are available. *Grosvenor*; 1850 Hotel Plaza Blvd.; Lake Buena Vista, FL 32830; 828-4444 (800-624-4109).

DOUBLETREE GUEST SUITES: Bright colors and whimsical patterns grace the public areas of this 229-unit property, the only all-suite hotel at Disney, across from the Crossroads of Lake Buena Vista shopping center. Guest units were redone in 1993, and other enhancements were completed last year at the former *Guest Quarters*. One innovation is a child's check-in desk near the regular one in the lobby, where each child receives a bag of gifts. A new children's theater has a big-screen television, toys, games, and weekly children's activities with clowns and storytellers. Each of the 643-square-foot suites has a living room (with a sleeper sofa), a large dressing room, and a separate bedroom, and can sleep up to six persons (there are some two-bedroom suites).

Amenities include two remote-control televisions, a small TV in the bathroom, a wet bar, a refrigerator, a coffeemaker (with daily coffee and tea refills), a microwave oven, and a hair dryer. Recreational facilities include a heated pool with a whirlpool, a gameroom, a children's play area, and two lighted tennis courts with tennis pro instruction. There are two new restaurants. The festive *Streamers* features American classics, while the *Cool Pool Deli & Market* has snacks, hot dishes, made-to-order sandwiches, and items for the microwave. There are suites for guest with disabilities. Nonsmoking rooms are available. Rates range from $109 to $239. *Doubletree Guest Suites*; 2305 Hotel Plaza Blvd.; Lake Buena Vista, FL 32830; 934-1000 (800-424-2900).

ROYAL PLAZA: A $10 million renovation has invigorated this 22-year-old hotel. The 396 guest units are divided between a 17-story high-rise and two-story lanai wings. The lower-level lanai units have gated patios, while the upper-level rooms have small balconies. Each luxurious tower room has a sitting area, a desk, a dresser, a double armoire with closet space, a television, an in-room safe, and an honor bar. The baths have marble counters (only one sink) and corner tubs (whirlpools on the concierge level). All rooms have VCRs, hair dryers, and coffeemakers. There also are four suites available—including two celebrity suites named the Burt Reynolds and the Barbara Mandrell—as well as 18 executive king/honeymoon suites. On-site recreation facilities include a heated pool, a spa, a sauna, a gameroom, and four lighted tennis courts.

The *Plaza Diner* serves family-style meals with table service or a buffet line. A delicatessen has yogurt, espresso, and carry-out items. The *Giraffe Lounge*, now a sports bar, retains its loyal local following (particularly Disney employees). Car rental is available. The *Royal Plaza* specializes in small meetings of fewer than 300 people. Depending on the season and the view, rates range from $95 to $150 for up to four in a room using existing beds. There are rooms specially equipped for travelers with disabilities. Nonsmoking rooms are available. *Royal Plaza*; Box 22203; 1905 Hotel Plaza Blvd.; Lake Buena Vista, FL 32830; 828-2828 (800-248-7890).

COURTYARD BY MARRIOTT: A $4.5 million refurbishment transformed this 323-room hotel from a *Howard Johnson* to the country's second-largest *Courtyard*. Recently redecorated guestrooms (some of the most spacious in Hotel Plaza) are divided between a 14-story tower and a 6-story annex. They all include sitting areas, computer-data ports, clock radios, marble vanities, in-room Nintendo, coffeemakers with china mugs, and pulsating showerheads. The atrium lobby has cheerful umbrella-shaded tables, a breakfast bar, and a lounge. The *Courtyard Café and Grille* is a full-service restaurant with a breakfast buffet, and the *Village Deli* serves snacks and sandwiches, and has *TCBY Yogurt* and *Pizza Hut* outlets. There are three heated pools, including one for children; a whirlpool; a playground; a gameroom; and an exercise room with Nautilus equipment. A pool bar is open seasonally. There are rooms for guests with disabilities. Nonsmoking rooms are available. Rates range from $79 to $149 year-round. *Courtyard by Marriott*; Box 22204; 1805 Hotel Plaza Blvd.; Lake Buena Vista, FL 32830; 828-8888 (800-223-9930).

Lake Buena Vista Accommodations

A full lineup of accommodations—moderately priced inns and comfortable suites with convenient kitchens to palatial villas and luxury hotels—abuts the crossroads at I-4 and S.R. 535, in the heart of Lake Buena Vista. Most of them offer free scheduled transfers to the three main Disney parks. Prices are highly competitive, so compare rates, size of accommodations, and amenities before you make a reservation. The following hotel listings are arranged according to standard room rates, from highest to lowest starting price.

HYATT REGENCY GRAND CYPRESS: When it opened in 1984, the 18-story *Hyatt Regency Grand Cypress* cost $110 million and was accorded worldwide attention for its dramatic 200-foot atrium lobby and its modernistic T-shaped design. It remains the centerpiece of the 1,500-acre resort, which is adjacent to Disney Village Hotel Plaza and just three miles from Epcot. Decor in the 750 guestrooms (including 74 suites) reflects the Florida location with wicker furniture, ceiling fans, and shutters. Guests have the choice of one king-size or two double beds. The 11th and 17th floors have been designated the Regency Club, and guests enjoy a complimentary breakfast buffet and concierge service. (There are three other concierges in the lobby.) The hotel has five restaurants and three bars; the formal *La Coquina* features nouvelle cuisine, while seafood, steaks, and game are highlights at the popular *Hemingway's*.

The secluded *Villas of Grand Cypress* are the resort's exquisite Mediterranean-style accommodations. Each club suite consists of a spacious bedroom with a separate dressing area, a large luxury bath with a separate shower, a sundeck, and a patio or a veranda. The actual villas also contain an oversize living room, a dining room, and a fully equipped kitchen. The *Villas* area has three dining possiblities, including the sophisticated *Black Swan* restaurant, where edible flowers and herbs are used in the gourmet dishes. *Fairways* is a casual eatery. The *Villas* have their own pool and whirlpool, both open 24 hours a day.

The *Hyatt Regency Grand Cypress* and the *Villas of Grand Cypress* share a half-acre freeform swimming pool with 12 waterfalls, 2 water slides, and 3 whirlpools; a 21-acre lake perfect for trying out one of the sailboats, sailboards, canoes, or pedal boats available for rent; and a tennis complex with 12 courts. There also is racquetball, volleyball, a playground, bicycling, a 4.7-mile jogging trail, a 45-acre nature area and Audubon walk, and a health club. Forty-five holes of Jack Nicklaus–designed golf separate the *Hyatt Regency* from the *Villas* (a 24-hour shuttle connects the two areas, which are actually 1½ miles apart!). The superb original course features two Scottish-style shared greens, grassy dunes, and elevated tees. This course is open to guests of the hotel and the *Villas*, and the greens fee will set you back $120 ($80 in the summer). The highly regarded Grand Cypress Academy of Golf is open year-round and provides full- and half-day instruction.

Grand Cypress Equestrian Center, the only resort center of its kind in North America, features a wide range of programs and lessons for riders of all levels as well as English and western trail rides. The Grand Cypress Racquet Club offers tennis camps and individual instruction on 12 courts (5 are lighted) as well as 2 open-air racquetball courts.

Shuttle service to the three Disney theme parks costs $5 round-trip. Rates at the *Hyatt Regency* range from $185 to $420; suites start at $600. Rates at the *Villas* range from $170 to $350 for a club suite, $245 to $425 for a one-bedroom villa, and $340 to $700 for a two-bedroom villa. Both have rooms for guests with disabilities. Nonsmoking rooms and villas are available. The resort has space for meetings for small groups and conventions of up to 2,500 people. *Hyatt Regency Grand Cypress*; One Grand Cypress Blvd.; Orlando, FL 32836; 239-1234 (800-233-1234); *Villas of Grand Cypress*; One North Jacaranda; Orlando, FL 32836; 239-4700 (800-835-7377).

VISTANA: If you drive near the intersection of I-4 and S.R. 535, you won't be able to miss this sprawling complex of more than 900 condominium units, only a mile from the Disney Village Marketplace. Its name is spelled out in floral landscaping adjacent to the interstate. *Vistana* was one of the area's earliest timeshare resorts—it still is one—but it also operates as a luxury resort behind its controlled-entry gate. All of the stylishly decorated 1,200-square-foot villas sleep six to eight people and have two bedrooms, two baths, living rooms (with sleeper sofa and VCR), and a fully equipped kitchen. The daily housekeepers do the dishes. Facilities include 13 tennis courts with clinics, 6 outdoor swimming pools, 5 children's pools, volleyball, a miniature golf course, and a video library. There are three recreational centers (each with a steam room and a sauna, one with an exercise room). A number of adult and children's activity programs are available for a nominal charge. Two restaurants are on the property, along with a general store and a deli. Complimentary bus service to the three Disney theme parks is provided. There are villas for guests with disabilities. Nonsmoking villas are not available. Rates range from $175 to $275 per villa per night. *Vistana*; 8800 Vistana Centre Dr.; Orlando, FL 32821; 239-3100 (800-877-8787).

SUMMERFIELD SUITES LAKE BUENA VISTA:

This all-suite hotel is popular because most of its 150 units feature two separate bedrooms, each with a private bath, joined by a living room and a fully equipped kitchen. Facilities are similar to those at the *Summerfield* on International Drive; the rates are slightly higher here but include shuttle service to the three Disney theme parks. Rates for one-bedroom units range from $169 to $209 for up to four guests; for two-bedroom units, $199 to $249 for up to eight guests. Prices include a breakfast buffet and a cocktail hour Mondays through Thursdays. There are suites for guests with disabilities. Nonsmoking suites are available. *Summerfield Suites Lake Buena Vista*; 8751 Suiteside Dr.; Orlando, FL 32836; 238-0777 (800-833-4253).

MARRIOTT'S ORLANDO WORLD CENTER:

The 27-story, Y-shaped tower dominates the landscape from its vantage point on the non-Disney side of the I-4 and S.R. 535 interchange. Its 1,503 guestrooms make it one of the largest hotels in Florida, and the hotel is sometimes near capacity for the substantial numbers of meetings held here. However, the property, set amid 200 manicured acres including an 18-hole Joe Lee–designed golf course, is so vast that leisure guests often are unaware that a sizable meeting is going on. The atrium lobby is filled with Sabal palms, banana trees, and jade plants, and there are museum-quality 16th- and 17th-century Chinese artifacts on the grounds. The guestrooms have tropical colors and corresponding theme, complete with wicker furniture. Each room has

a single-sleep sofa and a choice of two double beds or one king-size bed.

The extensive recreational facilities include four heated swimming pools (one indoors), eight lighted tennis courts, volleyball courts, a miniature golf course, a health club (free to guests), a whirlpool, a gameroom, and several shops. The Lollipop Lounge, a children's program for kids ages 3 to 12, operates from 8 A.M. to 11 P.M. The cost is $6 an hour for the first child, $4 for each additional child. There are six restaurants, including *Mikado's*, a Japanese steak house, and *Tuscany's Ristorante*, which features northern Italian dishes, homemade pastas and sauces, and authentic Italian wines. The hotel has three lounges. Rates range from $154 to $199; $250 to $2,000 for suites. There are rooms for travelers with disabilities. Nonsmoking rooms are available. *Marriott's Orlando World Center*; 8701 World Center Dr.; Orlando, FL 32821; 239-4200 (800-228-9290).

BEST WESTERN BUENA VISTA SUITES:

This 280-suite hotel, which opened in mid-1993, has been such a success that its owners plan to build a separate 1,250-unit luxury version on an adjacent lot. It has an ideal location for those who plan to tour Central Florida—S.R. 535 and the relatively new International Drive extension, about 1½ miles from Walt Disney World and close to the strip along I-Drive. The standard two-room suites have a separate bedroom and a living room with a queen-size sofa bed. Each unit has a coffeemaker, a refrigerator, two televisions, a VCR, two telephones, a safe, and a microwave oven. The phones are equipped with voice mail and data ports. The deluxe suites have a king-size bed and a whirlpool.

Other facilities include a fitness center, a heated pool, a whirlpool, a gameroom, a coin-operated laundry, a gift shop, a small market, and movie rentals. Sandwiches and snacks are sold at the *Patio Grille*. The *Citrus Lounge* provides poolside lunch and evening cocktails. The rates include a full American breakfast in the *Valencia Room*. Rates range from $99 to $149 for the standard suite and $109 to $169 for the deluxe suites. All suites accommodate up to four adults, or two adults and up to four children. There are rooms for guests with disabilities. Nonsmoking rooms are available. *Best Western Buena Vista Suites*; 14450 International Dr.; Orlando, FL 32830; 239-8588 (800-537-7737).

HOLIDAY INN SUNSPREE–LAKE BUENA VISTA:

About 1½ miles from the Disney Village Marketplace, this 507-unit property garnered attention with its innovative children's program and later became the prototype for *Holiday Inn's* mid-priced, family-related *SunSpree* chain. Each guestroom has a refrigerator, a microwave, and a coffeemaker (with a free coffee packet daily). Other in-room

amenities include a hair dryer, an electronic safe, and a VCR (movie rentals are available for a fee). Most of the rooms have two queen-size beds; some king-size beds with sleeper sofas are available.

Camp Holiday is a licensed child care and activity program for children ages 2 to 12. The hours are 8 A.M. to midnight and it's $1 an hour per child—a bargain compared with prices at many other properties, and unusual because it is open such long hours. Parents can rent a beeper for $5 so they can be reached when they leave the premises. Children receive a surprise when they register at the Kids' Check-In Desk, and a free bedtime tuck-in with Max, the hotel's mascot, upon reservation. Children under 12 eat breakfast, lunch, and dinner free when accompanied by a paying adult.

Recreational facilities include a heated pool, two whirlpools, a basketball court, a playground, and a fitness center. *Maxine's*, a family restaurant, serves a buffet for breakfast and dinner, along with an à la carte menu. *Pinky's Deli and Mini-Market* is a self-serve restaurant for eating in or taking out; it carries a variety of items to cook in the room as well as baby supplies and diapers. Free transportation to the three Disney theme parks is provided. There are rooms for guests with disabilities. Nonsmoking rooms are available. Rates are $79 to $129, depending on the season. *Holiday Inn SunSpree–Lake Buena Vista*; 13351 S.R. 535; Lake Buena Vista, FL 32821; 239-4500 (800-366-6299).

HOWARD JOHNSON PARK SQUARE INN & SUITES: A top-rated property within the chain for several years running, this is one of several hostelries in Vista Centre, which has assorted restaurants, clubs, and shops and is about five minutes from the Disney Village Marketplace. The pleasant lobby lounge has a big-screen television. There are 222 guestrooms and 86 suites, all with lake or courtyard settings. The rooms have two double beds, and the bathrooms are a decent size for the price.

Suites feature a microwave oven–refrigerator unit and a coffeemaker, as well as a sleeper sofa. Recreational facilities include two large heated pools, a whirlpool, a children's pool, and a gameroom. The *Courtyard Café* serves a buffet breakfast and an à la carte dinner. Children under 18 eat free with a paying adult. Complimentary shuttles carry guests to the three Disney theme parks. Room rates range from $65 to $105; suites run from $80 to $130, depending on the season. There are rooms for guests with disabilities. Nonsmoking rooms are available. *Howard Johnson Park Square Inn & Suites*; 8501 Palm Parkway; Box 22818; Lake Buena Vista, FL 32830; 239-6900 (800-635-8684).

COMFORT INN: This 640-room property in Vista Centre off S.R. 535 is one of the area's best-known bargains. The local owner's hotels generally have some of the most reasonable rates in town. Needless to say, this one also has a high occupancy in peak seasons, so it is wise to call in advance. The attractively furnished rooms have a direct-dial phone with a message light, two double beds, and a complimentary in-room safe. Bathrooms are small. Tropical landscaping surrounds the two swimming pools (one heated). Other facilities include a gameroom, a gift shop, a lounge, and a guest laundry. The *Boardwalk Buffet* restaurant serves breakfast and dinner. Up to three children under 12 eat free when accompanied by two adults. Free transportation to the three Disney theme parks is provided. Several rooms are designed for guests with disabilities. Nonsmoking rooms are available. Pets are permitted. Rates are reasonable: $39 to $69, depending on the season. *Comfort Inn*; 8442 Palm Parkway; Lake Buena Vista, FL 32836; 239-7300 (800-999-7300).

U.S. 192 Accommodations

The properties along this multi-lane highway (this stretch of U.S. 192 is also known as Irlo Bronson Memorial Highway), which intersects I-4 in the community of Kissimmee, are closer to the WDW theme parks than those along Orlando's International Drive. The area itself is less attractive and tends to be cluttered, although the motels on the west end of 192, near the so-called main gate to Disney World, are well maintained and offer few surprises. (The term "main gate" is now rather meaningless, since it originated when there was just one park, the Magic Kingdom.)

ROOM SERVICE

In this country's largest hotel market, with more than 82,000 rooms, visitors rarely discover that there is no room at the inn. Almost every type of accommodation from the all-suite hotel to the bed-and-breakfast inn to the budget motel is represented, and almost every U.S. brand name as well. However, these categories (and even the number of rooms) do not include the profusion of rental condominiums, apartments, and single-family houses that are also available. By shopping around and asking a few questions, it's possible to find the style of property you need, at a good price.

It's a good idea to contact a travel agent, or one of two local tourism organizations. The Orlando/Orange County Convention & Visitors Bureau is at 7208 Sand Lake Rd., Suite 300; Orlando, FL 32819; call 363-5871. The Kissimmee–St. Cloud Convention & Visitors Bureau operates a reservations system at 800-333-5477, which covers most of the properties along U.S. Highway 192, including a number of condominiums and houses. For information write Box 422,007; Kissimmee, FL 34724; or call 800-327-9159.

If you're making last-minute arrangements, save time and money by going to the Official Visitor Information Center (operated by the Orlando/Orange Country Convention & Visitors Bureau) in the Mercado Mediterranean Shopping Village at 8445 International Drive, Suite 152 (no phone; you have to show up in person). Ask a staffer to look in the "black book" for the rates and room availability of Orlando area hotels.

These motels are a short ride from Walt Disney World and are recommended for their value and convenience.

The following hotel listings are arranged by standard room rates, from highest to lowest starting price.

HOLIDAY INN MAIN GATE EAST: Like its sister property, the *Holiday Inn SunSpree* in Lake Buena Vista, this 670-room property, situated three miles from WDW, was designed with families in mind. Each guestroom has a refrigerator, a microwave oven, a coffee-maker, an ironing board, remote-control cable television, an electronic safe, and a VCR (movies can be rented in the lobby). There are two Olympic-size swimming pools, a kiddie pool, two playgrounds, two lighted tennis courts, and two gamerooms. Camp Holiday, a supervised activity program for children ages 3 to 12, is a bargain ($1 an hour for each child). The hours are 2 P.M. to 10 P.M. daily, and parents can leave the property and rent a beeper so they can be reached. Children receive free gifts and can be tucked into bed by the property's two hound-dog mascots. Children under 13 eat free when with a paying adult in the *Vineyard Café*, which serves breakfast and dinner, or in the six eateries at the *People's Choice Food Court*. A general store carries items that can be heated in microwave ovens. Free scheduled transportation to the three Disney theme parks is provided. There are rooms equipped for guests with disabilities. Nonsmoking rooms are available. Rates are $65 to $119, depending on the season. *Holiday Inn Main Gate East*; 5678 Irlo Bronson Memorial Highway; Kissimmee, FL 34746; 396-4488 (800-366-5437).

HILTON INN ORLANDO/KISSIMMEE GATE-WAY: This well-appointed 500-unit hotel has 24-hour security and is entered through a staffed gate. It does a brisk meetings business but has not forgotten its leisure visitors. All the units have small refrigerators, and the 147 luxury high-rise rooms have microwave ovens. There are two outdoor pools (one heated), an exercise room, a coin-operated laundry, an 18-hole putting green, a gameroom, a basketball court, and two shuffleboard courts. The *Palms Restaurant* is open for breakfast and dinner (buffets seasonally). Children eat free when accompanied by a paying adult. A self-service deli–snack bar offers items for eating in or taking out, and free coffee and tea, from 6 A.M. to midnight. Karaoke entertainment takes place nightly in the *Ficus Lounge*. Free

west of I-4, a pleasant choice. The spacious, newly redecorated rooms feature polished wood furniture in French Provincial style; each has a color television, a radio, and a VCR (movie rentals are available in the lobby). There are two medium-size heated swimming pools—rectangular to make for good lap swimming, a kiddie pool, an exercise room and sauna, a pair of lighted tennis courts, and a gameroom. The *Café Terrace* serves family-style breakfasts and dinners daily. Children under 12 eat free when accompanied by an adult. There also is a lobby lounge and a deli. Free shuttle service is available to the three Disney theme parks. Rates range from $49 to $89, depending on the season; rates for the hotel's three suites range from $120 to $140. The hotel has rooms equipped for guests with disabilities. Nonsmoking rooms are available. *Ramada Resort Maingate*; 2950 Reedy Creek Blvd.; Kissimmee, FL 34747; 396-4466 (800-365-6935).

KNIGHTS INN MAINGATE: This revamped 120-room hotel is one of the best bargains along the 192 strip. The refurbished rooms, all on the ground floor, are spartan but functional. The facilities include a heated pool, a laundry, an attraction ticket sales counter, and a gameroom. Complimentary shuttle service is provided to the three Disney theme parks. There are rooms for guests with disabilities. Nonsmoking rooms are available. Rates are $35 to $69. *Knights Inn Maingate*; 7475 West Irlo Bronson Memorial Highway; Kissimmee, FL 34746; 396-4200 (800-944-0062).

shuttle service is provided to the three Disney theme parks. Rates range from $60 to $125 a night; rates for suites are available on request. There are rooms equipped for guests with disabilities. Nonsmoking rooms are available. *Hilton Inn Orlando/Kissimmee Gateway*; 7470 West Irlo Bronson Highway; Kissimmee, FL 34747; 396-4400 (800-327-9170).

COURTYARD BY MARRIOTT MAINGATE: A $2.5 million renovation in 1994 turned this 198-room motel into a sleek hostelry. The Art Deco–style lobby has a pleasant-looking seating area. Rooms feature electronic locks, remote-control televisions, clock radios, and in-room coffee and tea (supplies are replenished daily). Almost half the rooms have a small refrigerator. An outdoor pool, a health club, a gameroom, a gift shop, and a guest laundry are available. The property's restaurant serves only breakfast, and the *Tiki Bar* at the pool offers sandwiches and light fare for lunch and dinner (children under 12 eat free). There is in-room pizza delivery as well. Free shuttle service is provided to the three Disney theme parks. There are rooms equipped for guests with disabilities. Nonsmoking room are available. Rates are $59 to $109. *Courtyard by Marriott Maingate*; 7675 West Irlo Bronson Highway; Kissimmee, FL 34747; 396-4000 (800-568-3352).

RAMADA RESORT MAINGATE: Attractive landscaping and a $2 million refurbishment in 1995 make this 391-room establishment, just

CAMPING OUTSIDE WALT DISNEY WORLD

The lush, cypress-hung woods of WDW's *Fort Wilderness* are unrivaled by any other Orlando-area campground. But not everyone can get a reservation at *Fort Wilderness*, and in any case, not everyone wants to spend the money. Consider one of the two Yogi Bear Camp Resorts in the WDW area: 8555 West Irlo Bronson Memorial Highway; Kissimmee, FL 34747 (239-4148; 800-776-YOGI); and 9200 Turkey Lake Rd.; Orlando, FL 32819 (351-4394; 800-776-YOGI). The two sites offer similar facilities, including a swimming pool, a miniature golf course, fishing, and boat rentals. Free shuttle service to WDW is provided. Rates are $18 for tents without hookups; $25 to $31 for full hookups. Rates are for two adults and any children under 12; it's $3 more for each additional adult.

International Drive Accommodations

Many well-known motel and restaurant chains, and one of Orlando's finest hotels, are represented on International Drive, or I-Drive, as it is known locally; most of the facilities on nearby Sand Lake and Kirkman roads are clustered close to their intersections with it. I-Drive has two distinct sectors: the more orderly south end that stretches from Sea World to the Orange County Convention Center to Sand Lake Road, and the more cluttered north end that is jammed with restaurants, T-shirt shops, and outlet stores.

Some of Orlando's most interesting restaurants are within walking distance of the hotels at the north end. If you are tired of being on your feet all day, however, catch the new I-Ride buses, which traverse the stretch of I-Drive and include stops at most of the properties listed here. The fare is 75 cents; exact change is required. Children under 13 ride free. Information may be obtained at hotel guest services desks.

The following hotel listings are arranged by standard room rates, from highest to lowest starting price.

PEABODY ORLANDO: The only sister property to the famed *Peabody* hotel in Memphis, this imposing 27-story, 891-room hostelry is one of International Drive's most luxurious establishments. And, of course, there are the famous *Peabody* ducks, which every day at 11 A.M. waddle from a private elevator into the enormous lobby, down a red carpet, then settle into a marble fountain—a spectacle that continues to attract hotel guests and locals. They waddle back at about 5 P.M.

Each of the *Peabody's* guestrooms has a hair dryer, a small television set in the bathroom, nightly turn-down service, and daily newspaper delivery. Facilities include an Olympic-size heated pool, four lighted tennis courts, tennis lessons, a pro shop, a gameroom, and a health club with personal trainers and aerobics classes. Babysitting services by a professional staff can be arranged.

Dux (where no duck is served) is the hotel's signature restaurant. *Capriccio* showcases northern Italian dining and mesquite-grilled specialties in an exhibition kitchen, and offers a Champagne brunch Sundays; and the *B-Line Diner*, a perfect recreation of a fifties-style diner, serves entrées, sandwiches, and homemade confections 24 hours a day. Afternoon tea is served Mondays through Fridays in the *Dux* foyer. There also are four bars. The

Peabody usually is the headquarters hotel for many of the groups attending meetings at the Orange County Convention Center across the street. The hotel's whimsical Double-Ducker bus provides unlimited shuttle service to the three Disney theme parks for guests (and the general public) for $6 a day. Rates run from $210 to $270; $395 to $1,300 for suites. There are rooms equipped for guests with disabilities. Nonsmoking rooms are available. *Peabody Orlando*; 9801 International Dr.; Orlando, FL 32819; 352-4000 (800-732-2639).

STOUFFER RENAISSANCE ORLANDO: When this luxury convention hotel opened in 1984 at International Drive's south end, it created a stir for its impressive atrium, which contains more than 292 tons of marble and seven glass-enclosed elevators. The 780 guestrooms are built around the atrium, many with balconies that overlook it. The standard rooms are spacious, and many have pullout sofas. Each suite has a large, separate sitting area. Coffee and a newspaper are provided with a wakeup call. There is a concierge floor with special amenities. Recreational facilities include an Olympic-size swimming pool, an oversize whirlpool, a children's pool, five lighted tennis courts, a gameroom, a supervised children's center, and a health club. There are four restaurants, a 24-hour deli, and three lounges. *Haifeng* serves cuisine from all four regions of China, as well as Chinese wines and beers. An elaborate, popular brunch is held in the atrium on Sundays.

WORTH NOTING

The driving time to the WDW theme parks from International Drive properties can be 15 to 30 minutes, depending on traffic conditions and the location of your hotel. Keep in mind that the traffic tends to be heavier at rush hour and when large conventions are in town, adding an extra 15 minutes to any schedule.

The area is relatively convenient to downtown Orlando (a 10 to 15 minutes' drive away), as well as Winter Park (about 30 to 40 minutes from parking space to parking space), which offers upscale shopping and a few enticing ethnic restaurants. Parking here is at a premium, but there is plentiful public parking in downtown Orlando.

There are rooms equipped for guests with disabilities. Nonsmoking rooms are available. Rates range from $199 to $269. *Stouffer Renaissance Orlando*; 6677 Sea Harbor Dr.; Orlando, FL 32821; 351-5555 (800-468-3571).

SUMMERFIELD SUITES INTERNATIONAL DRIVE: This variation of the all-suite hotel is particularly popular because at least half its units contain two bedrooms, which are completely separate from the living room area. The suites are roomy enough for large families or private enough for two couples traveling together. In fact, this 146-unit property on International Drive's south end requires plenty of advance notice during peak periods because it is frequently sold out. In addition to a fully outfitted kitchen, all units have a VCR, an iron and ironing board, a desk in each bedroom, computer hookups, and two telephones (three in two-bedroom units) equipped with voice mail.

Other facilities include a 24-hour convenience store with microwave entrées and movie rentals, a guest laundry, an exercise room, a heated pool, and a whirlpool. To have grocery items delivered to the suite by 6:30 P.M., guests leave a completed form with the front desk early in the morning. All guests are entitled to a breakfast buffet and a cocktail hour. Rates are $149 to $189 for a one-bedroom unit (sleeps four), $169 to $209 for a two-bedroom unit (sleeps six), and $189 to $229 for a two-bedroom trio unit (sleeps eight). There are units equipped for guests with disabilities. Nonsmoking units are available. *Summerfield Suites International Drive*; 8480 International Dr.; Orlando, FL 32819; 352-2400 (800-833-4353).

CLARION PLAZA: Adjacent to the Orange County Convention Center, this 810-unit hotel opened in 1991 and three years later was named "Inn of the Year" by Choice Hotels International, its franchisor. The oversize guestrooms have in-room safes, separate vanity areas, and in-room checkout. A coin-operated laundry is situated on every other floor. In addition to a heated outdoor pool and whirlpool, facilities include a gameroom and two restaurants, along with a 24-hour bakery and deli.

Jack's Place, complete with caricature sketches à la New York's legendary *Sardi's*, serves seafood, steaks, and memorable desserts. *Backstage*, its 400-person capacity nightclub, is open until 2 A.M. and features a deejay and a daily Happy Hungry Hour from 3 P.M. to 8:30 P.M. A babysitting service is available. An extensive business center is on the premises. There also are rooms equipped for guests with disabilities. Nonsmoking rooms are available. Rates range from $125 to $145 for doubles, although special-value rates as low as $79 are usually available during select periods of the spring and fall; suites range from $200 to $660. *Clarion Plaza*; 9700 International Dr.; Orlando, FL 32819; 352-9700 (800-627-8250).

EMBASSY SUITES INTERNATIONAL DRIVE SOUTH: The lobby is lined with gleaming marble, and waterfalls and a wishing pond highlight the tropical atrium. The eight-floor hotel contains 144 king suites, 95 suites with two double beds, and 6 conference suites. Each has a separate living room with a wet bar, a coffeemaker, a microwave oven, a refrigerator, and a sleeper sofa. As a special service to families, the property offers emergency delivery of infant supplies and free use of strollers and booster seats. Facilities include indoor and outdoor swimming pools, a whirlpool, a sauna, a steam room, a health club, a gameroom, and a laundry. There is a children's program. The property has a restaurant and lounge, and guests receive a daily cooked-to-order breakfast and an invitation to a two-hour cocktail reception. Free shuttle service to the three Disney theme parks is provided. Rates range from $109 to $159. There are suites equipped for guests with disabilities. Nonsmoking rooms are available. *Embassy Suites International Drive South*; 8978 International Dr.; Orlando, FL 32819; 352-1400 (800-433-7275).

HOLIDAY INN INTERNATIONAL DRIVE: This 650-room property's 13 tropically landscaped acres are occupied by five buildings, including a 14-story tower, all on the north end of International Drive. What space is left is laden with recreational opportunities, including a huge free-form heated pool, a tropical courtyard and large sundeck, and aquatic gardens. You'll also find a playground, a large gameroom, shuffleboard and volleyball courts, a fitness center, and a family fun center that provides scheduled activities for children. Kids under 13 eat free when accompanied by an adult in three restaurants, including the pleasant *Key Bar & Grille* (limit: four kids). The *Comedy Zone* nightclub features comedians nightly (for a cover charge). All guestrooms have a clock radio, a safe, and a hair dryer, and a small kitchenette with a microwave oven, a refrigerator, and a coffeemaker. There are rooms equipped for guests with disabilities. Nonsmoking rooms are available. Rates run from $89 to $145. *Holiday Inn International Drive;* 6515 International Dr.; Orlando, FL 32819; 351-3500 (800-465-4329).

WESTGATE LAKES: This property is a small resort with 320 one- and two-bedroom villas near International Drive. Each beautifully decorated villa features a living room, a dining room, one or two bathrooms, and a fully equipped kitchenette. The complex is set on 97 acres facing 300-acre Sand Lake, which is used for water sports. The hotel offers two tennis courts, 11 whirlpool spas, a swimming pool, a health club, three playgrounds, a gameroom, and a free supervised children's program for kids ages 4 to 15. *Fisherman's Cove* restaurant specializes in fresh seafood, and serves breakfast, lunch, and dinner. Other facilities include a lounge and a seasonally operated pool bar and grill. There's full maid service daily. Depending on the season, rates for a one-bedroom villa that sleeps six are $70 to $145; two-bedroom units sleep eight and are $115 to $235. There are villas equipped for guests with disabilities. Nonsmoking villas are available. *Westgate Lakes;* 10,000 Turkey Lake Rd.; Orlando, FL 32819; 354-0000 (800-424-0708).

COUNTRY HEARTH INN: The rocking chairs on the porch make this the closest thing to a quaint inn you'll find on International Drive. It is across the street from the convention center and does attract conventioneers, but it has always drawn a loyal following among locals. A patterned tin ceiling, hardwood floors, and an exquisite chandelier grace the lobby. The 150 guestrooms have French doors, polished cherry furniture, verandas, and cable television. Most have two double beds, although a few rooms have king-size beds. Deluxe rooms feature refrigerators, microwave ovens, and coffeemakers. A pool is nestled within a landscaped courtyard. The *Plantation Room* in the lobby serves a buffet and à la carte breakfast, a Sunday Champagne brunch, and an à la carte dinner. There is also a cocktail lounge. Rates range from $49 to $109. There are rooms equipped for guests with disabilities. Nonsmoking rooms are available. *Country Hearth Inn;* 9861 International Dr.; Orlando, FL 32819; 352-0008 (800-447-1890).

HOLIDAY INN EXPRESS: If you are seeking value on the north end of I-Drive, this former *Roadway Inn* is the ticket. The management has transformed the 217-room hotel into an attractive property that is close to a number of restaurants. The rooms, which are a comfortable size, have been redone in bright colors. Each features two double beds, a seating area, individually controlled heating and air conditioning, a VCR (movie rentals are available in the lobby), and a safe (for a nominal fee). Recreational facilities include an oversize heated swimming pool, a children's pool, and an electronic-games room. *Expressions Pool Café* is open seasonally from mid-morning to midnight for drinks and sandwiches. Rates range from $49 to $84 and include breakfast. Free shuttle service to the three Disney theme parks is provided. There are rooms equipped for guests with disabilities. Nonsmoking rooms are available. *Holiday Inn Express;* 6323 International Dr.; Orlando, FL 32819; 351-4430 (800-365-6935).

WYNFIELD INN WESTWOOD: Weather-beaten shutters give this motel, which is right off International Drive, the look of an inn, and the tropically landscaped grounds make it even more appealing. The 300 rooms are a decent size and functional. Each has two double beds, a television, phones with voice mail, and an in-room safe (for a nominal fee). Guest laundry facilities are spaced throughout the property. A gameroom is situated off the lobby, and a heated swimming pool and a wading pool are popular with guests. There are occasional barbecues on weekends. There is no restaurant on the premises, but a ten percent discount is available at nearby restaurants. The pool bar serves beer, wine, soft drinks, and snacks. Shuttle service to the three Disney theme parks is available for $3 per room per stay. Rates run from $29 to $72 and include coffee, tea, and fruit in the lobby each morning. There are rooms equipped for travelers with disabilities. Nonsmoking rooms are available. *Wynfield Inn Westwood;* 6263 Westwood Blvd.; Orlando, FL 32821; 345-8000 (800-346-1551).

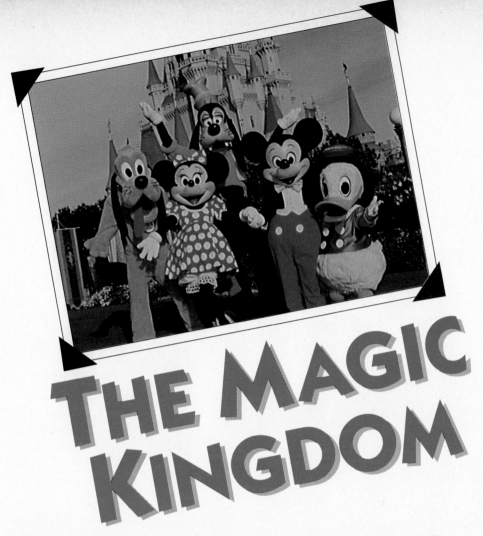

THE MAGIC KINGDOM

The Magic Kingdom is the most special part of the World. Few who have visited it are disappointed, and even the most blasé travelers manage a smile. The sight of the soaring spires of Cinderella Castle, the gleaming woodwork of the Main Street shops, and the crescendo of music that follows the parades never fail to have their effect. Even when the crowds are large and the weather is hot, a visitor who has toured this wonderland dozens of times still can look around and think how satisfying this place is for the spirit.

But the delight that most guests experience upon their first sight of the Magic Kingdom can quickly disappear when disorientation sets in. There are so many nooks and crannies, so many bends to every pathway, and so many sights and sounds clamoring for attention that it's too easy to wander aimlessly and miss the best that the Magic Kingdom has to offer. So we earnestly suggest that you study this chapter before you visit.

What makes the Magic Kingdom timeless is its combination of the classic and the futuristic. Both childhood favorites and space-age creatures have a home here. Every land has a theme, which is carried through from the hosts' and hostesses' costumes to the food served in the restaurants, the merchandise in the shops, and even the design of the trash bins. Thousands of details contribute to the overall effect; recognizing these touches makes any visit more enjoyable.

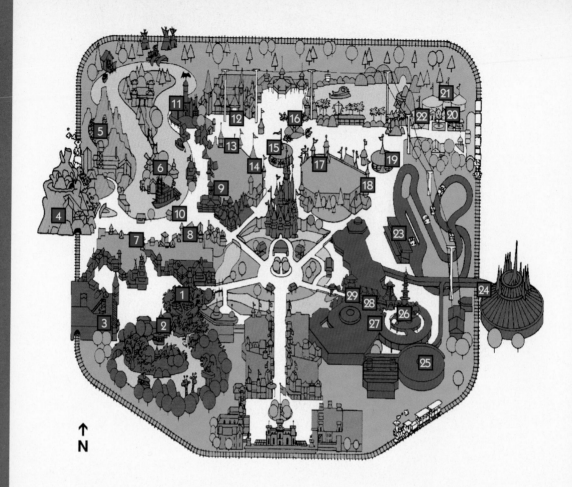

↑
N

ADVENTURELAND

1 Swiss Family Treehouse
2 Jungle Cruise
3 Pirates of the Caribbean

FRONTIERLAND

4 Splash Mountain
5 Big Thunder Mountain Railroad
6 Tom Sawyer Island
7 Country Bear Jamboree
8 Diamond Horseshoe Saloon Revue

LIBERTY SQUARE

9 The Hall of Presidents
10 Liberty Square Riverboat
11 The Haunted Mansion

FANTASYLAND

12 It's A Small World
13 Peter Pan's Flight
14 Legend of The Lion King

15 Cinderella's Golden Carrousel
16 Dumbo, the Flying Elephant
17 Snow White's Adventures
18 Mr. Toad's Wild Ride
19 Mad Tea Party

MICKEY'S STARLAND

20 Mickey's House
21 Mickey's Starland Show
22 Mickey's Hollywood Theatre

TOMORROWLAND

23 Grand Prix Raceway
24 Space Mountain
25 Walt Disney's Carousel of Progress
26 Astro Orbiter
27 Dreamflight
28 The Timekeeper
29 Alien Encounter

HOW TO GET TO THE MAGIC KINGDOM

From the *Contemporary* **resort, the** *Polynesian* **resort, and the** *Grand Floridian* **resort:** The monorail is the easiest way to go.

From the *Yacht Club* **or** *Beach Club* **resorts:** Take the bus directly to the Magic Kingdom.

From *Port Orleans* **and** *Dixie Landings:* Take the bus directly to the Magic Kingdom.

From the *Caribbean Beach* **resort:** Take the bus directly to the Magic Kingdom entrance.

From the *Dolphin* **or** *Swan* **resorts:** Take the bus directly to the Magic Kingdom entrance.

From *Wilderness Lodge:* Take the boat directly to the Magic Kingdom. Buses also make the trip.

From the *Disney Vacation Club:* Take the bus directly to the Magic Kingdom entrance.

From *The Villas at The Disney Institute:* Board a bus at one of the stops located throughout the villa area and take it to the Magic Kingdom.

From *Fort Wilderness:* Take a boat from the *Fort Wilderness* dock or take a bus to the Transportation and Ticket Center, then transfer to the ferry or monorail.

From the *All-Star Sports* **and** *All-Star Music* **resorts:** Take the bus to the Transportation and Ticket Center (TTC), then transfer to the ferry or monorail.

From the Disney Village Marketplace: Take the bus to the TTC, then transfer to the ferry or monorail to the Magic Kingdom.

From Epcot: Take the monorail to the TTC, then transfer to the other monorail or ride a ferry.

From the Disney-MGM Studios: Take the bus to the TTC, then transfer to the ferry or the monorail.

From the hotels at Disney Village Hotel Plaza: Take the bus to the Transportation and Ticket Center, then transfer to the ferry or the monorail.

From Orlando or Kissimmee: Follow the signs for Walt Disney World on I-4, take the Magic Kingdom turnoff (exit 25), and proceed to the Auto Plaza. Go straight ahead and then turn left into the parking lots. Grayline and Rabbit shuttle buses serve most hotels, but the per person charges are so high relative to the low local car rental rates that it usually makes economic sense to drive. Many of the hotels in the area offer free shuttle service to WDW.

GETTING THERE: One of Walt Disney's greatest personal disappointments was the fact that the citrus groves that originally rimmed the Disneyland site in Anaheim, California, soon gave way to unsightly commercial development. Finally, only the berm rimming the park protected it from surrounding eyesores. When planning Walt Disney World, he pledged to prevent a repeat of that situation and set the Magic Kingdom some four miles from the nearest public highway.

From the Walt Disney World exit off highway I-4, it's four miles to the Auto Plaza; from there it's under a mile to the main entrance complex known as the Transportation and Ticket Center (TTC). Even then, Magic Kingdom visitors have not completed their journey: There remains a five-minute ride by ferry

across the manmade Seven Seas Lagoon, or a slightly shorter trip by monorail around its shore. Each section of the trip—the drive from the I-4 exit to the Auto Plaza and then to the parking lot, then the lake crossing—serves to heighten the suspense, and by removing guests from the workaday world, to prepare them for the visual delights to come.

WHEN TO ARRIVE: Especially during the busy summer and holiday seasons—when the highways leading to the Auto Plaza can look like a Los Angeles freeway during rush hour, and when there are long queues at WDW monorails and ferries—it's advisable to plan on reaching the park at least a half hour before the posted opening time. Or, wait until later—about 1 P.M.—or even later than that during the seasons when the park is open late. During less congested periods, plan to arrive around the posted opening time. The Magic Kingdom is generally open from 9 A.M. to 6 P.M. During holiday periods and the summer months, hours are extended: The park stays open until 10 P.M. on weeknights and midnight on weekends.

PARKING: Parking in the Magic Kingdom lots costs $5 (free to guests at WDW resorts, upon presentation of their ID cards). After passing through the Auto Plaza, drive straight ahead and bear left for the parking lots. Parking attendants will direct you to a spot in one of a dozen areas. Each lot is named after a Disney character—Daisy, Donald, Sneezy, Bashful, Grumpy, Happy, Goofy, Pluto, Chip 'n' Dale, Minnie, Sleepy, and Dopey. Minnie, Sleepy, and Dopey are within walking distance of the TTC; other lots are served continuously by

tractor-drawn trams that make periodic stops to pick up and discharge passengers.

Before leaving your car, check the name of your section and your aisle number; there is a spot for noting this information on the back of your parking ticket. Roll up all windows and lock all doors. Also, do not leave any pets in the car! It is against the law in Florida. The Pet Care Kennel—it's air conditioned, far more comfortable for the animal, and far safer—is conveniently located right at the TTC.

Guests who leave the park at midday for their hotels should keep their parking tickets; the tickets are good for re-entry to the parking area throughout the day. Also remember that to re-enter the parks on the same day, you must have your valid ticket or admission pass *and* a hand stamp.

FERRY VS. MONORAIL: Once you've bought your admission ticket or pass and made your way through the TTC turnstiles, it's necessary to decide whether to travel to the Magic Kingdom by ferry or by monorail. (The bus loading area at the Magic Kingdom itself means that guests using WDW transportation can bypass the TTC entirely.) For guests arriving by car or tour bus, the monorails make the trip in a bit less than the five minutes required by the ferries—but the latter often will get you there more quickly during the busier seasons, because long lines can form at the monorails; most people simply don't make the short extra walk to the ferry landing. When there's no line for the monorail, it's your best choice.

Vacationers who use wheelchairs should note that while the monorails are accessible, the ramp leading to the boarding area is a bit steep.

GUIDED TOURS: A four-hour walking tour called Keys to the Kingdom is available during off-peak seasons for guests ages ten and older who would like an orientation to the history and workings of the Magic Kingdom. Guests visit five attractions (waiting in regular attraction lines) and take a peek at the

Production Center and the system of tunnels known as Utilidors. Cost is $45, excluding park admission. There is a maximum of 15 guests per tour. The tour departs daily at 10 A.M. from City Hall on Main Street. For details and advance reservations, call WDW-TOUR (939-8687). For same-day reservations stop by City Hall or call 824-4521.

MAGIC KINGDOM TIP BOARD: Located at the end of Main Street, this blackboard is a great source of information on the waiting times for the most popular attractions.

MONEY MATTERS: WDW resort guests who buy admission passes at WDW resorts may charge them to their rooms by using their resort ID cards. At the TTC, cash, traveler's checks, personal checks, MasterCard, Visa, American Express, and The Disney Credit Card are accepted as payment for all admission media; personal checks must be imprinted with your name and address and must be accompanied by a driver's license and a major credit card.

American Express, Visa, MasterCard, and The Disney Credit Card are accepted at sit-down restaurants and for merchandise. Traveler's checks and WDW resort identification cards also are accepted. No credit cards are accepted at fast-food eating spots. You must pay in cash or use traveler's checks.

Guests also may want to purchase Disney Dollars, available in one-, five-, and ten-dollar denominations. Disney Dollars are accepted

ADMISSION PRICES*

ONE-DAY TICKET
(Restricted to use in the Magic Kingdom only.)

Adult	$ 39.27
Child**	$ 31.80

FOUR-DAY VALUE PASS
(Valid for one day in each park, plus one optional day in the park of your choice. Includes use of WDW transportation system.)

Adult	$131.44
Child**	$102.82

FOUR-DAY PARK HOPPER PASS
(Valid in all three parks for four days and includes use of WDW transportation system.)

Adult	$145.22
Child**	$115.54

FIVE-DAY WORLD HOPPER PASS
(Valid in all three parks for five days, includes use of WDW transportation system, and allows admission to Typhoon Lagoon, Blizzard Beach, River Country, Discovery Island, and Pleasure Island for up to seven days from the first use of the pass.)

Adult	$197.16
Child**	$156.88

LENGTH OF STAY PASS
(Available to WDW resort guests only. Valid in all three parks, Typhoon Lagoon, Blizzard Beach, River Country, Discovery Island, and Pleasure Island for the duration of stay and includes use of WDW transportation system.)

Length of Stay	Adult	Child**
4 days	$166.42	$131.44
5 days	$193.98	$153.70
6 days	$217.30	$172.78
7 days	$241.68	$191.86
8 days	$259.70	$206.70
9 days	$277.72	$220.48
10 days	$288.32	$230.02

The cost of a **THEME PARK ANNUAL PASS** is $242.74 for adults and $210.94 for children; renewals are $221.54 for adults and $189.74 for children. The cost of a **PREMIUM ANNUAL PASS** is $338.14 for adults and $296.80 for children; renewals are $306.34 and $270.30 for children; in addition to the three theme parks, it includes admission to Typhoon Lagoon, Blizzard Beach, River Country, and Discovery Island.

Note: Multi-day passes need not be used on consecutive days.

These prices were correct at press time, but may change during 1996.

*The prices quoted include sales tax.
**3 through 9 years of age; children under 3 are free

at all Magic Kingdom, Epcot, and Disney-MGM Studios restaurants, shops, and food stands, and at all WDW resorts. They can be redeemed for greenbacks at any time. Many visitors, however, take at least one home as a souvenir. When purchasing tickets or passes at Walt Disney World ticket locations, guests can request Disney Dollars as change.

ADMISSION: Tickets and passes are available for one, four, and five days. The Disney organization defines a ticket as admission for one day only; other forms of admission media (for longer periods) are called passes. One-day tickets may be used at the Magic Kingdom, Epcot, or the Disney-MGM Studios, but not at more than one site on the same day. Four-Day Value Passes may be used for one day in each park, plus one optional day in the park of your choice, but not at more than one park on the same day. Four-Day Park Hopper Passes and Five-Day World Hopper Passes can be used at all three parks on the same day. Unlike one-day tickets, all multi-day passes also include use of the transportation system inside Walt Disney World. The Five-Day World Hopper Pass also allows admission to Typhoon Lagoon, Blizzard Beach, River Country, Discovery Island, and Pleasure Island for a seven-day period beginning with the first use of the pass. Guests staying at Walt Disney World resorts can purchase a pass valid for the length of their stay. The Length of Stay Pass offers savings over other passes, and includes unlimited admission to the Magic Kingdom, Epcot, the Disney-MGM Studios, Typhoon Lagoon, Blizzard Beach, River Country, Discovery Island, and Pleasure Island for the duration of your stay. Cash, traveler's checks, personal checks (with proper ID), American Express, Visa, Master-Card, and The Disney Credit Card can be used to pay for all admission media. When you purchase a Four-Day Park Hopper Pass, a Five-Day World Hopper Pass, or a Length of Stay Pass, you must have your photo mounted on the pass to validate it. Pass photos can be taken at the Transportation and Ticket Center and at the entrances to the Magic Kingdom, Epcot, and the Disney-MGM Studios. Multi-day passes do not have to be used on consecutive days.

Passes may be purchased at all WDW resorts (by WDW resort guests), at the entrances to the theme parks, at the Orlando International Airport, or at The Disney Store.

Passes by mail: Send a check or money order payable to Walt Disney World Company in the exact amount plus $2 for handling to:
Walt Disney World
Box 10,030; Lake Buena Vista, FL 32830-0030
Attention: Ticket Mail Order
Remember to include your return address. Allow at least three to four weeks for ticket requests to be processed.

The Lay of the Lands

Not long ago, one Magic Kingdom visitor spent an entire day in Tomorrowland, thinking it was the full extent of the place. To avoid having a similar experience, it's essential to understand the lay of all the lands before you arrive on Main Street.

There are seven sections, or "lands," in the Magic Kingdom—Main Street, U.S.A.; Adventureland; Frontierland; Liberty Square; Fantasyland; Mickey's Starland; and Tomorrowland. The monorail stations and ferry docks at which all guests arrive are just outside the Magic Kingdom gates; just inside them is Town Square, at the head of Main Street, which runs straight to Cinderella Castle. The area in front of the Castle is known as the Central Plaza, or, more aptly, the Hub. It is surrounded by small canals, the Hub Waterways, which are crossed by bridges to enter each of the lands. The first bridge to your left goes to Adventureland; the next, to Liberty Square and Frontierland. On your right, the first bridge heads to Tomorrowland, the second to Fantasyland and Mickey's Starland. The end points of the avenues lead-ing to the lands are linked by a roadway that is roughly circular, so that the layout of the Magic Kingdom resembles a wheel. All of the attractions, restaurants, and shops are arranged in various buildings along the rim of the wheel and along its spokes.

In theory, it couldn't be simpler; in practice, it's only too easy to get confused because of the many bends and curves in the pathways, the many entrances to each shop and restaurant, and the somewhat angular placement and architecture of many of the buildings. But if you keep mental notes of your own route, losing your bearings becomes fairly difficult. If you still manage to get confused, however, any park employee can help set you straight.

A note on north, south, east, and west: When you stand at the Magic Kingdom entrance and face Cinderella Castle, you're looking north. Main Street is straight ahead, with Fantasyland and Mickey's Starland beyond the Castle. Adventureland, Liberty Square, and Frontierland are to the west. Tomorrowland flanks the Hub on the east.

Main Street, U.S.A.

This is the Disney version of turn-of-the-century small-town Main Streets all over the country—freshly painted, full of curlicued gingerbread moldings and pretty details, and with its baskets of hanging plants and genuine-looking gaslights, a showplace both in the bright light of high noon and after nightfall, when the tiny lights edging all of Main Street's rooflines are flicked on.

What's particularly amazing is that all the variety of furbelows and frills that a real, growing Main Street would have enjoyed have been assimilated into the Disney version. Most of the structures along the thoroughfare are given over to shops, and each one is different, from the wallpaper and layout of displays to the flooring materials, the style of chandeliers, and even the lighting level. Some emporiums are big and bustling, others are relatively quiet and orderly; some are spacious and airy, others are cozy and dark. Floors are made of black-and-white tile or of wide oak planks set in with wooden pegs; some are covered with Victorian-patterned carpets. Where wallpaper is used, it is striped, or gaudily flowered; in contrast, some walls are paneled in subdued mahogany or oak. The effect is far more sophisticated than first-time visitors probably would have imagined, and it doesn't really matter that some of the "wood" is fiberglass.

Inside and outside, maintenance and housekeeping are superb. White-suited sanitation workers patrol the street to pick up litter and quickly shovel up any droppings from the horses who pull the trolley cars from Town Square to the Hub. The pavement, like all in the Magic Kingdom, is washed down every night with fire hoses. There's one crew of maintenance workers whose sole job is to change the little white lights around the roofs; another crew devotes itself to keeping the woodwork painted. As soon as these people have worked their way as far as the Hub, they start all over again at Town Square. The greenish, horse-shaped cast-iron hitching posts are repainted 20 times a year on the average—and totally scraped down each time. It's no wonder the professional painters who visit marvel at the quality of work they see.

Some visitors find all these details so fascinating that it takes them a good deal longer than the 40 minutes spent by the average guest to get from one end of Main Street to the other. There are only three real "attractions" along Main Street, and they are relatively minor compared to the really big deals such as Tomorrowland's Space Mountain and Frontierland's Big Thunder Mountain Railroad and Splash Mountain. But each and every shop has its own quota of merchandise

that is meant as much for show as for sale, for instance, the large Hummel figurines at Uptown Jewelers. It's also entertaining to watch the cooks stirring up batches of peanut brittle at the Main Street Confectionery. The windows at the Emporium also are worth a look.

While walking along the street, note the names on the second-story windows. Above Crystal Arts are the names of Roy Disney, Walt's brother, and Patty Disney; above the Shadow Box, that of Dick Nunis, Chairman of Walt Disney Attractions. Above the Main Street Athletic Store are the names of Ted Crowell, WDW's former Vice President of Facilities Support, who, among other things, was responsible for maintenance and for the World's own electric generating plants, and John de Cuir, the Disney artist in charge of the production of the paintings filmed for The Hall of Presidents show. Card Walker, the "Practitioner of Psychiatry and Justice of the Peace" mentioned nearby, is the company's former Chairman of the Executive Committee. Other names, as well as those on signs elsewhere in the Magic Kingdom, also are those of real people connected with the company.

Finally, some advice: Before heading toward the Castle, stop at City Hall and inquire about the times and places where live entertainment is scheduled to take place all around the park that day and night. Also, do your shopping in the early afternoon, rather than at day's end when the shops are normally jammed;

purchases can be stored in lockers under the Walt Disney World Railroad's depot or, in the case of very large items, behind the desk at City Hall. Guests staying at WDW resorts may arrange for purchases to be delivered to their hotel rooms free of charge, and guaranteed by noon the next day.

MAIN STREET CINEMA: The beauty of this prominent attraction on Main Street is that most vacationers bypass it in their rush to get to Space Mountain in Tomorrowland or Pirates of the Caribbean in Adventureland, or other thrill-a-minute attractions. Yet on a steamy summer afternoon—when everyone else is standing in line for these blockbusters—this air-conditioned theater is a fine place to relax. The feature attraction is *Mickey's Big Break*, a ten-minute film that shows how Mickey is chosen for his first starring role. As the story goes, Mickey is one of many actors auditioning for a part in *Steamboat Willie*, the first sound cartoon. Talent agents make their choice—and the rest is history. A vintage Disney cartoon follows the film. There are so many Mickey classics that it's impossible to predict what will be airing and when. But rest assured, *Steamboat Willie* is on the list of those that are shown. (By the way, Mickey was originally scheduled to be named Mortimer, but Mrs. Disney convinced Walt to make the change.)

WALT DISNEY WORLD RAILROAD: The best introduction to the layout of the Magic Kingdom, the 1½-mile 21-minute journey on this rail line is as much a must for the first-time visitor as it is for railroad buffs. For the former, it offers an excellent orientation, as it passes through Adventureland and Frontierland and skirts Fantasyland, Mickey's Starland, and Tomorrowland. The trains make stops here on Main Street and at the Frontierland and Mickey's Starland stations.

The 1928 steam engine happens to be exactly the same age as Mickey Mouse. Afi-

cionados of railroadiana may remember that Disney himself was among their number and perhaps, during the early years of television, saw films of him circling his own backyard in a one-eighth-scale train, the *Lilly Belle*, named for his wife. The Walt Disney World Railroad also has a *Lilly Belle* among its quartet of locomotives. The others are named *Roy O. Disney*, *Walter E. Disney*, and *Roger E. Broggie* (a Disney Imagineer who shared Walt Disney's enthusiasm for antique trains). All of these were built in the United States around the turn of the last century and later were taken down to Mexico to haul freight and passengers in the Yucatan, where Disney scouts found them in 1969. The United Railways of Yucatan was using them to carry sugarcane. Brought north once again, they were completely overhauled, and even the smallest parts were reworked or replaced.

MAIN STREET VEHICLES: A number of these can be seen traveling up and down Main Street—horseless carriages and jitneys patterned after turn-of-the-century vehicles (but fitted out with Jeep transmissions and special mufflers that make the putt-putt-putting sound); a spiffy scarlet fire engine, which can be seen in the Firehouse adjoining City Hall when not in operation; and a troop of trolleys drawn by Belgians and Percherons, two strong breeds of horses that once pulled plows in Europe. These animals—aged between six and ten, weighing in at about a ton each, and shod with plastic (easier on their hooves)—pull the trolley the length of Main Street about two dozen times during each of their three to four working days; afterward, they're sent back to their homes at the barn at the *Fort Wilderness* campground.

CINDERELLA CASTLE

Just as the courtly little mouse named Mickey stands for all the joy and merriment in the whole of Walt Disney World, the many-spired Cinderella Castle, childhood's storybook castle made real, represents the hopes and dreams of those youthful years when anything seems possible.

This Castle is different from Disneyland's Sleeping Beauty Castle: Measuring some 180 feet in height, the Florida castle is more than 100 feet taller; and with its slender towers and lacy filigree work, it's also more graceful, taking its inspiration not only from the architecture of 12th- and 13th-century France, the country where Charles Perrault's classic fairy tale originated, but also from the mad Bavarian King Ludwig's castle at Neuschwanstein, and from the designs prepared some three decades ago for the motion picture version of Perrault's story—and the imaginations of a whole troupe of creative Disney Imagineers who have collectively spent several lifetimes turning fantasies into reality.

Unlike real European castles, this one is not made of granite, but of steel beams, fiberglass, and some 500 gallons of paint. There are no dungeons underneath it, but rather service tunnels for the Magic Kingdom's day-to-day operations. In the Castle's upper reaches there are security rooms and the like; on one floor there's an apartment originally meant for members of the Disney family (but never occupied).

When mounting the curving staircase to *King Stefan's Banquet Hall*, the parapet-level restaurant, or when passing through the Castle's main gateway—or as seen by night from the *Contemporary* resort's observation deck, with fireworks exploding all around those slender towers—the Castle looks as if it had come straight out of some never-never land of make-believe.

The mosaic murals: The elaborate murals in the five panels beneath the Castle's archway entrance rank as one of the true wonders of the World. Measuring some 15 feet high and 10 feet wide, these creations of the Disney artist Dorothea Redmond, crafted by the mosaicist Hanns-Joachim Scharff, tell the familiar story of a little cinder girl, a hard-hearted stepmother, two ugly stepsisters, a fairy godmother, a pumpkin transformed, a handsome prince, a cer-

tain glass slipper, and one of childhood's happiest happily-ever-afters, using amillion bits of Italian glass in some 500 different colors, plus real silver and 14-karat gold. The renderings of the stepsisters and of the many small woodland animals are particularly faithful to images from the Disney film; but every passerby has favorite sections. Don't fail to stop and look.

Coats of arms: The one above the Castle on the north wall belongs to the Disneys. Others belonging to assorted Disney executives hang in the waiting hall just inside the door to *King Stefan's*; the hostess keeps a book behind the desk that details which belong to whom, for any interested party to see. Some of the same names show up as on the second-story windows of the Main Street shops.

Adventureland

Adventureland seems to have even more atmosphere than the other lands. That may be a result of its neat separation from the rest of the Magic Kingdom by the bridge over Main Street on the one end and by a gallerylike structure where it merges with Frontierland on the other; or possibly it's because of the abundance of landscaping. There are Canary Island date palms, the small Cape Sable palms, as well as pygmy date species, and more. On the Adventureland bridge alone, visitors will see Cape honeysuckle from South Africa, flame vines from Mexico, bougainvillea from Brazil, Chinese hibiscus, hanging sword ferns, spider plants, and Australian tree ferns, to name just a few.

As for the architecture, even though it derives from such diverse areas as the Caribbean, Polynesia, and Southeast Asia, there's a strong sense of being in a single place, a nowhere-in-particular that is both exotic and distinctly foreign, smacking of island idylls and tropical splendor. Shops offer imports from India, Thailand, Hong Kong, Africa, and the Caribbean islands.

Strolling away from Main Street, there is the sound of the beating of drums, the squawk of a couple of parrots, the regular boom of a cannon. Paces quicken. And the wonders soon to be encountered do not disappoint.

TROPICAL SERENADE: The first of the Audio-Animatronics attractions. This one laid the foundation for attractions such as Great Moments With Mr. Lincoln at the 1964–1965 New York World's Fair. Introduced at Disneyland in 1963, this 17-minute show features four emcees—José, Michael, Pierre, and Fritz—plus some 225 birds, flowers, and tiki god statues singing and whistling up a tropical storm with such animation that even the most blasé folks can't help but smile.

PIRATES OF THE CARIBBEAN: One of the very best of the Magic Kingdom's adventures, this ten-minute cruise through a series of sets depicting a pirate raid on a Caribbean island town is a Disneyland original added to WDW's Magic Kingdom, in revised form, because of popular demand. Here there are flowerpots that explode and mend themselves, drunken pigs whose legs actually twitch in the porkers' soporific contentment, chickens that look for all the world like the real thing (even when seen at close range); the observant will note that the leg of one swashbuckler, dangled over the edge of a bridge, is actually hairy. Each pirate's face has remarkable personality, and the rendition of "Yo-Ho-Yo-Ho"—the attraction's theme song—makes what is actually a rather brutal

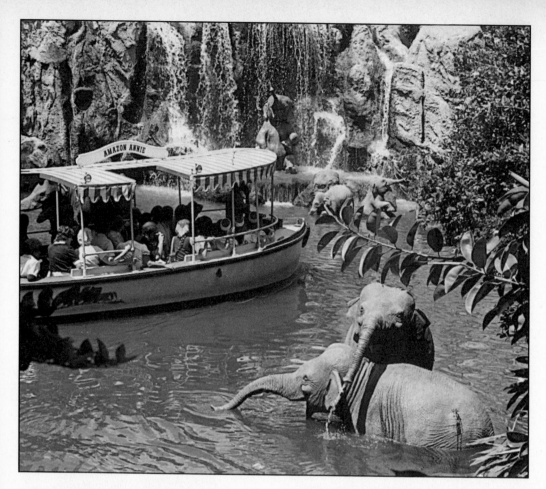

scenario into something that comes across as good fun. Before entering the queue area, be sure to stop and give a nod to the parrot, dressed in the pirate costume, near the Pirates of the Caribbean sign.

SWISS FAMILY TREEHOUSE: "Everything we need right at our fingertips" was how the father in Disney's 1960 rendition of the classic novel *Swiss Family Robinson*, described the treehouse that he and two of his three sons constructed to house the family after the ship transporting them to New Guinea was wrecked in a storm. When given a chance—several adventures later—to leave the island, all but one son decided to stay on. That decision is not hard to understand after a tour of the Magic Kingdom's version of the Robinsons' banyan-tree home. This is everybody's idea of the perfect treehouse, with its many levels and many comforts—patchwork quilts, lovely mahogany furniture, candles stuck in abalone shells, even running water in every room. (The system is ingenious.)

The Spanish moss draping the branches is real; the tree itself—unofficially christened *Disneyodendron eximus*, which translates roughly as "out-of-the-ordinary Disney tree"—was constructed by the props department. Some statistics: The roots, which are concrete, poke 42 feet into the ground; and some

300,000 lifelike polyethylene leaves grow on 1,400 branches, which stretch some 90 feet in diameter. "Boy, Dad sure went out on a limb for that one," quipped a Disney prop worker's son on hearing of his father's task.

JUNGLE CRUISE: Inspired in part by the 1955 documentary *The African Lion*, this ten-minute cruise adventure is one of the crowning achievements of Magic Kingdom landscape artists for the way it takes guests through landscapes as diverse as a Southeast Asian jungle, the Nile valley, the African veldt, and an Amazon rain forest. Along the way, passengers encounter zebras and giraffes, impalas, lions, vultures, and headhunters; they see elephants bathing and tour a Cambodian temple—and listen to the amusing spiel delivered by the skipper. For most passengers, this is all just in fun. Gardeners, however, are especially impressed by the variety of species coexisting in such a small area. To keep some of the more sensitive of subtropical specimens alive, gas-fired heaters and electric fans concealed in the rocks pump hot air into the jungle when temperatures fall to 36° F. This adventure, which is best enjoyed by daylight, is one of the Magic Kingdom's most popular attractions, and it does tend to be crowded from late morning until late afternoon, so plan accordingly.

Frontierland

With the Rivers of America lapping up at its borders and Big Thunder Mountain rising toward the rear, this recreation of the American Frontier encompasses the area from New England to the Southwest, from the 1770s to the 1880s. Hosts and hostesses wear denim, calf-length cutoffs, long skirts, or similar garb. Additionally, the shops, restaurants, and attractions have unpainted barn siding or stone or clapboard walls, and outside there are a few of the kind of wooden sidewalks down which Marshal Matt Dillon used to stride.

Near *Pecos Bill Café*, the landscape seems desertlike (even on humid summer days), with mesquite providing shade and Peruvian pepper trees nearby; the latter's twisted branches boast clusters of bright-red berries in fall and winter. Jerusalem thorns blossom with sweet-smelling yellow flowers in the spring. Century plants and Spanish bayonets also can be seen. Farther down the Frontierland avenue, slash pines provide some shade, along with other evergreens of a variety known as cajeput, which can be recognized by its spongy, light-colored bark and white flowers.

DIAMOND HORSESHOE SALOON REVUE: The hour-long show presented in this recreation of a western dance hall saloon is the kind of thing that makes sophisticated folk laugh in spite of themselves. The jokes range from corny to absolutely preposterous, yet seldom fall flat, thanks to the enthusiastic, energetic efforts of the talented crew of singers and dancers who perform here several times each day. Guests may drop in at any point during the performance. For guests who want to snack between laughs, there also is a fast-food counter here. See *Good Meals, Great Times* for more details.

FRONTIERLAND SHOOTIN' ARCADE: Silver bullets have given way to infrared beams at the completely electronic shooting arcade. Genuine Hawkins 54-caliber buffalo rifles have been refitted, and when an infrared beam strikes any of the 97 reactive targets, a humorous result is triggered. The arcade is set in an 1850s town in the Southwest Territory. Gun positions overlook Boothill, a town complete with bank, jail, hotel, and cemetery. Struck tombstones rise, sink, spin, or change their epitaphs; hit the cloud and a ghost rider gallops across the sky; a bull's-eye on a gravedigger's shovel causes a skull to pop out of the grave. Sound effects—howling coyotes, creaking bridges, and the shooting guns—are created by a digital audio system. Note that admission passes do *not* include use of the arcade, and there is an additional charge here.

COUNTRY BEAR JAMBOREE: An occasional determined sophisticate will remain impervious to the charms of this country-and-western hoedown in Frontierland's big stone-walled Grizzly Hall. But many guests, with the exception of the 10-to-18 crowd, call it one of the Magic Kingdom's best attractions. Ostensibly concocted by one Ursus H. Bear after an especially inspiring hibernation season, it is performed mainly by a cast of close to 20 life-size Audio-Animatronics bruins, with results more believable than almost anywhere else in the park, aside from The Hall of Presidents. Henry, the debonair, seven-foot-tall master of ceremonies, introduces the Five Bear Rugs (a C&W plinking group made up of Zeke, Zeb, Ted, Fred, and Tennessee); a big-bodied, tiny-headed pianist named Gomer; the girthy Trixie, the Tampa Temptation, sings "Tears Will Be the Chaser for Your Wine"; Teddi Barra floats down from the ceiling crooning "He Doesn't Know the Heart He's Breakin'"; Bubbles, Bunny, and Beulah, in sweet harmony, sing "All the Guys that Turn Me On Turn Me Down"; and assorted other bruins, including Terrence, the shank shaker; Wendell, the overbearing baritone; Liver Lips McGrowl; and Big Al, one of the few Audio-Animatronics figures with a following great enough to create a demand for his image on postcards and stuffed animals.

Since the 17-minute Country Bear Jamboree is a popular attraction, lines can get quite long during busy periods. They usually seem longer than they are, however, and it's

worth noting that huge bunches of people are admitted together so that once a line starts moving, it dwindles fast. Seats in the rear of the house are just as good as seats toward the front, if not a little better.

TOM SAWYER ISLAND: This small landfall in the middle of the Rivers of America has hills to scramble up, a working windmill, Harper's Mill, with an owl in the rafters and a perpetually creaky waterwheel, and a pitch-black (and scary) cave. To get to the island, guests take a raft across the river.

There are oaks, pines, and sycamores here, red maples and elms, and a number of small plants—dwarf azaleas; firethorn, an evergreen shrub that sprouts bright-red berries in December; Brazilian pepper trees, which also grow berries at the end of the year; and American holly plants, which acquire their masses of berries in fall. Dirt paths wind this way and that, and it's easy to get disoriented, especially the first time around. There also are two bridges—an old-fashioned swing bridge and a so-called barrel bridge, which floats atop some lashed-together steel drums. When one person bounces, everybody lurches—and all but the most chicken-hearted laugh. Both bridges can easily be missed, so keep your eyes peeled and ask for directions if the path eludes you.

Across the bridge is Fort Sam Clemens, where there is a guardhouse in which the figure of a ratty-looking drunk is Audio-Animatronically snoring off his last bender, accompanied by a mangy-looking dog, chickens, and a pair of horses. On the second floor of the fort, there are close to a dozen air guns for youngsters to trigger into ceaseless cacophony. This area offers a fine view across the Rivers of America to Big Thunder Mountain Railroad. Keep poking around and you'll find the twisting, dark, and occasionally scary escape tunnel out of the fort. Walk along the pathway on the banks of the Rivers of America, and you're back at the bridges.

The whole island seems as rugged as backwoods Missouri, and probably as a result, it actually feels a lot more remote than it is, enough to be able to provide some welcome respite from the bustle of the Magic Kingdom. One particularly pleasant way to pass an hour here is over lemonade and a snack on the porch at *Aunt Polly's Landing*. While adults in the party are giving their feet some rest, watching the sternwheelers plying the Rivers of America, kids can go out and burn up some more energy. Restrooms are located at the main raft landing. Note that this attraction closes at dusk.

SPLASH MOUNTAIN: As its name implies, guests are escorted on a waterborne journey through brightly painted backwoods swamps and bayous, down waterfalls, and, finally, over the top of a steep spillway, hurtling them from

the peak of the mountain to a briar-laced pond five stories below. Splash Mountain is based on the animated sequences in Walt Disney's 1946 film, *Song of the South*. The scenery is entertaining and there is a story line that follows Brer Rabbit through a variety of exploits as he tries to reach his "laughing place." It's tough for a first-timer to take in all the details, since the tension of waiting for the big drop is all-consuming.

There are three tame watery drops during the 11-minute trip, all leading up to the big fall—a 52-foot drop at a 45-degree angle at a top speed of 40 miles per hour—the steepest flume in the world. It is a bit terrifying at the top but once back on the ground it seems most riders can't wait for another trip. (Even though you may get drenched!) By the second or third time around, it's possible to relax and enjoy the interior design and also to take in the spectacular views of the Magic Kingdom from the top of the mountain.

Splash Mountain's designers not only borrowed the attraction's characters and color-saturated settings from *Song of the South*, they also included quite a bit of the film's Academy Award-winning music. As a matter of fact, the song in the attraction's finale, "Zip-A-Dee-Doo-Dah," has become something of a Disney anthem over the years.

Note: You must be at least 44 inches tall to ride Splash Mountain.

BIG THUNDER MOUNTAIN RAILROAD:

This attraction, located partly inside the red-stone mountain that pokes into the sky behind the Tom Sawyer Island rafts landing, is something of a cross between Tomorrowland's Space Mountain (an honest-to-goodness roller coaster) and Adventureland's Pirates of the Caribbean (a tame but very exciting and scenic boat tour). As any true coaster buff could tell you, this four-minute ride is a relatively mild one, despite the posted warnings; the thrills are there, but the experience is not so extreme that you'll be left with a determination never to subject yourself to it again. The pleasant rush of adrenaline that comes with some of the swoops and curves, as well as the attractive scenery along the 2,780 feet of track, gives most visitors the opposite reaction. There are bats, phosphorescent pools and waterfalls, and best of all, Tumbleweed, the flooded mining town (best seen to your left during one of the uphill climbs). There are some 20 Audio-Animatronics figures here—including real-looking chickens, donkeys, possums, a goat, a longjohn-clad resident spinning through the flood in a bathtub, and a rainmaker whose name is Professor Cumulus Isobar. Careful observers will note a party still going on in a not-yet-sunken second-story room of a saloon, whose weathered look (like that of some other sections of the Magic Kingdom) derives from a judicious mixture of plant food and paint. The $300,000 worth of real antique mining equipment sprinkled around the attraction's 2 1/2 acres—an ore-hauling wagon, a double-stamp ore crusher, a wooden mining flume, and an old ball mill used to extract gold from ore—were picked up at auctions all over the Southwest, at something less than bargain prices, since the high price of gold and the resulting profitability of small-scale mining operations had boosted demand by genuine miners themselves. As with Pirates of the Caribbean, every trip yields new sights, and even a second or third trip in a matter of days is as amusing as the first time.

The summit of the mountain, whose name refers to an old Indian legend about a certain sacred mountain in Wyoming that would thunder whenever white men took out its gold, is entirely Disney-made. It was in the planning for some 15 years and under construction for 2 years. Hundreds of rockmakers contributed, applying multiple coats of cement and paint, throwing stones at the mountain, kicking dirt on it, and banging on it with sticks and picks to make the whole thing resemble the rocks of Monument Valley, Utah—that is, as if Mother Nature herself had created it. Design was largely by Tony Baxter, whose name can be seen on one of the doors in the unloading and boarding area. The area inside the mountain that does not house the tunnels of the ride itself is occupied by the machinery that makes the ride go—pumps, electronic equipment, and part of the computer that runs the show. The total cost was about $17 million, which, give or take a few million, was as much as it cost to build all of California's Disneyland in 1955. Incidentally, that park's version of the attraction, which opened in 1979, is similar, but lacks the flash-flood scene and a few other details. You must be at least 40 inches tall to ride.

Note on timing: Certain aspects of the ride are more convincing after dark. Optimally, you should experience it first at night, then have a second go-round by the light of day. Since the trip is extremely popular, plan to take it in during the 9 P.M. running of Spectro-Magic (in season), or just before park closing, when the lines are generally shorter. By day, go during the early morning hours.

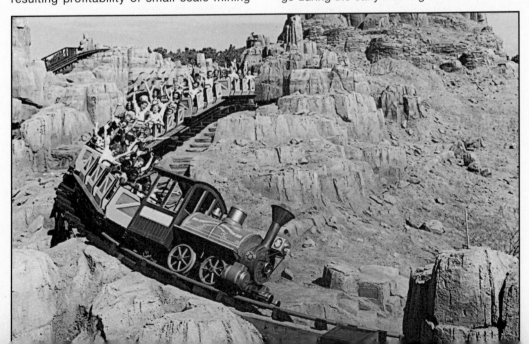

Liberty Square

The transition between Frontierland on one side and Fantasyland on the other is so smooth that it's hard to say just when you arrive, yet ultimately there's no mistaking the location. The small buildings are clapboard or brick and topped with weather vanes; the decorative moldings are Federal or Georgian in style; the glass is sometimes wavy, and there are flower boxes in shop windows, brightly colored gardens, neatly trimmed borders of Japanese yew, and masses of azaleas in a number of varieties and shades of white, pink, and red. There are a number of good shops, most notably the Yankee Trader and Olde World Antiques; plus two of the park's most popular attractions—The Haunted Mansion and The Hall of Presidents—and the *Liberty Tree Tavern*, one of the few Magic Kingdom restaurants to offer table service, and one of just three to take reservations. Liberty Square also is home of one of the most delightful nooks in all the Magic Kingdom—the small, secluded area just behind the Silversmith Shop. There are tables with umbrellas, plenty of benches, and big trees to provide shade—and the sound of the crowds seems a million miles away.

THE LIBERTY TREE: Not an attraction per se, this live oak (*Quercus virginiana*)—which recalls trees all over the colonies, on which the Sons of Liberty used to hang lanterns after the Boston Tea Party of 1773—was found on the southern edge of WDW's 27,400 acres, and then moved to its present site in one of the more complex of the Magic Kingdom's landscaping operations. Since the tree was so large, lifting it by cable was out of the question—the cable would have sliced through the bark and injured the tree. Instead, two holes were drilled through the sturdiest section of the trunk; the holes were fitted with dowels, and a 100-ton crane lifted the tree by these rods, which were subsequently replaced with the original wood plugs. Unfortunately, the wood plugs had become contaminated. To save the tree, the plugs again were removed, the diseased areas were cleaned out, the holes were filled with cement, and a young oak was grafted onto the tree at its base, where it grows even today. Careful observers will be able to spot the plugs and the portions of the trunk that were damaged. The 13 lanterns hanging on the branches represent the 13 original states.

THE HALL OF PRESIDENTS: This is not one of those laugh-a-minute attractions, like Pirates of the Caribbean or the Country Bear Jamboree; it's long on patriotism and short on humor. But the detail of this 20-minute show certainly is fascinating. After a film (presented on a sweeping 70mm screen) discusses the importance of the Constitution from the time of its framing through the dawn of the Space Age, the curtain goes up on what some guests have mistakenly called the "Hall of Haunted Presidents." A portion of today's Hall of Presidents presentation derives from the Disney-designed Illinois Pavilion's presentation Great Moments with Mr. Lincoln, from New York's 1964–65 World's Fair.

At the Magic Kingdom show, Bill Clinton and Abraham Lincoln have speaking roles. All 42 chief executives are announced in a roll call and each responds with a nod; careful observers will note the others swaying and nodding, fidgeting, and even whispering to each other during the proceedings.

Costumes were created by two famous film tailors coaxed out of retirement. Not only are the styles those of the period in which each president lived, but so are the tailoring techniques and the fabrics. Some had to be specially woven for the purpose. Each of the Audio-Animatronics figures has at least one change of clothes, and jewelry, shoes, hair texture, and even George Washington's chair are all recreated exactly as indicated by careful research of paintings, diaries, newspapers, and government archives. Perceptive viewers should be able to see the braces on Franklin Delano Roosevelt's legs. The effect is so lifelike that the figures look almost real, even at close range.

The paintings in the waiting area outside the hall are just a few of the 85 created for the pre-roll call film—in the style of the period during which the event depicted took place. Other paintings can be seen in Main Street's City Hall and in Liberty Square's *Liberty Tree Tavern* and *Columbia Harbour House*.

THE HAUNTED MANSION: Visitors who expect to get the daylights scared out of them inside this big old house, modeled on those built by the Dutch in the Hudson River Valley in the 18th century, will be a tad disappointed. In deference to the number of small children and other easily frightened souls who tour the Magic Kingdom every day, the most terrifying parts were expunged and a pleasant voice-over keeps things from getting too serious. Even then, the eight-minute experience is among the Magic Kingdom's best. Special effect is piled upon special effect, and just when you think you've seen it all, there's something new: the raven who appears over and over again; bats' eyes on the wallpaper; the plaque that reads "Tomb, Sweet Tomb"; the suit of armor that comes alive; the horrible transparent specter in the attic; the terrified cemetery watchman and his mangy mutt; the ghostly teapot pouring ghostly tea; the difficult-to-identify flying objects above the image in the crystal ball.

In the portrait hall (which you enter after passing through the mansion's front doors), it's amusing to speculate: Is the ceiling moving up—or is the floor descending? It's one way here, and the other way at the Haunted Mansion in California's Disneyland.

At both places, one of the biggest jobs of the maintenance crews is not cleaning up, but keeping things nice and dirty. Since each mansion's attic is littered with some 200 trunks, chairs, dress forms, shovels, harps, rugs, and assorted other knick-knacks, it requires a good deal of dust. This is purchased from a West Coast firm by the five-pound bagful and distributed by a device that looks as if it were meant to spread grass seed. Local legend has it that enough has been used since the park's 1971 opening to bury the mansion. Cobwebs are bought in liquid form and strung up by a secret process.

When waiting to enter, note the amusing inscriptions on the tombstones in the overgrown cemetery.

LIBERTY SQUARE RIVERBOAT: The *Richard F. Irvine*, built in dry dock at Walt Disney World and named for a key Disney designer, is a real steamboat. Its boiler turns water into steam, which is then piped to the engine, which drives the paddle wheel that propels the boat. It is not the real article in one respect, however: It moves through the ½-mile-long, nine-foot-deep Rivers of America on an underwater rail. The 15-minute ride is more pleasant than thrilling, but it's good for beating the heat on steamy afternoons. En route, a variety of props create a sort of Wild West effect: moose, deer, cabins on fire, and the like. (Best seats are in front or rear and center, so that you can see both riverbanks equally well.)

The trees framing the entrance to Riverboat Landing, which bear crinkly blossoms of bright red most of the year, are crepe myrtles.

Fantasyland

which were arranged in a rather decorous pose, were ingeniously rearranged to make the steeds look like real chargers. (Careful examination might reveal some of the cracks by which this change was effected.) For the wooden canopy above the horses, Disney artists hand-painted 18 separate scenes with images of the little cinder girl from Charles Perrault's fairy tale and Disney's 1950 film. Additionally, the original mechanical wooden parts were replaced by metal ones; the thick layer of paint that had obscured some of the finer points of the original carving was stripped away, and the horses were repainted white. The painting alone required about 48 hours per horse.

While waiting for the two-minute ride, it's worthwhile to take the time to study the animals carefully. No two are exactly alike. The band organ, which plays favorite music from Disney Studios (such as the Oscar-winners "When You Wish Upon A Star," "Zip-A-Dee-Doo-Dah," and "Chim-Chim-Cheree"), was made in one of Italy's most famous factories.

MAD TEA PARTY: The theme of this two-minute ride—in a group of oversize pastel-colored teacups that whirl and spin as wildly as many carnivals' Tubs of Fun—derives from a scene in the Disney Studio's 1951 production of Lewis Carroll's novel *Alice in Wonderland*. During the sequence in question, the Mad Hatter hosts a tea party for his un-birthday. Unlike many of the other rides in Fantasyland, this attraction is not strictly for younger children; the 9-to-20 crowd seems to like it best. Be sure to note the soused mouse that pops out of the teapot at the center of the platform full of teacups.

Walt Disney called this a "timeless land of enchantment," and his successors term it "the happiest land of all"—and it is, for some. Although it's not precisely a kiddieland, it is the home of a number of rides that are particularly well liked by children. The nursery-song cadences of "It's A Small World" appeal to them, as do the bright colors of the trash baskets, the flowers, and the tentlike rooftops; and they delight in the fairy-tale architecture and ambience, reminiscent of a king's castle courtyard during a particularly lively fair. Fantasyland also is one of the most heavily trafficked areas of the park. Parents of younger children should note that many of the attractions are dark and in some cases the special effects may be too intense. Those who remember 20,000 Leagues Under the Sea should be advised that it will be closed until further notice.

CINDERELLA'S GOLDEN CARROUSEL: Not everything in the Magic Kingdom is a Disney version of the real article. This carousel, discovered at the now-defunct Olympic Park in Maplewood, New Jersey, was built back in 1917. That was the end of the golden century of carousel building that began around 1825 (when the Common Council of Manhattan Island, New York, granted one John Sears a permit to "establish a covered circus for a Flying Horse Establishment"). During the Disney refurbishing, many of the original horses were replaced with horses made of fiberglass. Also, the original horses' legs,

DUMBO, THE FLYING ELEPHANT: This is purely and simply a kiddie ride—though personages as varied as Romanian gymnast Nadia Comaneci and Muhammad Ali have loved it. The character of the flying elephant was developed for the 1941 film release of *Dumbo*, one of the shortest of Disney's animated features and one of the best, starring a baby elephant born with inordinately large ears and an ability to fly that is discovered after he accidentally drinks from a bucket of champagne. The mouse that sits atop the mirrored ball in the middle of the circle of the ride's flying elephants is the faithful Timothy Mouse, who in the film becomes Dumbo's manager after the circus folk who had once laughed at the flying elephant hire him to be a big star. The ride lasts two memorable minutes.

LEGEND OF THE LION KING: Based on the animated film, *The Lion King*, this Fantasyland show combines 25 minutes of animation, puppetry, special effects, and music to make guests feel as if they have walked into a cel from the film. In the pre-show area guests meet Rafiki, the wise baboon who serves as the narrator. His voice is provided by stage and television actor Robert Guillaume. A clip from the film is shown and Rafiki recounts the legend that is about to unfold.

Once inside the 500-seat theater, visitors see the movie scene of the Circle of Life presented on stage. As the sun rises over Pride Rock, Mufasa assures his son, Simba, that he will always be with him. The characters are depicted by fully articulated puppets—when they speak their mouths move accordingly. Some of the puppets require up to four people to operate as their ears, heads, feet, and mouth move. The story advances to other scenes, introducing the assorted characters. Some of the more familiar voices you hear are Jeremy Irons as the evil Scar, James Earl Jones as Mufasa, Cheech Marin as Banzai, and Whoopi Goldberg as Shenzi. From the jungle to the plains, guests see Mufasa being trampled by the stampeding wildebeests and pushed to his death by Scar, Scar convincing Simba that he is responsible for his father's death and that he must go away, Scar declaring his power over the kingdom, Simba enjoying his freedom with Pumbaa and Timon, and the touching love scene in the jungle with Nala as she tries to convince Simba he must come back to take his rightful place as the Lion King.

Guests experience special environmental effects including warm winds during scenes in the Serengeti Plain and mists of rain and cold winds during the jungle nights. The highlight stampede scene begins on the screen; the noise builds and the theater shakes as smoke gives way to darkness. Later, special lighting helps create the image of Mufasa in the sky.

Songs in the show include "Circle of Life,"

"Hakuna Matata," "Can You Feel the Love Tonight?" and "I Can't Wait to Be King." The music was composed by Elton John and the lyrics written by Tim Rice. Presented by Kodak.

PETER PAN'S FLIGHT: The inspiration for this three-minute attraction was the Scottish writer Sir James M. Barrie's play about the boy who wouldn't grow up, which appeared as a Disney movie in 1953. Riding in flying versions of Captain Hook's ornate ship—which are suspended from an overhead rail once they leave the boarding area—visitors swoop and soar through a series of scenes that tell the story of how Wendy, Michael, and John get sprinkled with pixie dust and, heading for "the second star to the right and straight on till morning," fly off to Never-Never-Land with Tinkerbell; and meet Princess Tiger Lily, the evil Captain Hook, his jolly-looking sidekick Mr. Smee, and the

crocodile—who has already made off with one of Hook's hands and is on the verge of getting the rest of him as you sail out into daylight. As in the movie, one of the most beautiful scenes—one that makes this attraction a treat for adults as well as for smaller folk—is the sight of nighttime London, dark blue and speckled with twinkling yellow lights, complete with the Thames, Big Ben, London Bridge, and vehicles that really move on the streets. The song that accompanies the trip is "You Can Fly, You Can Fly, You Can Fly," by Sammy Cahn and Sammy Fain.

SKYWAY TO TOMORROWLAND: Entered from near Peter Pan's Flight, this aerial tram transports guests one-way to Tomorrowland in ten minutes. En route it's possible to see the striped tent tops of Cinderella's Golden Carrousel, Tomorrowland's Grand Prix Raceway, and the not-so-wonderful rooftops of the buildings where many Magic Kingdom adventures actually take place. This attraction is best boarded at its Tomorrowland terminus, where the lines are usually slightly shorter. Guests with disabilities who are able to leave their wheelchairs can take a round-trip ride from the Fantasyland station.

IT'S A SMALL WORLD: Originally created for New York's 1964–1965 World's Fair, with a tunefully singsong melody (written by the Academy Award-winning composers of the music for *Mary Poppins*, among other Disney scores), this favorite of young children and senior citizens involves an 11-minute boat trip through several large rooms where stylized Audio-Animatronics dolls—wooden soldiers, cancan dancers, balloonists, chess pieces, Tower of London guards in scarlet beefeater uniforms, bagpipers and leprechauns, gooseherds, little Dutch kids in wooden shoes, Don Quixote and a goatherd, yodelers and gondoliers, houri dancers, dancers from Greece and Thailand, snake charmers, Japanese kite flyers, hippos, giraffes, frogs, hyenas, monkeys, elephants, hip-twitching Polynesians, surfers, and even dolphins—sing and dance to a melody that will run through your head for hours after you float out of their wonderland. Of the two queues that are usually found here, the one to the left is almost always shorter.

SNOW WHITE'S ADVENTURES: This three-minute attraction near the carousel takes guests on a twisting, turning journey through a few happy moments and a bunch of scary scenes from the Grimm Brothers' fairy tale, which Walt Disney made into the world's first full-length animated feature in 1937. Snow White makes several appearances, as do cheery Audio-Animatronics dwarfs. But the wicked witch—evil, long-nosed, and practically toothless—appears more than once with such suddenness that some youngsters can be really frightened. The ride concludes on a happy note, as the dwarfs wave goodbye to Snow White and her prince.

MR. TOAD'S WILD RIDE: Wild in name only, this three-minute attraction is based on the 1949 Disney release *The Adventures of Ichabod and Mr. Toad*, which itself derives from Kenneth Grahame's classic novel *The Wind in the Willows*. It seems that a gang of weasels has tricked that memorable (but gullible) man-about-town Mr. J. Thaddeus Toad into trading the deed to his ancestral mansion for a motorcar that turns out to have been stolen.

In the attraction, flivvers modeled on this very car take guests zigging and zagging along the road to Nowhere in Particular, through dark rooms painted in neon colors and illuminated by black lights where the redoubtable Mr. Toad is trying to get out of the scrape. In the process, you crash through a fireplace, narrowly miss being struck by a falling suit of armor, hurtle through haystacks and barn doors and into a coop full of squawking chickens, then ride down a railroad track on a collision course with a huge locomotive. Some of this is scary enough that some children end up momentarily frightened. By and large, though, this is for kids.

Mickey's Starland

A 20-minute stage show starring Mickey Mouse, Bonkers, and characters from "Goof Troop," "Tale Spin," and "Dark Wing Duck," the popular Disney afternoon cartoons, is ranked by youngsters as WDW's best attraction. Adults will find it entertaining as well. The best way to get to Mickey's Starland is aboard the Walt Disney World Railroad.

Mickey's house is here, with his balloon-tired car and Pluto's doghouse out front. Once inside, visitors see Mickey's bedroom; a radio plays some old Disney song favorites in the den; the television set shows previews from The Disney Channel; and in the memorabilia room, photos of Mickey with Walt and other celebrities cover the walls.

From Mickey's house, guests head for the pre-show area, which is the entrance to Mickey's Magical TV World. The walls are lined with brightly colored cubes and individual Disney character cutouts. The screen looks like a large television set and guests are entertained by clips from "Goof Troop" and the other cartoons featured in the live show.

The countdown to showtime continues on the screen, and then Mickey Mouse appears to invite guests to enter his Magical TV World. The tunnel leading to the theater is brightly painted, and TV set cutouts are placed along the way. Mickey Mouse and his hostess sing a theme song and introduce the guest stars.

After the live show, guests are led into the Mickey Mouse Club Funland tent, where they are surrounded by a colorful cartoon version of a city skyline. An interactive video area allows guests to see themselves on TV screens, and there is a variety of activities waiting just outside the exit doors. A walkway features shops that offer interactive audio experiences. The Popcorn Shop, for example, has boxes out front that pop when opened. The firehouse features a working siren and rotating light activated when guests push the right button. In addition, Mickey's Walk of Fame replicates Hollywood's starred Walk of Fame. These stars, however, represent Disney characters, and when guests step on a star they hear a character's voice.

Guests have the opportunity to greet and meet Mickey Mouse at the Hollywood Theatre, and have their picture taken with him.

In the outdoor area of Mickey's Starland, Mickey's Treehouse and Minnie's Doll House offer opportunities for climbing, exploring, and having an all-around good time. There's Grandma Duck's Farm, where children can get up close to some extremely cuddly baby animals. Guests also can see Minnie Moo, a white cow that happens to have black spots in the shape of mouse ears on its side. A photograph of the cow was sent by its owner and Walt Disney World purchased it. When the cow is not touring, she lives at Grandma Duck's Farm. There's also a maze, called the Mouse-Ka-Maze, where topiary shrubs and trees create a not-too-confusing path for children. Drink, cookie, and ice cream carts are located all around the outdoor area.

Guests leave Mickey's Starland along a path guarded by topiary trees and shrubs that have been pruned into many shapes, including Disney characters. The path leads directly back to Fantasyland.

Tomorrowland

The original Tomorrowland attempted a serious look at the future. But as Disney planners discovered, it isn't easy to portray a future that persists in becoming the present. So the old Tomorrowland has given way to a friendlier, space-age town whose neighborhood atmosphere is more in keeping with the other lands in the Magic Kingdom. This is the future that never was, the fantasy world imagined by the science fiction writers and moviemakers of the 1920s and 1930s. It's a land of sky-piercing beacons and glistening metal, where shiny robots do the work, whisper-quiet conveyances glide along an elevated highway, and even time travel is possible.

SPACE MOUNTAIN: Rising to a height of over 180 feet and extending some 300 feet in diameter, this gleaming white steel and concrete cone (shaped vaguely like Japan's Mount Fuji) houses an attraction that most people call a roller coaster. Actually, it bears the same sort of resemblance to the traditional thrill ride as the Magic Kingdom does to the garden variety of theme park. It's the Disney version—a roller coaster and then some. While the 2 minute 38 second ride does not exactly duplicate a trip into outer

space, there are some truly phenomenal and quite lovely special effects—shooting stars and strobelike flashing lights among them; and the whole ride takes place in an outer spacelike darkness that gets progressively inkier—and scarier—as the journey progresses. The six-passenger rockets that roar through this blackness attain a maximum speed of just over 28 miles per hour. Just how terrifying this actually is to any given passenger depends on his or her level of tolerance. In general, the Space Mountain trip seems to inspire in lovers of thrill rides an immediate desire to go again; it's just wild enough to send eyeglasses, purses, wallets, and even an occasional set of false teeth plummeting to the bottom of the track, so be sure to find a safe place for your possessions before the ride starts. It's also turbulent enough to upset the stomachs of those so unwise as to ride it immediately after eating—but not so harrowing that passengers shake and weakened knees persist for more than a minute or two after "touchdown." Those in a quandary about whether or not to line up can get a preview from the Tomorrowland Transit Authority described below; and those who decide to pass after hearing the shrieks and the clatter of the cars from the queue area have their own exit.

After experiencing the space journey, it's interesting to note that the mountain itself occupies a ten-acre site. With the work lights on, the interior of Space Mountain looks humdrum and almost commercially common, with its tangled array of track and supporting scaffolding. Some of the shooting stars are produced quite simply, by aiming a beam of light at a mirrored globe; and legend has it that the meteors visible to guests in the queue area are actually projections of chocolate chip cookies! The whole ride is controlled by a computer and is monitored on a board full of dials and a battery of closed-circuit television screens by

Disney hosts and hostesses sitting in a control room (whose eerie blue glow is another striking feature of the queue area). As a result, any guest caught acting in an unsafe manner can be warned, and the ride stopped, if necessary.

Note: Children under seven years old must be accompanied by an adult; guests under 44 inches tall are not permitted to ride; and as the many signs at the attraction warn, "You Must be in Good Health, and Free from Heart Conditions, Motion Sickness, Back or Neck Problems, or Other Physical Limitations" to ride. It also is suggested that expectant mothers pass up the trip. Presented by Federal Express.

The Tomorrowland Power & Light Co., a new video arcade located at Space Mountain's exit, is a great place to wait for your party if you choose not to ride. A cart here sells video games and toys. An ATM also is available.

SKYWAY TO FANTASYLAND: This aerial cable car takes guests from Tomorrowland to a point near Peter Pan's Flight in Fantasyland in ten minutes. The cable car, built by Von Roll Ltd., in Bern, Switzerland, is notable for being the nation's first conveyance of its type able to make a 90-degree turn. If you're going to ride the Skyway, this is the place to get on: The lines at the Fantasyland end are usually slightly longer.

ALIEN ENCOUNTER: The centerpiece of Tomorrowland is the Tomorrowland Interplanetary Convention Center, home of the Magic Kingdom's newest and scariest attraction. Created by Disney Imagineers and director George Lucas, Alien Encounter features some

of the most elaborate special effects and show systems ever employed by a theme park.

The premise behind the attraction is a sophisticated one. The Convention Center is hosting X-S Tech, a mysterious corporation from a distant planet. Its objective is to impress earthlings, particularly Magic Kindgom

guests, with its line of high-tech products. Visitors learn more about X-S Tech in a glitzy corporate video presentation. They also meet Chairman Clench, X-S Tech's CEO. Then they are led into another room for a mini-demonstration of the company's premier product: a teleporter capable of "beaming" people or objects from place to place—even from one planet to another.

At the podium is a robot named S.I.R.. To his left and right are bell jars, one of which holds Skippy, a fuzzy, three-foot-tall character. S.I.R. tries to teleport Skippy from one jar to the next, but the demonstration doesn't go very well. He uses a little too much power, and Skippy's fur is singed and his eyes are rolling.

Despite the minor setback, the folks from X-S Tech continue with their presentation. Guests are shown to a circular auditorium with a large teleporter in the center. Screens around the theater display a live transmission from Planet X, asking visitors to take their seats. Restraints are suddenly lowered onto guests' shoulders. (Don't panic—this is not rough, just scary.) The Planet X broadcast informs guests that X-S Tech intends to demonstrate its invention by teleporting someone from the audience to Planet X. A scanner lights up each seat and lasers sweep the crowd in search of a specimen. Just then, Chairman Clench comes on screen and volunteers. He will have himself teleported to Earth, to meet this Magic Kingdom audience.

Special effects abound as the teleporter is fired up and guests await the arrival of Chairman Clench. But something goes terribly wrong and, instead of Clench, an alien is transported in their midst. Horrified, the technicians blow up the machine in hopes of destroying the hideous creature. The theater goes black and then there are a few flickers of light. But the strain on the equipment has been too great, and guests are plunged into darkness once more. There is a sound of breaking glass, and the audience realizes that the unthinkable has happened. The fearsome alien has escaped. Next comes a series of creepy sensations designed to convince members of the audience that the monster has found its way to their side. Ultimately, the X-S technicians regain control. They manage to repair the teleporter and to transport the creature back through space. Chairman Clench is retrieved, but too late to salvage any hope that the earthlings might purchase his product. Note that this 20-minute attraction may be too intense for young children or for anyone afraid of the dark.

TOMORROWLAND TRANSIT AUTHORITY: Boarded near Astro Orbiter, these small, five-car trains move at a speed of about ten miles per hour along almost a mile of track, alongside or through most of the attractions in Tomorrowland. If you have any doubts about riding Space Mountain, a ten-minute trip on the Tomorrowland Transit Authority—which travels through the queue area inside and offers a view of the rockets as they hurtle through the darkness—will probably help you decide. Just as important, from a technological and environmental standpoint, is the fact that this train shows off an innovative means of transportation: It is operated by a linear induction motor that has no moving parts, uses little power, and emits no pollution.

WALT DISNEY'S CAROUSEL OF PROGRESS: First seen at New York's 1964–65 World's Fair and moved here in 1975, this 20-minute show features a number of tableaux starring an Audio-Animatronics family, and demonstrates the improvements in American life that have resulted from the use of electricity. The audience moves around the scenes like a carousel, and kids enjoy this effect. An updated final scene has been added, in which guests see what life might be like about five or six years from now. A grandmother plays a virtual reality game and the oven talks. These technologically advanced products to be used in homes in the near future are now on display for hands-on inspection at Epcot's Innoventions.

THE TIMEKEEPER: A fantastic 20-minute multimedia presentation combining a Circle-Vision 360 film with Audio-Animatronics characters and special in-theater effects is hosted by Timekeeper, a wacky, mad scientist robot. Inspired by the likes of Jules Verne and H. G. Wells, who wrote about fantastic visions of the future, Timekeeper has created the world's first and only working time machine (at least as far as we know). Assisting Timekeeper in his time voyage demonstration is 9-Eye, a flying robot camera who is the test pilot for Timekeeper's invention. She has bravely volunteered to fly through history and transmit pictures of what she sees back to guests in the 360-degree time chamber. Guests are able to experience what it was like to hear the young Mozart play his first composition; to fly down a mountain on a speeding bobsled; to see Leonardo da Vinci working on a masterpiece; and to float in a hot air balloon above Moscow's Red Square, among many other exciting stops on this whirlwind trip through time and space. In a sweep of the 1900 Paris Exposition, guests even meet Jules Verne and H. G. Wells themselves. When Verne hitches a ride with 9-Eye to the present and beyond, he gets to see some of his visions realized. Guests will recognize the voice and zany antics of Timekeeper as those of Robin Williams. Other stars featured are Rhea Perlman as 9-Eye, Jeremy Irons as H. G. Wells, and Michel Piccoli as Jules Verne.

To create this blast through time, filmmakers took the 400-pound Circle-Vision nine-lens camera rig to a number of interesting locations: Innsbruck, Austria, where the rig was mounted on a bobsled and hurled down a 1,200-meter run at 60 miles per hour; Moscow's Red Square for the hot air balloon scene; the underwater world of the Bahamas; and Vienna, Austria, where the 1900 Paris Exposition was recreated for the historic, albeit fictional, encounter between Jules Verne and H. G. Wells.

ASTRO ORBITER: Spin around for two minutes in machine-age rockets, designed to look more like oversize Buck Rogers toys than 1990s space shuttles. Passengers are surrounded by whirling planets as they swing around, getting a good view of the newly designed Tomorrowland.

GRAND PRIX RACEWAY: Little cars that *vroom* down the tracks at this attraction opposite *Cosmic Ray's Starlight Café* provide most of the background noise in Tomorrowland—and that's another grim thought about the future. Kids love the ride and will spend as many hours driving the Mark VII-model gasoline-powered cars as they can; one 87-year-old grandmother comes here just to watch. Like true sports cars, the vehicles—which cost about $6,000 each—have rack-and-pinion steering and disc brakes; unlike most sports cars, these run on a track. Nonetheless, even expert drivers have a hard time keeping them going in a straight line until the technique is mastered: Just steer all the way to the right, or all the way to the left, and you've got it made. One lap around the track takes about five minutes, and the cars (which are manufactured by a Disney company called MAPO, short for Mary Poppins) can travel at a maximum speed of about seven mph. **Note:** You must be at least 52 inches tall to drive the cars by yourself. Presented by Goodyear.

DREAMFLIGHT: A whimsical look at the adventure and romance of flight—as seen through the eyes of a child—awaits guests at this 4½-minute attraction. A mixture of two- and three-dimensional media combine with special effects and digitally produced stereo music to take visitors on an entirely delightful journey. The attraction opens with a scene from a giant pop-up book, in which mankind's first attempts at flight are humorously depicted. Three-dimensional aircraft are used in a variety of scenes from the early days of flight. A barnstorming flying circus segment features a man and woman, each standing on a wing and keeping up a tennis match. The next segment highlights a 70mm live-action film, produced in the Northwest exclusively for this attraction, in which stunts are performed to the oohs and ahs of the audience.

In the next scene, a full-size segment of an M-130 Flying Boat, a popular plane during the late 1930s, is on view. An elegant dining room (particularly by today's standards) is displayed as monitors allow glimpses of the faraway places the M-130 made accessible. In one scene, two dancers perform outside a Japanese temple garden; in another, the sun sets over Paris as a flower merchant packs up his blossoms on the steps of Montmartre. Next stop on the journey is the jet age, in its most pure form. Guests actually ride through a real engine. Digitally prepared graphics and special effects recreate the rotation of the turbine in a realistic fashion.

In another 70mm film segment, visitors get that "you are there" feeling as they speed down a runway and fly off towards space. The moon, backlit by the sun, provides the lighting for some spectacular views over canyons, valleys, and flat terrain, where the suggestion of cities of the future are depicted. The finale features another pop-up book measuring 16 feet tall and 11 feet wide showing contemporary London and New York.

If this journey fuels the desire to travel, Delta is prepared to fulfill it. Brochures, ticket information, and flight schedules are available at the Delta counter at the *Contemporary* resort. Presented by Delta Air Lines.

Shops in the Magic Kingdom

No one travels all the way to the Magic Kingdom just to go shopping. But as many a first-time visitor has learned with some surprise, shopping is one of the most enjoyable pastimes there. Donald Duck key chains and Mickey Mouse lapel pins, Alice in Wonderland dresses for little girls, Walt Disney World sweatshirts, and other Disney souvenir items make up a large portion of the merchandise you see on display.

But the Magic Kingdom's boutiques and stores stock much more than just Disneyana. It's possible to buy antiques and silver-plated tea services, cookbooks and stoneware dishes, mock pirate hats and toy frontier rifles, 14-karat gold charms and filigreed costume jewelry in Main Street shops that also sell film and peanut brittle. In Adventureland, you can buy imported items from around the world—handcarved elephant statues from Africa, inlaid marble boxes from India, batik dresses from Indonesia, and much more. Shops stock items that complement the themes of the various lands (and so, in Tomorrowland, one finds contemporary wall hangings and futuristic-looking table lamps). Every store offers a selection of items from the inexpensive to the costly: In Tinker Bell's Treasures in Fantasyland, for instance, kids can beg for a $5 windup toy after requests for the larger-than-life-size $250 stuffed animals are denied. At Uptown Jewelers on Main Street, some three-foot-high Hummel figurines cost thousands of dollars. And in many shops, you can watch people at work—peanut brittle being poured in the Main Street Confectionery, a glassblower in Main Street's Crystal Arts, and the like.

Consequently, there's no need to spend a fortune to have a good time. Budget-watchers should note, though, that the temptation to nickel-and-dime yourself into penury is strong, and you need to be careful. It's a good idea to set a spending limit for each member of your party in advance—and try to stick to it. Keep in mind that Main Street shops stay open a half hour after park closing.

MAIN STREET
East Side

WHEELCHAIRS–STROLLERS: Just inside the turnstiles, to the right as you enter the park. A limited number of strollers and wheelchairs are available on a first-come, first-served basis, and assorted souvenirs may be purchased.

THE CHAPEAU: This Town Square shop is the place to buy Mouseketeer ears and have them monogrammed, and to shop for visors, straw hats, derbies, top hats, and other headgear. The decorated ladies' hats are fun to try on, if not necessarily worth the investment.

DISNEYANA COLLECTIBLES: Located next to *Tony's Town Square* restaurant. Limited edition Disney plates, cels from Disney movies, and other collectibles are sold here.

KODAK CAMERA CENTER: This high-ceilinged shop near Town Square is the spot for film, single-use cameras, two-hour film processing, and very minor camera repairs. Gleaming glass-fronted mahogany cases show off the Canon, Minolta, Pentax, Nikon, and other 35mm cameras for sale. Video cameras are available for rent (a deposit is required).

MAIN STREET CONFECTIONERY: Delicious chocolates are available in this old-fashioned pink-and-white paradise. A delight at any time of day, but especially when the cooks in the shop's glass-walled kitchen are pouring peanut brittle onto a huge tabletop to cool, and the candy is sending up clouds of scent that you could swear were being fanned right out into the street. About ten batches are made each day. The sweet product is for sale in small bags, along with pastilles, jelly beans, marshmallow crispies, nougats, mints, and dozens of other nemeses for a sweet tooth. When your stomach is growling, this is a good place to grab a snack.

UPTOWN JEWELERS: Fine china and other gift items—china figurines, swans, and flowers, Lladro figurines, all manner of pretty teacups, and Disney character figurines—priced from $3.50 to $3,500—are the stock-in-trade of this airy establishment. The most expensive item, at last look, was a giant Hummel statue, depicting ruddy-cheeked peasant children in an apple tree; at least peek at it, even if it is a bit rich for most pocketbooks. There's also a selection of good-quality and costume jewelry. One counter stocks wonderful souvenir charms in 14-karat gold and sterling silver: Tinkerbell, Cinderella Castle, and the Walt Disney World logo (a globe with mouse ears). Clocks and watches in all shapes and sizes, including Mickey Mouse watches in a variety of configurations, are available here. There even are some pocket watches and a Mickey Mouse telephone. Purchases can be shipped on request. Presented by Lorus.

DISNEY & COMPANY: The wallpaper at this shop on Center Street (the cul-de-sac just off Main) is Victorian and the woodwork elaborate; and old-fashioned ceiling fans twirl slowly overhead. This shop specializes in children's clothing, but also stocks clocks, watches, and an assortment of dolls and stuffed toys. The selection is not as vast as the Emporium, but neither is Disney & Company quite so overwhelming.

MARKET HOUSE: An old-fashioned spot, with pretzels, pickles, honey, and all kinds of tea and snack items arranged in oak cases. The floors are oak and pegged, the lighting comes in part from brass lanterns, and in one corner there's a real old-fashioned hand-crank telephone. Tobacco products also are available.

THE SHADOW BOX: Watching Rubio Artist Co. silhouette cutters snip black paper into the likenesses of children is one of Main Street's more fascinating diversions, and there's always a crowd on hand—some folks waiting their turn, some just inspecting the progress and the results. Silhouettes cost $5.

CRYSTAL ARTS: Cut-glass bowls and vases, urns and glasses, plates and shelves glitter in the mirror-backed glass cases of this high-ceilinged, brass-chandeliered emporium. An engraver or a glassblower is always at work by the bright light flooding through the big windows. Presented by the Arribas Brothers.

West Side

NEWSSTAND: No newspapers are sold in the Magic Kingdom—even at its newsstand, which is opposite Wheelchairs–Strollers near the park entrance. It's off to your left just inside the turnstiles. What the stand does sell is character merchandise and souvenirs. The selection is fairly limited, but you can usually pick up items you've forgotten during your travels through the rest of the park.

EMPORIUM: Framed by a two-story-high portico, this Town Square landmark, the Magic Kingdom's largest gift shop, stocks a little bit of everything—stuffed animals and toys, an array of dolls, sundries, film, and more. Everyone seems to have an armload of Walt Disney World T-shirts and sweatshirts, towels and handbags, Mouseketeer ears and other hats, and various items emblazoned with Mickey, Minnie, or Walt Disney World logos. The cash registers almost always seem to be busy, especially toward the end of the afternoon and before park closing. It's a good place to souvenir shop, though, since it's only a few steps from lockers (under the train station) where purchases can be stowed. Don't forget to note the window displays, which usually feature Audio-Animatronics displays ranging from themes of the season to the most recent Disney movie.

HARMONY BARBER SHOP: The setting of this working shop is quaint and old-fashioned, worth a peek even if you've no need for a trim. Nostalgic shaving items are for sale.

DISNEY CLOTHIERS: Disney character merchandise has always been popular, as evidenced by the number of T-shirts, Mouseketeer ears, wristwatches, and sweatshirts sold each year. This shop caters to fashion-conscious shoppers with a love for Disney gear. There is a vast array of men's, women's, and children's clothing and accessories, all of which incorporate Disney characters in some way. There are men's golf shirts with a small Mickey Mouse embroidered on the pocket, and jackets with Mickey embossed on the back. Hats, ties, and dress shirts round out the adult selections. Children's items include socks, suspenders, tops, pants, and bathing suits.

MAIN STREET ATHLETIC STORE: Sports-related gifts and apparel sure to be a hit with the active set are the hallmarks of this new shop. Merchandise features the logos of popular collegiate and professional teams and the Disney characters gamely pursuing their favorite sports. Other items will be themed to the 1996 Summer Olympics in Atlanta.

ADVENTURELAND

TRADERS OF TIMBUKTU: This shop is in a marketlike complex in the plaza opposite the Tropical Serenade, and displays a fine selection of the sort of handsome (but inexpensive) trinkets that travelers find while visiting parts of Africa—carved wooden giraffes and antelope, ethnic jewelry (including carved bangles and malachite and elephant-hair jewelry), dashikis, and khaki shirts.

BWANA BOB'S: A whimsical and colorful hut full of the critters you may have just seen on the Jungle Cruise or at the Tropical Serenade.

TIKI TROPICS: This tropical surf shop features a vast assortment of surfing clothing and accessories. Colorful T-shirts, baggies, sharks' teeth jewelry, and even surfboard wax can be found here.

ELEPHANT TALES: A variety of women's and men's clothing with a safari theme are featured at this shop. Women's accessories and safari plush toys also are available.

ISLAND SUPPLY: Discover nature at its finest through apparel and gifts representing gardening and the great outdoors. The merchandise here has an environmental theme: You'll find wind chimes, herb-garden kits, natural lotions, and a selection of T-shirts made of unbleached cotton.

CARIBBEAN PLAZA

HOUSE OF TREASURE: The only spot in the Magic Kingdom that sells pirates' hats, this swashbuckler's delight adjoins Pirates of the Caribbean on the west and stocks piratical merchandise—toy rifles and brass dolphins, a Pirate's Creed of Ethics printed on parchment, Jolly Roger flags, rings, old-looking maps, pirate dolls, sailing-ship models, ships in a bottle, and eye patches. There's as much for adults as for youngsters. Women's nautical apparel is available, as are fine nautical gifts such as lamps and brass items.

PLAZA DEL SOL CARIBE BAZAAR: Located next to the Pirates of the Caribbean, this market sells candy and snacks, a variety of straw hats (including colorful oversize sombreros), piñatas, pottery, straw bags, clothing, and artificial flowers.

FRONTIERLAND

FRONTIER TRADING POST: Stock your chuck wagon with venison chili, wild boar meat, and buffalo. Or outfit a youngster like a true child of the Great Frontier: Cowboy hats or feathered headdresses and moccasins, hefty brass belt buckles, sleeve garters, sheriff's badges, gold nugget and turquoise jewelry, and reproduction pistols and rifles should do the trick. Also available are western items like tom-toms, peace pipes, plastic toy horses, and forts. Film and sundries are in stock, too.

TRAIL CREEK HAT SHOP: Hats of all descriptions (though the specialties of the house are western styles), plus feathered hatbands and leather goods are on sale. It's tucked away near the arcade leading to Adventureland, between the ornamental Frontierland stockade, alongside the *Diamond Horseshoe Saloon Revue*.

PRAIRIE OUTPOST & SUPPLY: This is the place to go for clothing and other merchandise from Disney's animated film *Pocahontas*.

BRIAR PATCH: Cuddly creatures from *Song of the South* are featured at this shop near the exit to Splash Mountain. Country crafts and an unusual line of Disney character merchandise round out the offerings.

FRONTIER WOOD CARVING: The spot for personalized, wood-carved gifts. Presented by Rubio Artist Co.

BIG AL'S: Located along the river, this is a good place to acquire leather goods, harmonicas, rock candy, and assorted six-shooters.

LIBERTY SQUARE

OLDE WORLD ANTIQUES: One of the first of the Liberty Square shops that visitors pass after crossing the bridge from the Hub area in front of Cinderella Castle, this little, lace-curtained emporium stocks real antiques—hutches, drop-leaf tables, and assorted decorative items in brass, pewter, copper, mahogany, oak, and pine—as well as some reproductions. There also are antique-looking linens and jewelry. Both perfumes created to order and name-brand fragrances are available here. Prices range from reasonable to costly, but the browsing is good.

HERITAGE HOUSE: Among the early American reproductions that predominate in the stock of this store next to The Hall of Presidents, youngsters may go for the parchment copies of famous American documents, while homeowners might snap up pewter plates and candlesticks, creweled items, wooden candlesticks and pepper mills, busts of the presidents, souvenir spoons, mugs in early American motifs, wrought-iron knickknacks, or lovely enameled paintings of clipper ships.

YANKEE TRADER: No first-time Magic Kingdom visitor would expect to buy stoneware soufflé dishes and cast-iron muffin tins. But this shop, immediately to the right after you turn into the lane leading to the Haunted Mansion, is crammed like a too-small kitchen cabinet with just these kitchen items, and more. There's a great Mickey Mouse waffle iron, among other Disney-themed goods. The shop also has a wealth of countrified cookware and more varieties of jams and jellies than any supermarket shopper would have imagined existed. Gourmands will be pleased to find a cookbook selection that includes not only old favorites, but also unusual volumes of historic recipes. The store is located near the archway entrance to Fantasyland.

LIBERTY SQUARE PORTRAIT GALLERY: In the midst of Liberty Square next to The Hall of Presidents, guests can sit to have their portraits drawn.

ICHABOD'S LANDING: This small Liberty Square shop gives guests on their way to the Haunted Mansion a taste of things to come with a stock of horrific monster masks and assorted ghoulish goodies.

SILVERSMITH: The sign above the entrance to this tiny shop adjoining Olde World Antiques (just next to the Liberty Square bridge to the Hub) reads "J. Tremain, Prop." That refers to the main character in the 1957 Disney film of the Esther Forbes novel about a silversmith's apprentice who joins the Boston Tea Party and helps hang the lights on the Liberty Tree during America's colonial days. At this low-ceilinged, plank-floored establishment, antique-looking cabinets display tongs and teaspoons, Revere-style bowls, tea sets, silver-coated roses, candelabras, jewelry, and more—all in sterling or silver plate.

WHERE TO EAT IN THE MAGIC KINGDOM

A complete listing of all Magic Kingdom eateries—full-service restaurants, fast-food emporiums, snack shops, and food vendors—are found together with all other WDW eating spots in the *Good Meals, Great Times* chapter.

SHOPPING AWAY FROM THE PARKS

THE DISNEY CATALOG: T-shirts, stuffed animals, and many other souvenir items can be ordered through The Disney Catalog. Phone 800-237-5751 to receive one.

THE DISNEY STORES: Located in malls all around the country, these shops offer a wide selection of merchandise.

WDW MAIL ORDER: Merchandise found in shops at Walt Disney World also is available by calling 800-272-6201.

FANTASYLAND

THE KING'S GALLERY: This shop, situated inside Cinderella Castle, is one of the Magic Kingdom's best. The stock includes large tapestries, suits of armor, unicorns of all sizes, cuckoo clocks, Spanish-made swords, German beer mugs with lids, chess sets, and more—very little of it at rock-bottom prices. Also here, practiced artisans demonstrate the art of Damascening, a form of metalworking originated by the inhabitants of Damascus in the sixth century A.D. Painstakingly, these skilled workers dip steel pendants into acid to create tiny pores, then use a combination of sterling silver and 24-karat gold wire to outline designs onto the acid-blackened steel.

MICKEY'S CHRISTMAS CAROL: A wide selection of Christmas items, including tree-top dolls and souvenir ornaments—both Disney-themed and traditional—is available at this location year-round.

FANTASY FAIRE: It's difficult to miss this shop upon leaving the Legend of The Lion King show. It has everything imaginable featuring the characters from *The Lion King*, from plush Simba toys to Timon and Pumbaa T-shirts and souvenirs.

TINKER BELL'S TREASURES: One of the more wonderful boutiques in the Magic Kingdom, and a fine toy store by any standards. For sale are stuffed animals, miniature model cars and trucks, character patches, windup toys and wooden toys, bar soap emblazoned with Disney scenes, Mickey and Minnie toys and clothing, Alice in Wonderland dresses, Snow White dresses (with Dopey on the skirt), and a positively marvelous array of Madame Alexander dolls. A must.

THE ARISTOCATS: Most of the lands have one store that specializes in Disney souvenirs; this stone-walled, vaguely Gothic shop slightly to the northeast of Cinderella Castle is Fantasyland's spot for Donald and Mickey key chains, sweatshirts and T-shirts, china Disney figurines, salt-and-pepper shakers, Minnie tote bags, tennis balls with a Mickey logo, and hats.

SEVEN DWARFS MINING CO.: This souvenir stand next to Snow White's Adventures sells assorted Disney-motif key chains and stuffed animals, plus a colorful collection of Snow White merchandise.

KODAK KIOSK: A convenient location to buy film and other photo supplies.

MICKEY'S STARLAND

MICKEY'S STARLAND TENT: "Disney Afternoon" merchandise and Mickey Mouse character memorabilia are among the items available here.

TOMORROWLAND

MICKEY'S STAR TRADERS: One of the best places in the Magic Kingdom for Disney-themed items.

SKYWAY STATION SHOP: A small spot tucked away near the Tomorrowland terminus of the Skyway to Fantasyland; great for Disney souvenirs.

MERCHANT OF VENUS: Sells the kind of contemporary decorative gifts that teens and preteens seem to love: futuristic toys, games, jewelry, watches, clothing, and other such items. This is the only shop that carries Alien Encounter merchandise.

GEIGER'S COUNTER: This small shop features a variety of souvenir hats.

LET IT RAIN

The show doesn't stop just because of a storm. Instead, shops all over the Magic Kingdom stock bright yellow Mickey ponchos to outfit guests who have left their own back home, at their hotel, or in the car.

Happenings & Live Entertainment

Walt Disney World is constantly adding new live shows to its repertoire, so before heading down Main Street, check at City Hall to get times for special Magic Kingdom happenings, as well as a schedule of entertainment at the resorts, the Disney Village Marketplace, Epcot, the Disney-MGM Studios, and Pleasure Island. Others may be encountered serendipitously in the course of the day, and occasionally shows scheduled for a given place or time may be changed or canceled at the last minute—but more often than not, the shows proceed as planned.

DAPPER DANS: Likely to be encountered while you're strolling down Main Street. This barbershop quartet, its members clad in straw hats and striped vests, tap dance and let one-liners fly during their short four-part harmonic performances.

WALT DISNEY WORLD BAND: This concert band performs every morning in Town Square, and prior to the afternoon parade.

CASEY'S CORNER PIANO: A pianist tickles the ivories of a snow-white upright daily at the centrally located *Casey's Corner* restaurant on Main Street.

FANTASY IN THE SKY: Even those rare recalcitrant souls who resist fireworks displays as though they were other people's home movies have little quarrel with this spectacular show, which is presented nightly when the park is open until 10 P.M. or later. The 200-odd shells that were mortarized over a 15-minute period when the program was

first introduced are now ignited in a period of just 5 minutes—a rate of one shell every 2 seconds. The big symmetrical starburst shells are generally Japanese-made, while the ones whose explosions look as if they had been poured from a pitcher (with a concentrated area of particularly vivid color at the center) are manufactured in England.

ALL-AMERICAN COLLEGE MARCHING BAND: During weekdays in summer, this band featuring college students from around the country performs throughout the Magic Kingdom in the afternoon and early evening.

MICKEY MANIA PARADE: Literally everything in this parade, which wends its way down Main Street each day at 3 P.M., has been "Mickeyized." The costumes feature Mickey everywhere and even the tires on the vehicles are in the shape of the famed mouse's ears. The music is very contemporary—a combination of hip hop and rap. "Rock the House with the Mouse" is the theme song. Its driving beat pulses as a troupe of stilt walkers, skaters, and BMX bikers joins floats along Main Street. There also are characters who ride tricycles. Paraders involve onlookers as they hand out Mickey stickers and encourage spectators to sing and dance.

SWORD IN THE STONE CEREMONY: A child is appointed king or queen of the realm by pulling the magical sword, Excalibur, from the stone in front of Cinderella's Golden Carrousel. Merlin the Magician presides over this ceremony.

KIDS OF THE KINGDOM: This group performs often in front of the Castle. The show features lively singing and dancing to classic Disney tunes—plus appearances by Disney characters such as the portly Winnie the Pooh and Mickey Mouse himself.

FLAG RETREAT: Usually around 5:10 P.M., a small band and color guard march into Town Square, take down the American flag that flies from the flagpole there, then release a flock of snow-white homing pigeons symbolic of the dove of peace. Watch carefully lest you miss them: As one wag quipped, these are union pigeons; they flap away toward their lofthome (behind the Castle) practically before you can say "Cinderella." The whole flight takes just 20 seconds. Some trivia: The carts in which the birds are transported are fashioned from authentic peddlers' carts bought in England for the 1971 Disney film *Bedknobs and Broomsticks*.

DIAMOND HORSESHOE SALOON REVUE: A dance hall such as might have been found in 19th-century Missouri hosts a lively old-time show with cancan dancers several times daily. Guests may drop in at any time during the hour-long performances.

J. P. AND THE SILVER STARS: Play familiar tunes on the instruments so well known in the Caribbean islands, steel drums—oil barrels whose sides have been cut to a foot or less from the bottom (which itself has been pounded hollow). Near Adventureland's Pirates of the Caribbean.

RHYTHM RASCALS: This group plays specialty songs and comic ditties from the Roaring Twenties on washboards and banjos, usually on Main Street.

SPECTROMAGIC

Since its premier during Walt Disney World's 20th anniversary celebration five years ago, this parade has gotten rave reviews and has taken its place among WDW's must-sees. Even avid fans of the Main Street Electrical Parade (which, by the way, was shipped to Euro Disneyland) won't be disappointed with this display. SpectroMagic borrows from the prismatic holographic industry, military lighting developments, electro-luminescent and fiber-optic technologies, plus light-spreading thermoplastics, clouds of underlit liquid nitrogen, smoke, and some old-fashioned twinkling lights. The spectacle is choreographed to music composed just for the parade.

Fiber-optic cable and threads are conduits for shimmering lights that create everything from the strands of "hair" on King Triton's beard to the giant hibiscus blooms and daisy petals. Some 600,000 miniature bulbs light in wild patterns, moving in perfect concert with sound effects and music. Goofy's xylophone keys dance with light at his touch. Mickey's cape becomes a cascade of color sweeping from shoulder height to the base of the float and upward to 17 feet above his head.

SpectroMagic is a marvel of the computer age. Mini-computers are used and the audio is stored digitally on state-of-the-art microchips. A sequence of electronic triggers activates the visual and audio effects.

There are two SpectroMagic parades nightly during busy seasons. Spectro-Magic follows the traditional WDW parade route and of all the spots along the way, the single best vantage point is the very center of the platform of the Walt Disney World Railroad's depot. From there, it's possible to see the parade circling Town Square, and then follow it as it makes its way down Main Street. Unfortunately, only a couple of seats here have views that are not obstructed by trees.

The next-best viewing point is from the curbs on either side of Main Street. It's very crowded here, and you must claim your foot of curb as much as an hour before the parade (particularly for the busier 9 P.M. running).

If you hate crowds, head for *Pecos Bill Café*; park yourself on one of the restaurant's stools right next to the parade route.

Note that the 9 P.M. parade is always more crowded than the one at 11 P.M.

Holiday Doings

EASTER SUNDAY: A nationally televised holiday promenade helps make Easter extra special.

FOURTH OF JULY CELEBRATION: The busiest day of the summer—and with reason: There's a double-size fireworks display, whose explosions light up the skies not only above Cinderella Castle, but also over the Seven Seas Lagoon.

CHRISTMAS: A Christmas tree—a real Douglas fir that is as perfect among trees as Main Street is among small-town thoroughfares—goes up in Town Square, and the entire Magic Kingdom is decked out as only Disney can do it. There also are special Christmas parades, shows, and carolers. The crowds, of course, are thick. But the scenery is beautiful, and the weather is fine (if chilly)—so it's no wonder that some veteran Magic Kingdom lovers call this the very best time of year.

NEW YEAR'S EVE CELEBRATION: It has always been true that on December 31, the throngs are practically body to body. For a celebration, that's fun. (On an introductory visit, it could be less delightful; first-timers take note.) There is a double-size fireworks display, and the Main Street holiday decorations (including that almost surrealistically perfect Christmas tree presiding over Town Square) are still up. There's plenty of nip in the air as the evening wears on, so dress accordingly.

WHERE TO FIND THE CHARACTERS

Mickey's friends appear next to City Hall throughout the day. A queue has been set up to allow each guest a turn to meet the characters and perhaps have a photo taken. Disney characters also can be found near the Fantasyland Pavilion, located next to Dumbo, the Flying Elephant. But the best place to see the characters is at Mickey's Starland, where Mickey and friends are on hand for a spectacular show. At the Hollywood Theatre in Starland, Mickey is available for photo opportunities.

Tips From WDW Veterans

● Study before you arrive in the Magic Kingdom so that you're familiar with the layout and the things to see and to do in the park. Special services are occasionally available to guests during slack seasons, so be sure to peruse any printed information you find in your room.

● Allow plenty of time so that you can sample the Magic Kingdom in small bites. Trying to see it all in a day (or even just two) is like eating a rich ice cream sundae too quickly.

● Sunday morning ranks as the most peaceful time to visit the park.

● Consider taking advantage of early-bird admissions to the parks if you are staying at a WDW resort. Each day, sections of one park are open 1½ hours early for WDW resort guests. But keep in mind that the parks can get crowded on the designated days.

● If you are not staying at a WDW resort, you should still plan to start out early. Most people arrive between 9:30 A.M. and 11:30 A.M., when the roads approaching the Auto Plaza and the parking lots are jammed. If you're coming at Easter, Christmas, or in summer, plan to arrive before 8:30 A.M., or wait until late afternoon, when things are less hectic. Be at the gates to the Magic Kingdom

when they open, have breakfast at *Tony's Town Square* restaurant or the *Crystal Palace*, then be at the end of Main Street when the rest of the park opens.

● If you'd like to have a sit-down meal in the Magic Kingdom, make advance reservations for *Tony's Town Square*, *Liberty Tree Tavern*, or *King Stefan's Banquet Hall*, by calling WDW-DINE (939-3463).

● Check out the Magic Kingdom Tip Board at the end of Main Street for information on the waiting times for the most popular attractions.

● Organize your visit so that you don't hop around from area to area, for that wastes time. Plan to eat early or late; before 11 A.M. or after 2 P.M., and before 5 P.M. or after 8 P.M.

● At busy times on busy days, take in the following not-so-packed attractions:

Main Street:	Walt Disney World Railroad, Main Street Cinema
Liberty Square:	Liberty Square Riverboat
Tomorrowland:	Carousel of Progress, Dreamflight, Tomorrowland Transit Authority

● Break up your day. Go to Typhoon Lagoon, Blizzard Beach, or River Country (admission included in a Five-Day World Hopper Pass or a Length of Stay Pass), or head back to your hotel, if it's not too far, for some swimming. Be sure to have your hand stamped and hold on to your admission pass and your parking stub.

● Shop on Main Street in the early afternoon, not at day's end, when everybody else goes (since shops here are open a half hour after park closing). Besides, the stores are good places to escape the afternoon heat.

● If your party decides to split up, set a fixed meeting place and time that can't be confused. Avoid meeting in front of Cinderella Castle, since this area can become congested during showtimes and parades.

● Many attractions have two lines. Before getting into the one on the right-hand side, look at the one to your left. Most of the time it will be less crowded, since most Magic Kingdom visitors automatically head for the one on the right.

● Wear your most comfortable shoes: You'll be spending a lot of time on your feet. (Note that no bare feet are permitted in the Magic Kingdom.)

● Don't take food into the Magic Kingdom. (There are, however, picnic facilities and lockers at the TTC.)

● Guests staying at WDW resorts can have packages delivered to their hotels free of charge.

EPCOT

Imagine a place whose entertainment inventory includes both a rich sampling of world cultures and a fun, enlightening journey to the technological frontier. You now have an inkling of the eye-opening and mind-broadening potential of Epcot.

Walt Disney suggested the idea back in October 1966: "Epcot will be an experimental prototype community of tomorrow that will take its cue from the new ideas and new technologies that are now emerging from the creative centers of American industry." It would never be completed, he said, but would "always be introducing and testing and demonstrating new materials and systems." Now, more than ever, Walt Disney's dream is a reality. Innoventions, an ever-evolving showplace of the near future, is Epcot's newest highlight.

The theme park, which opened in 1982, consists of two distinct areas of exploration: Future World and World Showcase. The former examines the newest and most intriguing ideas in science and technology in ways that make them seem not only comprehensible but also downright irresistible. The latter celebrates the diversity of the world's peoples, portraying a stunning array of nations with extraordinary devotion to detail.

Think of Epcot as Disney's playground for the curious and the thoughtful. The experiences it delivers—all of them wonders of the real world—never fail to amaze, delight, inspire, and (rest assured) entertain.

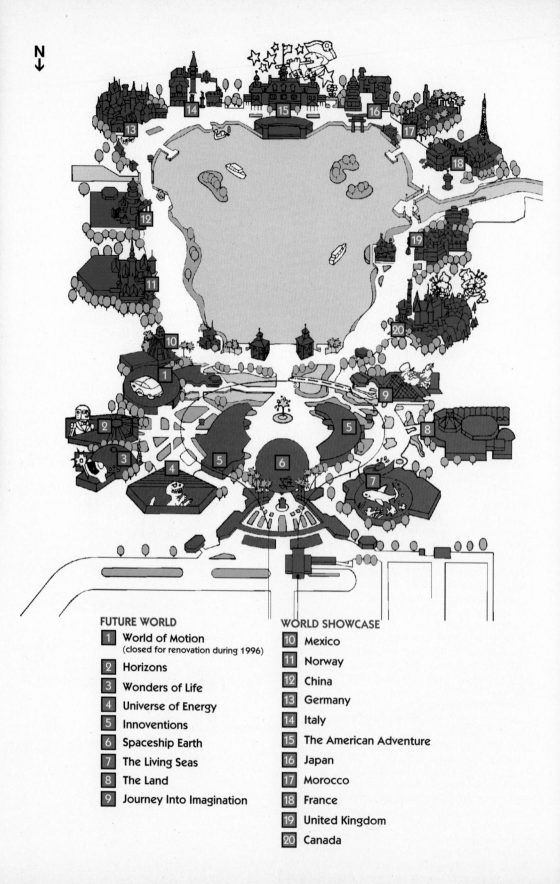

N
↓

FUTURE WORLD

1 World of Motion
(closed for renovation during 1996)

2 Horizons

3 Wonders of Life

4 Universe of Energy

5 Innoventions

6 Spaceship Earth

7 The Living Seas

8 The Land

9 Journey Into Imagination

WORLD SHOWCASE

10 Mexico

11 Norway

12 China

13 Germany

14 Italy

15 The American Adventure

16 Japan

17 Morocco

18 France

19 United Kingdom

20 Canada

Getting In & Around

TRANSPORTATION TO EPCOT: These two entertainment worlds are very easy to get to.

By car: Take Exit 26B off I-4 and follow the signs along Epcot Drive through Epcot's main gate. Epcot has a 9,000-space parking lot; daily parking costs $5. Parking is free for Walt Disney World resort guests with proper identification. Trams carry visitors from their parking space right to the ticket booths.

By monorail and bus: In general, allow about 30 minutes to get from one point to another, whether you go by bus or by monorail. Contact WDW Information (824-4321) before leaving your room to confirm the following routes and to check on the latest operating schedules. (Schedules coordinate with Epcot operating hours, so there's little chance of being stranded.)

- From the *Contemporary* resort, *Grand Floridian* resort, or *Polynesian* resort, take the local hotel monorail to the TTC, walk down the ramp and across the platform, and board the TTC-Epcot monorail.
- From the Magic Kingdom, take the express monorail to the TTC, then walk down the ramp and up the adjacent ramp to board the TTC-Epcot monorail.
- From the Disney-MGM Studios, take the bus directly to Epcot.
- From *Fort Wilderness*, take the bus to the TTC, then change to the TTC-Epcot monorail.
- From *Wilderness Lodge*, take the bus directly to Epcot.
- From *The Villas at The Disney Institute*, take the bus directly to Epcot.
- From Disney Village Hotel Plaza, take the bus directly to Epcot.
- From the *Caribbean Beach* resort, take the bus directly to Epcot.
- From the *Swan* and *Dolphin*, take a boat or walk directly to the World Showcase entrance.
- From the *Yacht Club* and *Beach Club* resorts, take a boat or walk to the World Showcase entrance.
- From *Port Orleans* and *Dixie Landings,* take the bus directly to Epcot.
- From the *Disney Vacation Club*, take the bus directly to Epcot.
- From *All-Star Sports* and *All-Star Music* resorts, take the bus directly to Epcot.

GETTING ORIENTED: Epcot is shaped something like a giant hourglass. Future World fills the northern bulb, while World Showcase occupies the southern half. In Future World, which is anchored on the north by the imposing "geosphere" known as Spaceship Earth, most pavilions are arranged around the bulb's perimeter. The exceptions are the two Innoventions buildings, which occupy the area at the center of the bulb. In World Showcase, pavilions are arranged around the edge of World Showcase Lagoon, with The American Adventure directly south of Spaceship Earth on the southernmost shore of the lake.

HOURS: Epcot is usually open from 9 A.M. to 9 P.M. Note that Future World hours are 9 A.M. to 7 P.M. (with the exception of Spaceship Earth and Innoventions, which stay open until 9 P.M.); World Showcase hours are 11 A.M. to 9 P.M. Hours may be extended during Presidents' week, spring school breaks, summer months, and certain holidays. Call 824-4321 for up-to-the-minute schedules.

GETTING AROUND: Five 66-foot water taxis, the *FriendShip* launches, shuttle guests back and forth across World Showcase Lagoon. Docks are located at both sides of World Showcase Plaza, in front of Germany, and near Morocco. Several double-decker buses, in styles once found all over New York City, London, and Berlin, can be boarded for a ride around the World Showcase Promenade, stopping at several points along the way.

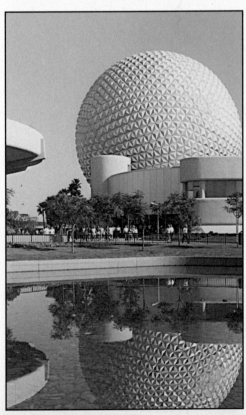

INFORMATION: Once inside Future World, visit Guest Relations, adjacent to Spaceship Earth, to use the computer terminals of the WorldKey Information Service there. Hosts and hostesses also are on hand. In World Showcase, visit the WorldKey satellite outside Germany.

EPCOT TIP BOARD: Be sure to check this board, set up in Innoventions Plaza in front of the fountain, for the latest waiting times for the most popular attractions. The board is updated often, so it's a great source of information about where the crowds are heading.

BABY CARE: Changing tables and facilities for nursing mothers can be found at Baby Services, near the Odyssey Center between World of Motion (in Future World) and Mexico (in World Showcase). Check at Guest Relations for operating hours. There also are changing tables in both men's and women's restrooms. Disposable diapers are kept behind the counter at many merchandise locations in both worlds; just ask.

CAMERA NEEDS: A large Camera Center is located on the west side of the Entrance Plaza. Video cameras may be rented here; film, photo supplies, and single-use cameras may be purchased; and two-hour film processing is available. There is a satellite camera shop in Journey Into Imagination. Film also is sold throughout World Showcase.

FIRST AID: Minor medical problems can be handled at First Aid, which is near the Odyssey Center, between the World of Motion (in Future World) and Mexico (in World Showcase).

VISITORS WITH DISABILITIES: Nearly all the attractions, shops, and restaurants in Epcot are completely barrier-free. Parking for guests with disabilities is available; inquire at the Auto Plaza. The monorail platform is accessible via elevator. Wheelchairs can be rented at the

Stroller and Wheelchair Rentals shop on the east side of the Entrance Plaza, at the Gift Stop on the west side, and at the International Gateway. The *Walt Disney World Guide for Guests With Disabilities* is available at Guest Relations. For hearing-impaired guests, Assistive Listening Devices, which amplify the audio in selected attractions, are available at Guest Relations. Guests must leave a $25 refundable deposit. Written scripts of all Epcot attractions also are available. For sight-impaired guests, special complimentary tour cassettes are available at Guest Relations. A refundable $25 deposit is required for the cassette player.

LOCKERS: These can be found at the Bus Information Center in the bus parking lot, just outside the Entrance Plaza, and in a small area on the west side of the plaza, underneath Spaceship Earth. There also are lockers at the International Gateway.

LOST AND FOUND: Located on the west side of the Entrance Plaza.

MEMORABILIA: Gateway Gifts, located alongside Spaceship Earth in the Entrance Plaza, Centorium in Future World's Innoventions, and Disney Traders in World Showcase Plaza are the three main sources for Epcot souvenirs. The Gift Stop and the Stroller and Wheelchair Rentals shop near the Entrance Plaza are good shopping spots, too. Souvenirs of the participating nations are found in each World Showcase pavilion and at Disney Traders in World Showcase Plaza.

PACKAGE PICKUP: Cumbersome or heavy purchases can be transported free of charge (by Disney hosts or hostesses) to this small office on the west side of the Entrance Plaza for later pickup. Ask your salesperson to arrange this service.

PETS: No pets are permitted in Epcot, but there is the Pet Care Kennel just east of the Entrance Plaza. *Do not leave pets in the car.* It is against the law in Florida. The cost for boarding pets is $6 per day per pet; overnight stays cost $11 (or $9 for WDW resort guests).

STROLLER AND WHEELCHAIR RENTALS: Available in the shop of that name on the east side of the Entrance Plaza, and at the International Gateway. Wheelchairs also are available at the Gift Stop. Replacement strollers and wheelchairs are available at the International Gateway. Remember to keep your rental receipt; it can be used on the same day in the Magic Kingdom, at the Disney-MGM Studios, or again in Epcot should you leave and return at a later hour.

MONEY MATTERS: Currency exchange can be handled at the Guest Relations window or at the American Express Travel Office on the

ADMISSION PRICES*

ONE-DAY TICKET
(Restricted to use in Epcot only.)

Adult	$ 39.27
Child**	$ 31.80

FOUR-DAY VALUE PASS
(Valid for one day in each park, plus one optional day in the park of your choice. Includes use of WDW transportation system.)

Adult	$131.44
Child**	$102.82

FOUR-DAY PARK HOPPER PASS
(Valid in all three parks for four days and includes use of WDW transportation system.)

Adult	$145.22
Child**	$115.54

FIVE-DAY WORLD HOPPER PASS
(Valid in all three parks for five days, includes use of WDW transportation system, and allows admission to Typhoon Lagoon, Blizzard Beach, River Country, Discovery Island, and Pleasure Island for up to seven days from the first use of the pass.)

Adult	$197.16
Child**	$156.88

LENGTH OF STAY PASS
(Available to WDW resort guests only. Valid in all three parks, Typhoon Lagoon, Blizzard Beach, River Country, Discovery Island, and Pleasure Island for the duration of stay and includes use of WDW transportation system.)

Length of Stay	Adult	Child**
4 days	$166.42	$131.44
5 days	$193.98	$153.70
6 days	$217.30	$172.78
7 days	$241.68	$191.86
8 days	$259.70	$206.70
9 days	$277.72	$220.48
10 days	$288.32	$230.02

The cost of a **THEME PARK ANNUAL PASS** is $242.74 for adults and $210.94 for children; renewals are $221.54 for adults and $189.74 for children. The cost of a **PREMIUM ANNUAL PASS** is $338.14 for adults and $296.80 for children; renewals are $306.34 for adults and $270.30 for children; in addition to the three theme parks, it includes admission to Typhoon Lagoon, Blizzard Beach, River Country, and Discovery Island.

Note: Multi-day passes need not be used on consecutive days.

These prices were correct at press time, but may change during 1996.

*The prices quoted include sales tax.

**3 through 9 years of age; children under 3 are free

west side of the Entrance Plaza. ATMs are located on the east side of the Entrance Plaza and at the International Gateway. Credit cards (American Express, Visa, MasterCard, and The Disney Credit Card) are accepted in shops and restaurants (except at fast-food locations, where you must pay with cash or traveler's checks only).

ADMISSION: Tickets and passes are available for one, four, and five days. The Disney organization defines a ticket as admission for one day only; other forms of admission media (for longer periods) are called passes. One-day tickets may be used at the Magic Kingdom, Epcot, or the Disney-MGM Studios, but not at more than one site on the same day. Four-Day Value Passes may be used for one day in each park, plus one optional day in the park of your choice, but not at more than one park on the same day. Four-Day Park Hopper Passes and Five-Day World Hopper Passes can be used at all three parks on the same day. Unlike one-day tickets, all multi-day passes also include use of the transportation system inside Walt Disney World. The Five-Day World Hopper Pass also allows admission to Typhoon Lagoon, Blizzard Beach, River Country, Discovery Island, and Pleasure Island for a seven-day period beginning with the first use of the pass. Guests staying at Walt Disney World resorts can purchase a pass valid for the length of their stay. The Length of Stay Pass offers savings over other passes, and includes unlimited admission to the Magic Kingdom, Epcot, the Disney-MGM Studios, Typhoon Lagoon, Blizzard Beach, River Country, Discovery Island, and Pleasure Island for the duration of your stay. Cash, traveler's checks, personal checks (with proper ID), American Express, Visa, Master-Card, and the The Disney Credit Card can be used to pay for all admission media. When you purchase a Four-Day Park Hopper Pass, a Five-Day World Hopper Pass, or a Length of Stay Pass, you must have your photo mounted on the pass to validate it. Pass photos can be taken at the Transportation and Ticket Center and at the entrances to the Magic Kingdom, Epcot, and the Disney-MGM Studios. Multi-day passes do not have to be used on consecutive days.

Passes may be purchased at all WDW resorts (by WDW resort guests), at the entrances to the theme parks, at the Orlando or at The Disney Store.

Passes by mail: Send a check or money order payable to Walt Disney World Company in the exact amount plus $2 for handling to:

Walt Disney World
Box 10,030; Lake Buena Vista, FL 32830-0030
Attention: Ticket Mail Order

Remember to include your return address. Allow at least three to four weeks for ticket requests to be processed.

Future World

A mere listing of the basic themes covered by the Future World pavilions—agriculture, communications, the ocean, energy, health, and imagination—tends to sound a tad academic, and perhaps even a little forbidding. But when these serious topics are presented with that special Disney flair, they become part of an experience that ranks among Walt Disney World's most exciting.

Some of these subjects are explored in the course of lively and unusual Disney "adventures," involving a whole arsenal of remarkable motion pictures, special effects, and Audio-Animatronics figures so lifelike that it is hard to remain unmoved. And Future World's newest attraction, Innoventions, offers a glimpse and an invitation to sample the near future of technology. The basic elements of Future World are appealing in their own right, from the palm-dotted Entrance Plaza and the massive buildings of Innoventions to the stupendous fountain just past Spaceship Earth and the many-faceted "geosphere" that has become the universal symbol of Epcot.

There is so much to see and enjoy that it's hard to know just what to do first. Many guests simply stop at Spaceship Earth on their way into Epcot and proceed to wander at random from one pavilion to the next through the morning. As a result, many of the pavilions are frustratingly crowded in the morning—especially Spaceship Earth, which has its largest crowds before lunch.

A wise alternative is to choose two or three pavilions from those described below, and then to head for World Showcase as soon as it opens at 11 A.M., moving clockwise around the lagoon on one day of your visit and counterclockwise on the next. Then in the afternoon, when the majority of guests have shifted over to World Showcase, return to Future World. Many of the pavilions have far fewer visitors during the late afternoon hours until Future World closes at 7 P.M. Innoventions is not only a fascinating spot to pass the exceptionally busy hours after lunch, but also a cool refuge when high temperatures prevail outdoors. And although queues can be found during peak seasons at Journey Into Imagination, The Land, and Wonders of Life throughout most of the late morning and afternoon, the period from late afternoon through closing at 7 P.M. is usually less hectic. Keep in mind that certain Future World pavilions—Innoventions and Spaceship Earth—stay open until World Showcase closes, usually 9 P.M.

Getting Oriented

As a guest crosses the enormous Entrance Plaza, the gleaming silver ball straight ahead (and facing south) is Spaceship Earth. Innoventions is housed in the two large crescent-shaped buildings that flank the large fountain just past Spaceship Earth. Universe of Energy, Wonders of Life, Horizons, and World of Motion lie to the left (east) of Innoventions; Journey Into Imagination, The Land, and The Living Seas are located to the right (west) of Innoventions. The World Showcase section of Epcot surrounds the shoreline of the large World Showcase Lagoon. Note that World of Motion will be closed during 1996 for renovation, and Horizons and Universe of Energy also are expected to be renovated at some point during 1996. Call 824-4321 to find out which pavilions will be closed during your visit.

Future World pavilions are described here as a visitor encounters them while moving counterclockwise (from right around to the left, that's west to east around the area).

Be aware that the two distinct worlds that comprise Epcot keep different hours. Future World usually is open from 9 A.M. to 7 P.M.; and World Showcase generally is open from 11 A.M. to 9 P.M. Exceptions are Spaceship Earth and Innoventions, which stay open until World Showcase closes. Hours may vary, depending on the season.

Spaceship Earth

As it looms impressively just above the earth, this great faceted silver geosphere—visible on a clear day from an airplane flying along either Florida coast—looks a little bit like the gigantic spaceship in *Close Encounters of the Third Kind* ready to blast off. It appears large from a distance, and seems even more immense when viewed from directly underneath. It's no surprise that most visitors simply stop beneath it and gawk. The show inside, which explores the continuing search by human beings for ever more efficient means of communication, remains one of Epcot's most visually compelling.

Weighing 16 million pounds, measuring 165 feet in diameter and 180 feet in height, and encompassing 2.2 million cubic feet of space, this geosphere is held aloft by six legs supported by pylons sunk 100 feet into the ground. The distinctive sheen of its covering derives from a sort of quarter-inch-thick sandwich made of two anodized aluminum faces and a polyethylene core. This sheath is made up of 954 triangular panels, not all of equal size or shape.

A common misconception about Spaceship Earth is that it is a geodesic dome. Not so. The designers had to make up the word *geosphere* because the structure is unlike any other pre-existing building. A geodesic dome is composed of only half a sphere, while Spaceship Earth is almost completely round. In fact, even the word geosphere is something of a misnomer. This extraordinarily large Disney creation is not a perfect sphere; the steelworkers' requirements dictated its slightly uneven dimensions. Presented by AT&T.

SPACESHIP EARTH RIDE: The noted science fiction writer Ray Bradbury, together with a number of consultants and advisers from the Smithsonian Institution, the Los Angeles area's prestigious Huntington Library, University of Southern California, and the University of Chicago (among others), collaborated with Disney designers in developing this memorable 15-minute journey. It begins in an inky black time tunnel complete with a musty smell that suggests the ages, and continues through history from the days of Cro-Magnon man (30,000 or 40,000 years ago) to the future.

En route, an Egyptian temple shows off the pictorial representations of words and sounds known as hieroglyphics, which were first used around 3,000 B.C., and hieratic writing, a form of script used to write on papyrus. A Phoenician scene set in the ninth century B.C. acknowledges civilization's debt to those tireless traders who introduced a 22-character alphabet (based on sounds) that put written communication, once the province of the intelligentsia alone, within the grasp of the masses. The Romans' system of roads, the Islamic empire, the efforts of 11th- and 12th-century Benedictine monks to handcopy religious and classical manuscripts, the Gutenberg press, the Renaissance in Italy, and a number of the 20th century's inventions are all represented, and in most cases it's not necessary to be a history scholar to understand why. The Greek theater scene, whose meaning here may not be as widely understood as it should be, reminds viewers that it was the Greeks who refined the alphabet (by the addition of vowels) and then went on to use the language so expressively. Then, as

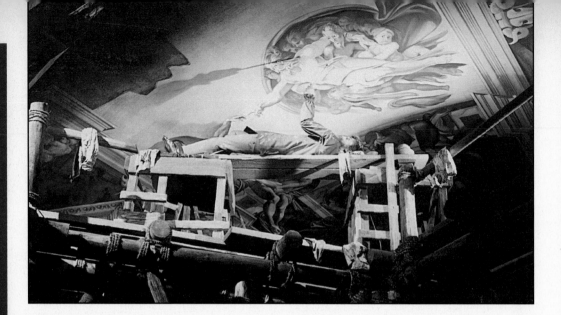

now, theater was an important means of examining and transmitting the moral and social questions of the time.

The attraction features some remarkable special effects, such as the flickering candles in the scene where a monk (himself crafted with such precision and authenticity as to appear to be breathing) has nodded off, and the smell of smoke coming from the fall of Rome.

Every scene is executed in exquisite detail. The symbols on the wall of that Egyptian temple really are hieroglyphics, and the content of the letter being dictated by the pharaoh was excerpted from a missive actually received by an agent of a ruler of the period. The actor in the Greek theater scene is delivering lines from Sophocles' *Oedipus Rex*. In the scene depicting the fall of Rome, the graffiti reproduces markings from the walls of Pompeii. In the Islamic scene, the quadrant—an instrument used in astronomy and navigation—is a copy of one from the tenth century. The type on Johannes Gutenberg's press actually moves, and the page that the celebrated 15th-century printer is examining is a replica of one from a Bible in the collection of the above-mentioned Huntington Library. In the Renaissance scene, the book being read is Virgil's *Aeneid*; the musical instruments in that scene are a lute and a *lyra da braccio*, both replicas of period instruments. During the 20th-century scenes, the steam-powered press is a reproduction of one that had been developed by William Bullock around 1863, notable because it used paper in continuous rolls rather than individual sheets.

Some visitors wonder as to the identity of the excerpts from the radio and television shows broadcast in this area. Take note: The former include "The Lone Ranger," "The Shadow," a commentary by Walter Winchell, and the Joe Louis–Max Schmeling 1938 rematch. It's the first round, and Schmeling, who had inflicted Joe Louis' first loss in a 1936 12th-round K.O., is on the mat. The ref-

eree is counting—and the crowd is going wild. Among the television programs are Walter Cronkite's reports from the March 10, 1964, New Hampshire Republican primary, Walt Disney introducing "The Wonderful World of Color," Ed Sullivan and the Harlem Globetrotters, the Colts versus Browns NFL championship game (1964), and "Ozzie and Harriet," featuring David and Ricky Nelson. Film buffs may recognize clips from the movies *Girl Shy* with Harold Lloyd (1924), *Top Hat* with Fred Astaire and Ginger Rogers (1935), and *20,000 Leagues Under the Sea* (1954).

All these sights are enough to keep necks craning and heads turning as the "time machines" wend their way upward. The most dazzling scene is the ride's new finale, when the audience is placed in the heart of a communications revolution amid interactive global networks that tie all the peoples of the world together. Magical special effects, animated sets, and audience-enclosing laser beams are used to create exciting visual sensations. Highlights include high-definition TV and virtual reality classrooms of the future. In one scene, an American boy and a Japanese girl exchange experiences via video telephone.

In the Global Neighborhood exhibit at the end of the journey, guests can directly interact with such emerging technologies as voice recognition, video telephones, and the information highway.

Note: The lines for this attraction are usually longest during the morning hours, and at their shortest just before park closing time.

GATEWAY GIFTS AND CAMERA CENTER: These two shops are located near the entrance to Spaceship Earth. The former sells Epcot souvenirs—T-shirts, mugs, toys, etc.—as well as suntan lotion, tissues, and the like. Film and various other Kodak products, including single-use cameras, are sold at the Camera Center. Video cameras may be rented here, and same-day film processing is available.

Innoventions

Imagine being able to get your hands on technological goodies fresh off the drawing board—gadgets that will one day change the way you live and work. At Innoventions, you can see, touch, and test products so new they won't be on the market for several months or years. The pavilion offers a fun, unintimidating environment where you needn't know how to program your VCR to be able to try out super computers, see a fully automated home in action, or take a shopping spree on the information superhighway.

Within the 100,000-square-foot area, formerly occupied by Communicore East and West, ever-changing exhibits are presented by major manufacturers including IBM, AT&T, Apple, LEGO Dacta, General Electric, General Motors, Motorola, Sega, Honeywell, and more. Computers, toys, games, phones, musical instruments, television sets, stoves, refrigerators, and even toilets are among the wide variety of products on display. Exhibits are constantly changing, making Walt Disney's original dream for Epcot a reality. Representatives from each manufacturer are on hand to answer questions from curious—or even skeptical—visitors. At some exhibits, visitors also can register via computer to receive additional information at home.

The entire area has a new look. The former monochromatic circle passage to Epcot's

EPCOT

pavilions is now filled with color, light, an assortment of spinning mobiles, neon stripes, and sidewalks glistening with fiber-optic lighting effects.

A good place to start a tour of Innoventions is at a multimedia show starring Bill Nye, the Science Guy, host of the popular television show. Bill Nye, seen on screens, offers an entertaining explanation and overview of the concept and purpose behind Innoventions.

Most of the areas are divided by company. Sega occupies the largest space, where kids love to try out the more than 140 new and proposed video games.

Family PC sponsors a new exhibit, showcasing multimedia technologies. Here, families get a chance to try the latest computer hardware and software. Highlights for kids include a Winnie the Pooh animated storybook.

IBM's Thinkplace features the opportunity to take an electronic "field trip," complete with sound and video, to just about anywhere in the world. Guests can surf the Internet on Prodigy and be among the first to try out IBM's newest technologies.

The LEGO display features computer-endowed LEGO blocks, sure to be a highlight with kids. They can construct buildings and learn about robotics at this spot.

For an initial lesson about the information superhighway, stop by the Oracle area. There guests can find out how they will be able to access motion pictures, remote shopping, and a vast library of information services through electronic networks.

General Electric's display features a jet engine, medical imaging systems, and an opportunity to be "interviewed" by Jay Leno.

At the AT&T area, a prototype model for a wrist telephone is on display. Other technologies include video phones, the Picasso system for transmitting voice and video images over the same phone line, and the first demonstrations of AT&T's PersonaLink Services. Also, AT&T has created a testing laboratory here, staffed by top Bell Labs

GUEST RELATIONS

Located adjacent to Spaceship Earth, this is not only the principal source of Epcot information, but it also is the spot to make dinner reservations via the easy-to-use touch-sensitive TV screens. For more specific details on making these reservations, see page 223. When the terminals are not being used to arrange tables for dinner, they can be used to get an overall picture of Epcot, to learn about each pavilion in considerable detail, and to discover nearly everything else that a guest could conceivably want to know about Epcot. If the system's electronic A-to-Z index to shops, restaurants, attractions, and services does not answer a question, it's possible to communicate with a specially trained human host or hostess, who will be able to hear and see the querying guest with the aid of a microphone and video camera unobtrusively placed adjacent to the screen. These hosts and hostesses also manage the message service for Epcot guests. Hosts and hostesses also keep records of any lost children who may be at Baby Services at any given time.

researchers. Guests will be able to help develop future technology by sharing their ideas with the researchers in focus groups.

Honeywell's Comfortville exhibit features products designed to make homes more energy efficient. Displays include motorized windows that close automatically when it rains and zoned climate-control systems.

At the General Motors display, guests get a preview of Impact, an experimental electric car. Also featured is the Ultralight, an alternative-fuel vehicle constructed with lightweight, super-strength materials. The Ultralight was seen in the movie *Demolition Man*.

Another interesting stop is the Hammacher Schlemmer display, where guests see how Hammacher Schlemmer tests new products for usefulness, wearability, and uniqueness. Guests can experience the most sophisticated application of interactive shopping under development. It is so advanced that it will not be on the market for several years.

Discover magazine holds an annual awards program at Epcot to honor the most innovative minds in science. Guests can learn about the technologies developed by finalists and winners in a permanent display area. The inventors may even appear to demonstrate their creations.

Among the other highlighted technologies on display at press time were electric-powered automobiles, voice-activated appliances, wrist telephones, virtual reality, wide-screen high-definition television, home security systems, a piano with a computer disk drive to record and play back, CD-ROM products, interactive computer and television games, and many more.

The **House of Innoventions**, presented by Masco, is an entertaining exhibit. In a sample kitchen, living room, bathroom, and bedroom, guests see the latest ideas to help make home life a little easier and more relaxing by fully automating some of our daily tasks.

Eclectronics houses a never-ending variety of the newest in consumer electronics. The area is completely interactive and allows guests to try out products newly released to the marketplace. Eclectronics is designed in a whimsical way—the idea being to make electronic goods less intimidating to the public. Leading the way is Alectronic, a see-through Audio-Animatronics figure that gives regular demonstrations to show guests how the technology actually works. The newest addition to this area is Info Byte's Virtual Museum, which takes guests through St. Peter's Basilica in Italy, as well as other places that are not easily accessible in real life, including recreated or torn-down buildings.

Perhaps the most exciting part of Innoventions is the **Walt Disney Imagineering Laboratory**. For the first time guests can actually see Imagineers at work on their latest attraction. As we went to press, an advanced form of virtual reality was being created and tested for a future Flying Carpet attraction. Based on

the animated film *Aladdin*, the Flying Carpet will combine animation with the most advanced computer graphics and interactive video techniques. Guests tour the lab before four "pilots" are chosen to test the ride. Wearing virtual-reality helmets, the brave souls climb on the carpet and holding onto handles, each pilot dives, turns, and soars through the animated city of Agrabah by twisting the carpet fringe. Every turn of the head makes the realistic scene even more exciting. Those not flying watch the action on four television screens to see what each pilot is up to.

Another area of interest at Innoventions is the two-story **Discovery Center**, a resource facility for teachers and anyone interested in learning more about the topics presented at Epcot. Complimentary discussion guides and resource materials are available. This area also serves as an information and resource center to answer any lingering questions you have about individual attractions and subjects showcased at Epcot. On the first floor is Field Trips, a shop featuring educational products of special interest to teachers.

There also are several restaurants and an espresso bar and bakery in the Innoventions complex. See the *Good Meals, Great Times* chapter for details.

CENTORIUM: This large, sleek shop stocks a vast selection of Epcot and Disney character memorabilia and souvenirs—watches, books, key chains, pennants, T-shirts, license plates, pencils, hats, visors, and much more. In addition, there are all kinds of items related to other areas of Future World, such as Figment dolls. There is a large selection of Disney-themed sports apparel and children's clothing. Youngsters particularly enjoy the glassed-in elevator.

The Living Seas

A trip four fathoms deep into the Caribbean Sea awaits visitors here. The Living Seas is the largest facility ever dedicated to mankind's relationship with the ocean and was designed by the Disney Imagineers, the company's creative design organization, in cooperation with a board of some of the world's most distinguished oceanographic experts and scientists.

At the entrance to The Living Seas is a stylized rockwork marquee that suggests a natural coastline with waves cascading into tidal pools. Upon entering, there's a 125-foot-long sea mural that leads to a display depicting the technological advances in undersea exploration, from Leonardo da Vinci's sketches of underwater breathing devices and submersibles to photos of John Lethbridge's diving barrel and Frederic de Drieberg's 1809 breathing device. Also featured is the diving suit from Walt Disney's classic film *20,000 Leagues Under the Sea*, and the actual 11-foot-long model *Nautilus* used in the movie. Next, as part of the introduction to The Living Seas, is a 2½-minute multimedia presentation that salutes the pioneers of ocean research, beginning with early ships, diving bells, submarines, and aqualungs. The show also features a seven-minute special effects film that attempts to demonstrate the critical role of the ocean as a source of energy, minerals, and protein. Some scenes were filmed in very remote parts of the world.

There's a ride through a Caribbean coral reef, housed in a huge tank 200 feet in diameter and 27 feet deep, plus Sea Base Alpha, where hands-on activities, underwater movies, video monitors, and the opportunity to communicate with the divers in the tank are sure to prolong visitors' stays. The *Coral Reef*

chickens' laying pellets, a complete amino-acid solution, and a vitamin B-complex solution, all held together by dental plaster. Yum! Following the three-minute ride, guests are conveniently deposited at the Visitors Center of Sea Base Alpha.

SEA BASE ALPHA: This proto-type undersea research facility, set up on two levels connected by escalators, includes a visitors center and six modules, each dedicated to a specific subject. One module focuses on ocean ecosystems and shows various forms of adaptation, including camouflage, symbiosis, and bioluminescence. A 6,000-gallon tank displays another coral reef where Bermuda morays, barracuda, and bonnethead sharks swim about. Another module is dedicated to the study of porpoises and manatees. A large holding tank features a step-in port, where guests can see the mammals up close. At another Sea Base Alpha station, a delightful show stars an Audio-Animatronics submersible named Jason who describes the history of robotics and their use in underwater exploration to visitors. In the same area, guests can try on a cut-away JIM suit, and test its maneuverability by doing a series of tasks as part of a game. There also are video screens around the Sea Base where visitors can test and expand their knowledge of oceanography.

SEA BASE CONCOURSE: Adjacent to the six modules, the concourse features three displays. The floor-to-ceiling diver lock-out chamber is where the crew enters and exits the ocean environment. Visitors can see the divers enter the chamber, ascend, and disappear through the ceiling of the concourse. A full-size mock-up of the latest one-person submersible vehicle, the Deep Rover, is suspended from the mezzanine of the concourse. The Deep Rover is capable of descending more than 3,000 feet below the ocean's surface.

restaurant offers fresh seafood in a setting where diners can look out at the coral reef through acrylic windows 18 feet high and 8 inches thick. Tables are arranged on tiers so that all patrons have an unobstructed view. Presented by United Technologies.

CARIBBEAN CORAL REEF RIDE: To reach the two-passenger sea cabs that make the trip to the coral reef, visitors enter "hydrolators," elevatorlike capsules that actually descend about an inch while creating the illusion of diving deep under the sea. The man-made reef exists in a 5.7 million-gallon tank where more than 200 varieties of sea life, ranging from tiny crustaceans to large predators, live in a simulated environment that accurately recreates the chemistry and life-support ecosystems of the Caribbean Sea. Among the 5,000 inhabitants are sea bass, parrot fish, puffers, barracuda, butterfly fish, angelfish, sharks, croakers, hog snappers, dolphins, and diamond rays.

In addition to the vast array of sea life and vegetation, guests also get to see scuba divers testing and demonstrating the newest diving gear and underwater monitoring equipment as they carry on training experiments with dolphins. Wireless radios allow the divers to talk to onlookers and explain their work. Other undersea attractions include a diver in a JIM suit, the latest in atmospheric diving-wear technology (at Sea Base Alpha, guests have the chance to try one on personally), two one-person submarines, and two mini-robotic submersibles.

Scientists had to develop foods to simulate the taste, chemistry, and nutritional value of natural coral. The resulting meal for parrot fish, for example, consists of dry dog food,

WHERE TO EAT IN EPCOT

For all the details on all the restaurants in Epcot—including both those in Future World and World Showcase—plus information about how to obtain restaurant reservations, see the *Good Meals, Great Times* chapter that begins on page 209.

ENTERTAINMENT

There are many shows and musical performances during the course of each day at Epcot. In addition to the larger shows that are described below, other entertainment includes musical performances in Future World by the Future Corps. In World Showcase, there usually is entertainment at each pavilion, presented by natives of each country. Performers vary, but you might find oompah music in Germany, Chinese dancers, a mariachi band in Mexico, Japanese music and dancing, live theater in the United Kingdom, bagpipers and a brass band in Canada, and much more. These performers are described in more detail in each country's description in the World Showcase section of this chapter. The America Gardens Theatre at The American Adventure also features entertainment. Always be sure to check the entertainment schedule for current offerings.

ILLUMINATIONS: A spectacular display of lasers, fireworks, and dancing fountains to the accompaniment of symphonic music is one of the highlights of any Epcot visit. The extravaganza is scheduled nightly at closing time throughout the year. Check for exact times upon arriving at the park.

WHERE TO FIND THE CHARACTERS: The Disney characters can be found in a variety of spots around the park. Dine with the characters for breakfast, lunch, or dinner at the *Garden Grill* restaurant in The Land pavilion in Future World. Reservations are required. (See the *Good Meals, Great Times* chapter for details.) In addition, the characters sometimes appear in international costumes and entertain along the World Showcase Promenade during the day. The American Adventure hosts characters from Disney's animated film *Pocahontas*. Check your entertainment schedule for times and places to find the characters.

The Land

Occupying six acres, this enormous sky-lighted pavilion examines the nature of one of everybody's favorite topics—food. A film, *Circle of Life,* uses characters from *The Lion King* to deliver an entertaining yet inspirational message about mankind and the world around us. A boat ride explores farming in the past and future, including a look at ongoing experiments in raising fish. Guided tours give interested visitors the chance to learn more about the experimental agricultural techniques actually being practiced in the pavilion and nearby greenhouses, and to get ideas about applications in the garden. In addition, the subject of nutrition is touched upon in one of Future World's wackiest attractions, a musical show called Food Rocks.

Since this also is the home of two of Epcot's most interesting eating spots—the *Garden Grill* and the *Sunshine Season Food Fair*—The Land is understandably popular. During peak seasons, lengthy queues do build up for the boat ride and the *Circle of Life* film. The best plan is to visit the pavilion first thing in the morning, have a quick breakfast at one of the food stands in the food court, and perhaps make reservations for the character lunch in *Garden Grill.* Or wait until later in the afternoon, when many people have left Future World for World Showcase. Count on spending about an hour at The Land, or longer if plans include eating here. Presented by Nestlé USA.

LIVING WITH THE LAND: This 13½-minute boat ride through the rain forest and greenhouses of this pavilion has been spruced up with a dramatic opening storm scene. Guests sail through tropical swamps, prairie grain fields, and a family farm. As the boat passes through each amazingly realistic setting, the guide offers a commentary on mankind's ongoing struggle to cultivate and live in harmony with the land. Note some of the details that make each setting so convincing, such as water dripping from leaves in the rain forest, sand blowing over the desert, and light flickering from the TV set in the window of the farmhouse. In the next segment, guests enter a fantastic living-plant research laboratory-solarium. Here, the earth's major food crops, fruits, and vegetables are being grown in high-tech research projects along with rare new crops that may someday help meet the earth's ever-growing dietary needs. The guide on each boat gives an interesting and educational talk on the crops being grown. Also of interest are the experiments being conducted to explore the possibilities of raising fish like other farm products, and the Desert Farm area where plants receive nutrients through a drip irrigation system that delivers just the right amount of water, and no more—important in an arid climate.

As fantastic and unreal as they appear, the plants on view in the experimental greenhouses are all living. In contrast, those in the biomes (ecological communities) were manufactured in Disney studios out of flexible, lightweight plastic that simulates the cellulose found in real trees. The trunks and branches were molded from live specimens; the majestic sycamore in the farmhouse's front yard, for example, duplicates one that stands outside a Burbank, California, car wash. Hundreds of thousands of polyethylene leaves, made in Hong Kong, were then snapped on. These are fire retardant, as are the blades of grass, which are made of glass fibers implanted into rubber mats. In the South American rain forest scene, the water on the leaves and trunks is supplied by a special drip system that provides a constant flow of moisture.

FOOD ROCKS: Classic rock and roll songs have been humorously altered to deliver a nutritional message at this 15-minute mock rock concert. The introduction, presented by a "heavy metal" group—three four-foot kitchen utensils atop a cartoon stove—perform Queen's "Bohemian Rhapsody" with new lyrics. The show is set in a kitchen of cartoon-ish proportion and life-size characters make this an entertaining show. The show is hosted by Füd Wrapper, inspired by rapper Tone Loc. He steers the audience through the kitchen, performing and introducing the guests.

The refrigerator door opens and the whole stage is filled with eerie blue light and fog. A group emerges led by a milk carton wearing

dark glasses. They are identified as The Refrigerator Police, and they perform a parody of The Police's hit "Every Breath You Take." The new words come with a message: "Every bite you take, every cake you bake, every milk you shake, every egg you break, will be part of you."

Other musical guests include the Peach Boys, an apple, pear, orange, and peach who harmonize a rendition of "Good Vibrations" called "Good Nutrition;" Pita Gabriel sings to the tune of "Sledgehammer;" and The Sole of Rock 'n' Roll, a fish inspired by Cher sings a new version of the "Shoop Shoop Song." Richard (Little Richard), Neil Moussaka, Chubby Cheddar, and Get-the-Point-Sisters also make humorous appearances.

It's interesting to note that Tone Loc, Chubby Checker, Neil Sedaka, Little Richard, and The Pointer Sisters actually recorded the parodies of their music. In the pre-show area, there are murals featuring fun food facts, three-dimensional food pyramids, and inter-active "meal kabobs" where guests can create their own nutritional menus. Six giant "smell boxes" open to reveal the aromas garlic, chocolate, coffee, bacon, orange, and seafood. Don't miss the colorful carpeting with its pattern of forks, knives, and spoons.

CIRCLE OF LIFE: This 20-minute film uses animation and live footage to illustrate some of the dangers to the environment, as well as potential solutions. Presented as a fable featuring *The Lion King* favorites Simba, Timon, and Pumbaa, the film takes an optimistic approach to a serious subject. *Circle of Life* is shown in the 428-seat Harvest Theater (near The Land's entrance) on a 23- by 60-foot screen. It opens with Simba, king of the Pridelands, beside a water hole where he is startled by the shout of "Timber!" and is drenched by the splash of a fallen tree. The culprits are none other than his friends, Timon and Pumbaa, who are clearing the savanna for the development of the Hakuna Matata Lakeside Village. Simba seizes the opportunity to tell the tale, passed on to him by his father, of a creature who sometimes forgets that everything is connected in the great Circle of Life. That creature, of course, is man. Simba's lessons are driven home by motion-picture views of man's mistreatment of the land. Many of these live-action shots, filmed on location throughout the world, are taken from the film previously shown in this theater. In this context, however, the shots take on a new tone. The overall effect is a nice mix of entertainment and an important message about being environmentally responsible.

GREENHOUSE TOUR: For guests who are interested in a more detailed look at the growing areas at The Land, guided, 45-minute tours take place throughout the day. The tour travels through four themed greenhouses where plants are grown hydroponically (without soil). Different areas of the greenhouses showcase pioneering research projects undertaken in cooperation with NASA and the U.S. Department of Agriculture. Highlights include two laboratories added in 1994 as part of the tenth anniversary renovation of The Land. In the biotechnology lab, researchers use tissue culture and genetic engineering to enhance plant life. The integrated pest management lab offers a look at the science of controlling insect and disease pests in plants. Because this walking tour is an expanded version of The Living with the Land boat ride, the ride is a suggested prerequisite. Reservations, which are required, must be made in person early on the day of the tour, at the Podium in front of the Green Thumb Emporium. Cost is $5 for adults and $3 for children ages three to nine.

GREEN THUMB EMPORIUM: This little shop between the *Sunshine Season Food Fair* and Food Rocks stocks merchandise such as hydroponic plants, seeds, books, topiaries, and kitchen accessories, including magnetized plastic stick-ons to embellish the front of a refrigerator, place mats, and more.

Journey Into Imagination

The oddly shaped glass pyramids that house Journey Into Imagination (as you face World Showcase Lagoon and then straight ahead to your right) are striking, but they pale by comparison with the experiences inside—which are among the most exciting at Epcot. Dreamfinder, a jolly, red-headed, professorial figure, who sports a carrot-colored beard and is accompanied by a purple baby dragon called Figment, is only one of the pavilion's delights. He appears in person outside and again inside when he escorts guests through the imagination world during a 14-minute ride.

There's also a dazzling 3-D movie, called Honey, I Shrunk the Audience. Not to mention the electronic fun house known as the Image Works. Or the quirky fountains outside—the Jellyfish Fountains that spurt streams of water that spread out at the top, look like their namesake sea creature for an instant, and then fall back to earth; or the Leap Frog Fountains, which send out smooth streams of water that arc from one garden plot to another in the most astonishing fashion.

Plant lovers will recognize the sculpted trees in this garden as *podocarpus*—the same type that is planted in many other locations (but pruned to many different shapes) throughout Epcot.

Count on spending an hour and 15 minutes at the very least at this pavilion—two hours wouldn't be too long at all. During peak seasons, the queue outside seems to be longest from about 10 A.M. to noon and remains fairly lengthy throughout most of the day. Early mornings and late evenings arethe least congested times to visit. Presented by Kodak.

JOURNEY INTO IMAGINATION RIDE: It is here that Dreamfinder creates Figment out of a lizard's body, a crocodile's nose, a steer's horns, two big yellow eyes, two small wings, and a pinch of childish delight—and commences the visitor's journey into the world of imagination.

First-timers may not realize that the 14-minute ride doesn't present a random assortment of scenes that are handsome and scary by turns, but rather an organized exploration of how the imagination works and the areas of life in which it functions.

First there is a visit to the Dreamport, the area of the mind to which the senses are constantly sending data to be stored for later use by the imagination. Subsequent scenes depict the way imagination suffuses the worlds of the visual and performing arts, of literature, and of science and technology. In the course of all this, laser beams dance, lightning crackles, and letters pour out of a giant typewriter like notes from an organ. The images are as fanciful as the imagination itself.

It's interesting to note that the iridescent painting in progress on the wall in the visual arts scene—a so-called "polage" produced by refracting light through polarized filters—is the largest of its kind anywhere. When you see flashing lights (about three-quarters of the way through the ride), be sure to sit up straight and smile—your picture is being taken. You'll see your photo at the end of the ride.

IMAGE WORKS: It's a rare Image Works visitor who doesn't experience at least some of the emotion felt by one four-year-old girl who cried every time her parents tried to take her home. That's not surprising, because Image Works is literally crammed with activities that give every visitor the chance to use his or her imagination.

For instance, at Dreamfinder's School of Drama, near the entrance to the Image Works, visitors have the opportunity to be in a TV show. Guests step onto a small stage and, thanks to a Chroma-Key video effects technique that involves foreground and background matting, perform in short video stories. Spectators and performers alike see the results as they happen via strategically placed video screens. It's *always* fun to watch the groups of senior citizens, teenagers, or families jumping crazily around on stage following on-screen instructions from Dreamfinder (and, in fact, having the time to spend more than just a few seconds watching these goings-on is sufficient reason to allot more time to your overall Epcot visit).

Another exhibit at Image Works is Figment's Coloring Book, where guests use state-of-the-art computer technology to paint giant coloring-book images of Figment and Dreamfinder. The Sensor is a sort of electronic maze whose various elements react to a visitor's presence by producing lights and sounds. Upon entering the Rainbow Corridor, you'll find a tunnel of neon tubes in all the

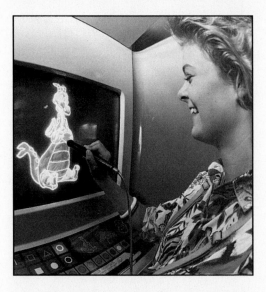

hues of the rainbow. Image Warp's pneumatically powered Mylar mirrors produce moving versions of old-style fun house reflections in a room wackily illuminated by strobe lights. Then there's the Lumia—a plastic ball seven feet in diameter, inside which swirling patterns of light and color appear in response to sounds of different frequencies and intensities. Another feature is Making Faces, a set of screens that allow you to electronically capture your own image and then apply different noses, hairstyles, ears, eyes, and even accessories. At Stepping Tones, hexagonal splotches of colored light on the floor correspond to sounds—a drumroll, a flourish on the harp, a couple of chords sung by a men's chorus, a

snippet of hoedown fiddling, and such—that are emitted when the area is trodden upon; the last red hexagon in the room, located in the farthest corner from the entrance, sends out the sound of a beautiful chord played on a harp. In fact, the first tones recreate the music heard in *Close Encounters of the Third Kind*. The floor was "orchestrated" by an avant-garde San Francisco Bay Area composer so that all possible combinations sound interesting at the very least—and the more the merrier. In the Mirage Room, Figment stars in a series of animated sequences using a unique holographic process. At Optical Illusion you'll see an animated hot-air balloon race between Figment and Dreamfinder.

Other activities include Light Writer, which involves drawing geometric patterns with laser beams, and the Magic Palette, where a special stylus and a touch-sensitive control surface can be used to create all kinds of images, mostly in Day-Glo colors. People often queue up to try these, while the huge kaleidoscopes and the unusual pin screens nearby are practically overlooked. Manufacturing the latter involved putting thousands of straight pins through a screen illuminated with colored lights from below (visitors run their hands across the bottom, thereby creating sweeping patterns of color).

The Electronic Philharmonic, one of the most amusing sections of the Image Works, allows guests to take turns conducting an orchestra. It's been renovated so now the feeling of conducting is even more realistic. Here's how this works: Each patch of light on the console represents a group of instruments (strings, woodwinds, brass, percussion). Raising and lowering one's hand above that patch of light increases and decreases the volume of the sound produced by that section of the "orchestra"; by covering three out of four patches of light, it is theoretically possible to bring up only the strings or only the brass.

Just outside Image Works, note the terrific photography display. The images are winners of Kodak's International Newspaper Snapshot Awards, and well worth a look.

HONEY, I SHRUNK THE AUDIENCE: Welcome to the Imagination Institute, workplace of Professor Wayne Szalinski, the featured character in the two hit "Honey" movies, *Honey, I Shrunk the Kids* and *Honey, I Blew Up the Kid*. Rick Moranis, Marcia Strassman, and the kids reprise their film roles at this 30-minute attraction.

In the pre-show area, guests see a movie about the imagination. Then they are welcomed to the Imagination Institute and given an overview of what they will see inside the theater. Szalinski will be presented with the Inventor of the Year Award and will demonstrate several of his inventions. On the way into the theater, guests are given "protective goggles" (3-D glasses), to shield their eyes

from flying debris that can get loose during new-product demonstrations.

Once the audience is seated, Szalinski is nowhere to be found. Then he zooms off the screen in his new HoverPod, out of control and miniaturized by his shrinking machine. Szalinski's son Nick steps in to demonstrate the "Dimensional Duplicator," a machine that can make exact copies of anything. As Nick switches on the machine, his little brother Adam drops his pet mouse into the duplicating chamber, hits the number 999, and suddenly hundreds of mice pour out of the screen in an almost 4-D effect that leaves guests squirming. It's so realistic, you might be inspired to stand on your chair!

Nick quickly gets rid of the mice with Professor Szalinski's No-Mess Holographic Pet System, which projects a 3-D cat out into the audience to scare away the mice. The cat morphs into a lynx and finally into a ferocious lion before overheating and exploding. Just then, Szalinski returns, blows himself up to normal size, and demonstrates his new, more powerful shrinking machine. The machine spins out of control and accidentally shrinks the audience and Nick. While the audience is miniaturized the theater shakes with every on-screen footstep. When apparent giants crouch down to ogle guests in the theater, it's a rare person who doesn't feel diminished to ant proportions. The effects are very believable, particularly when Adam picks up the theater and shows it to his mom. Motion effects in the theater add to the realism, as

does the full-size pet snake that gets loose. The audience is eventually brought back to normal size, of course, although not without incident. The attraction has one last surprise in store that we won't divulge.

CAMERAS AND FILM: A good selection of film is for sale here, along with a small selection of cameras, filters, cable releases, and other necessities of life for the traveling photographer. Some souvenir items also are available.

WORLD OF MOTION

The pavilion formerly devoted to chronicling the past, present, and future of transportation will be under renovation throughout 1996. A completely new General Motors pavilion is scheduled to open here mid-1997. This attraction will literally put guests through the motions of automobile testing. As ride vehicles progress along the test track, they will accelerate on long straightaways, hug hairpin turns, climb steep hills, and step on the brakes—not always on ideal road conditions. The wheels of change are in motion, so get ready to fasten your seatbelt.

Horizons

For generations, visionaries have been making predictions about life in the future. Jules Verne forecast rockets that would fly like bullets. The 19th-century French artist Albert Robida envisioned subways and dirigible taxis and sketched what life in Paris would be like in 1950. And in the 1930s, pulp science-fiction magazines circulated ideas about automatic barber chairs that would give their owners shoeshines and haircuts, about air conditioners that would pipe in alpine chills, about robots that would do housework, and about suntan lamps and televisions.

The three-acre Horizons show, which draws on the wisdom of countless scientists, adds its own predictions in a pavilion located between World of Motion and Wonders of Life, just beyond Innoventions. After a nod to the visions of earlier centuries in a Looking Back at Tomorrow sequence, the pavilion's continuously moving, suspended, four-passenger vehicles convey guests into the Omni-Sphere Theatre. Here, on a pair of spectacular hemispherical screens (80 feet in diameter), projectors with special lenses show filmed scenes of a Space Shuttle launch and of growing crystals, together with animated sequences of life in a space colony, a DNA chain, computer chips, and more. All this is a prelude to a voyage through a series of sets demonstrating aspects of life in the future.

In Nova Cite, the first destination, advanced transportation systems (such as trains that work by magnetic levitation) and sophisticated communication devices (including holographic telephones) keep members of far-flung families in touch with one another.

In the Mesa Verde sequence, voice-controlled crop-harvesting robots and genetically engineered fruits and vegetables populate a once-arid desert. Overhead, "hoverlifts" with spinning blades function as automatic shade controls, and "helium lifters" drop hooks down to fields to collect baskets of the harvest from the robots, and fly the produce off to market. In the future farmer's home, shown nearby, there's an electronic pantry that delivers food to the inhabitants at the push of a button and a home communications center where youngsters can study math (or other subjects) by computer.

In the Sea Castle sequence, depicting a movable—but otherwise islandlike—floating city in the Pacific, schoolchildren take underwater field trips to nearby mining and kelp-farming operations operated by robot devices. And in Omega Centauri, a free-floating colony in space, crystals are grown for use by computers back on Earth and colony inhabitants keep in shape in a health-and-recreation center that features games like zero-gravity basketball (seen in shadow along the rear wall), and rowing and bicycling in simulators that allow space folk the opportunity to pursue their favorite sport in any environment they choose. Boaters, for instance, may shoot the Colorado River's rapids in the Grand Canyon, or paddle a Louisiana bayou, or float through the canals of Venice. Home life is just like that on Earth, but with a couple of twists: When a boy newly arrived at the colony doesn't put on his shoes in the morning, he floats away. (They're magnetic shoes, designed for this zero-gravity environment.) And when the family gets together to celebrate a birthday, those who can't attend in person put in an appearance via a holographic telephone.

There's another fine experience at the ride's conclusion: Visitors pick the journey's ending. Just push a button, and a special audience-polling device inside your vehicle delivers the 30-second experience that the majority of your fellow riders have requested. The car tilts back and vibrates, and the sound effects enhance the sensation of great speed created by fast-moving, close-up filmed visuals of travel on land, in the sea, and in space, not unlike those found in the speed rooms in the nearby World of Motion.

Trivia buffs will be curious about the sources of the science-fiction clips presented in the Looking Back at Tomorrow sequence. These include the films *Metropolis* (1926) and *Woman in the Moon* (1928) by the director Fritz Lang; *Mars and Beyond* and *Magic Highways U.S.A.*, shown on the "Disneyland" programs of the 1950s; and Woody Allen's *Sleeper* (1973).

Note: This attraction will be open only periodically during 1996. Plans call for significant renovations to several Future World pavilions, including Horizons. A completely new attraction is scheduled for this pavilion in the future.

Wonders of Life

The 72-foot-tall steel DNA molecule at the entrance to this popular pavilion beckons guests to a humorous, informative, and healthful experience. Housed in a 100,000-square-foot geodesic dome and two attached buildings, this attraction allows guests to enjoy both a serious and amusing look at health, fitness, and modern lifestyles. Wonders also boasts Epcot's first authentic thrill ride called Body Wars—a fast and furious ride through the human body.

From outside the gold-topped dome, the Wonders of Life sign seems to rest on the flumes of water shot up by two fountains. Once inside the building, guests find themselves at the Fitness Fairgrounds. A mobile measuring 50 feet in diameter is suspended from the 65-foot ceiling and it swings gently in the air currents of the building.

At the Fairgrounds, a variety of shows and activities for both children and adults are offered. *Goofy About Health* is an eight-minute multi-screen montage that sees Goofy go from a sloppy-living guy to a health-conscious fellow. Using old Goofy cartoons that haven't been seen for many years, the show traces Goofy's ups and downs, and winds up with new footage of Goofy at his doctor's office. The film is shown in a 100-seat open theater where visitors can come and go as they wish.

At the Anacomical Players Theater, a corny (but nonetheless informative) show is presented by an improvisational theater group. Audience members are asked to participate,

and it's all a lot of fun. This theater seats 100 people. The third theater at the Fitness Fairgrounds is enclosed. The film shown here, *The Making of Me*, is a 14-minute story starring Martin Short. It is about a man who wonders how he came into existence. To find out, he travels back in time to the birth of his parents, their first few years together, and their decision to have a child—him. Footage from an actual delivery is part of the film, and it is sensitively done and provides a tangible and touching view of childbirth. It was written and directed by Glenn Gordon Caron, who directed the TV show "Moonlighting" and the film *Clean and Sober*. Parents should be aware, however, that the film is quite graphic and so may not be suitable for some children.

There are plenty of hands-on activities in areas surrounding the theaters. Guests can ride Wonder Cycles, computerized stationary bicycles that enable guests to pedal through a variety of locales including Disneyland and the Rose Parade. At Coach's Corner, golf, tennis, or baseball swings are analyzed, and a professional knowledgeable in each sport offers free, albeit taped, advice to help you on your way. The Sensory Funhouse offers hands-on activities for kids. It's the Disney version of a children's museum, where education and entertainment go hand in hand.

At the Met Lifestyle Revue, guests punch in such information as age, weight, height, exercise habits, whether they smoke, and perceived stress levels at an interactive computer terminal. The computer then processes the information and offers some advice on how to lead a healthier and less stressful existence.

Frontiers of Medicine, located toward the rear of the Fitness Fairgrounds, features the only completely serious segment of Wonders of Life. Here guests can see some scientific and educational exhibits of leading-edge developments in medicine and health sciences. The exhibits change regularly.

Pure & Simple offers a variety of healthy snacks, including oat bran waffles and smoothies (made with frozen yogurt). There is a pleasant seating area, and nearby Well & Goods, Ltd. features men's, women's, and children's athletic wear, most of which features Disney characters participating in a variety of sports, and some educational materials. Presented by Met Life.

CRANIUM COMMAND: The third major area of Wonders of Life welcomes guests into the mind of a 12-year-old boy in this 17-minute show. The pre-show sets the mood as an animated film explains what you are about to see. General Knowledge is recruiting pilots for an assortment of new brains. There are jokes aplenty, many of which go right over the heads of young kids. Buzzy, our star pilot, fumbles through basic training and gets assigned to the most volatile brain of all, that of an adolescent boy.

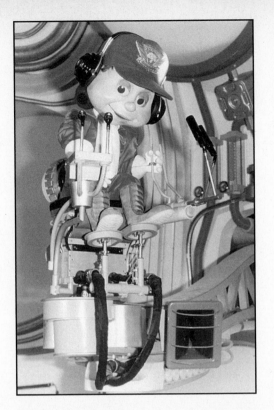

Inside a 200-seat theater, the enormously exaggerated head of our 12-year-old subject is piloted by Buzzy, a delightfully corny Audio-Animatronics figure. The two large eyes are actually rear-projection video screens, and it is through them that the audience gets an idea of how a 12-year-old thinks and reacts. The other animated participant, General Knowledge, helps Buzzy learn which portion of the mind is required for a particular situation. The right and left brain, the stomach, the heart, and the adrenal gland are all represented by familiar celebrities. Our personal favorite is George Wendt (Norm from "Cheers") operating the stomach. Other characters include Bobcat Goldthwait as the adrenal gland, Dana Carvey and Kevin Nealon (Hans and Franz of "Saturday Night Live" fame) as the heart, Charles Grodin as the left brain, and John Lovitz as the right brain. It's an altogether whimsical and entertaining show—one of the best at Epcot. This is such a fast-paced show with so many details that you'll notice new things even after seeing it many times.

BODY WARS: The same state-of-the-art technology that sends guests on a rollicking five-minute ride through space at the Star Tours attraction at the Disney-MGM Studios is also at Wonders of Life in the form of the thrill ride called Body Wars. After boarding the vehicles, which are actually the same type of flight simulators employed by military and commercial airlines in pilot training, guests are whisked away on a bumpy, rocky, and exciting ride through the human body. (Note that when instructed to fasten your seatbelt,

do so. This is a rough ride.) Movie buffs immediately will think of the film *Fantastic Voyage* and the more recent *Inner Space*. The queue area features exhibits from a fictional company specializing in the latest technology in the miniaturization of people. Guests pass through two special effects portals and are declared ready to do a routine medical probe of the human body—from the inside.

During the course of this bumpy trip, a scientist is dispatched to remove a splinter that has made its way beneath the patient's skin. Guests go along for the ride, but end up on a rescue mission when the scientist is attacked by a white blood cell. Of course, there are some problems along the way, making this trip seem out of control. **Note:** This is a rougher ride than Star Tours at the Studios.

Signs posted outside Body Wars warn that in order to ride passengers must be free of back problems, heart conditions, motion sickness, and other such physical limitations. Pregnant women and children under three are not permitted to board. Children under seven must be accompanied by an adult.

Universe of Energy

When strolling through Future World toward World Showcase Plaza, it's easy to spot this pavilion's mirrored, asymmetrical pyramid off to the left. But the facade doesn't provide any clue at all to the 45 minutes of surprises in store for those who venture inside. One of the most technologically complex experiences at Epcot, the Energy show consists of three motion pictures and a ride-through attraction. Not one of these is exactly what you might expect.

The first film, seen when you enter the pavilion, examines types of energy used today. Its vivid images of falling water, leaping fire, burning coal, enormous piles of logs, jet engines, and beautiful yellow flowers are the makings of a fine photo essay—but there's a twist: The projection surface is not at all a conventional flat motion picture screen, but is

made up of 100 solid triangular elements. These actually rotate on cue from a computer, in synchronization with the changing images, to produce what its creator (Czech filmmaker Emil Radok) described as a "kinetic mosaic."

The second film, shown in an adjoining area, is a short animated feature depicting the eras in which today's fossil fuels were created. This film was photographed with the multiplane camera developed by the Disney organization over 50 years ago, and the feeling of depth it gave to the forest scenes in famous films like *Bambi* and *Snow White* also enhances the cinemascape here.

But contrary to the expectations of some visitors, there's not an adorably Disneyesque creature in the show. The animals lumbering across the giant screen (which measures over half the length of a football field) are gigantic prehistoric beasts, and the landscape is an eerie one, full of volcanoes, exotic plants, and bizarre insects. Even more astonishing is the moment at the conclusion of the movie when the whole seating area suddenly begins to rotate, and then breaks up into six smaller sections that slowly move forward—usually to the accompaniment of a chorus of oohs and aahs from startled members of the audience.

Before very many people have even begun to grasp the transformation, the vehicles have embarked upon an odyssey through a three-dimensional recreation of the primeval world suggested in the film, an otherworldly region of sulfur-scented air, eerie blue moonlight,

unearthly fogs, and lava so ominously authentic that few visitors dare reach out and touch it—even when told that one of its main ingredients is a type of commercial styling gel.

Huge trees crowd the forest. Millipedes duel on a log to the left of the vehicles. Apatosauruses wallow in the lagoon out front. A lofty allosaurus battles dramatically with an armored stegosaurus a bit farther along, and an elasmosaurus bursts out of a tidal pool with frightening suddenness—all under the vulturelike gaze of winged creatures known as pteranodons. All of these were created only after months of research, including interviews with countless well-known paleobotanists and paleontologists. The Audio-Animatronics animals are the largest of their type ever to be fabricated, and the 250 prehistoric trees are the first ever to come off any production line. There are so many sounds, smells, and sights here that the time passes in a flash, and before you know it the vehicles have entered another theater.

Here a motion picture, shown on a 220-degree screen whose breadth intensifies the impact of every image, dramatizes sources of energy for the future. During the filming of the North Sea segment, temperatures dropped so low that the three 65mm cameras used in the filming—specially mounted to generate the almost seamless image projected on the curved screen—had to be taken indoors and defrosted before work could continue. Footage depicting the Space Shuttle's thunderous blastoff, so unusual that even NASA wanted a copy, serves as the film's grand finale and provides images that stay with you as you travel into another Energy adventure, a splendid computer-animated light show of what looks like dancing laser beams.

Fully as intriguing as the whole Energy experience is the advanced technology behind it. The traveling vehicles weigh about 30,000 pounds when fully loaded with their passengers. Yet they are guided along the concrete floor by a guide wire only 1/8-inch thick. And some of the pavilion's required energy is generated by two acres of photovoltaic cells mounted on the roof. These cells generate enough energy to run six average homes.

On leaving the pavilion, home gardeners should note that the Southern live oaks immediately to the east of the Universe of Energy (to your right as you face the entrance) are pruned to follow the slanted roofline of the pavilion. These trees were among a handful started from acorns for Walt Disney World's opening more than 20 years ago; a quartet of their siblings, in an unpruned state, can still be seen in front of The American Adventure, in World Showcase. Presented by Exxon.

Note: This attraction will be under renovation for at least six months during 1996. When the ride reopens, it is expected that the dinosaur segment will be similar, while the rest of the attraction will be updated.

World Showcase

Noble sentiments about humanity and the fellowship of nations, which have motivated so many world's fairs in the past, also inhabit World Showcase. But make no mistake about it: This half of Epcot, located to the south of Future World, is unlike any previous international exposition.

It is instead a group of pavilions that encircle World Showcase Lagoon (a body of water that, incidentally, is the size of 85 football fields) to demonstrate Disney conceptions about participating countries in remarkably realistic, consistently entertaining styles. You won't find the real Germany here; rather, the country's essence, much as a traveler returning from a visit might remember what he or she saw. Shops, restaurants, and an occasional special attraction are all housed in a group of structures that is an artful pastiche of all the elements that give that nation's countryside and towns their distinctive flavor. Although occasional liberties have been taken when scale and proportion required, careful research governed the design of every nook and cranny.

In the shops, all wares on display represent the country in whose pavilion they are offered for sale. The food focuses on native cuisine, and the entertainment is as authentic as the Disney casting directors can make it, with native performers consistently featured. And craftspeople are occasionally on hand to demonstrate their art in the appropriate shops. Thanks to special Epcot cultural exchange programs and the personnel department's energetic efforts to recruit nationals from around Central Florida, nearly all the World Showcase staff members in restaurants, shops, and attractions were born in the countries the pavilions represent (or at least spent many years living there), and that contributes still more atmosphere. The ongoing efforts of the entertainment department mean that festivities are always in the works, and that new performers are continually making Epcot debuts.

Home gardeners should be sure to note the World Showcase landscaping: Each pavilion's plantings closely approximate what would be found in the featured nation. The 1.3-mile World Showcase Promenade, which links pavilions on the shores of the World Showcase Lagoon, has its own interesting vegetation, beginning in World Showcase Plaza with 75-foot Washingtonia fan palms, Arizona-California natives that were imported to Central Florida. Underneath them is a garden full of rosebushes. All told, there are more than 10,000 tree roses, teas, grandifloras, and miniatures planted throughout World Showcase. The Y-shaped trees nearby are callery pears. The camphor trees encircling the lagoon on the promenade were planted to provide the walkway with abundant and welcome shade.

Keep in mind that since most of Future World closes at 7 P.M., World Showcase may become more congested at this time. We recommend taking in as many possible shows, rides, and films earlier in the day, and saving the shops for the pleasant, early evening hours.

Pavilions are described here in the order that they would be encountered while moving counterclockwise (west to east) around the World Showcase Lagoon after crossing the bridge from Future World.

Canada

Celebrating the beauties of America's neighbor to the north, the area devoted to the western hemisphere's largest nation is complete with its own mountain, waterfall, rushing stream, rocky canyon, mine, and splendid garden massed with colorful flowers. There's even a totem pole, a trading post, and an elaborate, mansard-roofed hotel similar to ones built by the Canadian railroads as they pushed west around the turn of the century. All this is imaginatively arranged somewhat like a split-level house, with the section representing French Canada on top, and another devoted to the mountains alongside it and below. From a distance, the Hôtel du Canada, the main building here, looks like little more than a bump on the landscape—as does Epcot's single Canadian Rocky Mountain. But up close they both seem to tower as high as the real thing, thanks to a motion picture designers' technique known as forced perspective, which exaggerates the relative smallness of distant parts of a structure to make the totality appear taller than it really is.

The gardens were inspired by the Butchart Gardens in Victoria, British Columbia, a famous park created on the site of a limestone quarry. The hotel is modeled after Ottawa's Victorian-style *Château Laurier.*

Willow, birch, sweet gum, plum, and maple trees can all be found in the Victoria Gardens; Canada's hemlocks are represented here by deodar cedars, a Himalaya native that can withstand torrid Florida summers with aplomb.

Entertainment is provided by the Caledonia Bagpipe Band, sometimes featuring two pipers and a drummer.

O CANADA!: This 17-minute motion picture, presented in Circle-Vision 360 inside Canada's mountain, portrays the Canadian confederation in all its coast-to-coast splendor—the prairies and the plains, the sparkling shorelines and rivers, and the untouched snowfields and rocky mountainsides. The Royal Canadian Mounted Police also put in an appearance. The maritime provinces are all pictured, with their covered bridges and sailing ships, as is Montreal, with its Old World cafés and imposing churches; the scene in the Cathédrale de Notre Dame, with its organ booming and choirboys in attendance, is particularly stirring. The great outdoors gets equal play. In one scene, Canada snow geese take off all around the screen, and the beating of their wings is positively thunderous. Eagles, possums, mallards, bobcats, wolves, bears, deer, bison, and herds of reindeer were all filmed. Filmed too were steers being roped at a rodeo and the chuck wagon race that takes place every year at that great provincial fair known as the Calgary Stampede. Skiers in the vast and empty Bugaboos, dogsledders, and ice skaters are featured in the winter scenes; in a hockey game, the sound system almost perfectly conveys the scratch of skates on ice and the sharp whack of sticks against a puck. And throughout, the motion picture conveys a sense of the vast size of Canada, providing a you-are-there feeling that makes all of this spectacular scenery still more memorable.

This is partly due to the filming technique, Circle-Vision 360, also used in the Magic Kingdom attraction, The Timekeeper. It involves a camera rig composed of nine individual cameras arranged around a tubular shaft containing the motor that drives the mechanisms for all the cameras. In some scenes the rig was suspended from a helicopter; when depicting the precision-flying Canadian Snowbirds, Canada's equivalent to the U.S. Air Force's Thunderbirds, it was mounted on a B-25 bomber; in the Calgary sequence, it was placed in one of the racing buckboards; and in the reindeer roundup scene, which took place on the edge of the Arctic Ocean, it was concealed by burlap. Note that there are no seats in this theater.

NORTHWEST MERCANTILE: The first shop to the left upon entering the pavilion's plaza on the way to the Hôtel du Canada, this emporium does a booming business in

Canadian sheepskins, which are piled high just inside the entrance. Heavy lumberjack shirts, maple syrup, and other wares that trappers might have purchased back in pioneering days round out the stock. Skeins of rope, tin scoops, lanterns, and a pair of antique ice skates hanging from the long beams overhead set the mood, together with the structure itself. That, like the adjacent Trading Post, is built of adze-hewn logs and ornamented by stone statues, masks, and paintings done in the style of the Ojibwa Indians. Located to the rear of the shop are Indian artifacts and assorted souvenirs—items like toy tomahawks, fur vests and moccasins, and sleek-lined sculptures (some made of imitation marble and some carved in soapstone by the Inuit). The small tepees are made from the bark of deciduous trees, which can be gathered up only once a year when the tree is dormant. These are among several hand-crafted Canadian items that are seldom seen elsewhere in the American market.

LA BOUTIQUE DES PROVINCES: At this shop you'll find Canadian merchandise with a French flavor.

United Kingdom

In the space of only a few hundred feet, visitors to this pavilion stroll from an elegant London square to the edge of a canal in the rural countryside—via a bustling urban English street framed by buildings that constitute a veritable rhapsody of historic architectural styles. But one scene leads to the next so smoothly that nothing ever seems amiss. Here again, note the attention to detail: the half-timbered High Street structure that actually leans a bit, the hand-painted "smoke" stains that make the chimneys look as if they had been there for centuries. When a thatched roof is required, it's right where it should be—though the roof may be made of plastic broom bristles because fire regulations prohibit the real thing. London plane trees, so common in British cities, are represented, and a sundial punctuates the promenade. Off to the side is a pair of scarlet phone booths identical to those that used to be found all around the U.K. And there are eight different architectural styles characteristic of the streetscapes, from English Tudor and Georgian to English Victorian.

There is no single major special attraction in this pavilion; instead, it features a half dozen fine shops and a pub that serves a selection of British-brewed beers and ales that would be the toast of any first class "local" in London itself. There's also plenty of good entertainment including a group of comedians called the World Showcase Players, who, when not engaged in general clowning on the World Showcase Promenade, coax audience members into participating in their farcical and altogether entertaining (if unsophisticated) playlets.

Sharp-eyed visitors with an interest in horticultural matters will have a field day

examining the landscaping here. The geometrically trimmed bush in front of The Toy Soldier shop is not an Irish yew, so common to the British Isles, but instead a *podocarpus*; Irish yews don't grow well in Florida. A *podocarpus*, left in its natural shape, also flanks the shop door just to the rear. A similar substitution had to be made for the London plane tree, also not suited to the Epcot climate; its replacement, crowding the half-timbered walls of The Magic of Wales, is a Western sycamore, which looks nearly identical and belongs to the same genus. Don't miss the perennial and herb garden next to Anne Hathaway's cottage (to the left of the entrance to The Tea Caddy as you face it), and the small path that leads to the garden courtyard. The characters often appear in the garden courtyard. A traditional English hedge maze surrounds the cottage.

THE TOY SOLDIER: All the necessities are here for such beloved youthful pastimes as sailing (wooden boats), creating works of art ("colouring" books), and just having a good time (Corgi toys).

No toy shop is complete without temptations for adults, and this one is no exception: There are elegant dolls designed expressly for collectors.

Be sure to notice the display at the shop's promenade entrance—a miniature, glitter-strewn medieval banquet hall peopled by royalty and nobles, musicians, jesters, and a host of other court figures. On the windows downstairs are the heraldic crests for eight of the U.K.'s principal cities, plus those for the three nations that make up the U.K. (Scotland, England, and Northern Ireland—but not Wales, which is a principality). In addition, there are

the three crosses that, combined, make up the Union Jack—the crosses of St. Andrew, St. George, and St. Patrick.

Outside, the shop resembles a stone manor built during the last half of the 16th century; the Scottish-stepped gable parapet and the round turrets are inspired by Scotland's Abbotsford Manor, where the novelist Sir Walter Scott lived for a period, wrote his most famous romances, and died in 1832.

LORDS AND LADIES: This shop looks like a backdrop for a child's fantasy of the days of King Arthur, with its high rafters decked out with bright banners, its vast fireplace (and crossed swords above), and its immense wrought-iron chandelier. Pottery replicas of British cottages, dart boards, fragrance products, "pub mugs," limited-edition chess sets, coin and stamp sets, and tapes and records are the stock in trade at this emporium adjoining The Toy Soldier.

PRINGLE OF SCOTLAND: On a sweltering summer day in Central Florida, trying on lamb's wool and cashmere may not hold terrific appeal. But the huge selection of styles and colors in men's and women's sweaters, knitted by Scotland's most famous maker, may well prove enticing despite the temperature outside. Tam-o'-shanters, socks, hats, ties, scarves, mittens, and kilts are only some of the items offered. Don't fail to look at the fascinating tartan map on the wall across from Lords and Ladies; this identifies plaids from Glen Burn and Gordon to Langtree and St. Lawrence.

THE QUEEN'S TABLE: Sponsored by the Royal Doulton, Ltd. china makers, this shop (opposite Pringle of Scotland) may be one of the loveliest in Epcot. This is particularly true of the store's elegant Adams Room, embellished with elaborate moldings, hung with a crystal chandelier, and painted in cream and robin's egg blue. The setting is a perfect background for the selection of superbly crafted collector's statuettes. The detail is almost photographically perfect, and the prices range from $5 to $12,500.

Among the Royal Doulton shop's more affordable delights are the company's famous Bunnykins cup-and-bowl sets for youngsters. Also intriguing are the small and large Toby mugs—cups that are shaped and painted to represent the visages of famous historical figures. A small selection of attractive Royal Doulton china dinnerware also is available.

Don't fail to inspect small, serene Britannia Square just outside the shop entrance furthest from World Showcase Promenade. But for its somewhat reduced scale and the distinctively Floridian climate, it almost feels like London itself. The crests on the shop's upstairs windows are those of three major U.K. schools—Oxford, Cambridge, and Eton.

THE MAGIC OF WALES: This small emporium offers pottery, slate, jewelry, souvenirs, and handcrafted gifts from Wales. Despite its modest size, it does the highest volume of business (per square foot of size) among the United Kingdom shops.

THE TEA CADDY: Fitted out with heavy wooden beams and a broad fireplace to resemble the Stratford-upon-Avon cottage of Shakespeare's Anne Hathaway, this shop, presented by R. Twinings & Company, Ltd., stocks various types of English teas, both loose and in bags in a variety of flavors. Other items include teapots, biscuits, and candies.

dusty rose-colored, lace-trimmed costumes that the hostesses wear were inspired by the dresses in the Impressionist painter Edouard Manet's *Le Bar aux Folies-Bergère*, and the park to the west of the pavilion, with its tall Lombardy poplars, was inspired by neo-Impressionist Georges Seurat's painting *A Sunday Afternoon on the Island of La Grande Jatte*. The main entrance to the pavilion recalls the architecture of Paris, most of which was built during the Belle Epoque ("beautiful age") years of the last decades of the 19th century when, following the designs of city planner Baron Georges-Eugène Haussmann, thoroughfares were widened and seven stories became the standard height for city buildings. The lane known as La Petite Rue ("the little street") is inspired by small provincial byways. The sinuously curved, Art Nouveau–style facade of the entrance to the arcade between La Signature and Plume et

France

The buildings here have mansard roofs and casement windows so Gallic in appearance that you expect to see some sad, bohemian poet looking down from above. A canallike offshoot of the World Showcase Lagoon seems like the Seine itself; the footbridge that spans it recalls the old Pont des Arts. There's a kiosk nearby like those that punctuate the streets of Paris, a sidewalk café at which to sip a glass of wine and watch the crowds go by, an elegant bookstore, and a bakery whose absolutely heavenly rich aromas announce its presence long before it's visible. Shops sell perfumes, fine leather wares, jewelry, crystal, and other luxury items. Their roofs are real copper or slate, and the cabinetry is crafted finely enough to dazzle even the most skilled woodworker. Galerie des Halles—the iron-and-glass-ceilinged market that Paris once counted as one of its most beloved institutions—lives again (near the Palais du Cinéma exit). But perhaps most special of all are the people. Hosts and hostesses who hail from Paris and the French provinces answer questions in lyrically French-accented English.

Some interesting background notes: The

Palette ("pen and palette") recalls the entrances to Paris's great underground transportation system, the Métro. Don't miss the quiet garden on the opposite side of this arcade—one of the most peaceful spots in World Showcase.

Horticulturally, France offers still other delights, beginning on the World Showcase Promenade. Here a row of Western sycamores that normally grow to 60 or 80 feet—planted in lieu of London plane trees—is being pruned French-style to a height of about 18 feet to develop knots on the end of each branch. These make a distinctive abstract pattern in winter, and in spring send out spiky leaf-bearing shoots that provide bountiful shade in summer. To the west, on the opposite side of the promenade, a small square edged with miniature rose bushes has been planted to outline the shape of a *fleur de lis*.

IMPRESSIONS DE FRANCE: Shown in the Palais du Cinéma, an intimate, elegant little theater not unlike the one at Fontainebleau. This enchanting 18-minute travel film takes viewers from one end of France to the other. The film shows off a beautiful tree-dotted estate; fertile fields and vineyards at harvest time; a village flower market and a luscious pastry shop; the ribbed tongue of a glacier and a harbor full of squawking gulls; black-clad Breton women with headdresses made of starched lace shaped into unique styles that reveal the wearer's origin; Paris on Bastille Day—in all some four dozen locations (out of 140 originally shot). Several scenes take place in world-famous landmarks like the Eiffel Tower; Versailles and its gilt Hall of Mirrors (just outside Paris); Mont St. Michel, close to the Brittany-Normandy border in the northwest corner of the country; the French Alps near Mont Blanc, in the southeast; and Cannes, the star-studded resort city on the Mediterranean coast. The automobile competition is Cannes's Bugatti Race; the chateau—which Francophiles will immediately recognize as one of those in the Loire River valley—is fabulous Chambord. (This scene, incidentally, was shot from a helicopter that could fly within three feet of any object being photographed.)

All this is even more appealing thanks to a superbly melodic sound track almost entirely made up of the music of French classical composers such as Jacques Offenbach (1819-1880), known for his operettas; Charles-Camille Saint-Saëns (1835-1921), a conductor, pianist, organist, and composer celebrated for his lush melodies; Claude Debussy (1862-1918), who did with sound what the Impressionist painters did with light; and Erik Satie (1866-1925), known for his piano works. Selections include Debussy's *Syrinx*, the haunting piece for solo flute, and his *Afternoon of a Faun*, which accompany an aerial shot of fertile fields. Listen for Offenbach's *Gaieté Parisienne* in the biking sequence and Satie's *Trois Gymnopédies* in the Alps scene. The Aquarium section from Saint-Saën's *Carnival of the Animals* accompanies the swamp scene, and the same composer's *Organ Symphony* is heard during the Eiffel Tower ascent. The whole is woven together with transitional segments written and arranged by long-time Disney musician Buddy Baker.

The exceptionally wide screen adds yet another dimension. This is not a Circle-Vision 360 film; it was not shot with the nine cameras needed for the motion pictures at China and Canada. Instead, the France film used only five cameras, but it is shown on a screen made up of five large projection surfaces—200 degrees around. It's one of Epcot's best films.

There is generally not a long wait here except during peak seasons, but it's still best to see the film soon after World Showcase opens or in the early evening.

PLUME ET PALETTE: This spot, devoted to art and crystal, is one of World Showcase's loveliest shops. The best of the art nouveau style is reflected in the curves embellishing the wrought-iron balustrade edging the mezzanine and the moldings that decorate the

shining cherry-wood cabinets and shelves. The woodworking is superb, and one case seems more beautiful than the next. Stained glass in purple, yellow, and lavender ornaments the top of one of them. Stylized tulips painted in a delicate antique rose color and pale green embellish still others. The curtains are a beautiful dusty pink with white lace.

The decor makes a fine backdrop for an array of merchandise that includes collectible miniatures, small china boxes, and tapestries. On the mezzanine level, a handful of fine oil paintings (by well-known French landscape artists) are for sale from $300 to $3,000 each, along with attractive prints of French countryside scenes.

LA SIGNATURE: Another beautiful spot, with wallpaper that resembles watered silk, a fine chandelier, brass-and-crystal sconces, and velvet curtains, this shop stocks lovely French fragrances and bath products, as well as French apparel.

GALERIE DES HALLES: French cookies and chocolate bars—plus souvenirs—are the stock in trade at this area located at the exit from the Palais du Cinéma. The area is modeled on Paris's now-demolished Les Halles, originally designed by the architect Victor Baltard (1805-1874).

LA MODE FRANCAISE: This shop presents a selection of sophisticated casual clothing with a French accent. Men's and women's fashions are available.

LA MAISON DU VIN: Selections in this lovely wine shop range from the inexpensive to the pricey, from a few dollars for *vin ordinaire* to upwards of $290 for a relatively rare vintage. Wine tastings are held here to sample the offerings (a small charge is levied, but you get to keep the glass). Those who don't want to carry their purchases all over World Showcase may have them dispatched to Package Pickup for retrieval at the end of the day.

Morocco

Nine tons of tile were handmade, handcut, and shipped to Epcot to create this World Showcase pavilion. To capture the unique quality of this North African country's architecture, 19 Moroccan artisans were brought to Epcot to practice the mosaic art that has been a part of their homeland for thousands of years. Koutoubia Minaret, a detailed replica of the famous prayer tower in Marrakesh, stands guard at the entrance. A courtyard with a fountain in the center—and flowers everywhere—leads to the Medina (Old City). Between the traditional alleyways and the more modern sections are the pointed arches

and swirling blue patterns of the Bab Boujouloud gate, a replica of the one that stands in the city of Fez. An ancient working waterwheel irrigates the gardens of the pavilion and the motifs repeated throughout the buildings include carved plaster and wood, ceramic tile, and brass. Native musicians perform Moroccan songs in the pavilion's courtyard.

GALLERY OF ARTS AND HISTORY: This museum houses ever-changing exhibits of Moroccan art, artifacts, and costumes.

MOROCCAN NATIONAL TOURIST OFFICE: An information center offers literature useful in planning a visit to Morocco, and the Royal Air Maroc desk makes it easy to book a trip if the mood strikes. There is a three-screen projection area where a continuous slide show depicts the lifestyles and landscapes of the country.

CASABLANCA CARPETS: Hand-knotted Berber carpets, Rabat carpets with brightly colored geometric designs, prayer rugs, wall hangings of lifelike scenes, and handloomed bedspreads and throw pillows are among the offerings here.

TANGIER TRADERS: Here's the perfect place to buy a fez, plus woven belts, leather sandals, leather purses, and other traditional Moroccan clothing.

MARKETPLACE IN THE MEDINA: Handwoven baskets, sheepskin wallets and handbags, assorted straw hats, and split bamboo furniture and lampshades are available.

THE BRASS BAZAAR: Brass, brass, and more brass—and it's all shiny. Pitchers, planters, pots, and serving sets.

BERBER OASIS: This shop on the promenade spills over with crafted brasswork. Baskets and leathergoods abound.

MEDINA ARTS: A representative selection of crafts from all parts of Morocco makes this an interesting and colorful stop.

Japan

Serenity rules in Japan. The principal entertainment is a young man known as Nasaji Teresawa, who pursues the 2,400-year-old art of snipping and swirling blobs of brown rice toffee into the shapes of swans, unicorns, crabs, and a score of other remarkable creatures. A drum-playing duo, known as One World Taiko, performs traditional Japanese music on World Showcase Promenade.

The landscaping, designed in accordance with traditional symbolic and aesthetic values, also contributes to the peaceful mood. Rocks, which in Japan represent the enduring nature of the earth, were brought from North Carolina and Georgia (since boulders are scarce in the Sunshine State). Water, symbolizing the sea (which the Japanese consider a life source), is abundant; the Japan pavilion garden has a little stream and a couple of pools inhabited (in good weather) by koi. A small bamboo device at the edge of one of these rivulets regularly fills up with water falling from above, and then, weighted by its contents, empties out and makes regular, but somehow soothing, clacking noises in the process. Evergreen trees, which in Japan are symbols of eternal life, are here in force.

Disney horticulturalists created this very Japanese landscape using few plants and trees native to that country because the climate there is so different from that of Florida. The evergreens near the brilliant vermilion *torii* gate are native Florida slash pines. The curly-leaved trees alongside the stream are corkscrew willows. Among the few trees actually native to Japan are the sago near the courtyard entrance to the *Yakitori House*, the two Japanese maple trees (identifiable by their small leaves) not far away (near the first stairway from the promenade on the left side of the courtyard as you face it), and the prickly monkey puzzle trees near the walkway to the promenade, on The American Adventure side of the pagoda; needle-sharp thorns make this the only species of tree that monkeys cannot climb.

Visitors who have been to Japan will be interested to observe that most of the structures inside the pavilion have their Japanese antecedents. The pagoda that occupies such a prominent place along World Showcase Promenade was modeled after an eighth-century structure located in the Horyuji Temple in Nara. The brilliant vermilion *torii* gate on the shores of World Showcase Lagoon derives from the design of the one at the Itsukushima shrine in Hiroshima Bay, one of the most beautiful sites on the inland sea.

BIJUTSU-KAN GALLERY: A changing cultural display, this small museum has offered, among other shows, "Echos Through Time—Japanese Women and the Arts," an exhibit of traditional and contemporary Japanese art forms.

MITSUKOSHI DEPARTMENT STORE: There are kimonos in silk, cotton, and polyester; attractive all-cotton T-shirts bearing Japanese characters; expensive, almost sculptural traditional headdresses that seem fabricated of lacquer-stiffened netting; and an excellent selection of bowls and vases meant for flower arranging. But on the whole, no one would ever apply the term "quaint" to this spacious store set up by Mitsukoshi—an immense, three-century-old retail firm that was once dubbed "Japan's Sears." Some of the china dinnerware is too often seen elsewhere in the U.S. in department stores or inexpensive chain import stores to arouse more than passing interest. It's unfortunate that this familiarity also makes it easy to dismiss some of the other merchandise that, though it appears to be of the same trinket quality, has considerable meaning in Japanese culture. One example is the dolls, of which there are literally rows and rows, priced from $3.50 to $3,000, and clad in elaborate kimonos sashed with wide, stiff *obis*. These are traditionally

given to female children on Girls' Day, a popular Japanese national holiday. The blank-eyed, egg-shaped papier-mâché scarlet masks, which come in a wide range of sizes from small to very large, are part of the traditional New Year celebration. The Japanese color in one eye when making a New Year's resolution, keep the one-eyed "face" in plain view throughout the next 364 days as a reminder of the holiday vow, and celebrate success when the year draws to its close by completing the face.

The structure housing the merchandise was inspired by a section of the Gosho Imperial Palace, which was constructed in Kyoto in the year 794 A.D., and is widely recognized as a fine example of early Japanese architecture.

The American Adventure

When it came to creating The American Adventure, the centerpiece of World Showcase, the Disney Imagineers were given virtually a free hand. So the 110,000 bricks of the imposing colonial-style structure that houses the show, a counter-service restaurant, and a shop are real brick—made *by hand* from soft, pinkish-orange Georgia clay. The show inside stands out because of its wonderfully evocative settings, its innovatively detailed sets, and the 35 superb Audio-Animatronics players, some of the most lifelike ever created by the Disney organization: The American Adventure's Ben Franklin even walks up stairs. The digital sound system also is the most advanced that the Disney organization has ever used, and the show is the most technically complex, involving the world's largest rear-projection screen (72 feet across) and a number of sophisticated sets that rise up from below the stage to the delight and awe of the audience. A superb a cappella vocal group called The Voices of Liberty serenades guests in the building's foyer before each show begins.

Be sure to note the four luxuriant trees out front. They were originally planted in 1969 on Hotel Plaza Boulevard, and have been moved four times in the intervening years. The Disney characters often appear here, including Pocahontas in her own meet-and-greet area. Presented by Coca-Cola and American Express.

THE AMERICAN ADVENTURE SHOW: One of the truly outstanding Epcot attractions, this 29-minute presentation celebrates the Ameri-

153

can spirit from our nation's earliest years right up to the present. The show is very current. Beginning with the arrival of the Pilgrims at Plymouth Rock and their hard first winter on the western shore of the Atlantic, the Audio-Animatronics narrators—an amazingly lifelike Ben Franklin and a convincing, cigar-puffing Mark Twain—recall certain key people and events in American history—the Boston Tea Party, George Washington and the grueling winter at Valley Forge, the influential black abolitionist Frederick Douglass, the celebrated 19th-century Nez Percé Chief Joseph, and many more. The Philadelphia Centennial Exposition is remembered, along with women's rights campaigner Susan B. Anthony, telephone inventor Alexander Graham Bell, and the steel giant and philanthropist Andrew Carnegie. Naturalist John Muir converses on stage with Teddy Roosevelt. Charles Lindbergh, Rosie the Riveter, Jackie Robinson, Marilyn Monroe, and Walt Disney are all represented. So are John Wayne, Lucille Ball, Margaret Mead, John F. Kennedy, Martin Luther King, Jr., Muhammed Ali, and Billie Jean King. The idea is to recall episodes in history, both negative and positive, which most contributed to the growth of the spirit of America, either by engendering "a new burst of creativity" (in the designers' words) "or a better understanding of ourselves as partners in the American experience." The presentation is hardly comprehensive; instead, it's "a hundred-yard dash capturing the spirit of the country at specific moments in time."

Throughout the show, the attention to historical detail is meticulous. Every one of the rear-projected illustrations was executed in the painting style of the era being described. The Chief Joseph and Susan B. Anthony figures are speaking their originals' own words. The exact dimensions of the cannon balls in another scene were carefully investigated—then reproduced. In the Philadelphia Centennial Exposition scene, Pittsburgh's name is spelled without the *h* that subsequent years have added.

For information about how each of the various historical figures actually spoke during their lifetimes, researchers contacted about half a dozen historians and cultural institutions—the Philadelphia Historical Commission, Harvard's Carpenter Center of Visual Arts, the State Historical Society of Missouri, the Department of the Navy's Ships Historical Branch, and others. When recordings were not available, educated guesses were made: Bell's voice was created on the basis of contemporary comments about his voice's clarity, expressiveness, and crisp articulation, coupled with the fact that his father taught elocution. To select Will Rogers's speeches for the Depression scene, whole pages of quotes were collected, reviewed, edited, and re-edited; the voice is the humorist's own, from an actual broadcast, as is that of FDR, here heard over the radio in the roadside gasoline stand scene. That particular scene was suggested by a *Life* magazine photograph; details are accurate down to the price of gasoline (18¢).

One of the most interesting aspects of the show is its inner workings. Underneath the entire theater is a movable carriage device

that designers have dubbed "the war wagon." The basement that supports "the war wagon" is itself supported by pilings driven approximately 300 feet into the ground; it carries ten different sets and during the presentation rolls forward or backward to position the appropriate set underneath the stage at the appropriate time. Also, because the height of the space underneath the theater is relatively limited, the sets themselves were specially designed to allow certain sections to contract telescopically as proved necessary. These operations are computer controlled.

The 12 life-size statues on either side of the stage represent the Spirits of America. These are, on the left, from front to rear, Individualism, Innovation, Tomorrow, Independence, Compassion, and Discovery; and, on the right, from front to back, Freedom, Heritage, Pioneering, Knowledge, Self-Reliance, and Adventure. The 44 flags flanking the Hall of Flags corridor in the escalator area are those that have flown over the United States. Revolutionary War flags, Colonial flags, and even flags representing the countries that had claims to American soil before Independence, can all be seen. A special highlight of the show is the majestic music played throughout by the Philadelphia Symphony Orchestra. The Golden Dreams sequence includes notables like Muppet creator Jim Henson, Ryan White—the young hemophiliac who succumbed to AIDS after a courageous battle with the disease—and basketball star Earvin "Magic" Johnson.

As one of the most compelling of all the World Showcase attractions, The American Adventure is often quite busy. Seats in the front of the house give the optimal view of the Audio-Animatronics characters (although all seats provide an acceptable view). Perhaps the best time to schedule a visit to the show is soon after World Showcase opens or in the early evening. Be sure to check your entertainment schedule for exact showtimes and arrive early. If you time it right, The Voices of Liberty a cappella group makes for an entertaining wait. Or read the quotes on the walls—Wendell Wilkie, Jane Addams, Charles Lindbergh, Ayn Rand, Archibald MacLeish, Herman Melville, Thomas Wolfe, and Walt Disney are all represented.

HERITAGE MANOR GIFTS: Visit this shop for pre-1940s Americana. Decorative gifts include glassware, hand-made wooden and cloth items, hand-painted porcelain, toys, and food products.

AMERICA GARDENS THEATRE: A variety of entertainment is presented several times a week in this lakeside amphitheater in front of The American Adventure pavilion. Check your entertainment schedule for details and exact times. Showtimes also are posted on the promenade at the east and west entrances to the amphitheater.

Be sure to note the pruning of the Western sycamores overhead; the old-fashioned pollarding method used, which involves trimming the treetops flat and allowing the lower branches to fill out and interlock, eventually produces a thick canopy. The flower beds outside are planted in red, white, and blue.

Italy

The arches and cut-out motifs that adorn the World Showcase reproduction of the Doge's Palace in Venice are just the more obvious examples of the attention to detail lavished on the individual structures in this relatively small pavilion. The angel atop the scaled down campanile was sculpted on the model of the original right down to the curls on the back of its head—then covered with real gold leaf, despite the fact that it was destined to be set almost 100 feet in the air. The other statues in the complex, including the sea god Neptune presiding over the fountain in the rear of the piazza, are similarly exact. Even the marblelike material used in the facade resembles that used in the real Doge's Palace. And the pavilion even has an island like Venice's own, its seawall appropriately stained with age, plus moorings that look like barber poles, with several distinctively Venetian gondolas tied to them. St. Mark the Evangelist also is remembered, together with the lion that is the saint's companion and Venice's guardian; these can be seen atop the two massive columns flanking the small arched footbridge that connects the landfall to the mainland. The only deviation from Venetian fact is the alteration of the site of the Doge's Palace in reference to the real St. Mark's Square.

The pavilion is equally interesting from a horticultural point of view. The island boasts a brace of kumquat trees, citrus plants typical of the Mediterranean, and a couple of olive trees that can be seen on both side walls of the Delizie Italiane; originally located in a Sacramento, California grove, they were moved to Anaheim and then were piled onto a flatbed truck, their branches spreading wide, for the trip to Florida. But they got only as far as the Arizona border. As Disney gardeners tell

the story, that state's regulation prohibiting loads beyond a given width is so erratically enforced that no problems had been anticipated. So it came as quite a surprise when the inspector on duty decreed that the trees be trimmed to ten feet. A chain saw soon materialized, and within minutes the ancient olives were shorn. Despite horticulturalists' fears, the trees survived, leaving only their scars to remind visitors of the ordeal; the darker bark is what remains of the original, while the lighter areas are the new growth. The tall, narrow trees that stand like dark columns at various points in the pavilion are Italian cypress, which are extremely common in Italy; Florida slash pines serve as stand-ins for Italian stone pines, which would not grow here.

DELIZIE ITALIANE: This open-air market on the western edge of the piazza is a good spot for a sweet snack with its selection of tasty Italian chocolates and other goodies for sale.

LA BOTTEGA ITALIANA: A selection of items from Benetton, the Italian casual wear manufacturer, is featured here. Colorful sweaters, shirts, slacks, jeans, and accessories are all available.

LA GEMMA ELEGANTE: Located to the rear of the piazza on its eastern edge, this small shop focuses on jewelry. There are gold and silver chains galore, and some are expensive, but it's also possible to find handsome—and affordable—beads, earrings, and pendants made of Venetian glass; intricate glass-mosaic brooches and pillboxes bearing images of tiny bouquets; cameos; and coral necklaces.

IL BEL CRISTALLO: The production of fine glassware has been a tradition in Italy for centuries, and so a shop like this one just off the promenade on the Germany side of the piazza was a must for the pavilion. Typical Venetian glass paperweights and other items, their bright colors trapped in smooth spheres or teardrops of clear or milky glass, small porcelain figurines and flower bouquets so finely crafted that they look almost real, pastel flowers made of beads, and lead crystal bowls and candlesticks are all on display. The name of the shop means "the beautiful crystal."

Germany

There are no villages in Germany quite like this one. Inspired in part by towns in the Rhine region and Bavaria, and in part by communities in the German north, it boasts structures reminiscent of those found in such diverse urban enclaves as Frankfurt, Freiburg, and Rothenburg. There are stair-stepped roof lines and towers, balconies and arcaded walkways, and so much overall charm that the scene seems to come straight out of a fairy tale. The beer hall to the rear is almost as lively as the one at Munich's famed Oktoberfest, especially during the later shows, and the shops, which offer a range of merchandise from wine and sweets to ceramics and cuckoo clocks, toys and books, and even art, are so tempting that it's hard to leave the area empty-handed. The various elements that make up the Germany pavilion are described here as they would be encountered while walking from west to east (counterclockwise) around the cobblestone-paved central plaza, which is known as the St. Georgsplatz, after the statue at its center. St. George, the patron saint of soldiers, is depicted with the dragon that legend says he slew during a pilgrimage to the Middle East.

Try to time your World Showcase peregrinations to bring you to Germany on the hour,

when the handsome, specially designed glockenspiel at the plaza's rear can be heard to chime in a melody composed specifically for the pavilion. Check the entertainment schedule to see if a strolling accordianist and a trio will be performing in the *Biergarten* restaurant.

DER BÜCHERWURM: This two-story structure, whose exterior is patterned after a merchants' hall known as the *Kaufhaus* (located in the southern German town of Freiburg in Breisgau), stocks prints and English books about Germany; handsome prints of German cities full of gabled old houses and gloriously spired cathedrals; and an assortment of souvenir items such as ashtrays and vases and spoons bearing images of German cities. The building itself is worth noting. In order to correctly

reproduce the statues of the German emperors on the facade, designers hired a photographer who shot from a "cherry picker" and submitted closeups from a number of angles. (Film and sundries also are available.)

VOLKSKUNST: This small, exceptionally appealing establishment is full of a burgher's bounty of German timekeepers, plus a smattering of other items made by hand in the rural corners of the nation. The latter include beer steins in all sizes, from the petite to the enormous and expensive ($2,800); wood carvings made in the southern German town of Oberammergau; bright, fringed Tyrolean scarves; nutcrackers; and a whole collection of "smokers," carved wooden dolls with a receptacle for incense and a hollow pipe for the smoke to escape. As for cuckoo clocks, some are small and unprepossessing, and some are so immense that they'd look appropriate only in some cathedral-ceilinged hunting lodge. The largest measures about five feet in height and is embellished not only with carvings of birds and rabbits and a hunting horn and crossed rifles, but also with a genuine pair of antlers. A must.

Schmitt Söhne, one of Germany's oldest and largest vintners. Wine tastings are held here daily. The selection includes not only those meant for everyday consumption, but also fine estate wines whose prices run into the hundreds of dollars per bottle. These are white (with a few exceptions), because white wine constitutes the bulk of Germany's vinicultural output. (Only 20 percent of all German bottlings are red.) Long, tall beer mugs and glasses, wine glasses in traditional German colors of greens and ambers, fragile crystal goblets, decanters, and other accessories also are available. The setting itself is quite attractive—low-ceilinged and cozy and full of fir cabinets that have been embellished with carvings of vines and bunches of grapes.

SÜSSIGKEITEN: It's a mistake to visit this tiny, tile-floored confectionery shop on an empty stomach: Chocolate cookies, butter cookies, and almond biscuits mix with caramels, nuts, and pretzels are on the crowded shelves; and there are boxes upon boxes of *Lebkuchen*, the spicy crisp cookies traditionally baked in Germany at Christmas, not to mention Gummi Bears (which the packages announce as *Gummibaeren*). Children enjoy the special alphabet cookies and animal crackers, both of which are different from those made in U.S. bakeries. Don't miss the attractive display of old Bahlsen cookie tins by the door. Incidentally, Bahlsen, the shop's sponsor, was among the first companies in the world to pack baked goods in airtight wrappers to preserve freshness; the firm's logo is an Egyptian hieroglyph that signifies *long life.*

DER TEDDYBÄR: Located alongside Volkskunst, this toy shop would be a delight if only for the lively mechanized displays high up on either side of the entrance and against the rear wall: Some of the stuffed lambs and the dolls in the full-skirted folk dresses (known as *dirndls*) have been animated so that tails wag and skirts swirl in time to German folk tunes. The shop also is home to one of WDW's best selections of toys. There are wonderfully detailed LGB-brand miniature trains and the expected assortment of expensive stuffed keepsakes from Steiff. Colorful wooden toys are tempting as well, along with all kinds of building blocks. Last but not least, the collection of dolls is simply wonderful.

WEINKELLER: The Germany pavilion's wine shop, situated between the cookie shop and the *Biergarten* toward the rear of St. Georgsplatz, offers about 250 varieties of German wines produced and bottled by H.

DIE WEIHNACHTS ECKE: This is a shop that can set a visitor's mind to thoughts of Christmas—even in the dog days of summer. Ornaments, decorations, and gifts manufactured by various German companies line the shelves of this store.

GLAS UND PORZELLAN: Featuring glass and porcelain items made by the German firm of Goebel, this is an attractive establishment with rope-turned columns, curved moldings, delicate scrollwork, and tiny carved rosettes. But no matter how attractive the backgrounds, the stars of the show are the M. I. Hummel figurines, which Goebel manufactures. Cherubic, rosy-cheeked children, shown carrying baskets, trays, umbrellas, and other items, as in the drawings of a young German nun named Berta Hummel, are favorites of collectors around the world. There is always an elaborate showpiece at the center of the shop, and a Goebel artist is here to demonstrate the process by which Hummel creations are painted and finished. An excellent display (which includes figurines in all stages of completeness) tells the story.

China

Dominated by a Disney equivalent of Beijing's Temple of Heaven, and announced by a pair of banners that offer good wishes to passersby (the Chinese characters translate: *May good fortune follow you on your path through life* and *May virtue be your neighbor*), this pavilion offers a level of serenity that makes an appealing contrast to the hearty merriment of nearby Germany and the Latin gaiety of Mexico. Part of this quiet environment is the byproduct of the soothing traditional Chinese music that plays over the sound system. The traditional Chinese Lion Dance is sometimes performed outside the pavilion. The attractive gardens also make a major contribution. They are full of rose-bushes native to China, and there is a century-old mulberry tree (to the left of the main walkway into the pavilion), with a pomegranate tree and a wiggly looking Florida native known as a water oak nearby. In addition, a spacious emporium devoted to Chinese wares has opened, and two Chinese restaurants add to the overall atmosphere. However, all this is secondary to the fabulous motion picture shown inside the Temple of Heaven—a Circle-Vision 360 film that is one of the best World Showcase attractions.

WONDERS OF CHINA: LAND OF BEAUTY, LAND OF TIME: This 19-minute presentation shows the beauties of a land that few Epcot visitors will ever see firsthand—and does it so vividly that it's possible to see the film over and over and still not fully absorb all the wonderful sights. The Disney crew was the first Western film group to film certain sites, and their remarkable effort includes such marvels as Beijing's Forbidden City; vast, wide-open Inner Mongolia and its stern-faced tribespeople; the 2,400-year-old Great Wall; the Great Buddha of Leshan, eight centuries old and dramatically imposing; the muddy Yangtze River and the 3,000-year-old city of Suzhou, whose location on the Grand Canal, which is generally believed to be the largest manmade waterway in the world, encouraged Marco Polo to call it the Venice of the East. There are shots of the Europeanlike city of Shanghai, as well as Hangzhou, where a handful of Chinese are shown doing their morning exercises along the river's edge. Also shown are Huangshan Mountain, wreathed in fog; the Shilin Stone Forest of jagged rock outcroppings in Yunnan Province; Urumchi, whose distance from the sea in Xinjiang Province earned it the title of the most inland city on earth; Lahsa, in Tibet, and its Potala Palace, boasting a thousand rooms and ten times that many altars. Just as fantastic are the Reed Flute Cave and the bizarrely shaped hills of Kweilin above. To complete the picture, there are fields of snow and of wheat, high meadows and beaches dotted with tropi-cal palms, harbors and rice terraces, calligraphers, checkers and Ping-Pong players, lightning-fast acrobats, championship horse-back riders, camels and a panda bear, glittering ice sculptures, and millions of bicycles.

Almost every step of the way, the film crews were besieged by curious Chinese, even in empty Inner Mongolia. For the Huangshan Mountain sequence, which lasts only seconds, the crew and about three-dozen hired laborers had to carry the 600-pound camera uphill for nearly a mile. The Chinese government would not permit Disney cameramen to shoot aerial footage in some areas, so Chinese crews were sent aloft to record the required scenes, first on videotape and later—after approval from the Disney director in charge of the project—on film. You can see for yourself just how well this collaboration worked.

Be sure to spend some time before viewing the film examining the details that embellish the building that houses the theater. The design is based on that of the Hall of Prayer for Good Harvest, the major section of Beijing's Temple of Heaven complex, which was built in the year 1420 (during the Ming Dynasty) and reconstructed after being damaged by lightning in 1896. The name of the World Showcase structure is represented by the characters above the entrance. The number of stones in the floor was chosen for auspicious associations; the center stone is surrounded by nine stones because nine is considered a lucky

number in China. Around the edge of the room rise 12 columns—because 12 is both the number of months in the year and the number of years in a full cycle of the Chinese calendar. Closer to the room's center, there are four columns—one for each of the seasons; the japonicus vines entwining each column symbolize long life, while the square beam that they all support alludes to earth, and the round beam above signifies heaven. The dragons on the beams allude to imperial strength, while the phoenixes are reminders of peace and prosperity. The measurements and proportions are all similarly symbolic. Be sure to stand on the round stone in the absolute center of the anteroom: Every whisper is amplified.

When exiting, pass by the House of the Whispering Willows, an exhibit of ancient Chinese art and artifacts. Changed about every six months, it invariably includes fine pieces from well-known collections. Note that the best time to see the film is during the first couple of hours that World Showcase is open and again just before closing.

YONG FENG SHANGDIAN SHOPPING GALLERY: This vast Chinese emporium, located off the narrow, charming Street of Good Fortune at the exit to the film, offers a huge assortment of Chinese merchandise—silk robes, prints, paper umbrellas and fans, embroidered items, change purses and glasses cases, and more. Trinkets, medium-priced items, and expensive antiques are all available in an array that may be matched in few other places in the U.S. The calligraphy on the curtains wishes passersby *good fortune, long life, prosperity, health, and happiness.*

Norway

Set between the Mexico and China pavilions is Norway, Walt Disney World's 11th World Showcase attraction. Built in conjunction with many Norwegian companies, the pavilion celebrates the history, folklore, and culture of one of the western world's oldest countries.

The cobblestone town square is an architectural showcase in the styles of such Norwegian towns as Bergen, Alesund, Oslo, and Setesdal. There's also a Norwegian castle fashioned after Akershus, a 14th-century fortress still standing in Oslo's harbor; the castle here houses the *Akershus* restaurant. Most can't resist walking into the bakery for a taste of its treats. In a show of modernity, a statue of Norway's living legend, Grete Waitz, may be found behind the bakery. Shops stock authentic Norwegian handicrafts and folk items: hand-knit woolens, wood carvings, and glass and metal artworks.

MAELSTROM: Most appropriately, visitors tour Norway by boat—16-passenger, dragon-headed longboats like those Eric the Red and his fellow Vikings used a thousand years ago—to begin a ten-minute voyage through time. The journey begins in a tenth-century Viking village where a ship is being readied to head out to sea. Seafarers then find themselves in a mythical Norwegian forest, populated by trolls who cause the boats to plummet backwards downriver, through a maelstrom to the majestic grandeur of the Geiranger fjord, where the vessel narrowly avoids spilling over a waterfall. Ultimately, after a harrowing plunge through a rocky passage, the boats wind up in the North Sea, caught in the fury of a full-blown storm. Lightning flashes reveal an enormous oil rig; as the boat passes the concrete platform legs, the storm calms and a friendly coastal village appears on the horizon.

Survivors disembark there and enter the village. Moments later, guests are invited to a theater where the journey continues on-screen, giving visitors a tangible sense of the natural scenic spectacles and unique personalities that make up modern Norway.

Maelstrom is an exciting ride that has quickly become one of World Showcase's more popular attractions. Try to visit in the evening, when it is least crowded.

STAVE CHURCH GALLERY: Inside the pavilion's reproduction of a wooden stave church, there is a small exhibit that explores Norwegian culture. It's interesting to note that only 30 stave churches remain in Norway today.

THE PUFFIN'S ROOST: A collection of Norwegian gifts, sweaters, activewear, handcrafted jewelry, fine leather goods, pewter, candy, toys, and trolls are the wares for sale at this shop.

Mexico

The tangle of tropical vegetation surrounding the great pyramid that encloses this pavilion and the *Cantina*, the Mexican restaurant at the lagoon's edge on the promenade, provide only the barest suggestion of the charming area inside. Dominated by a reconstruction of a quaint plaza at dusk, this area is rimmed by balconied, tile-roofed, colonial-style structures. Crowding a pretty fountain area is a quartet of stands selling Mexican handicrafts, and off to the left is an attractive shop stocked with other handsome wares. Mariachi bands keep things lively. To the rear, the *San Angel Inn*, a corporate cousin of the famous Mexico City restaurant, serves authentic Mexican fare. Behind it, the pavilion's main show chronicles Mexican culture from earliest times right up to the present. Take a look at the cultural exhibit inside the pyramid entrance on the way in. Note that the pyramid itself was inspired by Meso-American structures dating from the third century A.D. The serpent heads on either side of the stairway evoke the Aztec god Quetzalcoatl.

EL RIO DEL TIEMPO: THE RIVER OF TIME:
In the course of this six-minute boat trip, sprinkled with vignettes of pre-Columbian, Spanish-Colonial, and modern Mexican life, visitors greet a Mayan high priest, watch stylized dances by performers in vivid costumes, and are assailed by vendors at a lively market. A band costumed to look like skeletons entertains at one juncture (in a reference to the Day of the Dead, a holiday celebrated in Mexico with candies and sweets shaped like skulls or skeletons). In addition, there are a handful of film clips depicting present-day Acapulco (with its cliff divers and flying dancers), Tulum, Manzanillo (and its speedboats), and Isla Mujeres (with its gorgeous sea life). The assemblage of film, Audio-Animatronics figures, and props is reminiscent of the Magic Kingdom's It's A Small World. During peak seasons, long lines, which prevail from late morning on, usually thin out in the afternoon as the crowds drift into the more distant parts of World Showcase. If you are in the area, skip the boat ride the first time around and return in the evening or late in the afternoon when the crowds are likely to be far smaller.

PLAZA DE LOS AMIGOS:
Brightly colored paper flowers, sombreros, wooden trays and bowls, peasant blouses, baskets, and pottery make this shopping area (*mercado* in Spanish) at the plaza's center as bright and almost as lively as one in Mexico itself. The colorful papier-mâché piñatas that figure so strongly in the scenery here are so popular that Epcot has to buy them from suppliers by the truckload. Irresistible.

ARTESANIAS MEXICANAS:
This shop stocks more expensive versions of some of the merchandise sold in the *mercado*—onyx ashtrays, bookends, plaques, chess sets, malachite, and unique Mexican decorative gifts.

LA FAMILIA FASHIONS:
Mexican ready-to-wear and fashion accessories for women and children, plus examples of silver and turquoise jewelry are available here.

EL RANCHITO DEL NORTE:
Gifts and souvenirs from northern Mexico are the featured items at this spot.

World Showcase Plaza

PORT OF ENTRY: Features unique gifts, clothing, and accessories from around the world including countries not featured in World Showcase. Sunglasses, film, and cigarettes are available.

DISNEY TRADERS: Merchandise combining the charms of Disney characters and World Showcase themes are the stock in trade. Sunglasses, film, cigarettes, and sundries also are available.

International Gateway

SHOWCASE GIFTS: Disney memorabilia, convenience items, and a package pickup depot are located at this spot near the France entrance.

WORLD TRAVELER: Disney fashions and character merchandise, plus film, 35mm and video camera rentals, and a drop-off for two-hour film processing are conveniently located here.

STROLLER AND WHEELCHAIR RENTAL: Strollers and wheelchairs are available for rent at this location. Remember to keep your rental receipt; it can be used on the same day in the Magic Kingdom, at the Disney-MGM Studios, or again in Epcot should you leave and return at a later hour.

HOT TIPS

- Stop by Guest Relations for an entertainment schedule to be sure you won't miss any of the special shows scheduled for the day or evening.
- The best time to visit World Showcase is as soon as it opens (usually at 11 A.M.) See Future World in the late afternoon until it closes (usually at 7 P.M.) Remember that lines throughout Epcot are longest during midday, and shortest (sometimes nonexistent) during the early evening.
- Check the tip board in Innoventions Plaza for current waiting times for the most popular attractions, and alter your touring plans accordingly.
- During peak seasons, preferred reservation times at Epcot's full-service restaurants are usually fully booked by 10 A.M. So be sure to arrive at Epcot early to get a jump on the day and help assure that you get the restaurant and seating time of your choice. Remember, too, that non-prime dining hours are often available to those making late reservations, so adjustment of your eating schedule may well help you to try the restaurant of your choice. Most World Showcase restaurants seat guests until park closing. Guests also can make reservations in advance by calling 939-3463.
- Save the shops in World Showcase for the afternoon when just about everything else is very crowded.
- Guests staying at WDW resorts can have merchandise packages delivered to their hotels at no extra charge.
- Don't queue for the World Showcase Promenade buses. You'll get where you're going faster by walking.
- Don't see all the World Showcase films in one day, especially if you're traveling with children.
- Be sure to allow extra time for Innoventions, Image Works at Journey Into Imagination, and Sea Base Alpha at The Living Seas.
- The jumping fountains outside the Journey Into Imagination are a favorite with children of all ages.
- Note that Spaceship Earth and Innoventions stay open after the rest of Future World closes (usually 7 P.M.), making the evening hours a good time to take in these attractions. The *Fountain View Espresso & Bakery*, *Pasta Piazza Ristorante*, and the *Electric Umbrella* restaurants also stay open until 9 P.M.

DISNEY-MGM STUDIOS

Welcome to "the Hollywood that never was and always will be." So said Walt Disney Company Chairman Michael Eisner when he officially opened the Disney-MGM Studios. A bit corny—but also true.

In the solid Disney tradition, a dream Hollywood set in some indeterminate time in the 1930s and 1940s has been lovingly created. A rose-colored view of the movie-making capital has been combined with a backstage tour that breaks new ground, a variety of entertaining attractions, and a delightful selection of eateries to create this Walt Disney World enclave.

The Disney-MGM Studios is situated on a 110-acre site southwest of Epcot. The water tower, known to punsters (for obvious reasons) as the "Earffel Tower," is reminiscent of the types of towers looming over most Hollywood studios of the era. Here, however, it gets that special Disney touch and is capped by a mousketeer-style hat.

What makes this area of Walt Disney World different from other Disney creations is the extent to which guests can participate in the attractions. Our best advice is to volunteer, wherever and whenever possible. It's fun, and it adds enormously to the experience.

The Studios is still expanding. A brand-new parade may be rolling down Hollywood Boulevard this year. And Fantasmic!, the spectacular show that has been amazing Disneyland visitors for several years, is expected to come to the Studios by 1997. Other future plans may call for adding attractions to Sunset Boulevard, including Roger Rabbit's Hollywood.

163

N
↓

1 The Spirit of Pocahontas Stage Show

2 Jim Henson's Muppet★Vision 3-D

3 Star Tours

4 Monster Sound Show

5 Indiana Jones Epic Stunt Spectacular

6 SuperStar Television

7 Hollywood Boulevard

8 Sunset Boulevard

9 Beauty and the Beast Stage Show

10 The Twilight Zone Tower of Terror

11 The Magic of Disney Animation

12 Backstage Studio Tour

13 Voyage of the Little Mermaid

14 The Great Movie Ride

15 Working Sound Stages

16 Inside the Magic:
Special Effects and Production Tour

17 Catastrophe Canyon

18 Honey, I Shrunk the Kids
Movie Set Adventure

Getting In & Around

TRANSPORTATION TO THE DISNEY-MGM STUDIOS: It's very simple to get to this Disney theme park.

By car: Take exit 26B or exit 25 off I-4 and follow the signs for the Disney-MGM Studios. The entrance to the Studios is about half a mile from I-4. There is a 7,500-space parking lot. Parking is $5; free for Walt Disney World resort guests. Trams carry visitors from their parking space to the ticket booths.

By bus: Buses make the trip to the Studios from a variety of locations: from the Magic Kingdom and its surrounding resorts (*Contemporary*, *Grand Floridian*, *Polynesian*), from *The Villas at The Disney Institute*, from Disney Village Hotel Plaza, from the *Caribbean Beach* resort, from *Port Orleans*, from *Dixie Landings*, from the *Disney Vacation Club*, from *Wilderness Lodge*, from the *All-Star Sports* and *All-Star Music* resorts, and from Epcot. From *Fort Wilderness*, buses take guests to the TTC; transfer to the Disney-MGM Studios bus there. Call 824-4321 to confirm all the available transportation options.

By launch: Guests staying at the *Swan*, *Dolphin*, *Yacht Club*, and *Beach Club* can take a boat to the Studios.

HOURS: The Disney-MGM Studios is usually open from 9 A.M. to 7 P.M.; hours are extended during holiday weekends and the summer months. Call 824-4321 for up-to-the-minute schedules. Depending on the season, some of the Studios' attractions do not open until late in the morning. Be sure to check the Tip Board and your entertainment schedule for exact showtimes.

BABY CARE: Changing tables and facilities for nursing mothers can be found at the Guest Relations building at the main entrance.

CAMERA NEEDS: The Darkroom is located to the right as you enter the park. Camcorders are available for rent (with a deposit). Single-use cameras are sold, and two-hour film processing is offered. A wide assortment of film and accessories is sold. Film also is available in most of the shops.

STUDIOS TIP BOARD: Located at the end of Hollywood Boulevard, this information center is staffed by hosts and hostesses who can tell guests which attractions are about to begin a new show and which have the shortest lines. It is updated con-

stantly via a system of two-way radios, so the suggestions offered on the big blackboard are well worth following. The hosts also can provide general information. Restaurant reservations for several of the Studios' eateries can be made here as well.

FIRST AID: Minor medical problems can be handled at First Aid in the Guest Relations building at the main entrance.

VISITORS WITH DISABILITIES: Most of the attractions, shops, and restaurants are accessible to guests in wheelchairs. Special parking for guests with disabilities is available; be sure to inquire at the Auto Plaza. Wheelchairs can be rented at Oscar's Super Service, just inside the main entrance. Quantities are limited. The *Walt Disney World Guidebook for Guests with Disabilities* is available at Guest Relations. For hearing-impaired guests, an Assistive Listening Device is available at Guest Relations. A $25 deposit is required. Written scripts also are available at each show and attraction. For sight-impaired guests, descriptive audiocassettes and portable tape players (with a $25 refundable deposit) are available at Guest Relations.

LOCKERS: Large storage lockers, which cost 75 cents apiece, are located right next to Oscar's Super Service at the main entrance.

LOST CHILDREN: Report lost children to the Guest Relations building at the main entrance, call 560-4668, or tell an employee.

LOST AND FOUND: Claim or report lost articles at the Guest Relations building on the day of your visit. To claim or report lost articles after your visit, call 560-4245.

MONEY MATTERS: An ATM is located next to the ticket sales window at the main entrance. Credit cards (American Express, Visa, MasterCard, and The Disney Credit Card) and traveler's checks are accepted for merchandise, admission media, and at full-service restaurants. Only cash is accepted at food carts and counter-service establishments. Disney Dollars, available in colorful $1, $5, and $10 denominations, are good for dining and merchandise and can be exchanged at any time for U.S. currency, though many guests take a few home as inexpensive souvenirs.

STROLLER AND WHEELCHAIR RENTAL: Both are available for rent at Oscar's Super Service inside the main entrance, but quantities are limited. Remember to keep your rental receipt, because it can be used on the same day in the Magic Kingdom, Epcot, or again at the Studios.

ADMISSION: Tickets and passes are available for one, four, and five days. The Disney organization defines a ticket as admission for one day only; other forms of admission media (for longer periods) are called passes. One-day tickets may be used at the Magic Kingdom, Epcot, or the Disney-MGM Studios, but not at more than one site on the same day. Four-Day Value Passes may be used for one day in each park, plus one optional day in the park of your choice, but not at more than one park on the same day. Four-Day Park Hopper Passes and Five-Day World Hopper Passes can be used at all three parks on the same day. Unlike one-day tickets, all multi-day passes also include use of the transportation system inside Walt Disney World. The Five-Day World Hopper Pass also allows admission to Typhoon Lagoon, Blizzard Beach, River Country, Discovery Island, and Pleasure Island for a seven-day period beginning with the first use of the pass. Guests staying at Walt Disney World resorts can purchase a pass valid for the length of their stay. The Length of Stay Pass offers savings over other passes, and includes unlimited admission to the Magic Kingdom, Epcot, the Disney-MGM Studios, Typhoon Lagoon, Blizzard Beach, River Country, Discovery Island, and Pleasure Island for the duration of your stay. Cash, traveler's checks, personal checks (with proper ID), American Express, Visa, Master-Card, and The Disney Credit Card can be used to pay for all admission media. When you purchase a Four-Day Park Hopper Pass, a Five-Day World Hopper Pass, or a Length of Stay Pass, you must have your photo mounted on the pass to validate it. Pass photos can be taken at the Transportation and Ticket Center and at the entrances to the Magic Kingdom, Epcot, and the Disney-MGM Studios. Multi-day passes do not have to be used on consecutive days.

Passes may be purchased at all WDW resorts (by WDW resort guests), at the entrances to the theme parks, at the Orlando International Airport, or at The Disney Store.

Passes by mail: Send a check or money order payable to Walt Disney World Company in the exact amount plus $2 for handling to:

Walt Disney World
Box 10,030; Lake Buena Vista, FL 32830-0030
Attention: Ticket Mail Order

Remember to include your return address. Allow at least three to four weeks for ticket requests to be processed.

ADMISSION PRICES*

ONE-DAY TICKET
(Restricted to use in the Studios only.)

Adult	$ 39.27
Child**	$ 31.80

FOUR-DAY VALUE PASS
(Valid for one day in each park, plus one optional day in the park of your choice. Includes use of WDW transportation system.)

Adult	$131.44
Child**	$102.82

FOUR-DAY PARK HOPPER PASS
(Valid in all three parks for four days and includes use of WDW transportation system.)

Adult	$145.22
Child**	$115.54

FIVE-DAY WORLD HOPPER PASS
(Valid in all three parks for five days, includes use of WDW transportation system, and allows admission to Typhoon Lagoon, Blizzard Beach, River Country, Discovery Island, and Pleasure Island for up to seven days from the first use of the pass.)

Adult	$197.16
Child**	$156.88

LENGTH OF STAY PASS
(Available to WDW resort guests only. Valid in all three parks, Typhoon Lagoon, Blizzard Beach, River Country, Discovery Island, and Pleasure Island for the duration of stay and includes use of WDW transportation system.)

Length of Stay	Adult	Child**
4 days	$166.42	$131.44
5 days	$193.98	$153.70
6 days	$217.30	$172.78
7 days	$241.68	$191.86
8 days	$259.70	$206.70
9 days	$277.72	$220.48
10 days	$288.32	$230.02

The cost of a **THEME PARK ANNUAL PASS** is $242.74 for adults and $210.94 for children; renewals are $221.54 for adults and $189.74 for children. The cost of a **PREMIUM ANNUAL PASS** is $338.14 for adults and $296.80 for children; renewals are $306.34 for adults and $270.30 for children; in addition to the three theme parks, it includes admission to Typhoon Lagoon, Blizzard Beach, River Country, and Discovery Island.

Note: Multi-day passes need not be used on consecutive days.

These prices were correct at press time, but may change during 1996.

*The prices quoted include sales tax.

**3 through 9 years of age; children under 3 are free

Hollywood Boulevard

Enter the gates of the Disney-MGM Studios and the mosaic of flashy neon, chromed Art Deco and streamlined moderne architecture, and star-gazing street characters immediately plunge guests into the Hollywood of the 1930s and 1940s. Palm-lined Hollywood Boulevard conveys the spirit of a city that never existed, but one we all wish had. Assorted characters ask guests for autographs, while would-be starlets search for their big break. There's a guy selling maps to the stars' Beverly Hills homes and roving television reporters, all of whom populate this rosy image of Hollywood's heyday. Great movie music is piped in when small strolling bands aren't entertaining, the streets are spotless, and guests are transported to another time and place.

The shops of Hollywood Boulevard are described here. For details about the restaurants at the Studios, see the *Good Meals, Great Times* chapter.

East Side of the Street

MOVIELAND MEMORABILIA: Located just to the left of the main entrance, this kiosk stocks stuffed toys, hats, books, sunglasses, film, key chains, and other souvenirs.

CROSSROADS OF THE WORLD: In the middle of the entrance plaza, Mickey Mouse keeps watch from atop this Hollywood Boulevard landmark. The circular shop offers souvenirs, sunglasses, film, raingear, sundries, and information.

SID CAHUENGA'S ONE-OF-A-KIND: Authentic antiques and curios are the stock-in-trade here. Autographed photos, old movie magazines and posters, and assorted Hollywood memorabilia are among the collectibles with which Sid is willing to part—for a price.

MICKEY'S OF HOLLYWOOD, PLUTO'S TOY PALACE, DISNEY & CO.: These three shops are connected, similar to the setup at the Magic Kingdom's Emporium. This is the place to find T-shirts, sweatshirts, hats, plush toys, watches, jackets, socks, wallets, tote bags, books, and sunglasses, all emblazoned with the Disney-MGM Studios logo.

KEYSTONE CLOTHIERS: Ranging from flashy to classy, men's and women's fashions and accessories are the specialties of this shop. There's a wonderful pair of earrings—one Mickey and one Minnie—that will set you back $290. A favorite item sold here is a Mickey Mouse umbrella that sprouts two ears when opened.

LAKESIDE NEWS: A terrific selection of comic books is found here, along with souvenirs and a wide variety of movie magazines.

West Side of the Street

OSCAR'S CLASSIC CAR SOUVENIRS & SUPER SERVICE: The 1947 Buick parked out front gets plenty of attention. Automotive memorabilia, mugs, models, and key chains are for sale. The car, by the way, is not. Services offered here include stroller and wheelchair rental, lockers, and infant products. There also is a stamp machine.

THE DARKROOM: The Art Deco facade of this shop allows guests to enter through an aperture-like doorway. Kodak VHS video cameras are available for rent at $25 per day, with a refundable deposit of $300. Deposits can be charged on American Express, MasterCard, or Visa. Film is not included in the rental price. Although no 35mm cameras are available for rent, single-use cameras, film, and accessories are sold.

COVER STORY: Just through The Darkroom, this is where guests can have their images put on the front cover of a large choice of popular magazines. Costumes and appropriate accessories are provided by the shop.

CELEBRITY 5 & 10: Modeled after a 1940s Woolworth's, this large shop carries trinkets, costume jewelry, picture frames, shirts, jackets, aprons, teddy bears, magnets, and memorabilia associated with old Hollywood. This is the place to pick up a director's clapboard and other non-Disney, film-related merchandise.

SWEET SUCCESS: Specialty candies and more mundane treats are available at this sweet-smelling shop.

L.A. PROP AND STORAGE: A wide variety of children's clothing featuring characters from *Beauty and the Beast*, *Aladdin*, and *The Lion King* are among the offerings at this shop.

Sunset Boulevard

Anchored at its far end by the Hollywood Tower Hotel, home of The Twilight Zone Tower of Terror, Sunset Boulevard is the Studios' newest block. The wide palm-fringed thoroughfare is lined with a few shops (some are real while others are just facades with great window dressing), the *Sunset Ranch Market* where snack stands and tables with umbrellas look like an old-fashioned farmer's market, and the Theatre of the Stars amphitheater, home of the Beauty and the Beast Stage Show. Other shops are planned for the future. The shops are described here. For details about eating on Sunset Boulevard, see *Good Meals, Great Times*.

ONCE UPON A TIME: The exterior of this shop replicates exactly the Carthay Circle Theatre in Hollywood, where *Snow White* premiered in 1937. The focus here is on the classic Disney characters: Mickey, Minnie, Goofy, Pluto, Donald, Pinocchio, and of course, Snow White and the seven dwarfs. This is the place to find plain Mickey Mouse T-shirts, plus some great collectible items.

LEGENDS OF HOLLYWOOD: A tribute to legends of film. Celebrity items, photographs, autographs, and movie paraphernalia are available at this shop. Merchandise from other Disney divisions, including books, CDs, videotapes, and computer games, also is sold here.

Shopping Beyond the Boulevards

GOLDEN AGE SOUVENIRS: Located between the Monster Sound Show and SuperStar Television, there are gifts from television programs, plus The Disney Channel merchandise.

ENDOR VENDORS: Just outside Star Tours, this shop offers intergalactic souvenirs associated with the *Star Wars* films and the Star Tours attraction.

THE STUDIO STORE: Just outside the Backstage Studio Tour, this is the place for T-shirts, sweatshirts, hats, and accessories emblazoned with Pocahontas designs.

INDIANA JONES ADVENTURE OUTPOST: Located next to the attraction, this shop features an exclusive assortment of adventure clothing and memorabilia, all with the Indiana Jones insignia.

THE LOONY BIN: A perfect stop after the Backstage Studio Tour. Lots of Roger Rabbit merchandise and some gag gifts are on sale. There's a host of hands-on fun in the form of props from the movie *Who Framed Roger Rabbit?* that kids just love.

FOTOTOONS: Upon leaving the Backstage Studio Tour, visitors can have their photograph taken and then combined with an image of their favorite cartoon character.

ANIMATION GALLERY: Located in the Animation Building, this is the place to find original Disney animation cels, exclusive limited-edition reproductions, figurines, and other collectibles. It's a pleasant place to browse, even if buying isn't on your mind.

STAGE ONE COMPANY STORE: Near the exit of Jim Henson's Muppet*Vision 3-D, this is the shop where guests can find merchandise featuring the likenesses of Miss Piggy, Kermit the Frog, Fozzie Bear, and other Muppets in addition to a variety of Disney character items.

THE COSTUME SHOP: From Cruella DeVille to Queen Malificent, this shop stocks merchandise (and a great selection of masks) featuring the meanest and nastiest of Disney's villainous characters, plus racks of children's costumes. Next to the *Sci-Fi Dine-In Theater*.

UNDER THE SEA: Located near the Voyage of the Little Mermaid, this shop offers a variety of merchandise featuring Ariel, Sebastian, Flounder, and friends. T-shirts, sweatshirts, bathing suits, towels, and more are available.

The Twilight Zone Tower of Terror

The Hollywood Tower Hotel is the decrepit home of the Studios' newest thrill ride. A relic of Hollywood's Golden Age, the hotel clearly has had some problems. On the front of the 199-foot-tall building (the tallest attraction at any Disney theme park), is a sparking electric sign that reads Hollywood Tower Hotel. As the legend goes, during a violent storm on Halloween night in 1939, lightning struck the building. An entire guest wing disappeared along with an elevator carrying five people. The disappearances remain a mystery.

The line for the ride winds through the once glorious lobby, and guests are directed to enter a library. The furniture is dusty, and cobwebs and old newspapers circa 1939 add to the eerie atmosphere. On a television set, brought to life by a bolt of lightning, Rod Serling does a typical monologue inviting you to enter another part of the building—and The Twilight Zone. He introduces visitors to the one-time staff and guests of the hotel. Pay close attention because they will reappear later in the trip. During his spiel, Serling informs you that the only working elevator in the hotel is the maintenance elevator.

Guests are led through an old hallway past a passenger elevator and on toward the boiler room to enter the ride elevator. (This is your only chance to change your mind about riding. Guests who decide to forego the trip can take a real elevator to the exit. Remember, once you get on the ride elevator, you can't get off.) Once inside, passengers are seated on benches equipped with safety bars. The doors close and the elevator begins its ascent. At the first stop, the elevator doors open and guests have a view down an endless hotel corridor. Among the many special effects is a ghostly visit by the hotel guests who vanished. Suddenly, the view of the hall disappears and is replaced by stars. The doors close again and you continue your trip skyward. At the next stop, you enter the Fifth Dimension, a combination of strange sights and sounds reminiscent of "The Twilight Zone." In fact, Disney Imagineers watched each of the 156 original "Twilight Zone" episodes at least twice (over 174 hours) for inspiration. There is a clock that ticks incessantly as it hangs in mid-air, and a giant eyeball. Watch it closely and you may see your image floating inside. This is a disorienting experience, in part because the elevator is actually moving horizontally.

After this particularly eerie part of the ride, you are nearing the dreaded drop. What happens next depends upon the whim of Disney Imagineers, who have programmed the ride so that the drop sequence can easily be changed by computer. At press time the ride was taking an immediate plunge (of about eight stories)

before traveling very quickly back up to the 13th floor. The doors open during this ascent. When the elevator reaches the top (at a height of about 157 feet) passengers can see the Studios below. Then the elevator drops about five feet very fast. The flash of light you see is a camera capturing your look of horror, while the noises you hear may have you convinced the elevator cables are breaking. The doors shut and the *real* drop begins. It's over in about 2½ seconds but it certainly seems a lot longer. The elevator shaft is pitch black and the use of sound, wind, and flashing lights maintains the sense of speed even as you are slowing down. As you exit the hotel, Rod Serling reminds you that next time you enter an old hotel, be sure to use the stairs.

On the way out, you'll pass through Tower Hotel Gifts, where key chains, towels, T-shirts, and other merchandise with the Hollywood Tower Hotel logo are for sale. This is also the place to buy the photo taken at the top of the tower. Two bits of interesting trivia: The motors running the ride vehicles are three times as powerful as those that propel the elevators at New York City's 110-story World Trade Center; the cameras that take the pictures of horrified guests are mounted behind the Hollywood Tower Hotel sign.

From the time you enter the building, the entire trip takes about 12 minutes. Note that you must be at least 40 inches tall to go on the ride. It is not recommended that pregnant women or people with heart conditions or back and neck problems ride.

Beauty and the Beast Stage Show

The show that gave birth to the hit Broadway musical. Belle, Gaston, Mrs. Potts, Lumière, and the cast of the Disney film *Beauty and the Beast* come to life at the 1,500-seat Theatre of the Stars amphitheater on Sunset Boulevard five times each day. The 30-minute show is as entertaining as they come. The staging is just right and the music addictive. The tale is traced from Belle's dissatisfaction with her provincial life in a small French town to the battle between the staff of the Beast's castle and Gaston and the townspeople. Lumière and his group perform "Be Our Guest" with a delightful display of giant dancing spoons and Jell-O molds. The costuming of Lumière, Mrs. Potts, and Cogsworth is exceptional. The special effects used to transform the Beast into the dashing prince are effective. The happy-ending finale, complete with a send-off of white doves, is a delight.

The Magic of Disney Animation

This is one of the finest, funniest, and most entertaining of all the attractions at the Studios. Guests learn about the animation process, and they get to see the Disney animators at work on a forthcoming film. The animators who work in the building generally work Mondays through Fridays, so you might try to time your visit for a weekday. Also, they usually quit for the day between 5 P.M. and 6 P.M., so try to visit before then.

In the lobby, duplicates of 12 of the many Oscars won by the Disney Animation Team are on display along with a collection of character drawings and original cels from *Pocahontas* as well as works-in-progress. From the lobby, guests move into the Disney Animation Theater, where an uproariously funny film starring Robin Williams and Walter Cronkite offers a lesson in the basics of animation. It even allows guests a look at what it's like to be a cartoon character through the eyes of Williams.

The producers of this film will tell you that each scene was a struggle to complete, because Walter Cronkite had trouble keeping a straight face. Williams is at his best as one of the lost boys from *Peter Pan*. His nonstop banter is so funny that a second trip may be necessary to take it all in. In one segment, he's turned into a variety of recognizable characters, including Mickey Mouse. "I can even be a corporate symbol," he proclaims in his best Mickey Mouse voice. All in all it's great fun, and Cronkite is an absolutely perfect straight man.

The film is followed by a walk through the working animation studios, where the

35-minute tour continues to be narrated by Williams and Cronkite, who appear on overhead monitors. First stop is the story room, where animators develop story lines. Onward to the drawing boards where Mickey, Minnie, and other characters undergo the metamorphosis from pencil sketch to moving picture. Working at their desks in full view of visitors, animators are seen creating the drawings that will later appear in real films. During 1996, guests might see animators at work on *The Hunchback of Notre Dame* or *The Legend of Mulan*, two future Disney releases.

Guests also view the cleanup room, the special effects area, and the special camera that was designed to transfer drawings to cels. Then artists can be seen hand painting up to 25 different colors onto these transparent sheets. To produce one 24-minute

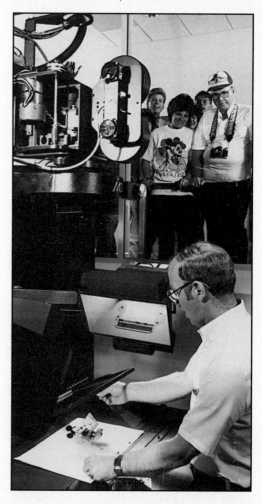

film, the animation team must complete 34,650 drawings, and add scenes from at least 300 background paintings before finishing the work with musical scores and special effects.

Be sure to stop in at the Animation Gallery, where original Disney animation cels, exclusive limited-edition reproductions, books, figurines, and other collectibles are for sale.

Backstage Studio Tour

On this 25-minute tram tour, guests go backstage to see work in progress on television shows and movies. The tour begins in the queue area with a presentation of the history of The Walt Disney Studios shown on overhead television monitors and narrated by Tom Selleck and Carol Burnett.

In typical Disney fashion, the line weaves up and back through a gallery of milestones and memories from the early days of the Disney Studios. On busy days there is a sign as guests enter the gate for the backstage tour that announces a 45-minute wait from that point. It takes about 30 minutes to wind through the main queue area when it's full, so be prepared. The crowds seem to thin out during the late afternoon hours, so if the line is beyond the 45-minute mark, your time will be better spent at one of the other attractions.

The Backstage shuttles are comfortable and roomy trams and tours are hosted by enthusiastic guides. (Note when boarding the trams, those who sit on the left side will get wet at Catastrophe Canyon, while those on the right will stay dry. Choose accordingly.) The trams pull out and guests have a view of bungalows housing television and movie production departments where actual work is being done. The tram then winds through a tunnel where guests can see the wardrobe department at work on the left through large windows. More than 100 artists produce the costumes for all of Disney's motion picture, television, and entertainment projects, and with 2.25 million garments, Walt Disney World has the world's largest working wardrobe.

The tram then passes through the camera, props, and lighting departments, where equipment is stored until it is needed both on and off the studio's sets. Disney's camera equipment is so advanced that many visiting network television crews often borrow it when covering Space Shuttle launches at the Kennedy Space Center, about 70 miles to the east. A look into the scene shop reveals carpenters at work on sets that are later finished on the soundstages.

The tram turns into the backlot residential street where empty, hollow facades give the outward appearance of a lovely neighborhood. Used mainly for exterior shots, the houses on the street include Vern's home from *Ernest Saves Christmas*. There's also the facade of "The Golden Girls" home and the house from "Empty Nest."

With a bit of flourish, the tour guide explains how landscapes can be created by set designers to fill certain needs and then asks, "Where in Central Florida can you find an active oil field in the middle of a dry, rocky, barren desert canyon prone to flash floods?" The answer is Catastrophe Canyon, which

produces some of the best special effects most visitors will ever experience. As the story goes, the crews are filming a movie in which a backstage tram gets stuck in the canyon during a flash flood. But the guide will tell you that it's safe to go in because they're not filming today. Astute guests will notice that the oil company, Mohave, is the same one represented at Oscar's Super Service on Hollywood Boulevard.

In a spectacular series of special effects, a rain storm begins; then there's an explosion, complete with flames that are so hot even riders on the right side of the tram feel them; followed by a flash flood that is so convincing it forces everyone to lean the other way. The road along which the tram rides shifts and dips hydraulically, lending even more reality to the scary adventure. A later behind-the-scenes look reveals the tanks that release enough water to fill ten Olympic-size swimming pools. Some of the water is blown out by air cannons, which can shoot 25,000 gallons of water over 100 feet. To put that in better perspective, if a basketball were stuck into one of the cannons, it could be shot over the top of the Empire State Building.

From Catastrophe Canyon, the tram rides by New York Street where meticulously re-produced facades line the urban streets. Though the brickwork looks authentic, these backless facades are constructed mostly of fiberglass and styrofoam. The skyscrapers, including the Empire State Building and the Chrysler Building, are actually painted flats. Forced perspective (the same technique that makes Cinderella Castle appear much taller than it is) is employed here to make the 4-story Empire State Building appear as if it's the real 104-story structure. Tour groups often encounter film crews setting up or tak-ing down equipment from shoots done on the lot. Though clearly a New York reproduction, the streets can be altered to fit the role for Any City, USA. Both the Empire State Build-ing and the Chrysler Building can be removed and facades changed to serve any purpose. If crews are not filming, guests can explore New York Street on foot.

The Making of...

Moviegoers have long been intrigued by the animation process. Be it Mickey Mouse or Snow White, Beauty or the Beast, audiences clamor for information on what it takes to bring their favorite characters to life. The answers, at least for Disney's most recent animated hits, are found in this attraction.

The Making of... is a movie produced by The Disney Channel that gives guests a fasci-nating, behind-the-scenes glimpse at the intricacies of animated film-making. It intro-duces the audience to the actors behind the characters, the composers and lyricists responsible for the memorable tunes, and the animators themselves, who go to great lengths to get into their characters. One senior animator for *Pocahontas*, charged with creating the mischievous Meeko, immersed himself in the world of raccoons, filling his office with raccoon posters, puppets, and stuffed animals.

There are lots of interesting, and perhaps surprising, bits of information throughout the film. Among them is the extensive research behind each Disney project. *The Lion King*, for example, required a field trip to East Africa. *Pocahontas*, four years in the making, included visits with Native American tribes.

The Making of... is updated periodically to keep up with the latest Disney releases. Depending on when you visit, you can expect to see either *The Making of Pocahontas*, *The Making of Toy Story*, or *The Making of The Hunchback of Notre Dame*. The theater entrance is located on Mickey Avenue.

Voyage of the Little Mermaid

One of the studio's most popular attractions, this live 15-minute musical production adapted from the instant animated classic is presented in a theater with an underwater feel to it. Characters such as Flounder, sea horses, snails, an octopus, and Sebastian are artfully created by puppeteers dressed com-pletely in black so that only the characters are visible. They perform the lively song, "Under the Sea," to open the show. Then clips from the movie are shown in the back-ground to help tell the tale as live actors join the puppets on stage.

Ariel is the star of the show and performs songs from the film, including "Part of Your World." Prince Eric also mades an appear-ance. An enormous Ursula glides across the stage and steals Ariel's voice. The story is a bit disjointed and hops from scene to scene, but most viewers are familiar enough with the plot that this does not detract from the show. Of course, there is a happy ending and Max the dog, Ariel, and Prince Eric live happily ever after.

There are some excellent special effects inside the theater, including cascading water, lasers, and a lightning storm that may be a bit intense for younger children. Some of the effects, particularly the lasers that make you feel as though you really are under the sea, are best seen from the rear of the theater. Expect to wait a while for this popular show.

while a convincing monster threatens riders with its slimy body from an overhead compartment. (Note that this scene and the gangster and western scenes are presented in a darkened setting and may be upsetting to younger children.) Next stop is the Well of Souls from *Raiders of the Lost Ark*, where Harrison Ford and John Rhys-Davies struggle to remove the ancient ark from its sepulcher. There is a Tarzan scene in a jungle, and the legendary farewell scene from *Casablanca* with Rick and Ilsa is depicted, complete with a real airplane that looks just like the one used in the movie.

Guests are taken from the airfield in *Casablanca* to the swirling winds of Munchkinland, where a house has just fallen upon the Wicked Witch of the East. Her sister, as portrayed by Margaret Hamilton, appears in a burst of black smoke. This Audio-Animatronics figure represents the third generation of this technology, and she is quite impressively lifelike. But happy endings prevail and guests follow Dorothy, the Tin Man, the Cowardly Lion, the Scarecrow, and Toto along the Yellow Brick Road to the Emerald City of Oz. As the ride draws to a close, a film montage of memorable moments from Academy Award–winning films is shown.

The 50 Audio-Animatronics figures created for this ride were done by many of the same artists who created the characters in The Hall of Presidents in the Magic Kingdom. Attention to detail is precise. John Wayne's horse and rifle, for example, match those he used in his westerns. The costumes worn by the Julie Andrews and Dick Van Dyke Audio-Animatronics figures are modeled after the originals from *Mary Poppins*. And Gene Kelly personally inspected his likeness before it was shipped from California to Florida.

The Great Movie Ride

Housed in a full-scale reproduction of historic Mann's Chinese Theatre, this 22-minute attraction captivates the imagination of guests from the start. The queue area winds through the precisely reproduced lobby and into the heart of filmmaking, where guests will see some famous movie scenes on a large screen. (Note that if the queue extends outside the building, you're in for a long wait. It takes about 25 minutes to reach the ride vehicles once you've entered the theater.)

More than 60 dancing mannequins atop a large-tiered revolving cake greet guests, in a replay of the "By a Waterfall" scene from the Busby Berkeley musical *Footlight Parade*. Gene Kelly's most memorable performance from *Singin' in the Rain* is the next scene on the tour. Rain seems to drench the soundstage, but doesn't dampen the spirits of the Audio-Animatronics representation of Kelly, who sings his heart out. Then Mary Poppins and Bert the chimney sweep entertain as Mary floats from above via her magical umbrella and Bert sings the tune "Chim Chim Cher-ee" from a rooftop.

From the world of musical entertainment, guests move on to adventure. James Cagney recreates his role from *Public Enemy* as the ride proceeds along Gangster Alley. A Prohibition-style mob shootout begins and guests find themselves in the midst of an ambush. An alternate route leads to a trip to a western town, where John Wayne can be seen on horseback eyeing some would-be bank robbers. The thieves blow the safe and flames pour from the building. The heat can be felt from the trams, so don't be too surprised.

The ride vehicles whisk guests past danger and into the spaceship *Nostromo* from the film *Alien*. Officer Ripley guards the corridor

SuperStar Television

Roles in famous television shows are up for grabs at this remarkable attraction. In the outdoor pre-show area, a host or hostess chooses members of the audience to star in a variety of famous television scenes. **Note:** Although a few guests are chosen from the rear of the area, most would-be stars are picked from nearer the front. While just being in the audience will provide a lot of laughs, if there's even a little ham in you, move up front and volunteer loudly.

Audience members are led into a 1,000-seat theater reminiscent of the days of live

television broadcasting. At the same time, would-be stars head backstage for costuming, makeup, and meetings with the directors.

The stage has several sets, and as the camera operators shoot the actors in action, the audience watches on one of eight six-foot-wide projection screens suspended from the ceiling. But the pictures on the screens vary significantly from the live events on stage because the use of "blue-screen" electronic techniques allows backstage editors to merge the live action with historic clips from the classic shows.

The first scene features a gentleman guest in the news reporter's seat on the "Today" show on July 17, 1955, the day Disneyland opened. Applause signs flash when appropriate, and audience members respond enthusiastically for their fellow tourists. Next, a woman guest gets to play the Ethel Mertz part opposite Lucille Ball's Lucy Ricardo in what is perhaps the single most famous scene from "I Love Lucy." Complete with white smock and tall white hat, the guest star tries to wrap chocolates as they quickly come along a conveyor belt, and though seen dozens of times, the scene is still funny, even with an amateur in the role of Lucy's second banana.

Another guest plays the part of Al Borlund opposite Tim "the Tool Man" Taylor in a scene from "Home Improvement." Several youngsters are chosen to star in the opening theme song from "Gilligan's Island." Other scenes include a classic from "Cheers," in which Woody the bartender, Norm, and Cliff star with four guests. One lucky youngster has the opportunity to hit a grand slam home-run at New York's Shea Stadium and then be interviewed by the late Howard Cosell.

There are no bad seats in the house since

the eight monitors can be seen easily by the entire audience. This attraction tends to be less crowded during the morning hours, so try it then, and if time permits go again as each new cast brings a fresh flavor to the presentation. The entire attraction takes about 45 minutes, from the choosing of stars to the end. Presented by Sony.

Monster Sound Show

Parents, don't be fooled by the name. There is nothing scary about this attraction, where guests have the opportunity to create the sound effects for a short film, with predictably funny results.

The pre-show begins outside the theater with a short video presentation starring David Letterman in a very funny introduction to what's inside. His comments close with an atypical (for a Disney attraction) warning that, "If you break anything, security guards in mouse suits will beat you senseless."

Upon entering the 270-seat theater, the host chooses several "Foley" artists from the audience. (Foley is the Hollywood sound-effects system named for its creator, Jack Foley.) The audience is then treated to a cute Martin Short/Chevy Chase comedy-mystery film that includes the sounds of thunder, rain, creaking doors, and falling chandeliers. The amateur sound crew watches the film a second time as they try to match the proper sound effects to the action on-screen. The third viewing of the film features the new soundtrack created by the studio's newest Foley artists. The thunder never seems to

match the storm and the crash of the chandelier seems most often to take place as the creaking door opens, but that's the whole point and it's all a lot of fun.

The 15-minute show features many original gadgets created by sound master Jimmy Macdonald. Macdonald, who became the voice of Mickey Mouse during the 1940s, was responsible for more than 20,000 sound gadgets during his 45 years with the Walt Disney Studios in California. There are some special artifacts, including Tinkerbell's chimes, a door used in *Alice in Wonderland*, and the coconut shells used to produce the hoofbeats in the *Legend of Sleepy Hollow*. But most of the sounds are created by the ingenious use of barrels, nails, sandpaper, and other gadgets that go bonk, buzz, zip, or bump.

The post-show area, SoundWorks, offers some hands-on fun for the rest of the audience. Earie Encounters allows visitors to reproduce the flying-saucer sounds from the 1956 film *Forbidden Planet*. At Movie Mimics, guests can dub in the voice of Roger Rabbit and other stars; and at Soundsations, our personal favorite, an adventure in "3-D audio" puts guests in an enclosed room filled with sound so realistic that the wind from a hair dryer can almost be felt. Presented by Sony.

Indiana Jones Epic Stunt Spectacular

Earthquakes, fiery explosions, and assorted other dramatic stunts give guests some insight into the science of movie stunts and special effects at this impressive 2,000-seat amphitheater. Stuntmen and women recreate scenes from Indiana Jones films to demonstrate the skill required to keep audiences on the edge of their seats. Show director Glenn Randall, who served as stunt coordinator of such well-known adventure films as *Raiders of the Lost Ark*, *Indiana Jones and the Temple of Doom*, *Poltergeist*, *Never Say Never Again*, *E.T.*, *Firestarter*, and *Jewel of the Nile*, calls the show "big, visual excitement."

But the 30-minute show isn't all flying

leaps. Guests also see how the elaborate stunts are pulled off—safely—while the crew and an assistant director explain what goes on both in front of and behind the camera.

In one segment, a scene from *Raiders of the Lost Ark* is staged. A 12-foot tall rolling ball chases a Harrison Ford lookalike out of the temple. There is steam and flame so intense that the audience can feel the heat. The crew dismantles the set, revealing the remarkable lightness of movie props, as two assistants roll it uphill for the next show.

In a scene at a busy Cairo street market, "extras" chosen from the audience participate. The famous scene in which Indiana Jones pulls a gun while others are fighting with swords is played out. The explosive action continues, and leads to a sensational desert finale in which the hero and his sweetheart make a death-defying escape.

There are moments during this presentation when the audience might wonder if, just for a minute, something has gone wrong. But by revealing the tricks of the trade, the directors and stars show that what appears to be very dangerous is actually a perfectly safe, controlled bit of movie magic. It's a great show.

Star Tours

Having witnessed the unyielding popularity of this attraction at Disneyland in Anaheim, California, Disney made the decision to open a counterpart here. The attraction, which was inspired by George Lucas's *Star Wars* film trilogy, offers guests the chance to board Star-Speeders that are actually the same type of flight simulators regularly employed by the military and commercial airlines to train pilots. Synchronizing a stunning film with the virtually

WHERE TO EAT AT THE DISNEY-MGM STUDIOS

A complete list of all Disney-MGM Studios eateries—full-service restaurants, fast-food emporiums, snack shops, and food vendors—can be found together with all other WDW eating spots in *Good Meals, Great Times*.

limitless motion of the simulator allows guests to truly feel what they see. (Note that when instructed to put on your seatbelt, do so. This is a very rough ride.)

Visitors enter an area where the famed *Star Wars* characters R2D2 and C-3PO are working for a galactic travel agency. They spend their time in a bustling hangar area servicing the Star Tours fleet of spacecraft. Riders board the 40-passenger craft for what is intended to be a leisurely trip to the Moon of Endor, but the five-minute ride quickly develops into a harrowing flight into deep space, including encounters with giant ice crystals and laser blasting fighters. The flight is out of control from the start, as the rookie pilot proves that Murphy's Law applies to the entire universe.

The sensations are extraordinary and the technology quite advanced. (By the way, this same technology is used at Body Wars in the Wonders of Life pavilion in Future World at Epcot. There guests take a rollicking ride through the human body.)

Signs outside Star Tours warn that passengers must be free of back problems, heart conditions, motion sickness, and other physical limitations to ride. Pregnant women and children under three are not permitted to board. Children under seven must be accompanied by an adult.

Jim Henson's Muppet*Vision 3-D

One of the most entertaining attractions at the Disney-MGM Studios, this spectacular 3-D movie is quite remarkable. Like so many Disney attractions, a lot of the appeal is in the details. A very funny 12-minute pre-show gives some clues of what's to come. Characters including Scooter, Gonzo, and Sam Eagle entertain on overhead screens.

Inside the theater specifically constructed for this show, many will notice that it looks just like the theater from the television series "The Muppet Show." Even the two curmudgeonly old fellows are sitting in a balcony, bantering with each other and offering some negative but humorous commentary on the film. The comedy comes directly from Muppet Labs, presided over by Dr. Bunson Honeydew—and his long-suffering assistant, Beaker—and introduces a new character, Waldo, the "Spirit of 3-D." The 3-D effects are convincing and most viewers can't resist reaching out at least once. Among the highlights are Miss Piggy's hilarious solo, which Bean Bunny turns into quite a fiasco. Sam Eagle's grand finale leads to trouble as a veritable war breaks out, and with an appearance by everyone's favorite Swedish Chef, a cannon blasts the screen from the rear balcony.

But the 3-D effects, spectacular as they are, are only part of the show: There are appearances by live Muppet characters, a clutch of fiber-optic effects, fireworks, and lots of very funny details built into the walls that surround the seating area of the huge theater. There are carryings-on for most of the senses—sight, smell, and touch, among them—and it's hard to know where to look first. It is more like a "4-D" experience. We're glad that they've put the 12-minute show in such a large theater, to allow the crowds to enjoy it without too long a wait.

The Spirit of Pocahontas Stage Show

Based on Disney's animated feature *Pocahontas,* this newest stage show weaves elements of nature and Native American folklore to deliver a compelling message—one of peace among different peoples and between man and the earth. From the moment guests enter the Backlot Theater, they are surrounded by the wonder of the outdoors. Trees adorn the stage to recreate the enchanted willow glade from the film. The air is filled with the sounds of whispering wind, rushing water, and animals in the wild.

Those who have seen the movie will recognize the opening notes of "Listen to Your

ENTERTAINMENT

The first thing to do when you reach the Disney-MGM Studios is stop at Guest Relations just inside the gates. Pick up an entertainment schedule, not only to check showtimes for attractions, but also to find out what entertainment will be taking place during your visit. You might even have the opportunity to see a celebrity make an appearance at the Studios.

Streetmosphere Characters are the entertaining troupe of performers along Hollywood Boulevard. Watch for autograph hounds, budding starlets, gossip columnists, and others who are doing their thing all day and evening.

During the seasons when the park is open late, don't miss **Sorcery in the Sky**, Disney's best fireworks. The ten-minute show, set to music from *Fantasia* with narration by Vincent Price, lights up the sky over the Chinese Theatre. Check the entertainment schedule for exact showtimes.

Some new entertainment was in the works when this book went to press. A brand-new afternoon parade—themed to Disney's 34th animated release, *Toy Story*—was expected to roll into the Studios sometime at the end of 1995. The film tells the comical tale of the adventures of toys that come to life when humans are not around. This theme should make for a very colorful and entertaining parade. No other details were available at press time, so be sure to check the entertainment schedule to find out when it's running. Fantasmic!, the spectacular laser, film, smoke, and fireworks show that has been playing to "oohs" and "aahs" at Disneyland, may premier here in 1997.

Heart," the song that signals the start of the show. The animal-hide curtain is drawn to reveal a ceremonial bonfire, which serves as the source of many of the show's special effects. Then the stage comes alive in celebration. The smoke builds, and seemingly from its midst, the narrator, Kekata the Powhatan medicine man, emerges. He welcomes the audience, explaining that it's a ceremony of hope for lasting peace among people of all tribes and colors. Then he invites everyone to join in celebrating the strength and spirit of the Powhatan tribe by paying tribute to the spirit of Pocahontas.

The story is told through dance and song, costumes, masks, giant puppets, and other props. In describing Pocahontas, Kekata calls her a free spirit who can travel wherever the wind takes her. That's precisely how she moves throughout this show, appearing and disappearing almost as an apparition. In one scene, she is in the enchanted glade, seeking the wisdom of Grandmother Willow. Later, she balances on the branch of a tree to spy on John Smith. In one of the show's highlights, after she and John Smith have fallen in love, there is a clap of thunder and Pocahontas appears to stop the war between the English and the Native Americans—and to save the life of John Smith.

The show is by no means a replay of the movie. It does, however, incorporate some of the film's most memorable tunes: "Just Around the River Bend," "Virginia Company," "Mine, Mine, Mine," "Savages," and, of course, "Colors of the Wind." It also provides a powerful reminder, in the words of Pocahontas, of "where the path of hatred has brought you." Then, in an uplifting finale, the show closes with a look at what is possible if we all live in peace.

Honey, I Shrunk the Kids Movie Set Adventure

The set for the backyard scenes of the popular Disney movie has been recreated as an oversize playground for kids (and adults, too). Stalks of grass soar 20 and 30 feet high and enormous tree stumps and extra-large Lego toys provide unusual climbing opportunities. Kids especially love to climb into the discarded film canister and slide back out along an oversize reel of film. A hose with a small leak also provides entertainment as it squirts in a slightly different location each time. It's all great fun, and these props serve to make the kids look and feel very tiny indeed.

Inside the Magic Special Effects & Production Tour

This is a 40-minute walking tour beginning in the queue area, where a Goldie Hawn/Rick Moranis video is presented to entertain tourers while they're waiting. The wait here averages 15 minutes.

First stop is an outdoor special effects area, where a guest plays the role of submarine commander "Captain Duck." This show demonstrates effects used to produce battle scenes at sea. Pyrotechnics, simulated depth charges, torpedo blasts, and strafing runs all combine in an action-packed adventure.

Two children are chosen from the crowd in the prop room to participate in the next portion of the tour. A giant bee, used in *Honey, I Shrunk the Kids*, is suspended from the ceiling. One of the children is put atop the bee and one on the wing. On this part of the tour, guests are shown how film shot against a blue screen can then be superimposed onto any background chosen by the producers. The kids are filmed, and the footage is cut in with real scenes from the movie.

Then it's on to the soundstages where specially designed, soundproof catwalks allow visitors to gawk and talk all they want. The tour takes in three soundstages, where at any given time filming may be in progress for movies or television shows. It also is possible, however, that nothing will be happening on the set.

From this area, guests are led into a walkway where a Bette Midler short film is presented on overhead monitors. The film was shot entirely at and exclusively for the Disney-MGM Studios. Guests will recognize the sets from New York Street. It's a cute tale in which Midler discovers she's holding a winning lottery ticket, and it graphically records her trials

and tribulations as she tries to retrieve it after it falls out of her window. At the film's conclusion, guests are led into a large soundstage in which the interior sets for the movie are displayed. On the soundstage a hostess explains some of the special effects used to create certain highlights of the film.

Studio Showcase

Costumes, props, and set pieces used in recent and past movies and television shows are on display in this ever-changing exhibition. Displays have included props from *Mary Poppins*, *Who Framed Roger Rabbit?*, *Three Men and a Baby*, and *Crimson Tide* as well as the hit television show "Home Improvement." Souvenirs with the "Home Improvement" logo also are on sale here.

HOT TIPS

- Arrive at the Disney-MGM Studios before the posted opening time. The gates usually open about 8:30 A.M.
- Check the Studios Tip Board to get an idea of showtimes and crowds.
- See Muppet*Vision 3-D, Voyage of the Little Mermaid, and Star Tours early in the day before the crowds build up.
- The Twilight Zone Tower of Terror has very long lines. See it early in the day and *never* right after a meal.
- See The Spirit of Pocahontas Stage Show either during the morning or during the hours just prior to park closing, as the show is performed in an open-air theater that is unprotected from the sun.
- If you'd like to have a sit-down lunch or dinner, make reservations when you arrive at the park for the *50's Prime Time Café*, the *Brown Derby*, the *Sci-Fi Dine-In*, or *Mama Melrose's Ristorante Italiano* either at the Tip Board or the individual eatery. Or make advance reservations by calling WDW-DINE (939-3463).
- Snag a good spot along Hollywood Boulevard to see the afternoon parade if it's running during your visit.
- You'll sometimes find the Disney characters—such as Mickey and friends, Belle and the Beast, and Aladdin and Jasmine—strolling along Mickey Avenue and Sunset Boulevard. In fact, Mickey is almost always standing by for photo opportunities on Sunset Boulevard. And Pocahontas is slated to have her own meet-and-greet area. Check the entertainment schedule for details.
- The shops on Hollywood Boulevard are open a half hour past park closing.

EVERYTHING ELSE IN THE WORLD

The Magic Kingdom, Epcot, and the Disney-MGM Studios take up only about 460 acres of the total Walt Disney World terrain, while the total turf of the entire World comprises 45 square miles! Quite a lot of this domain is crammed with all sorts of diverse and irresistible activities of a quantity and quality seldom found anywhere else on the globe.

There's superb golf and tennis, beaches for sunbathing, lakes for speedboating and sailing, canoes for rent and winding streams to paddle along, bicycles for hire, campfire sites, nature trails, and picnic grounds. And that list still doesn't include River Country, Disney's own old-fashioned swimming hole; Typhoon Lagoon, a state-of-the-art water park; Blizzard Beach, the newest watery wonderland; the Disney Village Marketplace, a wide assortment of shops and restaurants; and the 11-acre botanical garden and zoological park known as Discovery Island.

Add to all that Pleasure Island, an after-dark entertainment complex with nightclubs and restaurants. To satisfy guests' appetites to learn more about the World, there are a host of learning programs that allow youngsters and adults to slip behind the scenes. With the opening of The Disney Institute in February 1996, guests will have the opportunity to dabble in animation, the performing arts, and all manner of other areas in a whole new Disney adventure geared to discovery and learning.

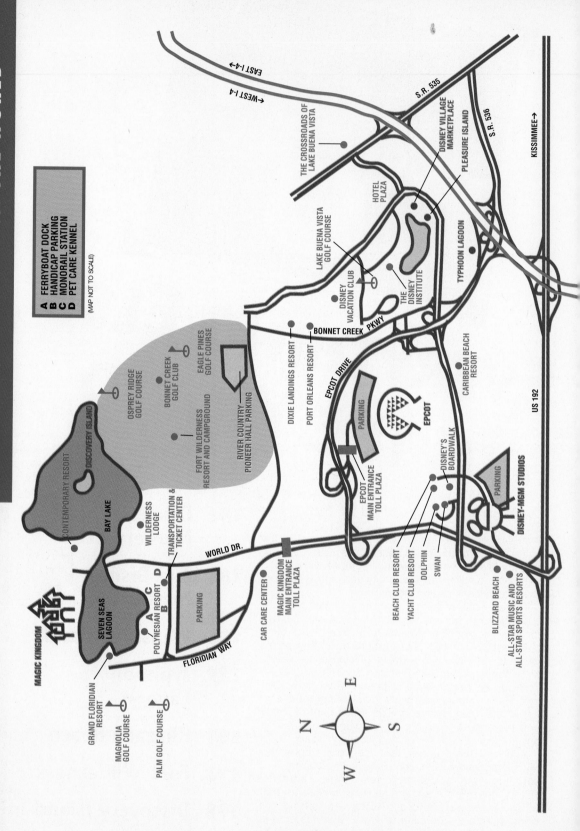

A FERRYBOAT DOCK
B HANDICAP PARKING
C MONORAIL STATION
D PET CARE KENNEL

(MAP NOT TO SCALE)

←EAST I-A
←WEST I-A

S.R. 535

THE CROSSROADS OF
LAKE BUENA VISTA

DISNEY VILLAGE
MARKETPLACE

PLEASURE ISLAND

S.R. 536

KISSIMMEE→

HOTEL
PLAZA

LAKE BUENA VISTA
GOLF COURSE

DISNEY
VACATION CLUB

THE DISNEY
INSTITUTE

TYPHOON LAGOON

CARIBBEAN BEACH
RESORT

BONNET CREEK PKWY

OSPREY RIDGE
GOLF COURSE

BONNET CREEK
GOLF CLUB

EAGLE PINES
GOLF COURSE

FORT WILDERNESS
RESORT AND CAMPGROUND

RIVER COUNTRY
PIONEER HALL PARKING

DIXIE LANDINGS RESORT

PORT ORLEANS RESORT

EPCOT DRIVE

PARKING

EPCOT

US 192

DISCOVERY ISLAND

CONTEMPORARY RESORT

BAY LAKE

WILDERNESS
LODGE

TRANSPORTATION &
TICKET CENTER

WORLD DR.

EPCOT
MAIN ENTRANCE
TOLL PLAZA

DISNEY'S
BOARDWALK

PARKING

DISNEY-MGM STUDIOS

MAGIC KINGDOM

SEVEN SEAS
LAGOON

A C
D
POLYNESIAN RESORT
B

PARKING

CAR CARE CENTER

MAGIC KINGDOM
MAIN ENTRANCE
TOLL PLAZA

BEACH CLUB RESORT

YACHT CLUB RESORT

DOLPHIN

SWAN

BLIZZARD BEACH

ALL-STAR MUSIC AND
ALL-STAR SPORTS RESORTS

FLORIDIAN WAY

GRAND FLORIDIAN
RESORT

MAGNOLIA
GOLF COURSE

PALM GOLF COURSE

N
E
S
W

Disney Village Marketplace

The Walt Disney World Village area is comprised of several hotel and villa accommodations, a few lakes, an 18-hole golf course, and the Disney Village Marketplace. The area also will be home to The Disney Institute when it opens in February. Despite all there is to do here, the pace is far more leisurely than that of the theme parks.

Although a year has passed since a revitalized Disney Village Marketplace began catching guests' attention, heads are still turning to take in the attractive waterside enclave's fresh features. Beyond the bright overhead sign that now greets visitors at the main entrance, broadened walkways sprinkled with gardens, interactive fountains, and outdoor seating wind through the shopping and dining complex. The place has also been spruced up with 17 topiaries, including a Cheshire Cat and a Lumière. Guests who have visited the Marketplace before will be happy to know that expanded parking was among the improvements made. Also, traffic flow is much better now that resort buses drop guests at a bus loop separate from the parking lot.

But all this is small potatoes compared with major expansion on the horizon that will ultimately blur lines between the Marketplace and Pleasure Island next door to create one huge entertainment district. Disney's plans call for the addition of two nightclubs, an expanded 24-screen movie complex, two restaurants, and a pair of Disney superstores. Highlights will include *House of Blues*, partly owned by Dan Aykroyd, *Wolfgang Puck's Café*, which will mark the L.A. chef's Florida debut; and a restaurant-nightclub created by singer Gloria Estefan and her husband, Emilio. The transformation will be completed sometime during 1997.

Shops

Located on the shores of Buena Vista Lagoon, the Disney Village Marketplace boutiques stock everything from toys and books to fashions and accessories for the whole family. There are several stores that carry the staggering range of merchandise related to the family of Disney characters. The shops are open daily from 9:30 A.M. to 11 P.M.

The best way to take it all in is simply to wander at will. The descriptions below suggest the types of things that each store offers. Particular items may not be there when you are, but comparable goods should be available. Note that weekends are fairly busy. Kids who get bored by their elders' browsing can be turned loose at the marina or at the innovative playground.

The Marketplace is easily accessible from exit 26B from I-4. The area can be reached from the Magic Kingdom, Epcot, and the Disney-MGM Studios via WDW's monorails and buses; holders of ID cards issued by WDW resorts, as well as bearers of certain admission passes, can ride them at no extra charge.

TOYS FANTASTIC: Located in the You & Me Kid building, this shop stocks a wide variety of Mattel toys and games, including the full line of Mattel-Disney merchandise.

CHRISTMAS CHALET: If anything can set a mind to dreaming of white Christmases when the mercury is hitting 95 degrees outside (and the humidity is just about the same), this lovely shop, also in the You & Me Kid building, is it. Arranged at the edges of the rooms are small treasures in traditional reds and greens—ornaments covered with feathers, others made of wood, metal, glass, felt, and calico. The selection is one of the best of its type anywhere. In addition, there are character collectibles and other unique Christmas trinkets.

CRISTAL ARTS: This shop sells roughly the same sort of cut-glass merchandise available at Main Street's Crystal Arts in the Magic Kingdom. Large green, blue, or red cut-glass bowls and vases are available, along with clear-glass mugs, glass sculptures, and other items engraved to customers' specifications with initials, messages, or pictures. If you bring a favorite photograph to this shop, the engraver can have it reproduced on a plate or other item.

THE CAPTAIN'S TOWER: At the center of the Disney Village Marketplace, this open-air shop is the focal point for major promotions. The merchandise changes three to four times a year depending on special events and the latest fashion trends.

LILLIE LANGTRY'S PHOTOGRAPHIC ARTIST: This is where guests can pose for sepia-toned prints in Edwardian suits or flounced gowns with a degree of frilliness rarely found outside a film studio's wardrobe department.

HARRINGTON BAY CLOTHIERS: Designed like a Bermuda plantation home, this shop stocks traditional and casual men's clothing from designers such as Nautica and Polo by Ralph Lauren. The store is located near the Captain's Tower, close to the parking lot.

DISCOVER: Concerns for Mother Nature are fully demonstrated in the relaxed atmosphere of this environmentally correct emporium. Among the offerings are birdhouses, herb-garden kits, wind chimes, educational toys for children, environmentally oriented music, and other unique gift items.

MICKEY'S CHARACTER SHOP: This is the largest Disney merchandise shop in all the World. As you enter, be sure to take a look up at Mickey, Minnie, and Donald flying high in a 20-foot-tall hot-air balloon. Dumbo, Jiminy Cricket, Minnie and Mickey, Chip 'n' Dale, Tigger and Eeyore, and Tramp and his Lady are all here, too—stuffed, in porcelain, and emblazoned on everything from T-shirts and back scratchers to pencils and carry-all bags. Be sure to check out the larger-than-life stuffed Mickey and Winnie the Pooh.

YOU & ME KID: This shop offers something for every member of the family. There are toys, clothing, gift items, stuffed animals, and lots of other things for kids, from infants to preteens.

USEFUL STOPS

GUEST SERVICES: Located at You & Me Kid, this information center also is the place for reservation assistance, lost and found, film and stamp sales, photo processing, an ATM, wheelchair and stroller rental, and gift wrapping.

BUS TRANSPORTATION: The Disney Village Marketplace bus stop is located next to 2R's Reading and Riting bookstore. Direct bus service is available to and from *The Villas at The Disney Institute, Caribbean Beach, Swan* and *Dolphin, Yacht Club* and *Beach Club, Port Orleans, Dixie Landings, Disney Vacation Club, All-Star Sports,* and *All-Star Music* resorts. The other WDW resorts are generally linked to the Marketplace via the TTC. For information on transportation within the rest of the World, see *Transportation & Accommodations.*

THE ART OF DISNEY: Disney animation cels, porcelain figures, ceramics, and unique collectibles are the goods available at this gallery next to 2R's Reading and Riting.

2R'S READING AND RITING: A large selection of hard-cover and paperback books on just about any subject can be found at this shop. Located near the new WDW bus drop-off, the shop also stocks greeting cards and stationery. In keeping with the national bookstore trend, you can order coffee or cappuccino to sip while browsing.

RESORTWEAR UNLIMITED: This shop features bright and classy fashions. An assortment of sportswear and swimwear is enhanced by bold jewelry, hats, and handbags. Lancôme cosmetics also are available.

24KT PRECIOUS ADORNMENTS: An elegant shop featuring a wide selection of gold fashion jewelry, ranging from unique designer items to Disney character charms and watches. Located next to *Chef Mickey's Village Restaurant*.

GOURMET PANTRY: Though escargots and smoked oysters can be found here, there also are breads and pastries, meats and cheeses, cereals, yogurt, beer and soft drinks, and many more items—both mundane and exotic. Unusual teas and specially blended, freshly ground coffees also are available, and occasionally free tastes are offered to passersby. Assorted chocolates, jellybeans, cookies, and fudge are sold both prepackaged and in an area where shoppers can select their own favorites. The shop stocks a large selection of wines and spirits. Godiva chocolates, specialty

CROSSROADS OF LAKE BUENA VISTA

Constructed by the WDW folks, the shopping center located just across the road from Disney Village Hotel Plaza is a convenient dining and shopping area for both visitors and Walt Disney World employees. The 137,000-square-foot retail center is anchored by a Gooding's supermarket, which is open 24 hours a day and has a full-service pharmacy inside. (Guests at the nearby villas will find this an especially convenient stop.)

Other shops include Fish Tale Freddy's, for island casual wear; Chico's, for casual clothing; Sunworks, which stocks women's sportswear and swimwear; Foot Locker, for athletic shoes; Character Connection, the Disney merchandise shop; Beyond Electronics, which stocks stereos, tape recorders, and gadgets; Crazy Shirts, featuring Florida and Orlando T-shirts; White's Books; and Mitzi's Hallmark. There also is a post office. Dining options include *T.G.I. Friday's, McDonald's, Taco Bell, Perkins, Pizzeria Uno, Red Lobster, Pebbles, Johnny Rocket's, Chevy's Tex-Mex,* and *Jungle Jim's.*

In addition to the shops and services, there's Pirate's Cove Adventure Golf, an innovative miniature golf course.

sandwiches, and salads also are available. The line of Gourmet Mickey cookware and utensils is fully represented. Guests at the nearby villas, take note: Purchases will be delivered to your villa; if you aren't going to be home, the delivery person will even stash perishables in your refrigerator. To order by phone, touch "Gourmet Pantry" on your room telephone or, when calling from outside the resort, dial 828-3886.

THE CITY: Trend-setting fashions and accessories for men and women can be found at this shop. Stussy, No Fear, Yaga, Mossimo, Paris Blues, Steel, Guess, and My Michelle collections are represented.

RESTAURANTS

For a complete listing of all Walt Disney World Village restaurants, bars, and snack shops, see *Good Meals, Great Times.*

TEAM MICKEY'S ATHLETIC CLUB: The locker room decor is the perfect setting for sports clothing, activewear, and sports equipment for the whole family. This is the place to find T-shirts, sweatshirts, and other items with Disney University logos, as well as Mickey and Goofy emblazoned on shirts. There also is a large selection of athletic shoes.

GREAT SOUTHERN CRAFT CO.: There is fine handmade pottery, plus a boutique featuring country and folk crafts. It's a showplace of Americana gift items.

EUROSPAIN: An array of handcrafted gifts and decorative items from prestigious Spanish artisans and designers. Presented by Arribas Brothers.

Lakeside Activities

The 35-acre Buena Vista Lagoon that borders this village of cedar-shingled shops also gives it much of its atmosphere: When the sidewalks radiate heat, the water looks cool and inviting; in the slanting rays of the late afternoon sun, it glistens like a sheet of silver.

There's always something going on. Little Water Sprites zip to and fro, speeding to the dock from feeder canals to the west, while more laid-back folks float gently along in pedal boats or canopy boats, and still others fish off the dock.

It's pleasant to sit and watch all this activity from the benches at the Buena Vista Lagoon marina, centrally located in Disney Village Marketplace; over ice cream sundaes or frozen yogurt at *Donald's Dairy Dip* on the lake's west shore; or over Maryland crab cakes and fresh frozen strawberry margaritas at *Cap'n Jack's Oyster Bar*.

Those who would rather participate need walk only a few steps to the marina, where several types of boats can be rented from morning until dusk. Opening and closing hours change from season to season; call 828-2204 for details. No swimming is allowed. (Prices are subject to state tax.)

WATER SPRITES: These tiny craft are extremely popular. Though they don't really move very fast, they feel as if they do; in any event, they get up enough speed to cover quite a lot of territory on Buena Vista Lagoon. Half-hour rentals cost $15. There are usually lines of people waiting for boats between 11 A.M. and 4 P.M.; plan accordingly. The minimum age to rent or drive one of these boats (even accompanied by an adult) is 14.

CANOPY AND PONTOON BOATS: Providing serenity rather than thrills, the 16-foot canopy boats accommodate up to six adults, while 20-foot pontoon boats hold up to ten adults. Some people stock up on picnic supplies at the Gourmet Pantry and turn an afternoon sail into a party. Cost ranges from $17.50 to $20 per half hour.

FISHING EXCURSIONS: A two-hour guided catch-and-release fishing trip, aboard a pontoon boat with room for five anglers, leaves the Disney Village Marketplace marina several times daily. The fee per boatload—$120 for two hours, $145 for three hours, or $175 for four hours—includes guide, gear, bait, and tackle. Reservations are required 48 hours in advance. Call 828-2204.

The Disney Institute

Tucked away in a tranquil, lakeside enclave in the Disney Village Resort area is The Disney Institute, a brand-new concept in vacations. Designed exclusively for adults and families with older children (ages ten and up), this resort is scheduled to open in February 1996 with more than 80 innovative, hands-on programs ranging from animation and topiary gardening to rock climbing and wilderness exploration.

Guests are encouraged to choose a variety of selections from nine different program tracks—entertainment arts, sports and fitness, lifestyles, story arts, culinary arts, design arts, environment, youth, and performing arts—to create their own customized vacation experience. Those traveling together do not have to sign up for the same programs. It's possible for a family of four to participate in totally different programs throughout the day and still spend evenings together.

Sample offerings include an animation workshop in which guests work on an actual Disney Institute animated film, a "swamp party" that takes the whole family canoeing along a Florida waterway, an outdoor youth adventure including overnight camping at the Disney Wilderness Preserve, and

"Taste of the World" sessions in which guests prepare international culinary specialties under the guidance of Disney Institute chefs.

An Artists-in-Residence program gives guests the opportunity to interact with creative professionals such as musicians, dancers, writers, and filmmakers, who will be present at The Disney Institute, taking part in programs, holding workshops, and practicing their crafts. Lecture forums present guest speakers on a variety of subjects, including politics, business, science, sports, literature, and the arts. Among those who have agreed to participate are former Senate Majority Leader George Mitchell; sports personalities Bill Walton, Bruce Jenner, and Lute Olsen; movie critics Gene Siskel and Roger Ebert; opera's Sherrill Milnes; composer Morton Gould; and architects Robert A. M. Stern, Frank Gehry, and Michael Graves.

Smaller in scale than other Disney resorts (it has only 457 rooms), The Disney Institute is self-contained and is designed to provide an intimate, personalized vacation experience. The architecture is reminiscent of a quaint American town. Community buildings are organized around a town green, and guest accommodations surround a private lake. Facilities include 28 program studios, a broadcast-quality performance center, an outdoor amphitheater, a state-of-the-art cinema, and a closed-circuit television and radio station. There also is a 38,000-square-foot sports and fitness center with full-service spa, clay tennis courts, an 18-hole championship golf course, five swimming pools, and a separate, supervised youth center.

For additional information about the Institute, call 800-496-6337.

Pleasure Island

A six-acre island entertainment complex with nightclubs, restaurants, shops, and movie theaters fills the need for evening and late-night entertainment options for Walt Disney World guests. Pleasure Island is connected to the Disney Village Marketplace by three footbridges. There are seven nightclubs, several restaurants (described in detail in *Good Meals, Great Times*), an unusual variety of shops, and the AMC multiplex cinemas. The nightclubs open at about 7 P.M. and don't close until 2 A.M. The Pleasure Island shops are open from 10 A.M. to 1 A.M., and the restaurants are open from about 11:30 A.M. to midnight.

There is no fee to enter the Pleasure Island premises, its shops, or restaurants until 7 P.M. After 7 P.M., a single admission of $15.95 allows access to all clubs and the nightly street party spectacular. Length of Stay Passes and Five-Day World Hopper Passes include Pleasure Island admission. Guests under age 18 must be accompanied by a parent. (Tickets are not required for *Portobello Yacht Club* or the *Fireworks Factory*.)

Remember, the drinking age in Florida is 21. Underage guests who are over 18 will be admitted to the clubs (except *Mannequins*), but not served alcohol. A valid U.S., foreign, or international driver's license with a photo, an active U.S. military identification card, or a passport must be presented as proof of age.

LATE-NIGHT STREET PARTY: Every night at Pleasure Island is like New Year's Eve. There is a fireworks show with special-effects lighting and confetti, and a talented troupe of dancers entertain along the streets.

AMC THEATRES: Current movies are featured at this multiplex cinema. The ten theaters are comfortable and have an exceptional sound system called THX that was developed by George Lucas.

MANNEQUINS DANCE PALACE: If a day of walking around Walt Disney World hasn't left your feet too weary, this is the place to head to dance the night away. Guests enter through an elevator that rises to the third floor. Lights, contemporary dance music, and an overall exuberant atmosphere dominate the scene. The name of the club is derived from the many mannequins strategically placed around the establishment. Each of the figures is tied to dance in some way. There are several "cats" from the musical of the same name, and wonderful recreations of Deborah Kerr and Yul Brynner dressed as Anna and the King of Siam from the "Shall We Dance?" scene in the film version of *The King and I*.

The main dance floor is actually a turntable, and the music is provided by a deejay whose audio booth is about as high-tech as they come. The lighting is a major attraction at *Mannequins*. There are 60 robotically controlled lighting instruments, and a matrix of lights behind the stage has been dubbed "the toaster oven" by Disney Imagineers (because it warms the entire room when lit). There also are machines that can cause bubbles to float in the air, hurl confetti, or even make it snow in the club.

Specialty drinks, beer, and wine are available at a number of locations within the club, which is restricted to guests 21 and older.

NEON ARMADILLO MUSIC SALOON: Live country-and-western music is performed nightly, and the dance floor is usually full. The Southwestern decor is highlighted by a wonderful brass chandelier in the shape of a spur and inlaid wood tabletops decorated in Navajo-blanket patterns. Specialty drinks, beer, and wine are served.

ADVENTURERS CLUB: "Explore the unknown, discover the impossible," states the credo posted at the entrance. Just about all the items on display were collected at garage sales and antiques shows and shops all around the world by Disney Imagineers. The place is modeled on the paneled libraries and elegant salons of similar clubs of the 19th century, and is jam-packed with photos, furniture, trinkets, books, letters, statuettes, and other memorabilia. The cozy recesses hide rooms where the masks on the walls come to life, and cast members portray members of the house staff, including the maid and the curator, and several club members, prime among them an inept pilot named Hathaway Brown, the club chairperson, and a world-renowned bug expert. These players interact with guests with amusing results.

Down the flight of stairs there is more "stuff" than anyone could ever hope to see in one visit, so just stroll around, read the captions

on some of the photos, and enjoy the cool, air-conditioned atmosphere. Drinks are served at the bar. If you have a seat on one of the stools, ask the bartender to work his or her magic; your stool (or the one of an unsuspecting friend) may very slowly sink toward the floor leaving you, or your friend, significantly shorter. Then it's on to the library, where a haunted organ sets the scene for the outrageous storytellers. The show is a little corny, but entertaining.

PLEASURE ISLAND JAZZ COMPANY: The newest club on the island is reminiscent of jazz clubs from the 1930s. It's situated in a building that looks like an old warehouse. There is live entertainment nightly featuring jazz tunes from the 1930s to the present. Guests sit at small cocktail tables on comfortable padded chairs. The music is not too loud, so conversation is possible. Tapas-style appetizers and wine by the glass are available, as are mixed drinks, beer, and soft drinks.

ROCK & ROLL BEACH CLUB: A novel combination of dancing, dining, and the beach awaits guests at this establishment. The dance floor is located on the lowest level of the building, and there are billiard tables and games on the second and third floors.

Live bands perform hits from the 1950s to the present. The band plays 45 to 50 minutes each hour, and a deejay takes over during the breaks to offer uninterrupted musical entertainment. The atmosphere is a little frenetic but nonetheless exciting. Alcoholic beverages and soft drinks also are available on the first level.

COMEDY WAREHOUSE: A comedy troupe performs five times each evening from 7 P.M. to 1 A.M. There are five comedians and one musician. It's a funny, entertaining show that features improvisational comedy based on audience suggestions. Guests perch on stools in a tiered arena, so every seat offers a good view, even if the stools are a little tough on bad backs. Popcorn is the snack of choice, and specialty drinks, beer, wine, and soft drinks are all available.

8TRAX: The seventies are back. Rock 'n' roll music from the early 1970s and sounds from the disco era fill this dance spot. To keep things in the 1970s mode, the staff dresses in polyester bell-bottom suits.

WEST END STAGE: Live bands, including some top-name groups, perform at this new, covered stage nightly. The Island Explosion, Pleasure Island's own dance troupe, also performs here.

Shopping at Pleasure Island

The variety of merchandise at Pleasure Island's shops is a little more eclectic than that found at the other Walt Disney World emporiums. Some items may not, however, be available at all times.

AVIGATOR'S SUPPLY: The *Adventurers Club* logo is emblazoned on a wide variety of merchandise, including T-shirts, sweatshirts, magnets, and tote bags. There also is a selection of aviation-related gifts, clothing, and accessories. Leather bomber jackets,

heavy-duty duffle bags, airplane clocks and sculptures, and a variety of collectibles round out the offerings.

CHANGING ATTITUDES: A shop with an assortment of merchandise in only black and white. T-shirts, unique electronic gadgets, and other items are among the goods.

DOODLES: Hats, horns, and other party items are available here. Logo merchandise from the various clubs also is for sale.

DTV: A collection of fun and colorful contemporary fashions featuring Mickey Mouse and his friends is available here.

THE MOUSE HOUSE: Pleasure Island's character shop stocks the usual selection of T-shirts, sweatshirts, plush toys, gift items, hats, books, and other such merchandise.

MUSIC LEGENDS: Compact discs, T-shirts, and memorabilia from the early days of rock 'n' roll to heavy metal and hip-hop are available at this spot. There are three sections highlighting different types of music. If a well-known band is being featured at the West End Stage, you'll be able to find its merchandise here.

PROPELLER HEADS: Pleasure Island's arcade features the usual array of blipping and bleeping video games, and is enormously popular with younger guests. It's open from 10 A.M. to 2 A.M.

REEL FIND MERCHANDISE: Movie- and television-themed memorabilia can be found here. Items once owned by stars also are on display.

STREET SMART: The shop features popular surfwear and active clothing, including T-shirts, shorts, backpacks, and hats. The No Fear and Mossimo collections are here, and casual watches and jewelry also are available.

SUPERSTAR STUDIOS: Star in your own music video. Guests lip-sync favorite songs for either audio or video recordings. A particular favorite with teens.

SUSPENDED ANIMATION: Posters, prints, lithographs, cels, and original Disney animation art are sold here. It's a pleasant place to browse, even if you don't plan to buy.

EATING AT PLEASURE ISLAND

For a complete list of Pleasure Island restaurants, fast-food emporiums, and snack spots, see *Good Meals, Great Times*.

Typhoon Lagoon

A furious storm once roared 'cross the sea
Catching ships in its path, helpless to flee
Instead of a certain and watery doom
The winds swept them here to Typhoon
* Lagoon!*

So reads the legend guests see (looking a bit like old Burma-Shave roadside signs) as they drive into Typhoon Lagoon, a 56-acre state-of-the-art aquatic theme park. The watery playground has been inspired by an imagined legend: A typhoon hit a small resort village years and years ago, and the storm—plus a resultant earthquake and volcanic eruption—left the village in ruins. The "local" residents, however, were resourceful and rebuilt their town as best they could. Trees toppled onto and into buildings, a ship was marooned atop a strangely magical mountain, and debris was strewn all around.

Whether the typhoon, earthquake, and eruption ever actually took place doesn't really matter, because Typhoon Lagoon is a delightful place to spend a day. The surf lagoon is larger than two football fields and normally kicks up 4½-foot waves, two speed slides whisk guests through a cave at 30 miles per hour, three winding storm slides offer a twisting journey, white-water routes give groups and families a chance to ride the rapids together, and a special area just for young kids duplicates the slides in miniature.

The centerpiece of Typhoon Lagoon is one of the world's largest manmade watershed mountains, Mt. Mayday. Atop its peak, the *Miss Tilly*, a shrimp boat out of Safen Sound, Florida, is precariously perched. The smokestack atop *Miss Tilly* erupts every 30 minutes, shooting a 50-foot flume of water into the air. Guests who make the 85-foot climb up Mt. Mayday will be rewarded with a great view of the action below.

What follows is a description of all the specific activities available at Typhoon Lagoon.

What we'll leave to your imagination is the pure joy of pulling up a lounge chair, and opening a book or just people-watching.

TYPHOON LAGOON: The main swimming area spreads out over 2½ acres and contains 2.75 million gallons of water. The Caribbean-blue lagoon is surrounded by a white-sand beach, and its main attraction is the four-foot-plus waves that come crashing to the shore every 90 seconds. Guests are welcome to bodysurf—just ride the waves with their bodies. Water collects in 12 huge chambers above the lagoon and falls through trapdoors, creating the waves. There also are two tidal pools, Whitecap Cove and Blustery Bay, where less adventurous guests can loll about in water made for bobbing, not riding.

CASTAWAY CREEK: This 2,100-foot circular river that winds through the park offers a lazy, relaxing orientation to Typhoon Lagoon. Tubes are free and are the most enjoyable way to make the trip along the three-foot-deep waterway that courses through a rain forest where guests are cooled by mists and spray; past caves and grottoes that provide welcome shade on hot summer days; and an area known as Water Works, where "broken" pipes from a water tower unleash showers on passersby. The current is calm, and aside from a few floating props, the journey is unimpeded. There are exits along the way where guests can hop out for a while and do something else, or just dry off a bit and then jump right back in. In the way that the Walt Disney World Railroad offers an overall perspective of the Magic Kingdom, so does Castaway Creek reveal the breadth of Typhoon Lagoon. It takes 25 to 35 minutes to ride around the park without taking a break.

HUMUNGA KOWABUNGA: These two speed slides, reported to have been carved into the landscape by the historic earthquake, will send guests zooming through caves at speeds of 30 miles per hour. The 214-foot slides offer a 51-foot drop, and the view from the top is a little scary. But it's over before you know it, and once-wary guests hurry back for another try. Modest maidens beware! A one-piece suit is far safer than a skimpy two-piece. Guests also are warned that they should be free of back trouble, heart conditions, and other physical limitations to take the trip. Pregnant women are not permitted to ride.

SHARK REEF: For those Walt Disney World guests who have longed to jump into the tank at Epcot's Living Seas, here's your chance. Guests obtain free snorkel equipment for a

swim through an artificial coral reef where they come face-to-face with lots of fish. The reef is constructed around a sunken, upside-down tanker (where guests who don't care to swim among the fish can get a close look from the portholes). There are 362,000 gallons of seawater around the reef. The sharks, by the way, are small leopard sharks and bonnethead sharks, both passive members of the species. They don't eat anything bigger than they are. Guests must shower before entering the reef's depths. Open during busy seasons only.

STORM SLIDES: The Jib Jammer, Rudder Buster, and Stern Burner body slides send guests off at about 20 miles per hour down winding fiberglass slides, in and out of rock formations and caves, and through waterfalls. It's a somewhat tamer ride than Humunga Kowabunga, but still offers a speedy descent. The slides run about 300 feet, and each offers a different view and experience. Altogether, it's a cooling and enjoyable trip.

GANGPLANK FALLS, KEELHAUL FALLS, AND MAYDAY FALLS: These three whitewater rides offer guests a variety of trips, all taken aboard oversize inner tubes. All the slides course through caves, waterfalls, and intricate rock work, making the scenery an attraction in itself.

KETCHAKIDDIE CREEK: Open only to those four feet tall or under (unless accompanied by a small child), this kiddie area offers the same rides scaled down for pint-size visitors. Children *must*, however, be accompanied by an adult. There are slides, fountains, waterfalls, squirting whales and seals, a mini rapid ride, and a grotto with a thin veil of water that kids love to run through again and again.

WHEN TO ARRIVE: Typhoon Lagoon gets very crowded early in the day, and the parking lot often closes before noon. Once the lot is full, only guests staying at Walt Disney World resorts using WDW transportation will be admitted to the park, so plan accordingly. Note that Typhoon Lagoon is usually closed for refurbishment during certain winter months. Call 824-4321 for schedules.

WHERE TO EAT: There are two restaurants at Typhoon Lagoon, both offering similar fare and outdoor seating at tables with colorful umbrellas. *Leaning Palms*, which was known as *Placid Palms* before the typhoon hit, was renamed to fit its somewhat unorthodox architecture. Burgers, hot dogs, salads, and assorted snacks are sold here. *Typhoon Tilly's Galley & Grog* offers a similar menu and has a separate area just for ice cream and frozen yogurt. Also on hand are picnic areas, where guests can bring their own food or enjoy a sampling from the restaurants.

RESTROOMS AND DRESSING ROOMS: Restrooms with showers and lockers are located near the entrance. Other restrooms are available farther into the park. These are labeled "Buoys" and "Gulls." Small lockers cost $3 plus a $2 deposit to rent for the day, while large lockers cost $5 plus a $2 deposit. Towels may be rented for $1, and life jackets are available with a $25 refundable deposit.

SHOPPING: Singapore Sal's, located just to the right of the main entrance, is set in a ramshackle building that was left a bit worn after the typhoon. Women's, men's, and children's clothing and bathing suits; sunglasses; hats; towels; suntan lotion; souvenirs; thong sandals; and beach chairs are among the wares available here.

FIRST AID: A first-aid station capable of handling minor medical problems is located just to the left of *Leaning Palms*.

ADMISSION PRICES*

ONE-DAY WATER PARK HOPPER PASS
(Includes admission to Blizzard Beach, Typhoon Lagoon, River Country, and Discovery Island.)

Adult	$23.85
Child**	$18.02

ONE-DAY WATER PARK HOPPER PASS
(Discounted after 3 P.M. in summer)

Adult	$16.96
Child**	$13.25

The **WATER PARK HOPPER ANNUAL PASS** costs $104.94 for adults and $83.74 for children.

Note: Admission is included with a Length of Stay Pass or a Five-Day World Hopper Pass. The park is typically closed for refurbishment during certain winter months.

These prices were correct at press time, but may change during 1996.

*The prices quoted here include sales tax.
**3 through 9 years of age

Blizzard Beach

The newest water park at Walt Disney World (it opened in April 1995) is said to be the result of a freak winter storm that dropped a mountain of snow on the western side of the WDW property. As plans were quickly made for Florida's first ski resort, temperatures soared and the ice and snow began to melt. Designers were ready to close the new resort when they spotted an alligator sliding down the slopes and realized that the melting snow created the tallest, fastest, and most exhilarating water adventure park in the world. The slalom and bobsled runs became downhill water slides. The ski jump is now the world's tallest (120 feet), fastest (60 miles per hour), free-fall speed slide. Instead of skiers, the chair lift carries swimmers to the top.

Once again, Disney Imagineers have concocted an interesting tale to explain the existence of their latest creation. And, of course, it doesn't really matter if the legend is true. This is the most action-packed water park yet, with enough cool activities for the entire family to fill at least a day.

The centerpiece of Blizzard Beach is the snow-capped Mt. Gushmore and its Summit Plummet, visible from almost anywhere in the

park. Most of the more thrilling runs are found on the slopes of this mountain, which tops out at 90 feet. "Skiers" travel to the peak via a chairlift that's been converted for beach-resort use. At the summit, they have their choice of speed slides, flumes, a white-water raft ride, and an inner-tube run. There also is an observation tower that offers a spectacular view of the 66-acre park and all the action below.

CROSS COUNTRY CREEK: This meandering 3,000-foot waterway circles the entire park. A slow current keeps visitors moving along. Inner tubes, which are free, are the most pleasant way to travel. The ride includes a trip through a bone-chilling ice cave, where guests are splashed with the "melting ice" from overhead.

MELT-AWAY BAY: This one-acre pool at the base of Mt. Gushmore is equipped with its own wave machine. No tsunamis here, however, just a pleasant bobbing wave. The pool is constantly fed by "melting snow" waterfalls and is perfect for swimming.

SKI PATROL TRAINING CAMP: An area designed specifically for preteens, the camp features a variety of activities. The Krinkle Tin Slide looks like an old pipe and drops sliders into eight feet of water. The Thin Ice Training Course tests agility skills as guests try to walk along broken "icebergs" without falling into the water. At the Ski Patrol Shelter, which begins in an A-frame building, guests grab on to a T-bar. At any point in the ride they can drop into the water below. Those who stay on until the end wind up springing into the pool.

MOGUL MANIA: It sure looks like snow on the way down this inner-tube slide. Visitors bounce over and around moguls in this first-of-its-kind run for water parks. All the while, jets spray a fine mist of water that resembles snowmaking in progress.

SUMMIT PLUMMET: The big thrill ride begins 120 feet in the air on a platform built 30 feet above the top of Mt. Gushmore. It looks just like a ski jump. Brave souls travel about 60 miles per hour down the 350-foot slide. Near the top, guests pass through the ski chalet. To those watching from below, riders seem to disappear into an explosion of mist. Female riders would be wise to make the trip in a one-piece suit.

SLUSH GUSHER: A tamer trip down Mt. Gushmore can be undertaken next door to Summit Plummet. Although shorter and less

severe than its neighbor, this double-humped slide still offers a quick journey through a snow-banked mountain gully. Topping out at 90 feet, Slush Gusher is the tallest slide of its kind.

TEAMBOAT SPRINGS: The longest family white-water raft ride in the world takes five-passenger rafts down a twisting, 1,400-foot series of rushing waterfalls.

TOBOGGAN RACER: An eight-lane water slide sends guests racing over a number of dips. Guests lie on their stomachs on a mat and travel headfirst down the 250-foot route.

SNOW STORMERS: A trio of flumes descends from the top of the mountain. Guests race down on a switchback course that includes ski-type slalom gates.

RUNOFF RAPIDS: On this inner-tube run, guests careen down three different twisting, turning flumes.

TIKE'S PEAK: A kid-size variation of Blizzard Beach, this attraction features miniature versions of Mt. Gushmore's slides and a snow-castle fountain play area.

WHEN TO ARRIVE: As the World's newest water park, Blizzard Beach becomes very crowded early in the day, and the parking lot may close before noon. Once the lot is full, only guests staying at Walt Disney World resorts using WDW transportation will be admitted to the park, so plan accordingly. Note that Blizzard Beach is usually closed for refurbishment during certain winter months. Call 824-4321 for schedules.

WHERE TO EAT: Burgers, hot dogs, fruit salads, and drinks are available at *Lottawatta Lodge*, a fast-food restaurant located in the main village area. Two other snack stands with limited offerings are located in more

remote areas: *Avalunch* and *The Warming Hut* offer snacks and soft drinks. There also are picnic areas for those who prefer to pack their own.

RESTROOMS AND DRESSING ROOMS: Restrooms with showers are located near the main entrance. Other restrooms and dressing rooms are located around the park. Small lockers cost $3 plus a $2 deposit to rent for the day, while large lockers cost $5 plus a $2 deposit.

SHOPPING: The Beach Haus, near the main entrance, stocks bathing suits, T-shirts, shorts, sunglasses, hats, suntan lotion, beach towels, and all the other accoutrements needed for a day in the park. Logo merchandise is in large supply.

FIRST AID: A first-aid station capable of handling minor medical problems is located near the main entrance.

ADMISSION PRICES*

ONE-DAY WATER PARK HOPPER PASS
(Includes admission to Blizzard Beach, Typhoon Lagoon, River Country, and Discovery Island.)

Adult	$23.85
Child**	$18.02

ONE-DAY WATER PARK HOPPER PASS
(Discounted after 3 P.M. in summer)

Adult	$16.96
Child**	$13.25

The **WATER PARK HOPPER ANNUAL PASS** costs $104.94 for adults and $83.74 for children.

Note: Admission is included with a Length of Stay Pass or a Five-Day World Hopper Pass. The park is typically closed for refurbishment during certain winter months.

These prices were correct at press time, but may change during 1996.

*The prices quoted here include sales tax.
**3 through 9 years of age

Fort Wilderness

In a part of the state where campgrounds tend to look like pastures—barren and very hot—the *Fort Wilderness* campground, located almost due east of the *Contemporary* resort, is an anomaly—a forested 700-acre wonder of tall slash pines, white-flowering bay trees, and ancient cypress hung with streamers of Spanish moss. Seminole Indians once hunted and fished here.

In all, there are some 1,192 woodsy campsites arranged in several campground loops; along some of them, Fleetwood homes are available for rent, completely furnished and fitted with all the comforts of home. For information about both lodging options, see *Transportation & Accommodations*.

Scattered throughout the campground loops are a number of sporting facilities, including two tennis courts, tetherball, basketball, and volleyball courts. *Fort Wilderness* has riding stables, two swimming pools, a marina full of boats, a canoe livery, a beach, bikes and electric golf carts for rent, and a nature trail. Some of these facilities are available for the use of campground guests only; some are open to guests at WDW-owned resort hotels and villas as well; some also can be enjoyed by guests lodging at the establishments at the Disney Village Hotel Plaza as well as off the property.

There's also a petting farm where goats, ducks, and other farm animals run free inside a white-rail fence, and it's fun to walk through the barn that houses the large, sleek horses that pull the Magic Kingdom's Main Street trolleys.

Two stores, the Settlement Trading Post and the Meadow Trading Post, stock campers' necessities, groceries, and some Disney souvenirs. And then there's Pioneer Hall, widely known as the home of the Hoop-Dee-Doo Musical Revue (described in *Good Meals, Great Times*). This rustic structure (made of western white pine shipped all the way from Montana) also has a cafeteria and lounge.

Last but not least in the *Fort Wilderness* catalog is River Country. This eight-acre expanse of water-oriented recreational facilities embodies everyone's idea of the perfect old-fashioned swimming hole. It's a separate attraction, with its own hours and admission fees.

How to Get There

BY CAR: From outside the World, take the Magic Kingdom exit off I-4 (number 25) onto U.S. 192, go through the Magic Kingdom Auto Plaza, and, bearing to your right, follow the *Fort Wilderness* or River Country signs. This is the most expeditious way to go, even for WDW resort guests.

BY BUS: There's a direct bus (or bike path) from the *Wilderness Lodge* to *Fort Wilderness*. From Epcot, the *Contemporary* resort, the *Polynesian* resort, and the *Grand Floridian* resort, take the monorail to the Transportation and Ticket Center (TTC), and transfer for the bus to *Fort Wilderness*. From Disney-MGM Studios, the Disney Village Marketplace, and Disney Village Hotel Plaza establishments, take a bus to the TTC. Change there to the bus to *Fort Wilderness*. From all other WDW resorts take a bus to the Disney Village Marketplace, switch for the bus to the TTC, then take the *Fort Wilderness* bus. To ride many of these buses, you must show an ID card from one of the WDW-owned properties or a multiday admission pass. Allow yourself plenty of time to make transfers.

BY BOAT: Guests at WDW-owned properties, and those with admission tickets to River Country or Discovery Island, also can go by boat from Magic Kingdom marinas (about a 30-minute ride) and from the *Contemporary* resort (about a 25-minute ride).

What to Do

SOUVENIRS AND SUPPLIES: Food staples and all sorts of other necessities of the camping life are available, along with souvenirs, at two stores—the Settlement Trading Post, located not far from the beach at the north end of the *Fort Wilderness* campground, and the Meadow Trading Post, which is conveniently located near the center of *Fort Wilderness*.

For a complete list of restaurants found at the *Fort Wilderness* campground, see the *Good Meals, Great Times* chapter.

BEACHES AND SWIMMING: The clear waters of Bay Lake, which lap the 315-foot-long, 175-foot-wide white-sand beach at the north end of the campground, are delightful. Swimming is allowed inside the roped-off areas, and there also are two pools for campers' use. Note that beaches and pools are open to *Fort Wilderness* guests only.

BIKE RENTALS: Tandems and other bikes can be hired at the Bike Barn for trips along the bike paths and roadways of *Fort Wilderness*—or just for getting around. Cost is $4 per hour or $8 per day.

BLACKSMITH SHOP: The pleasant fellow who shoes the draft horses that pull the trolleys down Main Street in the Magic Kingdom is on hand at some time every day to answer questions and talk about what he does; occasionally guests can watch him at work, fitting the big animals with the special polyurethane-covered, steel-cored horseshoes that are used to protect the horses' hooves.

BOAT RENTALS ON BAY LAKE: Zippy little Water Sprites, sailboats, pontoon boats, and pedal boats (described in *Sports*) are available for rent at the marina, at the north end of the campground.

CAMPFIRE PROGRAM: Held nightly near the Meadow Trading Post near the center of the campground, this evening entertainment program features Disney movies, a sing-along, and cartoons. It's free for WDW resort guests only. Also, Chip 'n' Dale always put in an appearance.

CANOE RENTALS: *Fort Wilderness* is ribboned with tranquil canals, sometimes in full sun and sometimes canopied by tall trees, which make for delightful canoe trips of one to three hours—or longer if you take fishing gear and elect to wet your line. Rentals are available at the Bike Barn (cost is $4 per hour or $10 per day).

ELECTRIC CART RENTALS: Available at the Bike Barn ($35.51 for 24 hours) for sightseeing or transportation. Renters must be 18 years old and have a valid driver's license.

ELECTRICAL WATER PAGEANT: This twinkling cavalcade of lights (described in more detail in *Good Meals, Great Times*) can be seen from the beach here nightly at 9:45 P.M.

FISHING EXCURSIONS ON BAY LAKE: WDW's restrictive fishing policy means plenty of angling action—largemouth bass weighing two to eight pounds, mainly—for those who sign up for the special 8 A.M., 11:30 A.M., and 3 P.M. fishing excursions. The fee is $125 for up to five people for a two-hour excursion (each additional hour is $50) and includes gear, a guide, and refreshments; no license is required. Guests whose accommodations have kitchens may keep their catch. Call 824-2621 for reservations.

FISHING IN THE CANALS: In addition to largemouth bass, catfish and panfish can be caught here as well. Those without their own gear will find cane poles and lures for sale at the trading posts; equipment also is available for rent at the Bike Barn. Cane poles are $2 per hour or $4 for the whole day. No license is required. *Fort Wilderness* resort guests may toss their lines in right from the shore.

HOOP-DEE-DOO MUSICAL REVUE

Sturdy, porch-rimmed Pioneer Hall is best-known Worldwide as the home of the Pioneer Hall Players, an energetic troupe of singing, dancing, wisecracking entertainers who keep audiences chuckling and grinning and whooping it up for two hours during a procession of barbecued ribs, fried chicken, corn-on-the-cob, strawberry shortcake, and other stomach-stretching vittles. If you have time for only one of the Disney dinner shows, make it this one (for more details see *Good Meals, Great Times*). Reservations are hard to come by. See the reservation chart on page 21 for details.

HAYRIDES: The hay wagon departs from Pioneer Hall and carries guests on a trip through wooded areas near Bay Lake. A ride lasts about an hour, and concludes back at Pioneer Hall. Tickets can be purchased from the hayride host. The price is $6 for adults; $4 for children ages 3 to 11. Children under ten must be accompanied by an adult.

THE HORSE BARN: The world-champion Percherons and all the draft horses that pull trolleys down Main Street in the Magic Kingdom call this corner of *Fort Wilderness* home. You can watch them chomping placidly on their food, and occasionally see young colts and fillies as well. The Tri Circle D insignia above the barn door—two small circles, Mouse-ears style, atop a large one with the letter *D* inside—also is the WDW brand.

LAWN MOWER TREE: The tree that somehow, mysteriously, grew around a lawn mower is a *Fort Wilderness* point of interest worth hunting down. It's just off the sidewalk leading to the marina.

PETTING FARM: This fenced-in enclave just behind Pioneer Hall is home to some friendly goats, sheep, rabbits, chickens, and other assorted barnyard critters. (A colony of prairie dogs didn't work out because its members persisted in burrowing out of their compound; no sooner would their Disney caretakers try to thwart them—by digging a bigger hole and installing a below-ground-level wire fence—than the little creatures would gnaw through it.) Pony rides are available for $2 between 9 A.M. and 5 P.M. Though mainly designed for youngsters, the Petting Farm also is fun for adults, and it's a good place to pass the time while waiting for seating at the Hoop-Dee-Doo Musical Revue in nearby Pioneer Hall.

TENNIS: Two tennis courts are available; play is on a first-come, first-served basis.

TRAIL RIDES: Offered from the middle of the campground, these horseback trips depart four times daily and take riders on a leisurely, meandering ride through the Florida wilderness, where it is not uncommon to see deer, wild birds, and even an occasional alligator. Galloping is not part of the game, so you don't need riding know-how to sign up. Cost is $17 per person for both day visitors and for guests at WDW-owned properties. No children under nine are allowed to ride. There is a weight limit of 250 pounds. Reservations are recommended; phone 824-2621 up to two weeks in advance.

VOLLEYBALL, TETHERBALL, AND BASKETBALL COURTS: Open only to guests at WDW-owned properties, these are scattered throughout the camping loops. No charge.

WATERSKI TRIPS: Ski boats with drivers and equipment can be hired for $75 an hour at the marina, including instruction; there is a minimum of two people and a maximum of five. Reservations can be made up to two weeks in advance. Call 824-2621.

WILDERNESS SWAMP TRAIL: A ¾-mile trail, this smooth footpath into the woods skirts the marshes along the shore of Bay Lake, then plunges into a forest full of tall, straight-standing cypress trees. It is near Marshmallow Marsh, at the northern end of the campground.

River Country

The Perfect Swimming Hole

It's next to impossible to go through childhood reading such classics as *The Adventures of Huckleberry Finn* and *The Adventures of Tom Sawyer* (and other great tales of growing up) without developing a few fantasies about what it would be like to swim in a perfect swimming hole. A group of Disney Imagineers have concocted a Disney version on a somewhat larger scale at River Country, a water-oriented playground that occupies a corner of Bay Lake at *Fort Wilderness* campground.

Fred Joerger—the same Disney rock builder who created Big Thunder Mountain, Schweitzer Falls at the Jungle Cruise, and the caves of Tom Sawyer Island in the Magic Kingdom—has helped design rocks used to landscape one of the largest swimming pools in the state. The rocks, scattered with pebbles acquired from stream beds in Georgia and the Carolinas, look so real that it's hard to believe they aren't.

More to the point, the place is great fun. Slipping and sliding down the curvy water chutes at top speed; getting tangled up, all arms and legs, in the whirlpools of Raft Rider Ridge; and whamming into the water from the swimming pool's high slides make even care-worn grown-ups smile, grin, giggle, chortle, and roar with delight. People who climb to the top with trepidation embark on the lightning-fast journey to the bottom only because it seems too late to back out; at the bottom they rush back for more. Line-haters queue up—over and over again. Those who associate lakes with muck and weeds get ecstatic over the way the soft sand on the River Country bottom squishes between their toes.

WHAT TO DO: There are several basic sections of River Country—the 330,000-gallon swimming pool; Bay Cove (aka the Ol' Swimmin' Hole), the big walled-off section of Bay Lake that most people consider the main (and best) part of River Country; an adjoining junior version of the above for small children, with its own beach; and the grassy grounds, with picnic tables and a squirting fountain in which to play. On the edge of the lake there's also a boardwalk nature trail through a lovely cypress swamp, and a wide (if not terribly long) white-sand beach.

Heated in winter, the oversize swimming pool has a pair of water slides that begin high enough above the water to make an acrophobe climb right down again. They plunge at such an angle that it's impossible to see the bottom of the slide from the top. Daredevils who don't chicken out are shot into the water from a height of about seven feet—hard enough, as one commentator observed, to "slap your stomach up against the roof of your mouth." Gutsy kids adore the experience; those who like their thrills a bit tamer might prefer to watch.

The heart of River Country, Bay Cove—actually a part of Bay Lake—is fitted out with rope swings, a ship's boom for swooping and plunging, and assorted other constructions designed to put hearts into throats as swimmers plunge from air to water. The big deals, however, are the two flume rides—one 260 feet long (accessible by a boardwalk and stairway to the far right of the swimming hole as you face it) and a smaller one, 100 feet shorter (accessible by a stairway to the left)—and the white-water raft ride.

The flumes, which are like overgrown, steep-sided water slides, corkscrew through the greenery at the top of the ridge known as Whoop-'N-Holler Hollow, sending even the most stalwart shooting into the water, usually like greased lightning. White Water Rapids, as the white-water raft ride mentioned above is known, involves a more leisurely trip through a series of chutes and pools in an inner-tube from the crest of Raft Rider Ridge (adjoining Whoop-'N-Holler Hollow) into Bay Cove. It's not a high-speed affair like the flumes, but some people like it better. The pools are contoured so that the water swirls through them in whirlpool fashion. You tend to get caught in the slow circling water, and when other tubers come sliding down the chutes at you, bare arms and legs get all tangled up.

ADMISSION: River Country is an attraction in its own right, with a separate admission charge that includes transportation to the site and use of all the facilities. A One-Day Water Park Hopper Pass, which includes transportation and admission to River Country, Typhoon Lagoon, Blizzard Beach, and Discovery Island for one day, also is available. The Length of Stay Pass and the Five-Day World Hopper Pass include

admission to River Country and Discovery Island. Note that children under ten must be accompanied by an adult. Some of the River Country adventures require swimming ability.

WHEN TO GO: Daytime temperatures in Orlando are such that it's possible to enjoy River Country almost all year-round, though it is perhaps most pleasant in spring when the weather is getting hot but the water is still cool. In summer, the place can be very busy indeed. Ticket windows close as the crowd approaches capacity. During Walt Disney World's busiest seasons, that may happen as early as 11 A.M. It's worth noting, however, that those who already have tickets will be admitted anyway. Consequently, if you plan to visit River Country in the afternoon of a summer day, it's smart to buy your ticket in the morning. River Country is usually closed for refurbishment during certain winter months.

River Country closes at 7 P.M. during the summer. Call 824-4321 for up-to-the-minute schedules.

HOW TO GET THERE: From the Transportation and Ticket Center, buses drop passengers off within walking distance of River Country. It's also possible to go by boat. Launches leave regularly from the dock near the gates of the Magic Kingdom. For guests arriving at River Country by car, a bus picks them up at the *Fort Wilderness* parking lot and takes them to the entrance.

TOWELS, DRESSING ROOMS, LOCKERS: Men's and women's dressing rooms with lockers are available. Small lockers cost $3 plus a $2 deposit to rent for the day; large lockers cost $5 plus a $2 deposit.

Towels are available for rent at $1 each at the concession window, but they're small, so you'll probably want to bring at least one beach towel.

FOOD: *Pop's Place*, the main snack spot, features quarter-pound burgers, hot dogs, salads, beer, and soda. During peak season the *Waterin' Hole*, a smaller stand nearby, offers a more limited selection. Picnicking is permitted. You can eat on the beach or seek out one of the tables located on the shady lawns.

ADMISSION PRICES*

ONE-DAY TICKET

Adult	$15.64
Child**	$12.19

ONE-DAY WATER PARK HOPPER PASS
(Includes admission to Blizzard Beach, Typhoon Lagoon, River Country, and Discovery Island.)

Adult	$23.85
Child**	$18.02

The **WATER PARK HOPPER ANNUAL PASS** costs $104.94 for adults and $83.74 for children.

Note: Admission to River Country and Discovery Island is included with a Length of Stay Pass or a Five-Day World Hopper Pass. The park is typically closed for refurbishment during certain winter months.

These prices were correct at press time, but may change during 1996.

*The prices quoted here include sales tax.
**3 through 9 years of age

Discovery Island

This 11½-acre zoological park (a member of the American Association of Parks and Aquariums), on a island located off the southeast shore of Bay Lake, is a delightful place to go for a change of pace from the theme parks. Here you're in the domain of the animals; human beings are just visitors. It is a natural marvel full of exotic birds and a whole United Nations of plants. The mood is different from anywhere else in the World, and the scenery is remarkably lush.

Before the World began, this island was flat and scrubby, just a tangle of vines. But Disney planners, thinking of Robert Louis Stevenson's classic *Treasure Island*, decided to turn it into a horticultural and zoological paradise. They cleared the vegetation, brought in 15,000 cubic yards of sandy soil, and added 500 tons each of boulders and trees. They built hills, carved out lagoons, sowed grass seed, and planted 20 types of palm trees, ten species of bamboo, and dozens upon dozens of other plants from Argentina, Bolivia, the Canary Islands, China, Costa Rica, Taiwan, the Himalayas, India, Japan, Peru, South Africa, Trinidad, and other far corners of the world. Then they added winding paths, built aviaries and filled them with birds, and added a few props to carry through the *Treasure Island* theme. A wrecked ship salvaged from off the coast of Florida was installed on the beach, and a Jolly Roger hung from the lookout post. The creation was dubbed Treasure Island.

Since then, that theme has been abandoned and the island's name changed. But the ship is still there, as is the vegetation (lusher than ever). And the avian population is flourishing so well that the droning of the Water Sprites' motors on Bay Lake almost is drowned out by chirps and tweets, crows and hoarse caws, cries and squeaks, and the lonely-sounding squawks of peacocks.

Today nobody makes any bones about the fact that the birds and the extraordinary vegetation constitute the island's chief attraction. Far from taking a backseat to the man-made, nature is the big deal on Discovery Island. The sweet-smelling flowers in pinks and reds and yellows that polka-dot the billowing greenery, the ferns that hang in the forests, the trees that canopy the footpaths, the butterflies, the dense thickets of bamboo, and the graceful palms—not to mention the birds themselves—are all very real; during Discovery Island hours—that is, from 10 A.M. to 5 P.M. (to 7 P.M. during the summer) every day—visitors provide a good show for the birds and animals. The last boat to the island leaves 1 hour 15 minutes before closing.

WHAT TO SEE: It's possible to walk the length of the paths and boardwalks that wind through the island in 45 minutes or so. But spending a good part of a day—or at least several hours—is a far better idea, since there is so much to see that it warrants more than just a rushed look. This is especially true in spring, when the birds are in breeding condition—looking their best, putting on courting displays, and sometimes collecting material for nests. Even during other seasons, however, each stop yields rewards. An ibis might be spotted building its nest. A sleeping tortoise—dinosaurlike, with the papery, wrinkled skin of an elderly person's neck—suddenly wakes and creeps forward to join a clump of rocks that turns out to be other tortoises.

Many animals run free. Peacocks trail their spotted trains of iridescent green, blue, and gold around the grounds. They lose their tail feathers every September and spend the winter growing new plumage in preparation for their springtime mating dance—a slow turning to and fro, sometimes punctuated by a quiver and a shudder of their graceful fans. The large rabbitlike animals are Patagonian cavies, members of the guinea pig family, who in the wild live in burrows to escape predators. By keeping calm and approaching slowly, you can examine them at close range.

One of the newest features at Discovery Island is the Center for Administration, Medicine, and Propagation (C.A.M.P.). Here guests can watch a veterinarian and animal-care specialists caring for and feeding animals behind large glass windows.

In addition, there are special points of interest, which are marked on maps available on the island:

Trumpeter Springs: The trumpeter swans who live here, the largest members of the waterfowl family, belong to a species that once was nearly extinct as a result of hunting in the early part of this century.

Parrots Perch: The macaws, cockatoos, and other trained birds that comprise the Discovery Island Bird Show make their home here. The show combines the birds' antics with a message about the efforts to help save them through captive breeding.

Bamboo Hollow: This is where you'll find lemurs, nimble primates from Madagascar. Lemurs are endangered in the wild.

Crane's Roost: Small demoiselle cranes, Asian muntjac deer, and white-crested hornbills can be seen at this spot on the island.

Avian Way: One of the largest walk-through aviaries in the world, this enclosure, occupying close to an acre, is the home of the United States' most extensive breeding colony of scarlet ibis. Their incredible color, even richer than that of ibis in the wild, is derived from a diet that is especially rich in carotenes. Even those in the forest are striking. The early South American explorers who first saw them thought that the trees were covered with blood.

Pelican Bay: Brown pelicans almost became extinct. The chemical DDT, washed into rivers and absorbed by fish that the birds subsequently ate, caused their eggs to have such thin shells that the weight of the mother pelican nesting on them broke them before hatching. It is only since Florida's 1965 ban on the chemical that the population has begun to grow again. The Discovery Island birds, though now healthy, have suffered injuries that have left them crippled in ways that would make it impossible for them to survive in the wild.

Flamingo Lagoon: Native flamingos—which nested in colonies some 20,000 strong when John James Audubon visited Florida in the early part of the 19th century—have not lived in the wild here since around 1920. The Discovery Island birds are Caribbean flamingos. They have grown accustomed to human presence, as the early Florida flamingos could not, and are breeding.

Alligator Pool: Native Florida gators can be seen swimming and sunning here.

Tortoise Beach: Early explorers used to lead Galápagos tortoises, now rare and endangered, onto their ships, because the animals can live for some time without food or water to provide the crews with fresh meat for the duration of a trip. There are five here; the largest weighs some 500 pounds.

HOW TO GET THERE: Watercraft from the Magic Kingdom, the *Polynesian* resort, the *Contemporary* resort, the *Grand Floridian* resort, the *Wilderness Lodge* resort, *Fort Wilderness*, and River Country all call regularly at Discovery Island. To ride these, you must show a Discovery Island admission ticket or a WDW resort ID.

ADMISSION: Cost is $10.60 ($5.83 for children three through nine) for a one-day ticket. Discovery Island admission also is included with a One-Day Water Park Hopper Pass, a Five-Day World Hopper Pass, or a Length of Stay Pass.

PHOTOS: The birds on Discovery Island offer wonderful photographic possibilities. Don't forget your camera. Film is available on the island.

BEACH: Swimming isn't allowed, but the peaceful strand flanking the shipwreck is great for sunbathing and sandcastle building—or just for sitting and watching the brightly colored sails of the Hobie Cats (from the *Fort Wilderness* marina) go by.

FOOD: It's fun to pack a picnic, with supplies from the Gourmet Pantry at the Disney Village Marketplace or one of *Fort Wilderness* campground's trading posts, for lunch on the beach near the handsome old wreck (which is still aging gracefully along the Bay Lake shore). Sandwiches, hot dogs, ice-cream sandwiches and bars, frozen-juice bars, and beer and soft drinks are available at the snack bar, the *Thirsty Perch*.

DISCOVERY ISLAND KIDVENTURE

Children 8 to 14 can explore Discovery Island and *Fort Wilderness* on four-hour guided tours. Cost is $32 per person and includes lunch, transportation, craft materials, and a souvenir photo. Reservations are required. Call 824-3784.

Learning Programs

Disney University Learning Programs offer a unique behind-the-scenes look at the Walt Disney World Resort through a variety of educational programs for guests of all ages. Young people (ages 10 through 15) can step backstage for a look at wildlife, art, entertainment, and international cultures. Adults can study the culture and landscapes of Epcot or participate in a series of multi-day business and educational programs. Here is a brief description of the programs available.

Wonders of Walt Disney World education programs spark imaginations and fuel ambitions of students interested in learning about wildlife, art, entertainment, or international cultures. Each six-hour learning adventure was developed in cooperation with leading educators and is recognized as an authentic learning experience. In many cases, students can earn school credit, special recognition, or an excused absence for completing the program. The cost is $79 and participants receive a colorful program book with follow-up activities, access to the theme parks and backstage areas during the program, lunch, and a personalized certificate of completion. Choose from four unique programs:

Wildlife Adventure: Exploring the Environment (Tuesdays and Thursdays) takes students on a safari through the pristine Walt Disney World conservation area. Discussions on environmental issues come to life as participants observe alligators, birds, and other creatures in their natural habitat. The day includes a visit to Discovery Island for an up-close look at caring for captive animals and a lesson in mankind's responsibility to protect wildlife environments.

Art Magic: Bringing Illusion to Life (Mondays through Fridays) shows how WDW artists create the illusion of reality in movies and theme parks. This adventure includes a behind-the-scenes look at the animation process. Following a discussion on the artists and steps involved in developing an animated film, participants get to paint a keepsake Mickey Mouse cel. The students then step back "on stage" to study the use of theme, color, and forced perspective. The day concludes with a hands-on experience: the participants learn tips on drawing Disney characters.

Show Biz Magic: The Walt Disney World of Entertainment (Mondays through Thursdays) introduces young people to the diversity of entertainment at WDW. Discussions on star quality, show preparation, and auditions are reinforced through talks with performers from a variety of entertainment areas. Highlights of this adventure include a visit to a rehearsal area and a costuming department, and a trip into the tunnel system beneath the Magic Kingdom for a look at other show preparation areas.

Passport: A Secret Mission to Other Lands (Wednesdays and Fridays) brings to life the traditions, art, culture, and history of Epcot's World Showcase. As students travel from country to country, they have the chance to talk with international cast members, study unique architectural styles, learn how to communicate in other languages, and uncover secrets "behind" world-famous landmarks. Participants will experience more than 3,000 years of history—all in one day.

Program content and prices are subject to change without notice. For individual reservations, call 354-1855. There are special rates for groups of 11 or more; phone 824-4730.

Adults can get in on the fun, too. **Adult Learning Programs** take guests 16 and older on guided behind-the-scenes tours of Epcot's World Showcase. In **Hidden Treasures of World Showcase**, participants discover the often overlooked art, architecture, costumes, landscape, and entertainment of the international pavilions at World Showcase. In **Gardens of the World**, a Disney horticulturist guides guests through a study of the plants, flowers, and trees of World Showcase. Each program is a three-hour walking tour and costs $25 per person in addition to theme park admission. For reservations phone 939-8687.

Disney University Professional Development Programs offer a variety of programs designed specifically for business and education professionals. **The Disney Approach Business & Management Programs** are packaged multi-day seminars offering business professionals insight into people management, quality service, creative leadership, and orientation strategies. A unique combination of classroom activities and behind-the-scenes field experiences helps participants see how Disney methods can be adapted to their organizations. **Disney Educator Programs** are professional development programs designed to help educators learn practical ways to adapt Disney communication, marketing, and motivation techniques to classrooms, schools, and districts. Graduate credit is available.

Special behind-the-scenes tours, team-building activities, and management presentations are available exclusively to convention groups of 15 or more staying on the Disney property. Call 828-3074 for more information.

For additional information about these programs, contact Disney University Professional Development Programs; Box 10,093; Lake Buena Vista, FL 32830-0093; 363-6000 or fax 824-4866.

SPORTS

Many first-time visitors don't realize that Walt Disney World is much more than just the Magic Kingdom, Epcot, and the Disney-MGM Studios. Within WDW's 27,000-odd acres there are more tennis courts than at most tennis resorts, more holes of championship-caliber golf than at most golf centers, and so many acres of other diversions—from fishing and bicycling to boating and swimming—that the quantity and variety are matched by few other vacation destinations.

So while the golfers in the family are pursuing a perfect swing on one of the five first-rate 18-hole courses, tennis buffs can be wearing themselves out on the courts, sailors can be sailing, waterskiers can be skimming back and forth across powerboat wakes, and anglers can be dangling a cane pole in a canal—in the hopes of bringing in a big bream.

Instruction (formal or impromptu), as well as guides, drivers, and assorted leaders and supervisors (as required), makes each sports offering as much fun for rank beginners as for hard-core aficionados. Moreover, the ready accessibility of all these WDW sporting activities—via an excellent system of public transportation (see *Transportation & Accommodations*)—means that no member of a visiting family or group need give up play time to chauffeur others around.

Note: Prices given in this chapter are subject to change, and do not include applicable state tax.

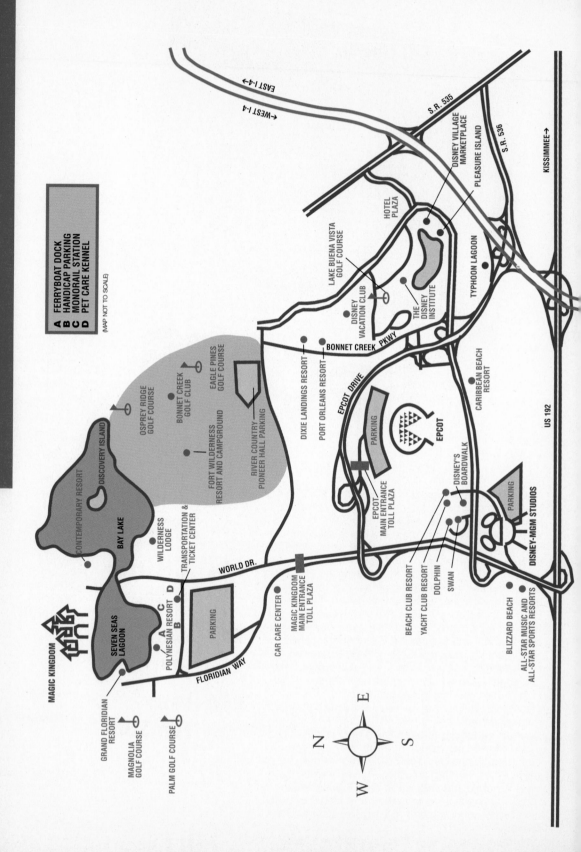

A FERRYBOAT DOCK
B HANDICAP PARKING
C MONORAIL STATION
D PET CARE KENNEL

(MAP NOT TO SCALE)

MAGIC KINGDOM

SEVEN SEAS LAGOON

GRAND FLORIDIAN RESORT

MAGNOLIA GOLF COURSE

PALM GOLF COURSE

CONTEMPORARY RESORT

DISCOVERY ISLAND

BAY LAKE

WILDERNESS LODGE

TRANSPORTATION & TICKET CENTER

A
B
C
D

POLYNESIAN RESORT

PARKING

CAR CARE CENTER

FLORIDIAN WAY

WORLD DR.

MAGIC KINGDOM MAIN ENTRANCE TOLL PLAZA

OSPREY RIDGE GOLF COURSE

BONNET CREEK GOLF CLUB

EAGLE PINES GOLF COURSE

FORT WILDERNESS RESORT AND CAMPGROUND

RIVER COUNTRY PIONEER HALL PARKING

DIXIE LANDINGS RESORT

PORT ORLEANS RESORT

BONNET CREEK PKWY

LAKE BUENA VISTA GOLF COURSE

DISNEY VACATION CLUB

THE DISNEY INSTITUTE

HOTEL PLAZA

DISNEY VILLAGE MARKETPLACE

PLEASURE ISLAND

TYPHOON LAGOON

S.R. 535

S.R. 536

KISSIMMEE →

EPCOT DRIVE

PARKING

EPCOT

EPCOT MAIN ENTRANCE TOLL PLAZA

DISNEY'S BOARDWALK

BEACH CLUB RESORT

YACHT CLUB RESORT

DOLPHIN

SWAN

CARIBBEAN BEACH RESORT

PARKING

DISNEY-MGM STUDIOS

BLIZZARD BEACH

ALL-STAR MUSIC AND ALL-STAR SPORTS RESORTS

US 192

EAST I-4 →

← WEST I-4

N
E
S
W

Tennis Everyone

No one comes to Walt Disney World just for a tennis vacation; there just isn't the country-club ambience of a tennis resort where everyone is totally immersed in the game. But the facilities and instruction program here are extensive enough that such holidays are certainly within the realm of possibility. And at the very least, a couple of sets of tennis on one of the World's 25 courts is a good way to unwind after a mad morning in the parks.

In February, March, April, June, and July the courts at the tennis locations endure fairly heavy use, but there is usually a lull between noon and 3 P.M., and again from dinnertime until 9 P.M. Even during these months, however, it's often possible to get a reservation.

WHERE TO FIND THE COURTS: With six tennis courts and a pro shop, Disney's Racquet Club at the *Contemporary* resort, located just beyond the Garden Wing to the north of the Tower, is WDW's major tennis facility; reopened in April 1995 after a complete overhaul, it features state-of-the-art hydrogrid clay courts. The *Grand Floridian* boasts two clay courts, as does *The Villas at The Disney Institute*. Facilities at the latter are new and, when not being used for Institute programs, are available for other resort guests. All other WDW tennis is played on hard courts. *Fort Wilderness* has two courts, the *Yacht Club* and *Beach Club* share a pair, the *Disney Vacation Club* has three, and the *Swan* and *Dolphin* have an eight-court facility. Courts are generally open from 8 A.M. to 9 P.M. daily (hours may vary during winter); lighted courts are available at each of the above-mentioned resorts.

COURT RESERVATIONS: Courts may be reserved up to 14 days ahead for play at the *Contemporary* (call 824-3578), up to 30 days ahead for the *Grand Floridian* courts (call 824-2433), and as far in advance as you wish for courts at the *Swan* and *Dolphin* (call 934-4396). The *Fort Wilderness* and *Disney Vacation Club* courts are available on a first-come, first-served basis. The limit on the number of hours a day any single group of players can occupy a court—a restriction in effect only during very busy periods—is two hours on any morning, afternoon, or evening. That means that you can spend six hours a day on a court even at the busiest times.

The "Tennis Anyone?" program helps solo players find an opponent. Just call Disney's Racquet Club at the *Contemporary* resort (824-3578) to get your name posted.

FEES: It costs $12 per hour to play at the *Contemporary* resort ($40 per family for an entire WDW resort stay); $12 at the *Grand Floridian* or *Swan* and *Dolphin* resorts. All other courts are free.

INSTRUCTION: The tennis program at the *Contemporary* resort offers clinics ranging in price from $35 to $50; a special clinic for families costs $75. Nobody will try to change your game radically; the idea is to help you play better with what you have.

Private tennis lessons also are available, by appointment, at the *Contemporary* resort. The cost is $40 per hour and $20 per half hour with a staff professional, all of whom are certified by the United States Tennis Association. For an additional $10, videotaped analysis can be included as part of hour-long lessons. For more information about lessons and clinics, call 824-3578.

Lessons also are available at the *Grand Floridian* for $40 per 45-minute session. For reservations call 824-2433.

TOURNAMENTS: Private tournaments may be arranged by calling Disney's Racquet Club at 824-3578. The fee for running a tournament is $40 per hour.

RACQUET RENTAL: Good-quality racquets are available for rent at $4 an hour for adults. New balls may be purchased ($5.50 per can) or used balls rented ($4 per basket).

LOCKERS: Locker facilities are available only at Disney's Racquet Club at the *Contemporary* resort. Use of the facility is free.

A Matter of Courses

Most people probably don't think of Walt Disney World immediately when they contemplate a golf vacation. Yet there are six superb courses right in the Vacation Kingdom: The Magnolia, the Palm, and the Oak Trail are across from the *Polynesian* resort and extend practically to the borders of the Magic Kingdom. Just a short drive away is the Lake Buena Vista, whose fairways are framed by *The Villas at The Disney Institute* and the *Disney Vacation Club*. Osprey Ridge and Eagle Pines play from the Bonnet Creek Golf Club near *Fort Wilderness*.

None of the original three Joe Lee-designed courses will set anyone's knees to knocking in terror from the regular men's or women's tees, though both the Palm and Magnolia are demanding enough to serve as the site of an annual stop on the PGA Tour tournament trail.

Depending on the tee from which a golfer chooses to play, the Disney courses are challenging and/or fun, and they are constructed to be especially forgiving for the mid-handicap player. What's more, they're remarkably interesting topographically, considering that the land on which Lee started was about as hilly as a tabletop.

Osprey Ridge was designed by Tom Fazio and was created to be a reasonable challenge for beginners as well as more advanced players. Eagle Pines, designed by Pete Dye, is a "low profile" layout built on the same level as, or lower than, the surrounding land. The LPGA Health South Inaugural tournament is contested on Eagles Pines each January.

At the five par-72 18-hole courses, greens fees (including the required cart) vary with the course and the season. Rates range from $85 to $100 for WDW resort guests or $95 to $115 for day visitors; twilight rates, usually in effect beginning at 3 P.M., are from $35 to $50. The fee to play Oak Trail is $23 for adults for 9 holes and $31 for 18 holes; juniors (under 17) pay $10 for 9 holes and $15 for 18 holes. Prices are subject to change. Call 824-2270 to confirm current rates and to secure tee-off times. From January through April, it's a good idea to reserve starting times well in advance for play in the morning and early afternoon (though starting times after 3 P.M. are almost always available at the last minute). Those with confirmed reservations at a WDW resort or Hotel Plaza property can reserve tee times 30 days in advance. Day visitors can reserve seven days in advance or four days ahead during peak season. Proper golf attire is required. Shirts must have collars, and if shorts are worn they must be Bermuda length.

The Golf Courses

PALM AND MAGNOLIA: The wide-open, tree-dotted Magnolia measures 5,232 yards from the front tees, 6,642 from the middle, and 7,190 from the back. The Palm is tighter, with more wooded fairways and nine water hazards and plays 5,398 from the front, 6,461 from the middle, and 6,957 from the back. The Palm has been ranked among the nation's top 75 resort courses by *Golf Digest* magazine. Together with the Lake Buena Vista course, the pair hosts the Walt Disney World/Oldsmobile Golf Classic every year. The Magnolia and Palm share two driving ranges and two putting greens.

Oak Trail: This nine-hole, par-36, 2,913-yard layout—a fun walking course nestled on a 45-acre corner of the Magnolia—was designed with the beginner in mind, though a recent renovation has added some challenging new holes.

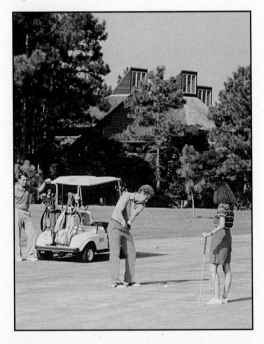

OSPREY RIDGE AND EAGLE PINES: These two courses play from the Bonnet Creek Golf Club. The Tom Fazio–designed Osprey Ridge plays 5,402 yards from the front tees, 6,680 from the middle, and 7,101 from the back. It escorts guests through some remote areas of WDW property as it winds through the wooded landscape near *Fort Wilderness*. Dramatic contouring puts some tees 20 feet to 25 feet above the basic grade. In contrast, the Pete Dye–designed Eagle Pines is a low-profile layout. It plays 4,838 yards from the front tees, 6,309 from the middle, and 6,772 from the pro tees. Many of the fairways are bordered by scrub and pine needles; water comes into play as well. Osprey Ridge and Eagle Pines share a driving range and a putting green.

LAKE BUENA VISTA COURSE: This Joe Lee design measures 5,176 yards from the front tees, 6,268 from the middle, and 6,829 from the rearmost markers. Among the shortest of the 18-hole courses, it has a fair amount of water, and its tree-lined fairways are the World's narrowest. This course is well suited for beginners but equipped to challenge more experienced players. A driving range and putting green are available. Note that once *The Villas at The Disney Institute* opens in early 1996, this course will largely be given over to Institute programming.

INSTRUCTION: Skill clinics are offered from 9 A.M. to 10 A.M. daily at the Palm and Magnolia courses, with Saturdays and Sundays designated for beginners; cost is $25. Private lessons are available for $35 per half hour with an assistant pro. The Walt Disney World Golf Studio, based at the Palm and the Magnolia, offers 90-minute sessions that focus on building skills through video analysis; the studios cost $60 and are held at 10:30 A.M. and 1:30 P.M. daily. Playing lessons are $100. Reservations are necessary for all lessons; call 824-2270.

EQUIPMENT RENTAL: Titleist clubs ($20), range balls ($5 a bucket), and shoes ($6) are available for rent at all pro shops.

TOURNAMENTS

The Walt Disney World/Oldsmobile Golf Classic is among the biggest spectator events on WDW's sports calendar. It takes place in the fall, usually in October, and features most of the pro tour's top players. Guests who plan to golf during their WDW vacation are advised *not* to schedule a visit during tournament week.

You can, however, play alongside the pros if you are willing to pay for it: One-year membership in the Classic Club starts at about $5,000. As tourney sponsors, members play with competing pros for three of the Classic's four rounds. While the pros are competing for cash prizes, the amateurs vie for trophies in a separate competition. Some Classic Club memberships include lodging during the tournament at WDW resorts, reduced greens fees for a year, and admission to the Magic Kingdom, Epcot, and the Disney-MGM Studios for a week. For details, phone 824-2250.

At other times of the year, private tournaments may be arranged at no charge beyond the normal greens and cart fees (contact the tournament coordinator at 824-2275).

Waters of the World

Boating

Walt Disney World is the home of the country's largest fleet of pleasure boats. Cruising on Bay Lake and the Seven Seas Lagoon can be excellent sport, and a variety of boats are available for rent at the marinas at the *Contemporary*, on the western shore of Bay Lake; *Wilderness Lodge*, on the south shore of Bay Lake; *Fort Wilderness*, to the southeast beyond Discovery Island; the *Polynesian*, which occupies the southern edge of the Seven Seas Lagoon; and the *Grand Floridian*, just east of the *Polynesian*. The *Caribbean Beach* resort leases watercraft for use on its own 45-acre Barefoot Bay. The *Yacht Club*, *Beach Club, Swan,* and *Dolphin* share a boating haven in 25-acre Crescent Lake. And marinas at *Dixie Landings*, *Port Orleans*, the *Disney Vacation Club*, and the Disney Village Marketplace send guests out on the Disney Village waterways and the 35-acre Buena Vista Lagoon.

To rent, day visitors and resort guests alike must show a resort ID, a driver's license, or a valid passport. Rental of certain craft may carry other special requirements (described below). Note that no privately owned boats are permitted on any of the WDW waters.

SPEEDBOATS: Particularly when the weather is warm, there are always dozens of small boats zipping back and forth across Bay Lake, the Seven Seas Lagoon, and the lakes at the Disney Village Marketplace and the *Caribbean Beach* resort. These are called Water Sprites, and they are just as much fun as they look. Though they don't go very fast, they're so small that a rider feels every bit of speed, and they zip around quickly enough so that a lot of watery terrain can be covered in a half-hour rental period ($15). You can rent them at the *Contemporary*, *Polynesian*, *Grand Floridian*, *Wilderness Lodge*, *Yacht Club* and *Beach Club*, *Fort Wilderness*, *Caribbean*

Beach, and Disney Village Marketplace marinas. During warm weather, lines usually form at about 11 A.M. and remain fairly constant until about 4 P.M. The minimum rental age is 12, except at the Marketplace, where the minimum age is 14. Children under the minimum age are not allowed to drive.

SAILBOATS: The size and usually reliable winds of Bay Lake and the adjoining Seven Seas Lagoon make for good sailing, and the *Contemporary*, *Polynesian*, *Grand Floridian*, *Wilderness Lodge*, and *Fort Wilderness* resort marinas rent a variety of craft so that guests might get a little wind in their sails on the 650-acre expanse. Sailboats also are available at *Caribbean Beach*, where guests have their own private lake to explore, and at the *Yacht Club* and *Beach Club*, where the nautical feel of the resorts extends out to Crescent Lake. Various types of sailboats are available; models accommodate two to six people and rent for $10 to $15 per hour. Experience is required for rental of catamarans, available at the *Contemporary*, *Polynesian*, and *Grand Floridian*. Sailing conditions are usually best in March and April, and before the inevitable late-afternoon thundershowers in the summer—and that's when demand is greatest. So don't tarry. Head for the marina as soon as the urge to sail strikes.

PONTOON BOATS: Flotebotes—motorized, canopied platforms-on-pontoons, really—are perfect for families, for inexperienced sailors, and for older visitors more interested in serenity than in thrills. Available at most resort marinas, the 20-foot boats hold up to ten adults and cost $20 per half hour.

CANOPY BOATS: These 16-foot, V-hulled motorized boats with canopies are good for slow cruises, and can accommodate up to six adults. They can be rented for about $17.50 per half hour at the Disney Village Marketplace, *Polynesian*, *Contemporary*, *Grand Floridian*, *Wilderness Lodge*, *Yacht Club* and *Beach Club*, *Disney Vacation Club*, *Port Orleans*, *Dixie Landings,* and *Caribbean Beach*.

PEDAL BOATS: These craft are for rent for $5.50 per half hour or $8 per hour at most WDW lakeside marinas. They're also available, for resort guests only, at the Bike Barn at *Fort Wilderness*, and at the *Yacht Club* and *Beach Club*, *Caribbean Beach*, *Port Orleans*, and *Dixie Landings* resort marinas.

CANOEING: A long paddle down the glass-smooth, wooded *Fort Wilderness* canals is such a tranquil way to pass a misty morning that it's hard to remember that the bustle of the Magic Kingdom is just a launch ride away. Canoes are for rent at the Bike Barn at *Fort Wilderness* ($4 per hour, $10 per day). Most trips last one to three hours; those who take fishing gear can easily stay out longer. Canoes also may be rented at *Port Orleans*, *Dixie Landings*, and *Caribbean Beach* resorts.

WATERSKIING: Ski boats with driver and equipment ($75 an hour, with a minimum of two guests and a maximum of five) are available at the *Fort Wilderness*, *Wilderness Lodge*, *Polynesian*, *Grand Floridian*, and *Contemporary* resort marinas. Reservations must be made at least two days in advance; call 824-2621 up to two weeks ahead.

PARASAILING: Excursions are offered at the *Contemporary* marina, where the man who invented the high-flying adventure sport supervises seven- to ten-minute flights over Bay Lake. Cost is $40 for a single rider or $65 for two; reservations are necessary (call 824-1000, ext. 3586).

Fishing

The 70,000 bass with which Bay Lake was stocked in the mid-1960s have grown and multiplied as a result of WDW's restrictive fishing policy. No angling is permitted on Bay Lake or the Seven Seas Lagoon, except on the guided two-hour *Fort Wilderness* fishing expeditions. The excursions depart the campground marina at around 8 A.M., 11:30 A.M., and 3 P.M. every day; five fishing persons can be accommodated on each trip. The fee per boatload is $125 for two hours ($50 for each additional hour) and includes guide, gear, tackle, and refreshments (coffee and pastries in the morning, soft drinks in the afternoon). Largemouth bass weighing two to eight pounds are the most common catch. Guides will pick up guests at the *Contemporary, Polynesian*, and *Grand Floridian* resort marinas.

Other guided fishing excursions leave the Disney Village Marketplace marina at 7 A.M., 9 A.M., and 11 A.M. Reservations must be made at least 48 hours in advance; call 828-2204. Cost for up to five people, including guide, gear, tackle, and refreshments, is $120 for two hours.

At *Dixie Landings*, a two-hour guided fishing adventure takes guests on the Sassagoula River and the Buena Vista Lagoon at 6:30 A.M. daily. The trip accommodates up to five people; includes gear, artificial bait, and soft drinks; and costs $35 per person. Reservations must be made 24 hours in advance by calling 934-5409. Children under ten must be accompanied by an adult.

Fishing on your own is permitted off the dock at the Disney Village Marketplace, in the canals of the Disney Village resort area and *Fort Wilderness*, and at the stocked fishing hole at *Dixie Landings*. *Fort Wilderness* guests may toss in their lines from any campground shore. Licenses are not required. Canoes, rods and reels, and cane poles are available for rent at the *Fort Wilderness* Bike Barn, and cane poles also may be rented at *Dixie Landings* and the Disney Village Marketplace.

Swimming

Between Bay Lake and the Seven Seas Lagoon, Walt Disney World resort guests have five miles of powdery white sand beach at their disposal. And that doesn't include the many swimming pools that come in all shapes and sizes. River Country, Typhoon Lagoon, and Blizzard Beach (see *Everything Else in the World*) only add to the fun.

BEACHES: All WDW resort beaches are open only to guests staying at that hotel. When Walt Disney World was under construction during the mid-1960s, Bay Lake, with an eight-foot layer of muck on its bottom, was found to be unpolluted. It was drained and cleaned, and below the muck, engineers unearthed the pure, white sand that now edges WDW resort shorefronts, most notably at the *Contemporary* resort, the *Grand Floridian* resort, the *Caribbean Beach* resort, and *Fort Wilderness*. These four sections of beach, plus the ones at the *Polynesian, Wilderness Lodge, Yacht Club* and *Beach Club*, and *Dolphin* and *Swan* make up WDW's sandy areas. They aren't the walk-forever strands found on Florida's coasts, but they are long enough that most people don't bother to go to the end.

POOLS: With the exception of the sister resorts (*Yacht Club* and *Beach Club*, *Dixie Landings* and *Port Orleans*, and *Dolphin* and *Swan*), which share their recreational facilities, all WDW hotel pools are open only to guests staying at that resort. This policy was initiated to prevent overcrowding and unsafe conditions. Featuring one pool apiece are the *Grand Floridian, Wilderness Lodge*, and *Port Orleans*. The *Contemporary, Polynesian, Fort Wilderness, All-Star Sports*, and *All-Star Music* resorts have two pools each. The *Disney Vacation Club* has four swimming holes, *Dixie Landings* and *The Villas at The Disney Institute* each have six, and the *Caribbean Beach* resort has seven. The *Yacht Club* and *Beach Club* resorts have between them two quiet pools plus a small water park called Stormalong Bay that features slides, jets, and a sand-bottomed wading area. The *Dolphin* and *Swan* share a themed grotto pool with slide, a huge rectangular pool, and a third smaller pool. There are no diving boards at any of the pools; to practice cannonballs, head for River Country, Blizzard Beach, or Typhoon Lagoon. Lifeguards are on duty during most daylight hours. In addition, each of the seven hotels that make up Disney Village Hotel Plaza has its own pool.

More Fun Stuff

VOLLEYBALL AND BASKETBALL: Except for the volleyball courts at River Country and Typhoon Lagoon, all courts are reserved for WDW resort guests' use. Volleyball courts are located at the *Grand Floridian*, *Contemporary*, *Yacht Club* and *Beach Club*, *Fort Wilderness*, and *The Villas at The Disney Institute*. Basketball hoops are found at *Fort Wilderness* and the *Disney Vacation Club*.

JOGGING: Except from late fall to very early spring, the weather is usually too steamy in Central Florida for comfortable jogging. If you run early in the morning in warm seasons, the heat is somewhat less daunting. The 1.4-mile promenade around the *Caribbean Beach* resort's lake is perfect for jogging. *Fort Wilderness* and the *Wilderness Lodge* share a ¾-mile path with exercise stations. *Dixie Landings* and the *Disney Vacation Club* also offer scenic routes. Maps are available from each WDW resort's Guest Services desk; courses range from one mile to just over three.

BIKING: Pedaling along the rustic pathways and lightly trafficked roads at *Fort Wilderness* and *The Villas at The Disney Institute* can be a pleasant way to spend a couple of hours—especially during cooler seasons. Both areas are sufficiently spread out that bicycles are a practical means of getting around. Bikes are available for rent at *Fort Wilderness*, the *Disney Vacation Club*, *Wilderness Lodge*, *Port Orleans*, *Dixie Landings* and *The Villas at The* *Disney Institute*. The cost for rentals is about $4 an hour or $8 per day; tandem bicycles are available at some locations for $4 an hour or $9 per day.

SKATING: In-line skating enthusiasts who bring their own gear will find the paths and roadways at the *Disney Vacation Club*, *Fort Wilderness*, and *The Disney Institute* especially conducive. Beginners may find the wooded trails at *Fort Wilderness* somewhat tough going.

HEALTH CLUBS: Of the seven fitness centers located within WDW hotels, all but two are reserved for guests staying at the resort that houses them. These are for the Olympiad Health Club at the *Contemporary* resort (open to any WDW resort guest) and the Body By Jake Health Club at the *Dolphin* (open to anyone). The small facility at the *Swan,* complimentary to the hotel's guests, offers basic fitness equipment. The *Contemporary's* Olympiad features Nautilus, a variety of cardiovascular machines, a sauna, and massage; rates are $8 per day or $18 per family for length of stay. R.E.S.T. at the *Disney Vacation Club* (complimentary to guests) and St. John's Health Club at the *Grand Floridian* ($5 per day or $10 for length of stay) are directly comparable to the Olympiad. The Ship Shape Health Club at the *Yacht Club* and *Beach Club* resorts ($7 per day or $20 per family for length of stay) features all the aforementioned equipment and services plus whirlpool, steamroom, personal trainers, and a more extensive collection of weight machines. Body By Jake at the *Dolphin* ($8 per day or $16 for length of stay) offers aerobics, personal trainers, massage, and sophisticated equipment such as Polaris machines. The vast health and fitness center at *The Villas at The Disney Institute* (complimentary to Institute guests) features a gymnasium, aerobics, and an equipment inventory that includes Cybex machines.

HORSEBACK RIDING: Trail rides into the pine woods and scrubby palmetto country leave from the middle of *Fort Wilderness* campground four to six times daily depending on the season. This is not for gallopers—you can't ride off on your own—and the horses have been culled for gentleness so that the trips are suitable even for novices. Cost is $17 a person. No children under nine are permitted to ride, and there is a weight limit of 250 pounds. Reservations are suggested, and can be made up to two weeks in advance by calling 824-2621.

GOOD MEALS, GREAT TIMES

Although fast food is in great supply, it is by no means all of the Walt Disney World food story. Epcot adds international flavors to the WDW palate. Tempting options at the Disney Village Marketplace, the Disney-MGM Studios, and Pleasure Island—not to mention new frontiers in the WDW resorts—make deciding where to dine a mouth-watering dilemma.

Because the number and variety of eateries around the World is so large, this chapter presents meal information in three different ways. To find a specific restaurant, we've provided an alphabetized directory to all restaurants on the property with their exact locations. If you are getting hungry in a particular part of the World, the second section of this chapter offers an area-by-area rundown of all operative eateries. Finally, this chapter also contains a meal-by-meal selection of eating places. These restaurants are organized by breakfast, lunch, and dinner specialties, and we've indicated certain entrées for which we think it's worth going a bit out of your way. Menus and prices vary during the year. **Note:** All Walt Disney World restaurants (except those with outside seating) are nonsmoking only. Smoking is prohibited in lines for fast-food counters as well. The letters that conclude each entry are a key to the meals served there: breakfast (B), lunch (L), dinner (D), or snacks (S).

The list below includes all the restaurants, lounges, and snack spots currently operating in Walt Disney World—at the hotels, at *Fort Wilderness*, at the Disney Village Marketplace, at Pleasure Island, and at the Magic Kingdom, Epcot, and the Disney-MGM Studios.

In the sections following this listing, all the restaurants are described in detail. As an indication of what you should expect to spend for a meal, we've classified restaurants as very expensive (dinners $50 and up); expensive (lunches over $25, dinners $30 and up); moderate (lunches $15 to $25, dinners $20 to $30); inexpensive (lunches under $15, dinners under $20). These prices are for an average meal for two, not including drinks, tax, or tips.

Acadian Pizza 'n' Pasta: *Dixie Landings* resort; in Colonel's Cotton Mill food court

Akershus: Epcot; in the Norway pavilion in World Showcase

Ale and Compass: *Yacht Club* resort; in the lobby

Aloha Isle: Magic Kingdom; in Adventureland, near the Swiss Family Treehouse

Ariel's: *Beach Club* resort; on the first floor

Artist Point: *Wilderness Lodge* resort; in the main lodge building

Aunt Polly's Landing: Magic Kingdom; in Frontierland, on Tom Sawyer Island

Auntie Gravity's Galactic Goodies: Magic Kingdom; near Merchant of Venus in Tomorrowland

Au Petit Café: Epcot; on the World Showcase Promenade in the France pavilion in World Showcase

Avalunch: Blizzard Beach

Backlot Express: Disney-MGM Studios; near the Epic Stunt Theater

Banana Cabana: *Caribbean Beach* resort; near the pool

Barefoot Bar: *Polynesian* resort; near the pool

Beaches & Cream Soda Shop: *Yacht Club* and *Beach Club* resorts; in the central area between the two hotels

Beverage Base: Epcot; in Innoventions, in the *Electric Umbrella* restaurant

Biergarten: Epcot; to the rear of the St. Georgsplatz in the Germany pavilion, in World Showcase

Bistro de Paris: Epcot; upstairs at the France pavilion, in World Showcase

Bleu Bayou Burgers and Chicken: *Dixie Landings* resort; in Colonel's Cotton Mill food court

Boatwright's Dining Hall: *Dixie Landings* resort; adjacent to the Cotton Co-Op Lounge

Bonfamille's Café: *Port Orleans* resort; off the main lobby, across from the front desk

Boulangerie Pâtisserie: Epcot; France pavilion, around the corner from *Chefs de France*, in World Showcase

Bridgetown Broiler: *Caribbean Beach* resort; at Old Port Royale food court

Cabana Bar & Grill: *Dolphin* resort; at the pool

Cajun Broiler: *Dixie Landings* resort; in Colonel's Cotton Mill food court

California Grill: *Contemporary* resort; on the 15th floor

California Grill Lounge: *Contemporary* resort; on the 15th floor

Cantina de San Angel: Epcot; on the World Showcase Promenade opposite the Mexico pavilion's pyramid

Cape May Café: *Beach Club* resort; in the lobby

Cap'n Jack's Oyster Bar: Disney Village Marketplace; on the edge of Buena Vista Lagoon

Captain Cook's Snack and Ice Cream Company: *Polynesian* resort; on the lobby level of the Great Ceremonial House

Captain's Tavern: *Caribbean Beach* resort; at Old Port Royale court

Casey's Corner: Magic Kingdom; on the west side of Main Street

Catwalk Bar: Disney-MGM Studios; above the *Soundstage* restaurant

Chef Mickey's Village Restaurant: Disney Village Marketplace; on Buena Vista Lagoon

Chefs de France: Epcot; in the France pavilion in World Showcase

Churro Wagon: Magic Kingdom; at the entrance to Frontierland

Cinnamon Bay Bakery: *Caribbean Beach* resort; at Old Port Royale food court

Columbia Harbour House: Magic Kingdom; in Liberty Square near the entrance to Fantasyland

Commissary: Disney-MGM Studios; near The Great Movie Ride

Concourse Steak House: *Contemporary* resort; Grand Canyon Concourse (fourth floor)

Contemporary Café: *Contemporary* resort; on the fourth floor

Copa Banana: *Dolphin* resort; on the lobby level

Coral Café: *Dolphin* resort; on the lower level

Coral Isle Café: *Polynesian* resort; on the second floor of the Great Ceremonial House, around the corner from *'Ohana*

Coral Reef: Epcot; in Future World's The Living Seas

Cosmic Ray's Starlight Café: Magic Kingdom; at the Fantasyland edge of Tomorrowland

Cotton Co-Op: *Dixie Landings* resort; in the main reception area

Crew's Cup Lounge: *Yacht Club* resort; next to the *Yachtsman Steakhouse*

Crockett's Tavern: *Fort Wilderness*; in Pioneer Hall

Crystal Palace: Magic Kingdom; near the Adventureland bridge at the north end of Main Street

Diamond Horseshoe Saloon Revue: Magic Kingdom; in Frontierland at the edge of Liberty Square

Dinosaur Gertie's: Disney-MGM Studios; on Echo Lake

Dolphin Fountain: *Dolphin* resort; on the lower level

Donald's Dairy Dip: Disney Village Marketplace

D-Zertz: Pleasure Island; near Propeller Heads

Egg Roll Wagon: Magic Kingdom; in Adventureland, near the Swiss Family Treehouse

Electric Umbrella: Epcot; in Future World's Innoventions Plaza

El Pirata y el Perico: Magic Kingdom; in Adventureland, opposite Pirates of the Caribbean

Enchanted Grove: Magic Kingdom; east side of Fantasyland, opposite *Cosmic Ray's Starlight Café*

End Zone: *All-Star Sports* resort; in Stadium Hall

Fantasyland Pretzel Wagon: Magic Kingdom; between Pinocchio Village Haus and Cinderella's Golden Carrousel

50's Prime Time Café: Disney-MGM Studios; on the south side of Echo Lake

Fireworks Factory: Pleasure Island

Flagler's: *Grand Floridian* resort; on the second floor of the main building

Food and Fun Center: *Contemporary* resort; first floor

Fountain View Espresso & Bakery: Epcot; next to Innoventions

Garden Grill: Epcot; on the second floor of Future World's The Land

Garden Grove Café: *Swan* resort; on the first floor

Garden View Lounge: *Grand Floridian* resort; on the Windsor Level

Gasparilla Grill and Games: *Grand Floridian* resort; on the first floor of the main building

Good's Food to Go: *Disney Vacation Club* resort; on the boardwalk

Goofy's Grill: Disney Village Marketplace; near Crystal Arts

Grand Floridian Café: *Grand Floridian* resort; on the first floor of the main building

Gurgling Suitcase: *Disney Vacation Club* resort; on the boardwalk

Handwich Wagon: Disney-MGM Studios; near Echo Lake

Harry's Safari Bar & Grille: *Dolphin* resort; on the third floor

Hill Street Diner: Pleasure Island; near Avigators Supply Company

Hollywood & Vine: Disney-MGM Studios; on Hollywood Boulevard

Hollywood Brown Derby: Disney-MGM Studios; on Hollywood Boulevard

Hook's Tavern: Magic Kingdom; in Fantasyland, next to Peter Pan's Flight

Hot Dog Wagon: Disney-MGM Studios; near The Great Movie Ride

Hot Dog Wagon: Epcot; near The American Adventure, in World Showcase

Hurricane Hanna's Grill: *Yacht Club* and *Beach Club* resorts; near Stormalong Bay

Intermission: *All-Star Music* resort; in Melody Hall

Juan & Only's Cantina and Bar: *Dolphin* resort; on the lower level

Kimono's: *Swan* resort; on the first floor

King Stefan's Banquet Hall: Magic Kingdom; in Cinderella Castle

Kingston Pasta Shop: *Caribbean Beach* resort; at Old Port Royale food court

Kringla Bakeri og Kafe: Epcot; in the Norway pavilion, in World Showcase

Leaning Palms: Typhoon Lagoon; near the main entrance

Liberty Inn: Epcot; alongside The American Adventure

Liberty Square Market: Magic Kingdom; in Liberty Square

Liberty Square Potato Wagon: Magic Kingdom; in Liberty Square

Liberty Tree Tavern: Magic Kingdom; in Liberty Square

Little Big Top: Magic Kingdom; in Fantasyland, near Legend of The Lion King

Lobby Court Lounge: *Swan* resort; in the lobby

L'Originale Alfredo di Roma Ristorante: Epcot; on the east side of the piazza in the Italy pavilion, in World Showcase

Lottawatta Lodge: Blizzard Beach; near the main entrance

Lotus Blossom Café: Epcot; China pavilion, in World Showcase

Lumière's Kitchen: Magic Kingdom; in Fantasyland, near Dumbo, the Flying Elephant

Lunching Pad at Rockettower Plaza: Magic Kingdom; at the base of the Astro Orbiter in the center of Tomorrowland

Main Street Bake Shop: Magic Kingdom; on the east side of Main Street, halfway between the Hub and Town Square

Mama Melrose's Ristorante Italiano: Disney-MGM Studios; on New York Street

Mardi Grogs: *Port Orleans* resort; near the pool

Marrakesh: Epcot; Morocco pavilion, in World Showcase

Martha's Vineyard Lounge: *Beach Club* resort; near *Ariel's*

Matsu No Ma Lounge: Epcot; in the Japan pavilion, in World Showcase

Meadow Trading Post: *Fort Wilderness*; near the playing fields

Mickey's Tropical Revue: *Polynesian* resort; Luau Cove

Min & Bill's Dockside Diner: Disney-MGM Studios; on Echo Lake

Minnie Mia's Italian Eatery: Disney Village Marketplace; near the Gourmet Pantry

Mitsukoshi: Epcot; on the second floor of the large building on the west side of the plaza in the Japan pavilion, in World Showcase

Mizner's Lounge: *Grand Floridian* resort; on the Alcazar Level

Montego's Deli: *Caribbean Beach* resort; at Old Port Royale food court

Mrs. Potts' Cupboard: Magic Kingdom; in Fantasyland near Cinderella's Golden Carrousel

Muddy Rivers: *Dixie Landings* resort; near Ol' Man Island

Narcoossee's: *Grand Floridian* resort; at the end of the dock near the marina

Nine Dragons: Epcot; China pavilion, in World Showcase

1900 Park Fare: *Grand Floridian* resort; on the first floor of the main building

Oasis: Magic Kingdom; in Adventureland, near the Jungle Cruise

'Ohana: *Polynesian* resort; second floor of the Great Ceremonial House

Olivia's: *Disney Vacation Club* resort; on the boardwalk

Only's Bar: *Dolphin* resort; in *Juan & Only's Cantina*

Outer Rim Cocktail Lounge: *Contemporary* resort; on the fourth floor

Palio: *Swan* resort; on the first floor

Pasta Piazza Ristorante: Epcot; in Future World's Innoventions Plaza

Pecos Bill Café: Magic Kingdom; near the Walt Disney World Railroad's Frontierland depot

Pinocchio Village Haus: Magic Kingdom; in Fantasyland, adjoining It's A Small World on the east

Planet Hollywood: Pleasure Island; near the AMC movie theater

Plaza: Magic Kingdom; on Main Street around the corner from *Plaza Ice Cream Parlor*

Plaza Ice Cream Parlor: Magic Kingdom; on the east side of Main Street

Plaza Pavilion Terrace Dining: Magic Kingdom; east of the *Plaza Restaurant*, on the edge of Tomorrowland

Pop's Place: *Fort Wilderness*; inside River Country

Portobello Yacht Club: Pleasure Island

Port Royale Hamburger Shop: *Caribbean Beach* resort; at Old Port Royale food court

Potato Wagon: Epcot; in the United Kingdom pavilion in World Showcace

Pretzel Wagon: Epcot; in the Germany pavilion in World Showcase

Pure & Simple: Epcot; in Future World's Wonders of Life pavilion

Refreshment Outpost: Epcot; between China and Germany pavilions, World Showcase

Refreshment Port: Epcot; next to the Canada pavilion, in World Showcase

Rip Tide Lounge: *Beach Club* resort; in the lobby

Riverside Market and Deli: *Dixie Landings* resort; in Colonel's Cotton Mill food court

Roaring Forks: *Wilderness Lodge* resort; in the main lodge building

Rose & Crown Pub & Dining Room: Epcot; in the United Kingdom pavilion

Royale Pizza Shop: *Caribbean Beach* resort; at Old Port Royale food court

San Angel Inn: Epcot; inside the Mexico pavilion's pyramid, in World Showcase

Sand Bar: *Contemporary* resort; near the beach

Sand Trap Bar & Grill: Bonnet Creek Golf Club

Sassagoula Floatworks & Food Factory: *Port Orleans* resort; just off the main lobby

Scat Cat's Club: *Port Orleans* resort; next to *Bonfamille's Café*

Sci-Fi Dine-In Theater: Disney-MGM Studios; near Star Tours

Settlement Trading Post: *Fort Wilderness*; near the marina

Singing Spirits Pool Bar: *All-Star Music* resort; near the pool

Sleepy Hollow: Magic Kingdom; in Liberty Square, opposite Olde World Antiques

Sommerfest: Epcot; in the Germany pavilion, in World Showcase

Soundstage: Disney-MGM Studios; near the Animation Building

Southern Trace Bakery: *Dixie Landings* resort; in Colonel's Cotton Mill food court

Splash Grill: *Swan* resort; near the pool

Starring Rolls Bakery: Disney-MGM Studios; on Hollywood Boulevard

Studio Catering Co.: Disney-MGM Studios; near The Loony Bin

Sum Chows: *Dolphin* resort; on the lower level

Summerhouse: *Grand Floridian* resort; near the beach

Sunset Ranch Market: Disney-MGM Studios; on Sunset Boulevard

Sunshine Season Food Fair: Epcot; on the first floor of Future World's The Land

Sunshine Tree Terrace: Magic Kingdom; in Adventureland, adjoining Tropical Serenade

Tambu Lounge: *Polynesian* resort; on the second floor of the Great Ceremonial House

Tangaroa Terrace: *Polynesian* resort; in a separate building on the eastern edge of the property

Team Spirits Pool Bar: *All-Star Music* resort; near the pool

Tempura Kiku: Epcot; on the second floor of the Japan pavilion

Teppanyaki Dining Rooms: Epcot; on the second floor of the Japan pavilion

Territory Lounge: *Wilderness Lodge* resort; in the main lodge building

Thirsty Perch: Discovery Island

Tony's Town Square: Magic Kingdom; east side of Town Square

Trail's End Buffet: *Fort Wilderness* resort; in Pioneer Hall

Trout Pass: *Wilderness Lodge* resort; at the pool

Tubbi Checkers Buffeteria: *Dolphin* resort; on the lower level

Tune-In Lounge: Disney-MGM Studios; adjacent to the *50's Prime Time Café*

Turkey Leg Wagon: Magic Kingdom; in Frontierland, near *Pecos Bill Café*

Typhoon Tilly's Galley & Grog: Typhoon Lagoon; near Shark Reef

Victoria & Albert's: *Grand Floridian* resort; on the second floor of the main building

Village Lounge: Disney Village Marketplace; next to *Chef Mickey's Village Restaurant*

Warming Hut: Blizzard Beach; near Summit Plummet

Westward Ho: Magic Kingdom; in Frontierland, near *Pecos Bill Café*

Whispering Canyon Café: *Wilderness Lodge* resort, in the main lodge building

Yacht Club Galley: *Yacht Club* resort; off the lobby

Yachtsman Steakhouse: *Yacht Club* resort; overlooking Stormalong Bay

Yakitori House: Epcot; on the east side of the Japan pavilion's plaza, in World Showcase

SPECIAL REQUESTS

The World's full-service eateries can accommodate special dietary needs, providing kosher, low-sodium, lactose-free, and other requested selections with 24 hours' notice. Make your request when booking your table by calling 939-3463.

In the Magic Kingdom

Main Street

FULL SERVICE

Tony's Town Square: One of the best bets for Magic Kingdom meals. The menu offers Italian specialties, steaks, and seafood. Pizzas with selected toppings are perennial favorites. Other lunch specialties include Caesar salad, sandwiches, fresh pasta salads, and a fresh-fruit plate. At dinner there are grilled fresh fish, New York strip steaks, spaghetti with meatballs, and daily specialties. For dessert, Italian pastries and spumoni complement a cup of freshly brewed espresso or cappuccino. Children's menus and menus for guests with special dietary needs are available. The decor comes straight out of Walt Disney's film, *Lady and the Tramp*. It is genteelly Victorian, with plenty of polished brass and curlicued, beautifully painted woodwork. The terrazzo-floored patio gives diners a fine view over the action in Town Square. Full breakfasts also are served: eggs, *Lady and the Tramp* character waffles, cold cereals (with low-fat milk on request), and freshly baked pull-apart sweet rolls. Reservations suggested. Moderate. B, L, D.

Plaza: This airy, many-windowed establishment, around the corner from the *Plaza Ice Cream Parlor*, is done in mirrors with sinuous Art Nouveau frames. The menu offers fresh salads, hamburgers, turkey burgers, and hot and cold sandwiches—plus milk shakes, ice cream, floats, and the biggest sundaes in the Magic Kingdom. Café mocha, which combines chocolate and coffee, is another specialty. Moderate. L, D, S.

CAFETERIA SERVICE

Crystal Palace: One of the Magic Kingdom's landmarks, and its only cafeteria. Modeled after a similar structure that once stood in New York and after another that still graces San Francisco's Golden Gate Park, it serves standard cafeteria fare. Menu offerings include carved beef, spit-roasted chicken, pasta

dishes, and healthy salads. A wide assortment of tempting desserts also is available.

This is civilized fare, and the fact that it's here at all is just more proof—as if any were needed—that the Magic Kingdom is not just for kids. The place is huge but not overwhelming, because the tables are well-spaced throughout a variety of nooks and crannies. Tables in the front look out onto flower beds and the passing throng beyond, while those at the east end have views into a secluded courtyard.

The *Crystal Palace* also is one of the few spots in the Magic Kingdom to serve full breakfasts—scrambled eggs and hashed brown potatoes, biscuits, sausage, bacon, ham, hotcakes, french toast, Danish pastry, and cold cereal. Moderate. B, L, D, S.

FAST FOOD & SNACKS

Casey's Corner: The small, round tables at this spacious, old-fashioned, red-and-white stop on the west side of Main Street (located near the *Crystal Palace*) spill out onto the sidewalk. Except when the weather is terrifically hot, it's a delightful spot for fast food—hot dogs in jumbo sizes, french fries, brownies, soft drinks, and coffee. During busy periods a pianist is on hand to plink away on the restaurant's white upright. Inexpensive. L, D, S.

Main Street Bake Shop: This genteel little tearoom, with its small, round tables and cane chairs, is a good place for a light breakfast, a mid-morning coffee break, or a mid-afternoon rest stop. Assorted pastries, cakes, and pies are the main temptations. Also offered are delicious chocolate chunk, oatmeal raisin, Snickerdoodle, sugar, and Nestlé's Original Toll House cookies, and cinnamon rolls baked fresh on the premises. Inexpensive. B, S.

Plaza Ice Cream Parlor: Ice cream lovers from all over the country converge on this corner of the Kingdom, which boasts the Magic Kingdom's best variety of ice cream flavors. Inexpensive. S.

Adventureland

FAST FOOD & SNACKS

Aloha Isle: This refreshment stand near the Swiss Family Treehouse often sells pineapple spears and juice along with other tropical offerings including Dole Whip soft serve. Inexpensive. S.

Egg Roll Wagon: Located just outside the Swiss Family Treehouse, this wagon features an assortment of egg rolls. Inexpensive. S.

El Pirata y el Perico: The Spanish name of this snack stand, directly across from Pirates of the Caribbean, means "The Pirate and the Parrot." The offerings feature Mexican items such as tacos, taco salads, and nachos. Open during busy seasons. Inexpensive. L, S.

Oasis: Tucked away near the Jungle Cruise, this is the perfect spot for a soft drink. Inexpensive. S.

VENDORS

Throughout the Magic Kingdom, there are ice cream wagons that sell the unique Nestlé's King Crunch Bars, Mouseketeer Bars, and two especially wonderful frozen treats—lowfat strawberry yogurt and strawberry bars.

Popcorn wagons all over the park contribute their lovely aromas all day long. The Center Street Wagons near the intersection of Main Street, U.S.A. and Center Street sell hot dogs, fresh fruit, juices, and soft drinks.

At Epcot and the Disney-MGM Studios, vendors purvey soft drinks, strawberry bars, popcorn, and ice cream galore.

Sunshine Tree Terrace: So close to the Tropical Serenade that you can hear the Audio-Animatronics parrot José squawking his spiel. Offerings here are some of the tastiest in the Kingdom: orange slush, nonfat frozen yogurt shakes, frozen yogurt, soft drinks, and the excellent citrus swirl—soft-serve nonfat frozen yogurt swirled through with a not-too-sweet frozen-orange-juice concentrate. Cappuccino and espresso also are available. Inexpensive. S.

Frontierland

FAST FOOD & SNACKS

Diamond Horseshoe Saloon Revue: From about 10 A.M. until early evening, a troupe of singers and dancers presents a sometimes corny, occasionally sidesplitting, always entertaining show in this Wild West dancehall saloon. Sandwiches, potato chips, and cookies are available. Inexpensive. L, S.

Pecos Bill Café: This is not one of those Magic Kingdom eateries that is tucked away so that only those who look will find it. Sooner or later, almost every guest passing from Adventureland into Frontierland—ambling by the Frontierland depot of the Walt Disney World Railroad on the way to Splash Mountain— walks by *Pecos Bill*. And as a sidewalk café, this establishment—fitted out with leather-seated chairs, ceilings made of twigs, and red-tile floors—has few peers. There are tables indoors (in air-conditioned rooms) and outdoors, under umbrellas and in an open-air courtyard. Cheeseburgers, barbecued-chicken sandwiches, salads, and hot dogs are the staples. Inside, three shaggy animal heads hang on the walls in keeping with the Wild West theme. Guests who stand around long enough will see one animal turn to another and wink, for these are Audio-Animatronics figures, just like the ones on the walls at the Country Bear Jamboree. Inexpensive. L, D, S.

Aunt Polly's Landing: The much-trumpeted sense of getting away from it all that islands always convey comes home once again out on Frontierland's Tom Sawyer Island. Though only a couple of minutes' ride across the Rivers of America via the Tom Sawyer Island rafts, this landfall manages to seem remote even when there are dozens of youngsters clambering through its caves, over its hills, and across its rickety barrel bridges. Therein lies the charm of *Aunt Polly's*. While the adults in a party get some well-needed R&R sipping lemonade in the shade of the old-fashioned porch and watching the gleaming white riverboats docking or chugging by, the kids can go out exploring. And, at nearby Fort Sam Clemens, kids can ping the toy rifles perched on the gunholes as if there were no tomorrow. It doesn't even matter that *Aunt Polly's* offers a selection barely wider than the fare that that lady might have served her youthful nephew— peanut-butter-and-jelly and ham-and-cheese sandwiches, cold fried chicken, apple pie, soft-serve ice cream, cookies, iced tea, lemonade, and soda. Inexpensive. L, S.

Turkey Leg Wagon: Located just outside *Pecos Bill Café*, this stand features extra-large smoked turkey legs. Inexpensive. L, D, S.

Westward Ho: Soft drinks, cookies, pretzels, and potato chips are available at this stand across from *Pecos Bill Café*. Inexpensive. S.

Liberty Square

FULL SERVICE

Liberty Tree Tavern: At this pillared and porticoed eatery opposite the riverboat landing, the floors are made of wide oak planks, the wallpaper looks as if it might have come from Williamsburg, the curtains hang from cloth loops, and the venetian blinds are made of wood. The rooms reflect mementoes that might have been found in the homes of Thomas Jefferson, George Washington, and Ben Franklin. The window glass was made using 18th-century casting methods, but most of the tables and chairs were mass-produced (for sturdiness' sake). So the *Liberty Tree Tavern's* charm is not of a random type.

Dinner is served family-style, is hosted by Disney characters, and includes fresh fish, shrimp, prime ribs, chicken, and lobster. Oysters and New England clam chowder are served at both meals. The character dinner costs $19.50 for adults and $9.95 for children ages three to nine. Reservations are necessary for dinner, suggested for lunch; call 939-3463. Expensive. L, D.

FAST FOOD & SNACKS

Columbia Harbour House: A fast-food fish house with some class. Clam chowder, salads, assorted sandwiches, and chicken also are available. There are enough antiques and other knickknacks decking the halls to raise this place, located near the Liberty Square entrance to Fantasyland, above the ordinary. Model ships, copper measures, harpoons, and nautical instruments, and little tie-back curtains, small-print wallpaper, and low-beamed ceilings give the place a cozy air—despite its size. Operates seasonally. Inexpensive. L, D, S.

Liberty Square Market: Bananas, apples, juices, pickles, and sliced melon on ice are among the offerings at this refreshing spot. Inexpensive. S.

Liberty Square Potato Wagon: Baked potatoes and sweet potatoes with a variety of toppings are the fare here. Inexpensive. S.

Sleepy Hollow: Sandwiches made with whole-wheat pitas or potato bread, vegetarian chili served in a bread bowl, and a special Legendary Punch (fruity and not half bad) are for sale at this snack stand located opposite Olde World Antiques, near the Liberty Square bridge. Eat on the secluded brick patio outside. Inexpensive. L, D, S.

Fantasyland

FULL SERVICE

King Stefan's Banquet Hall: The hostesses at this establishment (named for Sleeping Beauty's father) wear 13th-century-style French headdresses and long medieval gowns with overskirts. The hall itself is high-ceilinged and as majestic as the old mead hall

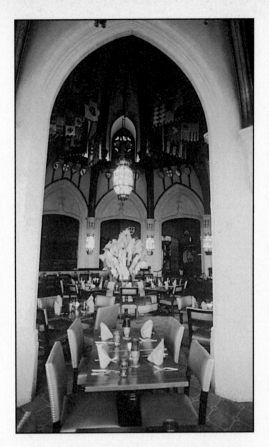

it is supposed to represent. The delightful salads and roast-beef sandwiches on the noontime menu make lunch here pleasant indeed. At dinner, there are prime ribs, seafood, and chicken. There's also a children's menu, and Cinderella is usually on hand to entertain children and grown-ups alike.

The "Once Upon A Time" character breakfast is held here every morning. This all-you-can-eat breakfast is $14.95 for adults and $7.95 for children ages three to nine. Reservations are necessary for the breakfast, suggested for lunch and dinner. To make them, either call 939-3463 or present yourself at the Castle door as soon after arriving in the Magic Kingdom as possible. Expensive. B, L, D.

FAST FOOD & SNACKS

Enchanted Grove: A small stand that's the perfect spot for lemonade, lemonade slush, or a soft-serve swirl. Inexpensive. S.

Hook's Tavern: Soft drinks and chips are available at this small refreshment stand west of Cinderella's Golden Carrousel. Inexpensive. S.

Little Big Top: Soft drinks, milk shakes, and chips are the draw here. Open seasonally. Inexpensive. S.

Lumière's Kitchen: Located near Dumbo, the Flying Elephant, this spot caters to kids with a variety of selections, including chicken nuggets and grilled cheese, to please even finicky eaters. Adult menus are available. Inexpensive. L, D, S.

HEALTHIER OPTIONS

Dieters need not abandon all restraint for want of suitable foodstuffs at WDW. Most restaurants offer lowfat, low-cholesterol, low-salt, and vegetarian entrées. Most restaurants, including fast-food stands, are now featuring fresh salads, grilled-chicken sandwiches, fresh fruit, turkey burgers, and nonfat frozen yogurt.

MAGIC KINGDOM MEALTIME TIPS

- The hours from 11 A.M. to 2 P.M., and again from about 6 P.M. to 8 P.M., are the mealtime rush hours in Magic Kingdom restaurants. Try to eat earlier or later whenever possible.
- When a restaurant has more than one food-service window, don't just amble into the nearest queue. Instead, inspect them all, because the one farthest from a doorway occasionally will be almost wait-free.
- Sit-down restaurants offering full-scale meals are usually less crowded at lunch than they are at dinner.
- To avoid queues, eat lunch or dinner at a restaurant that offers reservations—*Tony's Town Square* in Town Square on Main Street, *Liberty Tree Tavern* in Liberty Square, or *King Stefan's Banquet Hall* in Cinderella Castle. Reservations for these restaurants can be made at the restaurants or in advance by calling WDW-DINE (939-3463).
- Consider taking the monorail to the *Contemporary*, *Polynesian*, or *Grand Floridian* to have lunch or dinner in a resort restaurant, and then return to the Magic Kingdom later. (Remember to have your hand stamped and keep your ticket for reentry to the park.)

Mrs. Potts' Cupboard: Ice cream gets top billing here. There are soft-serve cones in chocolate, vanilla, and chocolate-vanilla swirl; hot-fudge sundaes; and root-beer floats. Inexpensive. S.

Pinocchio Village Haus: This is another of those Magic Kingdom restaurants that seems a lot smaller from the outside than it really is, thanks to a labyrinthine arrangement of a half-dozen rooms decorated with antique cuckoo clocks, European tile-fronted ovens, oak peasant chairs, and murals depicting characters from Pinocchio's story—Figaro the Cat, Cleo the Goldfish, Monstro the Whale, and Geppetto, the puppet's creator. The menu offers hot dogs, cheeseburgers, hamburgers, turkey burgers, cold sandwiches, and pasta salad. Inexpensive. L, D, S.

Tomorrowland

FAST FOOD & SNACKS

Auntie Gravity's Galactic Goodies: This small spot between Merchant of Venus and Mickey's Star Traders serves natural foods, fruit smoothies, soft-serve frozen yogurt, soft drinks, and fresh fruit. Inexpensive. S.

Cosmic Ray's Starlight Café: The largest fast-food spot in the Magic Kingdom, where three distinctive menus are offered. Cosmic Chicken serves rotisserie chicken dinners and drummettes; Blast-off Burgers has cheeseburgers, double cheeseburgers, and vegetarian burgers; and Starlight Soup, Salad, Sandwich offers soups, Caesar salad, chef salad, grilled-chicken sandwiches, and cheese steak sandwiches. In addition, a child's menu and soft drinks are available. Inexpensive. L, D, S.

Lunching Pad at Rockettower Plaza: Located at the base of the Astro Orbiter in the center of Tomorrowland's vast concrete plaza, this small spot offers chips as well as assorted desserts and a variety of soft drinks. Inexpensive. S.

Plaza Pavilion Terrace Dining: Just east of the *Plaza* restaurant, this sleek spot on the edge of Tomorrowland serves pan pizzas, fried chicken strips, and Italian specialty sandwiches. Some particularly pleasant tables look past the graceful willow trees nearby, toward the Hub Waterways and an impressive topiary sea serpent. Inexpensive. L, D, S.

A WORD TO THE WISE

Ride Space Mountain *before* eating, not afterward. The trip can uncomfortably jostle even the strongest stomach.

In Epcot

Restaurants within each area of Epcot are described as they would be encountered in Future World while moving counterclockwise from Spaceship Earth, and in World Showcase while walking counterclockwise around World Showcase Lagoon. **Note:** Reservations are an absolute must at certain Epcot restaurants, and they may not be easy to come by without following the instructions in the box on page 223.

Future World

FULL SERVICE

Garden Grill: Sleek upholstered wood-trimmed booths illuminated with handsome brass lamps, make this an exceptionally attractive eatery.

The restaurant revolves, past a mural of giant sunflowers, as well as the thunderstorm, sandstorm, prairie, and rain forest scenes of the Living with the Land boat ride down below. The scenes were designed with diners in mind, and provide them with a peek into a farmhouse window out of viewing range of the waterborne passengers below. Farmer Mickey and Farmer Minnie join Chip 'n' Dale to host three character meals here each day. The all-you-can eat country breakfast is $14.95 for adults and $7.95 for children ages three to nine. Lunch and dinner menus feature rotisserie chicken, hickory-smoked steaks, and fish, with a separate menu for children. The character lunch costs $16.95 for adults and $9.95 for children ages three to nine, and the character dinner is $19.50 for adults or $9.95 for children. Necessary reservations may be made by calling 939-3463. Moderate to expensive. B, L, D.

Coral Reef: Decorated in cool greens and blues to complement its Living Seas surroundings, this restaurant offers diners a panoramic view of the living coral reef through large, clear windows. The acrylic windows are eight feet high and more than eight inches thick. The dining room is constructed on several tiers, so all 264 guests have an unobstructed view. The menu features fresh fish and shellfish, including baked clams, oysters on the half shell, pan-fried swordfish served with a Thai curry lobster sauce, Mediterranean shrimp baked with tomatoes, leeks, and onions, and Maine lobster with crabmeat stuffing. Landlubber selections also are available. The menu varies seasonally, and reservations are necessary. Expensive. L, D.

FAST FOOD & SNACKS

Pasta Piazza Ristorante: Pizza, pasta, and antipasto salad are the specialties at this eatery located in Innoventions, opposite the *Electric Umbrella* restaurant. The decor is traditional Italian, accented by some unusual neon lights. Inexpensive. B, L, D, S.

Fountain View Espresso & Bakery: Delicious baked goods and desserts—croissants, cheesecake, tiramisù, éclairs—can be found at this spot located next to Innoventions, adjacent to the *Pasta Piazza Ristorante*. Espresso, cappuccino, wine, beer, and other beverages are available here. Inexpensive. B, S.

Sunshine Season Food Fair: One of the most interesting of the Epcot eateries, and a wrinkle on the Walt Disney World fast-food scene, this handful of special counter-service stands is located on the lower level of The Land pavilion. Each of these stands boasts a unique menu. Soup & Salad offers Florida

chicken, and vegetable lasagne. A Sandwich Shop regales the hungry with several types of hefty combinations, including the Disney Handwich, while an ice cream stand tempts guests with cooling cones and cups, frozen yogurt, and sundaes. The Potato Store serves steaming baked potatoes stuffed with oriental-style chicken and vegetables, cheddar cheese with bacon, or other fillings. Even the Beverage House here offers something special—not just an array of soft drinks, beer, and wine, but also alcoholic and nonalcoholic frosty frozen drinks.

Each stand has a farm-style facade done in bright colors, not unlike those that might be found in agricultural exhibit buildings at a

seafood chowder, impressive fruit salad, and rottini pasta salad. The Bakery Shop's morning offerings include fresh fruit, bagels with cream cheese, jumbo cinnamon rolls, Danish pastries, apricot crumb cake, and muffins. After 11 A.M., apple pies appear, along with cheesecake and chocolate cake, strawberry shortcake, rich double-chocolate brownies, hermit cookies with cinnamon—plus chocolate chip cookies baked on the premises. (These are so delicious that some Disney employees make special trips to The Land just to nibble on them.)

The Barbecue stand sells barbecued chicken and ribs smoked on the premises; barbecued beef, pork, or chicken-breast sandwiches; and sides of beans, corn-on-the-cob, and cornbread muffins. The Cheese and Pasta stand offers baked macaroni with ham and cheese, tortellini or fettuccine with meat sauce, noodles with Asian-style

Midwestern state fair. With bright, umbrella-topped tables nearby, the effect is cheery. Because of the wide variety of foods available here, this is one of the best bets in Epcot for a family that can't agree on what to eat. It's also a good spot for weight watchers. Inexpensive. B, L, D, S.

Pure & Simple: Located in the Wonders of Life pavilion, this snack spot offers a variety of healthy treats including waffles with fruit toppings, sandwiches, salads, frozen yogurt, yogurt shakes, muffins, fruit juices, and more. Inexpensive. B, L, S.

Electric Umbrella: This large fast-food establishment, located in Innoventions, is handsomely decorated in shades of blue, mauve, and magenta. It's a particularly good bet when the weather is temperate enough to allow dining at the tables on the terrace outside—or when bound for World Showcase with finicky eaters in tow. At lunch and dinner, offerings include chicken sandwiches, hot dogs, hamburgers, fruit salads, and chef's salads. The *Beverage Base* is located inside and features soft drinks and frozen yogurt. Inexpensive. L, D, S.

FUTURE WORLD DINING AFTER HOURS

Guests who wish to dine in Future World after its attractions close at 7 P.M. can choose from three fast-food restaurants. The *Electric Umbrella* serves burgers, chicken sandwiches, and salads. *Pasta Piazza Ristorante* offers pasta, pizza, subs, and chicken parmesan. For espresso, specialty coffees, pastries, and assorted desserts, try the *Fountain View Espresso & Bakery.*

All World Showcase restaurants stay open until park closing, usually 9 P.M.

World Showcase

FULL SERVICE

Rose & Crown Pub & Dining Room: The fare here is called "pub grub"—that is, fish and chips, steak-and-kidney pie, chicken-and-leek pie, and roast lamb. For lunch, however, it's possible to order hot roast beef with gravy and mashed potatoes, and a really delicious fresh vegetable platter served with Stilton cheese and walnut dressing. At dinner the standard offerings are supplemented with roast prime ribs and horseradish sauce and a dish known as Scotch eggs—hard-boiled eggs, covered with sausage and fried, then chilled and served with mustard sauce on the side. (It's usually inedible back in Great Britain, but it's really quite tasty here in Florida.) For dessert there's traditional sherry trifle, a confection of layered whipped cream, custard, strawberries, and sherry; and raspberry fool, strictly whipped cream and raspberry purée. Bass India Pale ale from England, Tennent's lager beer from Scotland, and Harp lager beer and Guinness stout, both from Ireland, are on tap. They're served cold, in the American fashion, not at room temperature, as Britons prefer.

The decor is beautiful, mainly polished woods, etched glass, and brass accents. In fine weather it's pleasant to lunch under the sunny yellow umbrellas on the terrace outside and watch the sleek *FriendShip* ferries chugging across World Showcase Lagoon. On the little island just to the east, the wind ruffles the leaves of the Lombardy poplars, a species of tree that is found along roadsides all over Europe.

Horticulturally speaking, it's also interesting to note the vines on the pub's northwest wall. These Virginia creepers grow amazingly fast and, when Epcot opened, showed only a few tentative tendrils close to the ground. The spreading tree nearby is a laurel oak, distinguished from the southern live oaks more widely seen at Epcot by its upright growth and its leaves, which are shiny on both sides instead of just one.

As for the pub's architecture, it incorporates three separate styles. The wall facing the World Showcase Promenade is reminiscent of urban establishments popular in Britain since the 1890s, while that on the south evokes London's *Cheshire Cheese* pub, with its brick-walled flagstone terrace, slate roof, and half-timbered exterior. The canal facade, with its stone wall and clay-tile roof, reminds visitors of the charming pubs so common in the British countryside.

The pub section of the *Rose & Crown* serves such snacks as Stilton cheese and fresh fruit platters, and the above-mentioned Scotch eggs—along with all the brews noted above and traditional British mixed drinks such as shandies (Bass ale and ginger beer), lager beer with lime juice, black velvets (Guinness stout and champagne), and black and tans (Bass ale and Guinness stout). This drinking-and-snacking spot is quite popular, so it's often necessary to queue up at the door. But the wait is seldom very long since few guests linger over their drinks. Reservations are not accepted in the pub area but are suggested for the adjacent dining room. Moderate to expensive. L, D, S.

Chefs de France: Multiple-star restaurants are rare even in France, so it's a notable coup that WDW has somehow managed to lure three of France's finest chefs to run this rather remarkable restaurant. Paul Bocuse and Roger Vergé operate three- and two-star restaurants respectively in France (Bocuse's is outside Lyons, Vergé's just north of the French Riviera), and together with Gaston Lenôtre (widely recognized as France's premier preparer of pastries and other delicious dessert delicacies), they form a most unusual, absolutely formidable gastronomic trio.

Bocuse, Vergé, and Lenôtre operate this unique World Showcase restaurant, and they have designed a menu that features fresh ingredients readily available from Florida purveyors. One or more of the French chefs makes regular visits to WDW to supervise and adjust certain items on the menu, though there has been very little need to tinker.

As you might expect, the fare here is fiercely French, but the foundation of the menu is nouvelle cuisine, which involves lighter sauces, using much less cream and butter than the classic style of French cooking. At dinner, appetizers include chilled potato, leek, and Lyons-style onion soup; salmon soufflé served with lobster sauce, hot pâté of chicken and duck en croute, and a casserole of snails in herb butter with garlic. Diners choose from entrées such as fillet of snapper and spinach baked in puff pastry with sautéed scallops and crab dumplings, braised half duck in red wine sauce, and marinated chicken breast baked in puff pastry with port wine cream sauce. At lunch, the menu offers various soups, salads, cheeses, and pâtés. Hot dishes such as fillet of orange roughy with hazelnut butter, brochette of prawns, salmon tartar, and a beef filet with bordelaise sauce are available. A beef stew redolent of wine and a rich onion soup are available at lunch and dinner, as are an array of absolutely fabulous pastries and desserts (some wonderful Lenôtre specialties) and the thick, strong coffee known as café filtre. The atmosphere is as much a delight as the food. Tablecloths are crisp linen, and decorative touches of brass and etched glass abound. A modest wine list accompanies both lunch and dinner menus. Note that this can be one of the most expensive of all World Showcase restaurants. (There's a separate menu "for the little gourmet"—kids under 12—at reduced prices.) Reservations necessary. Expensive. L, D.

Bistro de Paris: One flight above *Chefs de France*, this restaurant evokes early 20th-century Paris. Peach and green curlicues decorate the ceiling above brass light fixtures and sconces, large mirrors, leaded colored glass, and simple wood chairs. A traditional bistro menu (created by the same trio of French chefs responsible for the fare at *Chefs de France*) features roast red snapper topped with potato scales and red-wine lobster sauce, seafood casserole with garlic sauce, roasted rack of lamb, and sautéed breast of duck. The heartiness of the fare makes it an especially good dining choice in cool weather. Reservations necessary. Expensive. L, D.

Au Petit Café: Located prominently in front of the France pavilion, along the World Showcase Promenade, this sidewalk café is a delightful place to stop for a snack or light meal. Under a large canopy with small round tables and black-jacketed waiters, it's as pleasant as it can be, and it can't be beat as a people-watching headquarters. No reservations are accepted, and long lines can develop. So don't stop if you're tired or ravenous. Moderate to expensive. L, D, S.

Akershus: The Norwegian castle of Akershus, which dominates Oslo's harbor, is the most impressive of Norway's medieval fortresses. It is actually half fortress and half palace, and many of its grand halls continue to be used for elaborate state banquets. At Epcot's *Akershus*, guests are treated to an authentic royal Norwegian buffet called the *koldtbord*, literally "the cold table." The diverse mix of offerings includes both hot and cold meats and seafood, and a selection of salads, cheeses, and breads. Traditional Norwegian desserts also are served, as are cocktails and Norwegian beer. Hosts and hostesses are on hand to answer any questions about the menu that guests may have. Reservations accepted. Moderate to expensive. L, D.

EVERYTHING YOU NEED TO KNOW ABOUT EPCOT RESTAURANT RESERVATIONS

Because restaurant reservation procedures have changed more than once since Epcot opened, it's important to confirm that the policies described below are still in effect at the time you arrive. To check, call WDW-DINE (939-3463). Also, try to arrive five minutes before your reserved seating time.

For dinner reservations: All guests—those staying at WDW hotels or off-property hotels—can make reservations up to 60 days ahead by calling 939-3463. Advance reservations are strongly recommended for nearly all full-service restaurants at Epcot. (The number of tables available for advance reservations varies depending upon the restaurant and the season.)

Otherwise, reservations must be made *on the day of the meal* at the WorldKey Information System screens in Guest Relations. Shortly after Epcot opens for the day, a line of would-be reservation-makers usually develops, and those at the end have less chance of booking a table at a popular restaurant at a popular time. For this reason, it's helpful to arrive at the Epcot turnstiles about half an hour before the published park opening. Preferred seating times (5:30 P.M. to 7:30 P.M.) are usually booked early in the day, so plan your evening meal with that in mind. Decide in advance where you want to eat and when (and choose a couple of possible alternate dining times and locales), and then send a member of your party on ahead to Guest Relations to make reservations. (It will help if you've familiarized yourself with the location of Guest Relations and the WorldKey Information System stations.) Each of the restaurants has something

special about it, and there's always a good menu selection even for unadventurous eaters—even in the more exotic restaurants of World Showcase. If you're undecided, ask at Guest Relations to see a book of menus. Don't arbitrarily dismiss the idea of an early seating if you can get it: If you have lunch at 11 A.M., a 5 P.M. dinner will not only be welcome, but more important, it will provide the opportunity to spend the most pleasant and uncrowded evening hours enjoying the Epcot attractions. And don't abandon an Epcot restaurant experience altogether.

For lunch reservations: This meal provides guests with another chance to enjoy the most popular Epcot restaurants. It also has another important appeal: With a reservation for 1 P.M., it's possible to spend some of the most crowded hours in the park consuming a pleasant meal while less fortunate visitors are waiting in some of the longest lines of the day. Reservations for lunch can be made by calling 939-3463, at the WorldKey Information System, or in person at the restaurant of your choice on the day you wish to dine. Complete this chore as early in the day as possible. Also note that you may be able to walk right in—say, if the time you have in mind is not too popular (like 10:45 A.M.). Most restaurants open for lunch between 10:30 A.M. and 11 A.M.

If all else fails: It sometimes happens that someone holding a reservation does not show up at the appointed seating time (reservations are held for only 15 minutes), so it certainly doesn't hurt to stop and inquire when passing a restaurant for which you have a sudden appetite.

Marrakesh: The tastiest part of the Morocco pavilion features a variety of examples of traditional and modern Moroccan cuisine. Waiters are dressed in traditional Moroccan costumes. Moroccan menu specialties include roast lamb, chicken brochette, couscous (steamed semolina served with your choice of lamb, chicken, or vegetables). Sampler platters also are available. The beautiful tilework was done by Moroccan craftsmen. Belly dancers and Moroccan musicians entertain diners at both lunch and dinner. A children's menu is available. Reservations accepted. Expensive. L, D.

Mitsukoshi: This complex of dining and drinking spots, all operated by the Japanese firm for which it is named, occupies the sec-

ond level of the large structure on the west side of the Japan pavilion plaza. There are two options:

Tempura Kiku: This small corner of the *Mitsukoshi* restaurant is devoted to the batter-dipped, deep-fried chicken, beef, seafood, and fresh vegetables that are collectively known as tempura. The individual tidbits are crisp and delicious. Expensive. L, D.

Teppanyaki Dining Rooms: The style of these five rooms is not unlike that popularized by the *Benihana* chain all around America: Guests sit counter-style around large flat grills, while white-hatted chefs chop vegetables, meat, and fish at lightning speed and then stir-fry it all just as quickly. Whether or not all the chopping and cooking is accompanied by a mildly comic routine depends on the sense of humor of the chef, but in any case the establishment is quite convivial. The seating arrangements make it quite natural to strike up a conversation with fellow diners; in fact, it's almost impossible to keep to yourself. Reservations necessary. Expensive. L, D.

L'Originale Alfredo di Roma Ristorante: This restaurant's *trompe l'oeil* ("trick the eye") perspective paintings make diners believe they're seeing real scenes rather than mere murals, and lend character to the decor of this popular establishment. As in the famous Roman restaurant of the same name, the specialty is fettuccine Alfredo—wide, flat noodles tossed in a sauce made of butter and imported Parmesan cheese. But many other sizes and shapes of pasta, all of it made right on the premises, also are available; they are significantly enhanced by tomato, meat, pesto (basil, garlic, and Parmesan), or carbonara (egg, bacon, cream, and pecorino cheese) sauces. There also are a number of less familiar Italian preparations involving chicken, eggplant, seafood, sausage, and veal, which are all very good. For dessert, choose from a number of specialties such as ricotta cheesecake, spumoni, tortoni, or gelato. Even if you don't eat here, it's fun to stop and just peer through the glass kitchen windows to watch the cooks cranking out the rigatoni, ziti, linguine, lasagne, fettuccine, and spaghetti (which, the eminently readable menu reminds guests, were brought to America by Thomas Jefferson from Europe in 1786). Reservations necessary. Expensive. L, D.

Biergarten: Located at the rear of the St. Georgsplatz in the Germany pavilion, this huge, tiered restaurant is set in a courtyard rimmed with geranium-studded balconies and punctuated by an old mill. It's every bit as jolly as Italy's *Alfredo's*, especially in the evenings, partly because of the long tables that encourage a certain togetherness among guests, partly because Beck's beer is served in 33-ounce steins. But equal credit for the gemütlich atmosphere must go to the restaurant's lively shows, in which yodelers, dancers, and other traditional southern-German musicians—each appropriately clad in lederhosen or dirndls—play accordions, cowbells, a musical saw, and a harplike stringed instrument known as the "wooden laughter." The performances are exceptional, and the

WHERE TO EAT IN EPCOT IF YOU DON'T HAVE RESERVATIONS

It's important to remember every establishment offers unique delights. If you can't get dinner reservations in advance, don't despair. France offers the informal full-service eatery known as *Au Petit Café* (though there are sometimes queues), and Japan has its *Yakitori House*, good for skewered bits of barbecued beef and chicken. Or sample Mexican specialties at Mexico's *Cantina de San Angel* (whose lagoonside tables provide a fine view of the sun setting behind Epcot). Also try the open-face sandwiches at *Kringla Bakeri og Kafe* in Norway, or the sweet-and-sour pork at China's *Lotus Blossom Café*.

Cravings for more conventional fast foods will be satisfied at the *Electric Umbrella* in Innoventions; and at the *Liberty Inn* in The American Adventure. The *Pasta Piazza Ristorante* in Innoventions serves Italian fare. The *Sunshine Season Food Fair* in The Land pavilion offers a little bit of everything.

Biergarten offers an extremely entertaining time. Diners are usually invited to join the fun on stage. The food is hearty and exquisitely presented on an all-you-can-eat German buffet, featuring assorted sausages (grilled bratwurst, debrizinger, bauernwurst), frankfurters, rotisserie chicken, homemade spatzle, assorted cold dishes, potato salad, cucumber salad, and many more German specialties. Because entertainment is intermittent, there's plenty of time to enjoy the pleasant setting, with the big mill waterwheel slowly turning and the sound of water splashing into the millstream blending with the rousing oompah music. Reservations suggested, particularly during peak seasons. Moderate to expensive. L, D.

Nine Dragons: One more item on Epcot's varied international restaurant list offers provincial Chinese cooking styles, including Mandarin, Cantonese, Hunan, Szechuan, and Kiangche. Entrées include braised duck (served Cantonese style), Kang Bao chicken (stir-fried chicken, peanuts, and dried hot peppers), and beef and jade tree (sliced steak and Chinese broccoli). Appetizers range from Chinese pickled cabbage to pan-fried dumplings and hot-and-sour soup. A selection of Chinese teas, beers, and wines also is available. The dessert menu is varied and features red-bean ice cream, toffee apples, and assorted Chinese pastries. Reservations necessary. Expensive. L, D.

San Angel Inn: A corporate cousin of the famous Mexico City restaurant of the same name, the food at this establishment, located to the rear of the plaza inside the Mexico pyramid, may come as a surprise to most visitors. Although the tacos and tortillas and other specialties that usually fall under the broad umbrella of Mexican food are available, the menu also offers a wide variety of more subtly flavored fish, poultry, and meat dishes. To start, there's queso fundido for two (melted cheese and Mexican pork sausage with corn or flour tortillas). As entrées, the menu offers sopes de pollo (fried corn dough shells topped with refried beans, chicken with green tomatillo sauce, and cheese); grilled tenderloin of beef served with chicken enchilada, guacamole, and refried beans; mole poblano (chicken simmered with spices and a bit of chocolate); huachinango à la Veracruzana (fresh fillet of red snapper poached in wine with onions, tomatoes, and peppers); and much more that is good and tasty. Mexican desserts are largely unfamiliar to North Americans, with the possible exceptions of the custard known as flan, and arroz con leche, best known in the United States as rice pudding. Still, such desserts as chocolate Kahlua mousse pie and helada con cajeta (vanilla ice cream with a milk caramel topping) are well worth trying. Dos Equis brand beer, tart lemon-flavored water, and delicious margaritas make good accompaniments. Reservations necessary. Expensive. L, D.

CAFETERIA SERVICE

Le Cellier: This low-ceilinged, stone-walled establishment tucked away on the lowest level of the pavilion near Victoria Gardens, looks a little like the ancient wine cellars for which it is named. It offers a full menu of Canadian foods, with hearty sandwiches also available for lunch, and roast prime ribs added to the offerings at dinner. The savory, Quebec-born pork-and-potato-filled pie known as tourtiére is dished out in enormous slices, each one fully three inches high and covered with a tempting golden crust. Tangy Canadian cheddar cheese serves as the base of a rich soup and adds zip to some appetizing fruit platters. Chicken and meatball stew, poached fresh salmon in spinach velouté sauce, and carved Canadian bacon—all served with choice of potatoes or rice, and vegetables—round out the selection of entrées. For dessert there's maple-syrup pie, a sweet cousin to pecan pie, and apple-berry-rhubarb pie. Canada's own Molson and Labatt's beers are served in bottles. Children's selections include macaroni and cheese. The combination of all this makes *Le Cellier* a prime destination for those who haven't been able to get a reservation at one of the more publicized World Showcase restaurants but still want something more substantial than what the fast-food eateries are offering. Operates seasonally. Moderate. L, D, S.

FAST FOOD & SNACKS

Refreshment Port: A perfect spot for a quick thirst quencher, next to the Canada pavilion. Canadian beer and wine are served. Fresh fruit, frozen yogurt, and cookies also are available. Inexpensive. S.

Yakitori House: The nature of the food offered at this small but comfortable establishment in the Japan pavilion is representative of the pace of life in that country. The average Japanese spends about seven minutes consuming his or her guydon, a stewlike concoction flavored with soy sauce, spices, and the Japanese rice wine known as sake—all served over rice. That, together with skewered chicken known as yakitori (which is basted with soy sauce and sesame oil as it broils), teriyaki sandwiches, and Japanese sweets and beverages, makes up the offerings here. Located in the Japanese gardens to the left of the plaza, the restaurant occupies a scaled-down version of the 16th-century Katsura Imperial Summer Palace in Kyoto; sliding screens, lanterns, and kimono-clad hostesses add to the atmosphere. Inexpensive. L, D, S.

Liberty Inn: To many foreigners, American food means hamburgers, hot dogs, and french fries, and these are the staples at the *Liberty Inn*, located alongside The American Adventure on the far end of the World Showcase Lagoon. Grilled-chicken sandwiches, salads, ice cream, apple pastries, and chocolate chip cookies round out the selections. As a result, the place is a delight for small children, and also quite a pleasant spot for their parents. There's veranda seating, a pretty fountain, and a full complement of antique-looking decoys and chests. Inexpensive to moderate. L, D, S.

Refreshment Outpost: Another good spot for a refreshing cold drink. Frozen yogurt and ice cream are served. Between the Germany and China pavilions. Inexpensive. S.

Lotus Blossom Café: Adjacent to Yong Feng Shangdian shopping gallery in the China pavilion, this fast-food counter offers sweet-and-sour pork, egg rolls, and soup. There's a covered, outdoor seating area for 200 people. Inexpensive. L, D.

Boulangerie Pâtisserie: This bakery-and-pastry shop in the France pavilion is not hard to find: Just follow the wonderful aroma and then watch the crowds line up to consume the establishment's flaky croissants and brioches, éclairs, fruit tarts, and chocolate mousse. These are served by women wearing black pinafores with ruffled white blouses, under the management of the stellar trio of chefs who run the popular *Chefs de France* restaurant not far away—Paul Bocuse, Gaston Lenôtre, and Roger Vergé. Hint for those who hate to wait: Arrive early (this has become a favorite breakfast stop among Epcot veterans) or stop here about half an hour before park closing. Inexpensive. S.

Sommerfest: Bratwurst sandwiches, soft pretzels, apple strudel, Black Forest cake, Beck's beer and wine are offered at this outdoor establishment near the Germany pavilion. Inexpensive. L, D, S.

Cantina de San Angel: Located along the World Showcase Promenade, just outside the entrance to Mexico's pyramid, this fast-food stand serves beef-filled soft tortillas; tacos al carbon, flour tortillas filled with grilled chicken breast strips, onions, and peppers, served with refried beans and salsa; and—perhaps best of all—churros, a sort of fried dough rolled in cinnamon and sugar. The *Cantina* is first rate for a tasty rest stop on a hot afternoon. Dos Equis beer, margaritas, and watermelon juice are available, and the establishment's plant-edged terrace makes a fine grandstand for people-watching. Inexpensive. L, D, S.

Kringla Bakeri og Kafe: Tucked between an ancient wooden church and a cluster of Norwegian shops, this eating spot serves kringles, sweet candied pretzels eaten on special occasions in Norway; vaflers, heart-shaped waffles topped with powdered sugar and jam; kransekake, almond-pastry rings; and smörbrods, open-face sandwiches of smoked salmon, roast beef, or turkey. Ringnes Beer, brewed in Norway, also is available. There is a 55-seat outdoor eating area. Inexpensive. L, S.

In the Disney-MGM Studios

The restaurants in the Disney-MGM Studios are the only places in the entire complex where a hint of the present meets the Hollywood of the 1930s and 1940s. It's true that the decor and atmosphere of the Studio eateries fiercely clings to eras gone by, but the ingredients in the food have been updated and most menus offer lowfat items. The chili at the *50's Prime Time Café*, for example, is made with vegetables and served over angel hair pasta. And in a tribute to the Hollywood image, most establishments also offer a couple of trendy California creations.

FULL SERVICE

Hollywood Brown Derby: The home of the famous Cobb Salad is alive and well. This re-creation of the former Vine Street mainstay is quite faithful, right down to the caricatures (lovingly reproduced from the original *Derby* collection) that cover the walls. Arch rivals Louella Parsons and Hedda Hopper (portrayed by convincing actresses) still reign over the restaurant from reserved tables, just as they did when the *Brown Derby* was in its heyday.

The 235-seat restaurant is predominantly decorated in teak and mahogany, and the elegant chandeliers and perimeter lamps (shaped like miniature derbies) are reminiscent of the original eatery. The china is embossed with the *Brown Derby* logo. The atmosphere is just about authentic save for the theme park clientele who show up in shorts and tennis shoes.

The menu features the famed Cobb Salad, created by owner Bob Cobb in the 1930s. It's a mixture of finely chopped fresh salad greens, tomato, bacon, turkey, egg, blue cheese, and avocado. It's tossed tableside

and served with old-fashioned French dressing. The modern incarnation of the salad also is available with shrimp or lobster. Other menu selections of note include Fettuccine Derby, pasta in a Parmesan cheese sauce with chicken and red and green peppers, and fillet of grouper. The dessert tray is tempting—particularly the grapefruit cake, a *Brown Derby* institution. A children's menu is available, although the slightly formal atmosphere is not likely to enchant most youngsters. Reservations suggested. Expensive. L, D.

50's Prime Time Café: The setting is straight out of the favorite sitcoms of the 1950s. Each of the plastic-laminate kitchen tables is set under a pull-down lamp, and the

idea is to evoke a suburban kitchenette. Video screens set all around the room show black-and-white clips (all related to food) from favorite 1950s TV comedies, and these nostalgic bits are visible from each of the 226 seats. The place mats pose television trivia quizzes and meals are served either on Fiesta Ware plates or TV dinner-style on three-compartment trays. The waitresses play "Mom" with considerable enthusiasm; they make recommendations and encourage guests to clean their plates (*or no dessert!*).

The menu is packed with "comfort foods." For openers there's alphabet soup, chili, and the French Fry Feast, served either plain or with chili and cheese. Specialties of the house include Magnificent Meat Loaf, served with mashed potatoes and mushroom gravy;

broiled chicken and spuds; chicken pot pie; and Granny's Pot Roast. There also are burgers with a variety of toppings, turkey burgers, hot roast beef sandwiches, club sandwiches, Aunt Selma's Chicken Salad, and the Apple-A-Day TV Tray (an apple served with cottage cheese and assorted fruits). Milk shakes, ice-cream sodas, and root-beer floats are filling accompaniments. And when you've finished everything on your plate, "Mom" will ask if you'd like dessert. Standouts include S'mores (you'll feel like you're back at summer camp), a graham cracker topped with chocolate and toasted marshmallows; sundaes; banana splits; and apple pie à la mode. Beer and wine are served. Kids love this place and a children's menu is available. Reservations necessary. Moderate. L, D, S.

Sci-Fi Dine-In Theater: This 250-seat eatery recreates a 1950s drive-in theater. The tables are actually flashy, 1950s-era cars, complete with fins and whitewalls. Fiber-optic stars twinkle overhead in the night sky, and there are real drive-in theater speakers mounted next to each car. All the tables face a large screen where a 45-minute compilation of the best (and worst) of science fiction trailers and cartoons plays in a continuous loop. Popcorn is served before the meals, which include the Monster Mash—actually roasted turkey with dressing and mashed potatoes. Tossed in Space is the (huge) chef's salad and They Grow Among Us is a sampling of fruits. The Red Planet is an assortment of vegetables with linguini, and Towering Terror, a platter of barbecued pork ribs with corn-on-the-cob and cole slaw. There also are hot and cold sandwiches and a variety of desserts, including the Cheesecake that Ate New York; Twin Terrors, a banana-split cake; Science Gone Mad, Dutch apple pie served warm; and The Black Hole, a chocolate layer cake. There also is a children's menu. Reservations accepted. Moderate to expensive. L, D.

Mama Melrose's Ristorante Italiano: A pizzeria has opened in a warehouse that has been converted into a dining room. Pizzas are prepared in a wood-burning oven. Fresh fish and steaks are grilled over a hardwood charbroiler. Other menu items include lasagna, chicken, veal chops, and pasta with a variety of toppings. Reservations accepted. Moderate to expensive. L, D (during busy seasons).

CAFETERIA SERVICE

Hollywood & Vine: The distinctive Art Deco facade ushers guests into a contemporary version of a 1950s diner—all stainless steel with pink accents. An elaborate 42- by 8-foot wall mural depicts notable Hollywood landmarks, including the Disney Studios, Columbia Ranch, and Warner Brothers (back when they were the only studios in the San Fernando Valley). At the center of the mural is the Carthay Circle Theatre, where *Snow White* premiered in 1937.

The 368-seat cafeteria presents a varied menu. At breakfast, there's the Hollywood Scramble, two eggs served with bacon or sausage and a choice of potatoes or grits and a breakfast biscuit; french toast; pancakes; omelettes; assorted hot and cold cereals; and fresh fruit. Muffins, Danish pastries, and croissants also are served. Lunch features a variety of salads, including the Seafood Serenade, a chilled salad of shrimp, grilled chicken, garden greens, and fresh fruit. Baby-back ribs, roasted chicken, and spaghetti and meatballs also are served. Pies head the dessert list. Beer and wine are available, and a children's menu is posted. Inexpensive to moderate. B, L, D.

FAST FOOD & SNACKS

Soundstage: The split theming of this 560-seat food court reflects the settings of two animated features—*Aladdin* and *Pocahontas*. Guests can find Pocahontas, John Smith, and Aladdin at a character breakfast, held daily. This all-you-can-eat breakfast is $12.95 for adults and $7.95 for children ages three to nine. Make necessary reservations by calling 939-3463. Music from the films play in the

background, and the characters also make regular appearances throughout the day. Deep-dish pizza, linguine, spaghetti and meatballs, stacked turkey sandwiches, and chilled pasta salad are on the menu. Ham sandwiches, hot dogs, and macaroni and cheese are available for the kids. Inexpensive. B, L, D.

Commissary: Fast food with a healthy twist is the bill of fare at this streamlined moderne eatery. The 550-seat restaurant is located between the Chinese Theatre and SuperStar Television. In the open kitchen, chefs prepare chicken-breast sandwiches and fresh salads. There is a children's menu. Inexpensive. L, D.

Starring Rolls Bakery: Freshly baked rolls (not roles), pastries, muffins, and croissants are sold at this sweet-smelling shop. Coffee, tea, and soft drinks also are served, making this a good place for an eat-and-run breakfast. Inexpensive. B, S.

Dinosaur Gertie's: "Ice Cream of Extinction," claims the sign at this life-size dinosaur set on Echo Lake where ice cream has been replaced with frozen slush drinks in a variety of flavors. Inexpensive. S.

Backlot Express: This 600-seat counter-service restaurant looks like the old crafts shops on a studio backlot. There's a paint shop, a stunt hall, a sculpture shop, and a model shop. The paint shop has paint-speckled floors, chairs, and tables; the prop shop

has car engines, bumpers, and fan belts. There is outdoor seating available amidst stored streetlights, plants, and trees. Menu offerings include charbroiled chicken, chicken-breast sandwiches, burgers, hot dogs, chef's salads, and chili. For dessert, there's chocolate-chip cheesecake, apple pie, carrot cake, and fresh fruit. Beer and wine are available by the glass. Inexpensive. L, D, S.

Min & Bill's Dockside Diner: "There's good eats in our galley," proclaims the welcoming sign posted on the *S.S. Down the Hatch*, a bit of "California crazy" 1950s architecture. The little tramp steamer, complete with a cartoonlike smokestack, mast, and booms, doesn't sail. *Min & Bill's* sandwich offerings (served during busy seasons only) include the Portside Sandwich (turkey ham and turkey salami, lettuce, tomato rolled in a soft tortilla). Other specialties are the Cucamonga Cocktail, marinated Gulf shrimp and fresh vegetables; San Pedro Pasta, tricolored pasta with crab and shrimp; and fresh fruit with yogurt. Soft-serve frozen yogurt is served year-round in cups or cones with a variety of toppings. Inexpensive. L, D, S.

Studio Catering Co.: Guests on the Backstage Studio Tour come across this eatery at the end of the tram tour. Situated just behind The Loony Bin, the menu features desserts and snacks. Beer also is available. Inexpensive. S.

Sunset Ranch Market: Three food stands on Sunset Boulevard feature good opportunities for snacking. Popcorn, hot dogs, frozen yogurt, fresh fruit, fruit juices, and soft drinks are among the options. Inexpensive. L, D, S.

In the Hotels

Contemporary

Most of the hotel's restaurants are located on the Grand Canyon Concourse on the fourth floor—with one notable exception. The hotel's newest eatery, *California Grill*, is found on the 15th floor, where it offers a beautiful view of the entire property. There also are snacks available by the marina and in the first-floor Food and Fun Center.

California Grill: On the 15th floor, with spectacular views of sunsets and Magic Kingdom fireworks. This new restaurant offers the best in West Coast cuisine in a colorful, relaxing atmosphere. The menu includes wood-fired California pizzas, spit-roasted and grilled meats, alderwood-smoked salmon, market-fresh vegetables, seafood, and jumbo

soufflés, all prepared to order. Fresh produce plays an important role in the menu, so expect items to change depending on what's in season. Reservations suggested. Expensive. D.

Contemporary Café: On the Grand Canyon Concourse. Serves a bountiful, all-you-can-eat international buffet—one of the World's best buys—every evening. Six days a week, there's a buffet-style character breakfast hosted by Goofy and pals from 7:30 A.M. to 11 A.M. The same crew gathers for brunch on Sundays. Reservations necessary for character meals, accepted for dinner. Moderate. B, D, Sunday brunch.

Concourse Steak House: On the Grand Canyon Concourse, this spot offers a variety of eggs, omelettes, pancakes, and fresh fruit for breakfast. At lunch there are salads, soups, burgers, and sandwiches. Dinner

entrées include chicken, fresh fish and seafood, and steaks. Reservations accepted. Moderate. B, L, D.

Outer Rim Cocktail Lounge: On the Grand Canyon Concourse, opposite the *Contemporary Café*, with a good view over Bay Lake. Specialty drinks, cocktails, and appetizers are served from noon to 1 A.M. Moderate. S.

Food and Fun Center: On the first floor adjacent to the gameroom; serves light fare from 6 A.M. to midnight. Inexpensive. B, L, D, S.

Polynesian

Some of WDW's more interesting eating spots are located here.

'Ohana: On the second floor of the Great Ceremonial House, this new restaurant features a 16-foot-long open fire pit. Dinner choices in the all-you-can-eat feast include shrimp, poultry, pork, beef, and lamb, all

roasted on skewers up to three feet long. Meats are marinated in original combinations of soy, ginger, lemon grass, or garlic, and are served family-style with an assortment of fresh vegetables, salads and homemade bread. Dessert offerings include passion fruit crème brûlée. The room itself is large and open and offers fine views across the Seven Seas Lagoon all the way to Cinderella Castle. Minnie's Menehune character breakfast is held every day from 7:30 A.M. to 10:30 A.M. Reservations are necessary for Minnie's Menehune breakfast and suggested for dinner. Expensive. B, D.

Coral Isle Café: Also on the second floor of the Great Ceremonial House, it's around the corner from 'Ohana. This standard coffee shop with a faintly South Seas decor serves the usual assortment of eggs every morning, plus granola and other cereals, and wonderful banana-stuffed french toast, one of the many unique Walt Disney World dishes. At lunch, the house does a booming business in burgers and a variety of sandwiches. At dinner, 20-ounce New York strip steaks, ribs, and tempting desserts are served. Drinks, including the special Polynesian concoctions served at the *Tambu Lounge*, are available. A good choice when you want a no-fuss meal. Moderate. B, L, D, S.

Tangaroa Terrace: This sprawling establishment, on the eastern edge of the property near the Oahu longhouse, serves Mickey-shaped Belgium waffles with hot toppings and banana-stuffed french toast. Eggs and other more usual breakfast selections also are

available à la carte or buffet-style. The dinner buffet features Asian dishes, chicken, and salads; à la carte entrées include prime ribs, steaks, and fresh seafood. Children's selections are available. Reservations accepted. Moderate. B, D, S.

Captain Cook's Snack and Ice Cream Company: A good spot for continental breakfasts, hamburgers, hot dogs, fruit salad, soft-serve ice cream, and snacks; cans of beer also are available. Open 24 hours. Inexpensive. B, L, D, S.

Grand Floridian

There are several good restaurants at the *Grand Floridian*, including one of the finest dining spots in the entire Orlando area.

Victoria & Albert's: The premier restaurant not only of the *Grand Floridian*, but probably of the entire Walt Disney World complex. The small dining room seats only 65, and elegant touches include Royal Doulton china, Sambonet silver, and Schott-Zweisel crystal. There is no formal, printed menu. Each night there are fish, fowl, red meat, veal, and lamb selections, which depend on the best ingredients in the market, and which are described in detail by your waiter. The chef may even make a personal appearance to accommodate special requests from patrons. There also are choices of two soups, two salads, and desserts, including the specialty soufflés of fresh berries, chocolate, or Grand Marnier. There is an extensive wine list.

Once guests have selected their meal they are presented a handwritten souvenir menu. Women receive a long-stemmed rose. Jackets are required. One oddity of note: Every host and hostess here is named Victoria or Albert. Reservations are necessary. Very expensive. D.

Flagler's: There are Italian influences at the hotel's largest restaurant. Pasta dishes, fresh seafood, veal, and steaks, all served with an Italian flair. Dessert offerings include homemade gelato. There are strolling musicians, and the restaurant offers a lovely view of the hotel's marina. Reservations suggested. Expensive. D.

1900 Park Fare: The all-American menu takes a backseat to the decor in this 248-seat buffet restaurant. Big Bertha, a band organ built in Paris nearly a century ago, sits 15 feet above the floor in a proscenium. The bellows-

powered instrument simultaneously plays pipes, drums, bells, cymbals, and xylophone. Mary Poppins joins other Disney characters here during breakfast. The dinner buffet features seafood, salads, vegetables, breads, and prime ribs. Mickey Mouse and Minnie Mouse entertain at dinner. The offerings change weekly. Reservations necessary for character meals, otherwise suggested. Expensive. B, D.

Narcoossee's: The open kitchen is the focal point at this casual, airy, octagon-shaped restaurant on the shore of the *Grand Floridian* beach. Specialties include grilled swordfish marinated in garlic, olive oil, and

BONNET CREEK GOLF CLUB

Sand Trap Bar & Grill: A variety of appetizers, sandwiches, and snacks are offered at this pleasant spot. Hamburgers, Reuben sandwiches, barbecued pork, and grilled-chicken sandwiches are on the menu. There is a full bar, and ice cream and milk shakes also are available. Moderate. L, D, S.

basil; grilled steaks; double lamb chops; veal chops; and grilled chicken. The Seven Seas, Seven Scoops Spectacular is a 48-ounce snifter filled with berries, seven scoops of ice cream, and topped with whipped cream and a touch of amaretto. Reservations suggested. Expensive. L, D.

Grand Floridian Café: Southern cooking is the specialty, and selections include a sandwich of roast turkey, smoked ham, tomatoes, bacon, cheddar cheese, and crispy onions, and honey-dipped fried chicken. There also are salads and an assortment of more traditional entrées. Moderate. B, L, D.

Gasparilla Grill and Games: Grilled chicken, hamburgers, pizza, hot dogs, and soft-serve ice cream are the mainstays at this take-out, self-service restaurant near the pool. Continental breakfast also is available. Inexpensive. B, L, D, S.

Wilderness Lodge

The American West theme is carried out with flair in the hotel's three restaurants.

Artist Point: Decorated with artwork representing the painters who first chronicled the Northwest landscape. This fine dining spot offers a creative menu that incorporates wild game as well as more traditional items such as steaks, salmon, and other Pacific seafood. There also is a good wine list featuring wines from the Pacific Northwest. A character breakfast is served every morning. Reservations necessary for breakfast, suggested for dinner. Expensive. B, D.

Whispering Canyon Café: A traditional family-style coffee shop is open for all-day dining. Hearty fare includes warm apple cakes and biscuits for breakfast, barbecued beef brisket for lunch, and apple-rosemary rotisserie chicken for dinner. Moderate. B, L, D.

Roaring Forks: Light snacks and salads are available at the hotel's arcade 24 hours a day. Inexpensive. B, L, D, S.

Caribbean Beach

Captain's Tavern: Prime ribs, chicken, and crab legs are on the menu at this cozy 200-seat restaurant located within Old Port Royale. Tropical drinks, beer, wine, and cocktails also are served. Moderate. D, S.

These six counter-service restaurants are located in Old Port Royale. A 500-seat common dining area serves all guests. Each counter has a variety of breakfast items as well. Moderate. B, L, D, S.

Cinnamon Bay Bakery: Freshly baked rolls, croissants, pastries, ice cream, and other caloric treats are available.

Port Royale Hamburger Shop: Grilled chicken sandwiches, burgers, and soft drinks are on the menu.

Kingston Pasta Shop: A variety of Italian specialties are available.

Bridgetown Broiler: Spit-roasted chicken and homestyle meals are the offerings.

Montego's Deli: Soups, salads, and hot and cold sandwiches round out the selections at this stand.

Royale Pizza Shop: Pizza by the slice or the pie is available.

Swan

Palio: This Italian bistro gets high marks for its homemade pasta and pizza. Other specialties include veal and fish dishes. There also is a strolling musician. Reservations suggested. Expensive. D.

Garden Grove Café: Situated in a five-story greenhouse, this dining spot offers a complete breakfast menu, and fresh fish and shellfish at lunch and dinner. The desserts baked fresh daily in the open pastry kitchen are worth special note. As you approach the restaurant take a look through the glass windows to see the chefs at work. Character breakfasts and dinners are held here on certain days. Reservations necessary for character dinner. Moderate. B, L, D, S.

Kimono's: Attractively decorated in a Japanese design, this small spot features sushi and a variety of oriental specialties. Moderate to expensive. D, S.

Splash Grill: Breakfast, lunch, and snacks are available at this poolside spot. Drinks also are served. Moderate. B, L, S.

Dolphin

Harry's Safari Bar & Grille: Grilled beef, seafood, and chicken seasoned with herbs bought by "Harry" during his world travels are the specialties. On Sundays there is a character brunch. Reservations suggested for dinner, necessary for brunch. Expensive. D, Sunday brunch.

Sum Chows: A broad spectrum of Asian dishes is found at this ambitious eatery. Dishes such as steamed Dungeness crab with black-bean sauce and sautéed pheasant with almonds, lime, and honey are on the menu, served in a relaxed but stylish setting. Reservations suggested. Expensive. D.

Juan & Only's Cantina and Bar: This festive restaurant features authentic Mexican food amid an atmosphere of the warm hues and rich fabrics of old Mexico. Specialties include fresh pico de gallo served with blue corn and spicy red chips; grilled beef, chicken, shrimp, and a special meatless fajita from the fajita bar; chimichangas; burritos; taco salads; and other Mexican fare. The bar offers rare tequilas and beers from every region of Mexico. Reservations suggested. Expensive. D.

Coral Café: Buffet breakfast and dinner are served daily, with à la carte menus available for breakfast, lunch, and dinner. The Sunday brunch is quite extravagant. Moderate. B, L, D, S, Sunday brunch.

Tubbi Checkers Buffeteria: Checkerboard decor makes this cafeteria look a bit more interesting than the norm. The food is fresh and hot, and the lines are seldom very long. There also is a convenience store (open 24 hours), where snacks and baby-care items are available. Moderate. B, L, D, S.

Dolphin Fountain: Homemade ice cream, including some very unusual flavors, is the highlight here. It comes in waffle cones, cups, or as part of assorted super sundaes served by an energetic young staff who break into song and dance several times during the day. Burgers and sandwiches also are available. Moderate. L, D, S.

Cabana Bar & Grill: Burgers, grilled-chicken sandwiches, fresh fruit, and yogurt are offered at this poolside eatery. Moderate. L, S.

Yacht Club

Yachtsman Steakhouse: As its name implies, aged beef is the specialty of the house. Guests can see the house butcher choosing cuts of meat in the glassed-in shop, and then see the meals prepared in the display kitchen. Fresh seafood and chicken also are available. Reservations suggested. Expensive. D.

Yacht Club Galley: Brightly colored ceramic-tile tabletops help emphasize the yachting theme. Breakfast features a buffet and a full menu; lunch and dinner are à la carte only. Reservations accepted. Moderate. B, L, D.

Beaches & Cream Soda Shop: Patterned after a turn-of-the-century ice cream parlor, the menu features oversize sundaes, cones, floats, shakes, and sodas, as well as the Fenway Park Burger—which can be ordered as a single, double, triple, or a homerun. There are some breakfast items available as well. Moderate. B, L, D, S.

Hurricane Hanna's Grill: Located in the Stormalong Bay area shared by the two hotels. Hot dogs, hamburgers, sandwiches, french fries, and ice cream are on the menu. There also is a full bar. Moderate. L, S.

Beach Club

Cape May Café: An all-you-can-eat New England clambake is held every evening. A cooking pit used for steaming is in full view of diners, and menu items include clams, mussels, chicken, shrimp, corn, red-skin potatoes, and chowder. Lobster is available for an extra charge. There also is a character breakfast buffet each morning. Reservations necessary for breakfast, suggested for dinner. Moderate to expensive. B, D.

Ariel's: The *Beach Club's* signature restaurant, named for the star of *The Little Mermaid*, features a 2,500-gallon saltwater aquarium. The menu is strong in fresh seafood (not straight from the tank, though). Linen tablecloths and seaworthy china accent the restaurant's theme. Reservations suggested. Expensive. D.

Port Orleans

Bonfamilles Café: The name of the full-service restaurant comes from the Disney movie *The Aristocats*. Steaks, seafood, and Creole cooking highlight the menu. Breakfast is also served. Moderate. B, D.

Sassagoula Floatworks & Food Factory: The stands at this food court feature pizza, pasta, Italian specialties, burgers, fried chicken, sandwiches, soups, salads, spit-roasted chicken, barbequed ribs, ice cream, frozen yogurt, and a full selection of fresh bakery products. Moderate. B, L, D, S.

Sassagoula Pizza Express: Hand-tossed pizza, salads, desserts, and soft drinks can be delivered directly to guestrooms.

Dixie Landings

Boatwright's Dining Hall: Be sure to notice the boat being built in this 200-seat, full-service eatery. The specialties of the house include Cajun dishes from the rural South, as well as American homestyle favorites. Moderate. B, D.

Acadian Pizza 'n' Pasta: Fresh pizza with a variety of toppings and pasta dishes and calzones are on the menu at this food-court location. Moderate. B, L, D, S.

Bleu Bayou Burgers and Chicken: Fried and grilled chicken and an interesting assortment of burgers are the offerings here. Moderate. B, L, D, S.

Cajun Broiler: Spit-roasted chicken, barbeque ribs, and Tex-Mex specialties are available at this stand. Moderate. B, L, D, S.

Riverside Market and Deli: This convenience store stocks sandwiches, beer, wine, snack items, and prepared salads. Moderate. B, L, D, S.

Southern Trace Bakery: Pastries, freshly baked pies, and sticky cinnamon buns are the specialties here. Moderate. B, L, D, S.

Sassagoula Pizza Express: Hand-tossed pizza, salads, desserts, and soft drinks can be delivered directly to guestrooms.

Disney Vacation Club

Olivia's: An assortment of Key West favorites—including Key lime pie and conch fritters—is featured on the menu alongside more traditional items like turkey pot pie and crab cakes. A Winnie the Pooh character breakfast is held every Wednesday and Sunday. Moderate. B, L, D.

Good's Foods to Go: Snacks, burgers, grilled-chicken sandwiches, ice cream, and frozen yogurt are among the offerings here. Inexpensive. L, D, S.

All-Star Sports & All-Star Music

Each of the resorts features a themed central food court. The **End Zone** food court in Stadium Hall at the *All-Star Sports* resort and the **Intermission** food court in Melody Hall at the *All-Star Music* resort have similar food stands. The selections include pasta, hand-tossed pizza, chicken, ribs, burgers, hot dogs, sandwiches, salads, frozen yogurt, and a wide variety of baked goods. Inexpensive. B, L, D, S.

Fort Wilderness

Most people cook their own meals here; ample supplies are available at both the Meadow Trading and the Settlement Trading Post (open from 8 A.M. to 10 P.M. in winter, to 11 P.M. in summer).

Trail's End Buffet: This informal, log-walled, beam-ceilinged restaurant offers standard breakfasts, plus grits, biscuits, gravy, and a seven-inch "breakfast pizza" that vaguely resembles an omelette; and during the rest of the day serves hearty lunches and dinners featuring barbecued chicken, fish, chicken pot pie, and spare ribs. There are sandwiches and a taco bar at lunch. Specially priced children's portions are available. Saturday nights feature a Hoe Down supper where an all-you-can-eat buffet of lasagne, spaghetti, and fried chicken is served from 4:30 P.M. to 9:30 P.M. Pizza is served every night from 9 P.M. until 11 P.M. (until midnight on weekends). Beer and sangría are available by the glass or by the pitcher. Moderate. B, L, D, S.

Crockett's Tavern: Appetizers, steaks, ribs, and chicken are available in this Pioneer Hall eatery. A children's menu is offered and cocktails are served. Moderate. D.

Pleasure Island

The six acres of Pleasure Island mostly bustle with activity during evening hours, but the restaurants are open for both lunch and dinner and offer a few tempting dining options for WDW guests. The restaurants operate from 11:30 A.M. to midnight; most of the snack spots are open from 11 A.M. to 2 A.M. For up-to-the-minute details on opening hours call 824-4321.

Portobello Yacht Club: The elegant Bermuda-style house combines high gables and beamed ceilings, bright Mediterranean colors and earthy tones. This is one of two dining spots operated by the Levy Restaurants of Chicago, and one of our favorites on the WDW property. The 326-seat establishment is divided into several informal dining rooms, each of which displays an impressive collection of maritime memorabilia.

Food is the highlight of the *Portobello Yacht Club*. The bustling open kitchen turns out grilled meat and fish and absolutely delicious small, gourmet pizzas baked in their wood-burning oven. Try the quattro formaggi, a four-cheese pie that's a true taste treat, and a great appetizer or snack. Pasta offerings include *spaghettini alla Portobello*, pasta with shrimp, scallops, clams, mussels, crab legs, tomatoes, garlic, olive oil, wine, and herbs, and *bucatini all'amatriciana*, long pasta tubes with plum tomatoes, Italian bacon, garlic, and fresh basil. Be sure to save some room for desserts such as *crema bruccioto*, Italian custard with a caramelized sugar glaze or *cioccolato paradiso*, a rich layer cake with chocolate ganache frosting, chocolate toffee crunch filling, and warm caramel sauce. A children's menu is available. No reservations are accepted. Moderate to expensive. L, D, S.

Fireworks Factory: The other of the duo of eateries operated by the Levy Restaurants. The 400-seat dining spot features high ceilings juxtaposed with antique brick walls, metal stairs, and a floor stained with black gunpowder. Some of the props around the restaurant are on loan from the Gruccis, the famous fireworks family of New York. There are two dining rooms and a bar.

Upon entering, guests are invited into a casual atmosphere where they sit at bench tables topped with yellow tablecloths. Ribs are the specialty of the house: baby backs and Texas beef. They are seasoned with a blend of spices, slowly smoked over an applewood grill, and then doused in *Fireworks Factory's* own barbecue sauce.

MARDI GRAS JAZZ BRUNCH

Mardi Gras is every Sunday at the *Pleasure Island Jazz Company*. The Mardi Gras Jazz Brunch is an all-you-can-eat feast featuring such authentic Creole fare as crab cakes, red beans and rice, and chicken Louisianne. The menu also offers made-to-order omelettes, apple-cinnamon crêpes, and Champagne to wash it all down. The Dixieland Jazz Band keeps things lively.

And if you're still in the mood to groove, reentry to Pleasure Island that evening is included. Tickets cost $22 for adults and $12 for children under 12, including tax and gratuity; prepayment is required by credit card. There are two seatings; Reservations are necessary and can be made by calling 828-5636.

If you like what you eat—and hear—you might want to check out Pleasure Island's full-blown Mardi Gras celebration (this year, February 17–20).

But ribs aren't the only thing on the innovative menu. If all the appetizers sound good, try the appetizer sampler of spicy hot chicken wings, rock shrimp, quesadilla and applewood-smoked baby-back ribs. Entrées include grilled chicken, grilled steaks, and grilled pork chops. Dessert selections include Atomic Chocolate Cake, topped and filled with chocolate mousse, and coated with chocolate chips; turtle pie; Key lime pie; Edy's ice cream; and the Tollhouse Cookie Sundae, a large, warm Tollhouse cookie served in a cast-iron skillet and topped with vanilla ice cream and hot fudge.

A children's menu is available, as is a selection of T-shirts, sweatshirts, hats, and other items bearing the *Fireworks Factory* logo. *Fireworks'* special barbecue sauce also is available in jars to take home. Expensive. L, D.

Planet Hollywood: The newest Pleasure Island eatery, this branch of the international chain would be a stand-out if only for its unique architecture—it is designed in the shape of a sphere. Co-owned by Arnold Schwarzenegger, Sylvester Stallone, Bruce Willis, and Demi Moore, this globe is built on

three levels. Movie and television memorabilia abound. The wide-ranging menu features salads, sandwiches, pasta dishes, burgers, appetizer pizzas, fajitas, and dessert specialties. Moderate to expensive. L, D, S.

Hill Street Diner: Located next to Avigators Supply. Individual pizzas, sausage subs, chili dogs, and beer are served here. Inexpensive. L, D, S.

D-Zertz: Pastries, chocolates, candy, frozen yogurt, and other such sweet treats are the mouth-watering fare available here. Coffee and cappuccino also are served, making it a pleasant spot for a quick snack. Inexpensive. S.

Disney Village Marketplace

A couple of the World's more popular dining spots are located in this shopping enclave on the southeastern edge of the property. It's worth noting that while the restaurants hereabouts really hop at dinnertime, none is terribly crowded at lunch, except on Saturdays and Sundays, when Orlando and Kissimmee residents make the trip to the Disney Village Marketplace for a day of shopping. And these restaurants have the advantage of being just a couple of hundred yards' dash from the marina, so kids can go hire a pedal boat or a Water Sprite (during lunchtime and in late afternoon) while parents linger over coffee or drinks. **Note:** Those who have dined on the *Empress Lilly* riverboat, which is docked on the western edge of Buena Vista Lagoon, should know that the restaurants are now closed. Keep watch for something new here.

Donald's Dairy Dip: This is a perfect spot for ice cream. Milk shakes and hot-fudge sundaes are only a couple of the many tasty creations here. Assorted ice cream flavors, chocolate and vanilla soft-serve ice cream, and frozen yogurt are served. Inexpensive. S.

Cap'n Jack's Oyster Bar: The menu at this waterside spot is so full of good things—seafood marinara, shrimp, ceviche, crab claws, Maryland crab cakes, and baked garlic clams—that it's as good for a light lunch or dinner as it is for a snack, even though the place is nominally a lounge. *Cap'n Jack's* is a terrific place to be, especially in late afternoon, as the sun streams through the narrow-slatted blinds and glints on the polished tables and the copper above the bar. And the house's special frozen strawberry margaritas—made with fresh fruit, strawberry tequila, and a couple of other potent ingredients—are as tasty as they are beautiful. They're served in big balloon-shaped goblets, with a slice of lime astraddle the rim: tart, fruity, and altogether delightful. Moderate. L, D, S.

Minnie Mia's Italian Eatery: Pizza, pasta, and pasta salads are on the menu at this restaurant. Beer and soft drinks also are available. Inexpensive. L, D, S.

Goofy's Grill: This is the shopping area's fast-food spot, serving hamburgers and french fries—to eat inside or out, plus soft drinks, thick milk shakes, and beer. Inexpensive. L, D, S.

Chef Mickey's Village Restaurant: This unassuming dining room is one of the most pleasant restaurants in Walt Disney World. There are fine views of Buena Vista Lagoon, and the sunshine keeps a whole garden's worth of house plants robust and green all year. The restaurant serves a daily character breakfast in addition to dinner, and offers fresh Florida seafood and a variety of pasta dishes. Chef Mickey strolls through the dining room every evening. Adjoining the restaurant is the living-roomlike *Village Lounge*. Fitted out with comfortable club chairs, it's a great spot for after-dinner drinks. Reservations are necessary for Breakfast à la Disney, suggested for dinner, and can be made by calling 939-3463. Walk-ins are welcome but

there can be a wait. The hostess will provide you with a pager so that you can walk around the Marketplace and easily be alerted when your table is ready. Moderate. B, D.

Village Lounge: Located adjacent to *Chef Mickey's*, this relaxing spot is a good place to wait for a table at the restaurant. At Mickey's Cartoon Theater, located in the lounge, Disney classic cartoons are shown from 5 P.M. to 10 P.M. There also is a full-service bar.

CROSSROADS AT LAKE BUENA VISTA

WDW visitors also have several restaurants from which to choose at the Crossroads of Lake Buena Vista shopping center, across from Disney Village Hotel Plaza. These include *T.G.I. Friday's, Red Lobster, McDonald's, Taco Bell, Pebbles, Jungle Jim's, Johnny Rocket's, Chevy's Tex-Mex,* and *Pizzeria Uno.*

DISNEY VILLAGE HOTEL PLAZA

At the Buena Vista Palace: One of the state's finest restaurants, *Arthur's 27*, is here. It boasts a wonderful view over Walt Disney World Village, and the food and service are both excellent. Very expensive. D. The *Outback*, decorated in an Australian theme, serves dinner. Expensive. D. The gardenlike *Watercress Café & Bake Shop* offers full meals and snacks, as well as a character breakfast on Sundays. The bakery portion of the café is open 24 hours a day. Moderate. B, L, D, S.

At the Courtyard by Marriot: *Courtyard Café and Grille* serves an eclectic menu ranging from salads and sandwiches to seafood. There is a breakfast buffet, but guests also may order from an à la carte menu. Moderate. B, L, D. The *Village Deli* features sandwiches and items from *Pizza Hut* and *TCBY Yogurt*. Inexpensive. D, S. The *2 Go* is a breakfast bar and take-out facility adjacent to a casual dining area in the atrium lobby. Inexpensive. B.

At the Doubletree Guest Suites: *Streamers* offers classic American dishes as well as shrimp tortellini and filet mignon. There is a breakfast buffet. Moderate. B, L, D. The *Cool Pool Deli & Market* is a great spot for a snack, meal, or drink with sandwiches, salads, and hot items for eat-in or take-out service. Inexpensive. B, L, D, S.

At the Grosvenor: This highrise hotel features *Baskervilles*, a casual restaurant serving breakfast, lunch, and dinner in an atmosphere with a Sherlock Holmes theme. There is a Mystery Show here on Saturday nights as well as character breakfasts on Tuesdays, Thursdays, and Saturdays, and a character dinner on Wednesdays. Moderate. B, L, D. The *Crumpets* lobby café—open 24 hours—serves continental breakfast, snacks, and lighter fare. *Crickets* lounge serves espresso, cappuccino, and alcoholic beverages. Inexpensive. B, L, S.

At the Hilton: *Finn's Grill* offers fresh seafood and steaks in an old Key West atmosphere. Moderate. L, D. At the *Beni-*

hana Japanese steak house, chefs put on a tableside show as they cook up Japanese favorites. Moderate to expensive. D. The *County Fair* serves breakfast (with characters putting in an appearance on Sundays), lunch, and dinner. Moderate. B, L, D. For salads, sandwiches, or hamburgers alfresco, there's the *Rum Largo Pool Bar and Café*. Inexpensive. L, D, S. Or try the *County Fair Terrace*, an outdoor café offering salads, sandwiches, and pasta. Inexpensive. B, L, S. The *Old-Fashioned Soda Shoppe and Arcade* has everything from ice cream to pizza. Inexpensive. L, D, S.

At the Royal Plaza: The *Plaza Diner* serves family-style meals, table service, or buffet. Moderate. B, L, D, S. There is a deli for yogurt, espresso, and takeout.

At the Travelodge: *Traders* has a breakfast buffet and serves à la carte breakfast and dinner, with a focus on fresh seafood and steaks. Moderate. B, D. The *Parakeet Café* offers pizza, baked goods, salads, and snacks. Inexpensive. B, L, D, S.

Meal by Meal

When you're looking for something special in the way of a meal, and you're willing to go a bit out of your way to find it, the descriptions below should provide sufficient suggestions to sate your appetite. What follows are the highlights of WDW breakfasts, lunches, and dinners, as well as some suggestions for avoiding mealtime crowds at the eatery of your choice. This is a selective, not a comprehensive, list; for complete information see the preceding listings under "Restaurants of WDW."

DINING WITH DISNEY CHARACTERS

At some sites, food takes second place to Mickey Mouse, Donald Duck, Minnie Mouse, Goofy, and the rest of the Disney gang, who take turns making special appearances at these especially delightful affairs. Options abound, as the characters host meals throughout the day all over the World. Unless otherwise noted, character meals below are offered daily, and necessary reservations generally can be made up to 60 days in advance, by calling WDW-DINE (939-3463). Walk-ins are possible but highly unlikely for any except the *Swan*'s first-come, first-served character breakfasts (held Wednesdays and Saturdays at the hotel's *Garden Grove Café*). Bottomless buffets and all-you-can-eat family-style dining are the rule, particularly for breakfast, but specific offerings vary from place to place, so ask the reservationist to describe the food that's served at the character meal you'd like to attend. Finally, as you make note of the following menu of character affairs—organized by meal—keep in mind that the lineup is subject to change.

Breakfasts: Breakfast à la Disney, at *Chef Mickey's Village Restaurant* in the Disney Village Marketplace, is served banquet-style. The *Contemporary Café* in the *Contemporary* resort hosts an all-you-can-eat breakfast buffet with characters Mondays through Saturdays. Guests may also breakfast with characters at *1900 Park Fare* in the *Grand Floridian* resort; at *Cape May Café* in the *Beach Club* resort; at *Olivia's* at the *Disney Vacation Club* (Winnie the Pooh and friends hold court); at *Artist Point* in the *Wilderness Lodge* (here, it's called the Character Stampede); and at *'Ohana* in the *Polynesian* resort (where Minnie Menehune carries the South Seas theme). Character breakfasts also are served forth in the theme parks. More specifically, there is a "Once Upon A Time" breakfast at *King Stefan's* in the Magic Kingdom (for which reservations can be made just seven days ahead by calling 939-3463). At Epcot's *Garden Grill* restaurant, Farmer Mickey and Farmer Minnie put in appearances for special family-style breakfasts. And in the Disney-MGM Studios, Pocahontas, Captain John Smith, and Aladdin preside over breakfast at the *Soundstage* restaurant. Prices range from $12.95 to $14.95 for adults; cost is $7.95 for children ages three to nine.

Sunday brunches: The *Contemporary Café* in the *Contemporary* resort skips its usual character breakfast in favor of an equally bountiful character brunch each Sunday, while other Disney favorites are off hosting brunch at *Harry's Safari Bar & Grille* in the *Dolphin* resort (call 934-4025 ahead for reservations). Prices are about $15.95 for adults and prices range from $5.95 to $9.25 for children.

Lunches: The *Garden Grill* in Epcot's Future World offers homey fare, including rotisserie chicken and garden vegetables, in a lunch hosted by Farmer Mickey, Farmer Minnie, and friends. Cost is $16.95 for adults and $9.95 for children.

Dinners: The *Liberty Tree Tavern* in the Magic Kingdom hosts a character supper. The *Garden Grill* in Epcot's Future World offers an evening character meal that, like lunch, includes such menu choices as rotisserie chicken and fresh fish. Character dinners also are held at *1900 Park Fare* in the *Grand Floridian* resort. At the *Garden Grove Café* in the *Swan*, character dinners are offered Mondays, Thursdays, and Fridays (call 934-1609 to make necessary reservations). Prices are about $19.50 for adults, $9.95 for children.

Breakfast

Most people opt for eggs and bacon or something similar at their own hotel. But those who decide to go farther afield will be amazed at the choices available. For instance, the french toast served at the *Polynesian* resort's *Coral Isle Café* and *Tangaroa Terrace* restaurants is made with thick slices of real sourdough bread, stuffed with bananas, deep fried, and then rolled in cinnamon and sugar—and is one of the best breakfast concoctions ever.

At most breakfast spots in the hotels, there are likely to be lines between 8 A.M. and 10 A.M., the morning rush hour. So allow plenty of time at these hours, eat earlier or later, or stop at a snack shop for something light to stave off hunger until it's time for a lineless breakfast (or an early lunch). At many of the WDW resorts, it's also possible to order breakfast from room service the night before.

Except during the busiest periods, restaurants in the Magic Kingdom are good choices for quick morning meals. Most fast-food spots serve coffee and pastry from park opening until about 11 A.M. For a hearty breakfast, try the *Crystal Palace*.

In Epcot, the *Sunshine Season Food Fair* in The Land offers bagels and cream cheese, as well as eggs and delicious pastries. *Fountain View Espresso & Bakery* next to Innoventions has a great selection of pastries and coffees to enjoy in the morning.

At the Disney-MGM Studios, try a home-cooked breakfast at *Hollywood & Vine* or a coffee and a croissant at the *Starring Rolls Bakery*.

Lunch

Breaking up a day in the theme parks with lunch at one of the resorts can provide the energy needed to keep you going until closing time. A few of the eating spots do get crowded around midday, but the *Coral Isle Café* at the *Polynesian* resort tends to be exceptionally peaceful.

Choice lunch spots in the Disney Village Marketplace are *Minnie Mia's Italian Eatery* and *Cap'n Jack's Oyster Bar*. At Pleasure Island, there are delicious pizzas-for-one at the *Portobello Yacht Club*. Barbecued ribs and chicken are on the menu at the *Fireworks Factory*. Burgers, unique salads, and desserts are good at *Planet Hollywood*. Or for something lighter try the frozen yogurt at *D-Zertz*.

If you can't tear yourself away from the Magic Kingdom for even an hour to go elsewhere for lunch, there's still no lack of selection. Burgers and french fries are for sale at practically every turn, but better yet there are the salads, sandwiches, and pizza at *Tony's Town Square* restaurant; the sandwiches and seafood salads served (seasonally) at *Columbia Harbour House* in Liberty Square; the pasta dishes and salads available at the *Crystal Palace* on Main Street; the clam chowder and oysters served at the *Liberty Tree Tavern* in Liberty Square; the pizza at *Plaza Pavilion Terrace Dining* in Tomorrowland; and the salads at *King Stefan's Banquet Hall* in Cinderella Castle.

As at breakfast, crowds can be a problem; the three hours between 11 A.M. and 2 P.M. are the busiest. To avoid the rush, eat a light breakfast and a big early lunch—or have a late breakfast and a late lunch. If necessary, snatch a mid-morning snack to tide you over until things get less hectic.

In Epcot, midday is a good time to sample some of the full-service restaurants offering ethnic specialties. Linger over their culinary delights, out of the heat of the midday sun, while crowds of other guests are lining up for attractions. Try not to miss the Scotch eggs in the *Rose & Crown*, the beef stew and the pastries at *Chefs de France*, and the Mexican

court; salads, ribs, grilled chicken, and fresh fruit at the *Hollywood & Vine Cafeteria*; chili, charbroiled chicken, and burgers at the *Backlot Express*; salads and healthful fast food at the *Commissary*; or sandwiches, salads, and barbecued pork ribs at the *Sci-Fi Dine-In Theater* restaurant.

Dinner

There's an awesome choice, from the humblest snack center to *Victoria & Albert's*. Walt Disney World is not exactly a bastion of haute cuisine, but that doesn't mean that dinner experiences are anything less than pleasant. Service is almost unfailingly good (slipping just slightly during the busiest seasons), and the best of Walt Disney World's dinners are just fine. For a night on the World, some good choices are the *Portobello Yacht Club* at Pleasure Island; *Chef Mickey's Village Restaurant* at the Disney Village Marketplace; *Victoria & Albert's* at the *Grand Floridian* resort; *'Ohana* at the *Polynesian* resort; *Ariel's* at the *Beach Club* resort; the *Yachtsman Steakhouse* at the *Yacht Club* resort; *California Grill* at the *Contemporary* resort; and the *Hollywood Brown Derby* at the Disney-MGM Studios.

FOR FAMILY FARE: Children are welcome at every WDW restaurant, but the leisurely pace of service at some places can make kids fidget. Still, there are plenty of choices that are well suited to dining *en famille*. Restaurants at the resorts especially good for families are the *Concourse Steak House* and the *Contemporary Café* at the *Contemporary* resort, *Boatwright's Dining Hall* at *Dixie Landings*, and *Bonfamille's Café* at *Port Orleans*. The buffet-style clambake held in *Cape May Café* at the *Beach Club* resort is a hit with kids, (as is any other buffet-style meal where they can

queso fundido at Mexico's *San Angel Inn* restaurant. The *Biergarten* has lively entertainment throughout the day and evening. But for burgers and other standard fast-food fare, try the *Electric Umbrella* restaurant in Innoventions or *Liberty Inn* in The American Adventure. The *Sunshine Season Food Fair* in The Land offers a huge variety, from baked potatoes, soups, and salads to barbecued sandwiches and more—and is therefore a good choice for a family that can't arrive at a consensus. The pizza quiche offered at the *Cheese Shoppe* there is a favorite, and the chocolate chip cookies from the nearby bakery make a good dessert. Ethnic fast foods are available at Japan's *Yakitori House*, China's *Lotus Blossom Café*, Norway's *Kringla Bakeri og Kafe*, and Mexico's *Cantina de San Angel*.

Among full-service eateries, the *Garden Grill* is special for its imaginatively conceived regional American offerings. In World Showcase, meat pies and Epcot's best salad (the fresh vegetable platter) may be found at the *Rose & Crown Pub & Dining Room*; stir-fried meats and vegetables are the prime fare in the *Mitsukoshi* restaurants; Moroccan sampler platters are offered at *Marrakesh*; Chinese specialties are served at the *Nine Dragons* restaurant; hearty German food is offered in Germany's *Biergarten*; and fairly authentic Mexican fare comprises the menu in Mexico's *San Angel Inn* restaurant. An enormous buffet is served at *Akershus* in Norway. The delightful *Au Petit Café* on the World Showcase Promenade in France is the only sit-down restaurant that doesn't require reservations, but the waiting line is often long. The most elaborate cooking is done at Italy's *Alfredo's* and at France's *Chefs de France*.

At the Disney-MGM Studios, try the famous Cobb Salad at the *Hollywood Brown Derby*; a good home-cooked meal served by "Mom" at the *50's Prime Time Café*; soups, salads, pastas, and sandwiches at the *Soundstage* food

serve themselves). The food courts at the *Caribbean Beach*, *Port Orleans*, *Dixie Landings,* and the *All-Star Sports* and *All-Star Music* resorts are other good choices for finicky eaters. The best choice for villa guests, and a favorite with kids and adults alike, is *Chef Mickey's Village Restaurant*.

Most of the restaurants at the Magic Kingdom cater to kids, but *Pecos Bill Café* (for burgers and fries) and *Tony's Town Square* (for pizza) get particularly high marks. At Epcot, *Pasta Piazza Ristorante* and *Liberty Inn* are top picks for kids who love fast food.

At the Disney-MGM Studios, kids particularly enjoy the *50's Prime Time Café* and the *Sci-Fi Dine-In Theater*. Other options include a quicker meal at one of the other eateries: the *Soundstage* food court, the *Hollywood & Vine,* the *Commissary*, *Min & Bill's Dockside Diner*, or the *Backlot Express*.

WDW restaurants outside the Magic Kingdom are busiest in the evening between 7 P.M. and 9 P.M. Those in the Magic Kingdom are busiest between 5 P.M. and 7 P.M.

During busy seasons, guests visiting the Magic Kingdom will do well to eat a late lunch and have dinner after 8 P.M. in order to catch the second, less crowded showing of SpectroMagic. Those traveling with young children should plan to eat their meals on the early side and take in the first show.

About Reservations

In some WDW restaurants, it's first-come, first-served. The lines that result can be avoided by eating early or late—or by choosing one of the many restaurants that accept dinner reservations. There is one central phone number for making meal reservations; call WDW-DINE (939-3463). All guests can book tables at the resort and theme park restaurants listed below up to 60 days in advance; the number of tables available depends upon the season. If you are unable to book a table in advance, we suggest you call again, since it is possible that more tables will open up. If all else fails, try to make reservations in person on the day of your visit.

There are several exceptions. Reservations for dinner shows—the Hoop-Dee-Doo Musical Revue, Mickey's Tropical Luau, and the Polynesian Luau—can be made up to two years in advance for all guests. If you can't get a place for an early performance, try for a later one (usually less heavily booked). Reservations for the restaurants at the *Swan* and *Dolphin* resorts can be made through each hotel's concierge; phone numbers are listed below.

See the reservation chart in *Getting Ready to Go* for more information. Walt Disney World reservation policies are subject to change. With this in mind, call to check which policy will be in effect during your visit. **Note:** Reservations are held for only 15 minutes.

BEACH CLUB RESORT: *Ariel's, Cape May Café.*

CONTEMPORARY RESORT: *California Grill, Concourse Steak House, Contemporary Café.*

DOLPHIN RESORT: *Harry's Safari Bar & Grille, Sum Chows,* and *Juan & Only's Cantina* (934-4025).

GRAND FLORIDIAN RESORT: *Victoria & Albert's, Flagler's, Narcoossee's,* and *1900 Park Fare.*

POLYNESIAN RESORT: *'Ohana, Tangaroa Terrace.*

SWAN RESORT: *Palio* (934-1609).

WILDERNESS LODGE RESORT: *Artist Point.*

YACHT CLUB RESORT: *Yachtsman Steakhouse, Yacht Club Galley.*

MAGIC KINGDOM: Reservations are accepted at *Tony's Town Square* restaurant, *King Stefan's Banquet Hall* in Cinderella Castle, and *Liberty Tree Tavern* in Liberty Square. Reservations also can be made in person on the same day.

EPCOT: Refer to the box on page 223.

DISNEY-MGM STUDIOS: Reservations are accepted at the *Hollywood Brown Derby*, *Mama Melrose's Ristorante Italiano*, the *Sci-Fi Dine-In Theater*, and the *50's Prime Time Café.* You also can make reservations in person on the same day.

DISNEY VILLAGE MARKETPLACE: *Chef Mickey's Village Restaurant.*

DINNER SHOWS

The fact that the Disney organization is the king of family entertainment is nowhere more strongly apparent than amid the whooping and hollering troupe of singers and dancers who race toward the stage at *Fort Wilderness* resort's Pioneer Hall. As you plow through barbecued ribs, fried chicken, corn-on-the-cob, and strawberry shortcake, those enthusiastic performers sing, dance, and joke up a storm. This is the Hoop-Dee-Doo Musical Revue, presented nightly at 5 P.M., 7:15 P.M., and 9:30 P.M. Cost is $36.04 per adult, $26.50 for juniors (12 through 20), and $18.02 for children (3 through 11).

Mickey's Tropical Luau, presented daily at 4:30 P.M. at the *Polynesian* resort, is a Polynesian show aimed at the younger set. Disney characters, dressed in traditional costumes, dance along with the Polynesian performers. A full dinner complete with dessert is served. Cost is $29.68 for adults, $22.79 for juniors, and $13.25 for children.

The Polynesian Luau at the *Polynesian* resort, presented nightly at 6:45 P.M. and 9:30 P.M., also has its moments. The performers' dancing is some of the most authentic this side of Hawaii. Many of the WDW dancers have studied at the well-respected Polynesian Cultural Center in Hawaii. A full Polynesian-style meal, including frozen piña coladas and a tropical fruit dessert is served. Cost is $33.92 for adults, $25.97 for juniors, and $17.49 for children.

The *Biergarten* at Epcot's Germany pavilion entertains diners both during lunch and throughout the evening with intermittent shows, featuring traditional German musicians, yodelers, and dancers. A hearty buffet is served. Lunch is $9.95 for adults, $3.99 for children; dinner is $14.50 for adults, $3.99 for children.

Plan to arrive 15 minutes or so before starting time, and allow enough time for transportation and parking. (Prices, which include tax, are subject to change and do not include gratuity.)

Reservations for all these shows can be made by calling WDW-DINE (939-3463); they are required well in advance and are generally hard to come by. Groups of eight or more should call 939-7707.

SCOOPS, SUNDAES, AND SOFT SERVE

BY THE SCOOP

HOTELS: Assorted flavors and sundaes at the *Dolphin Fountain* at the *Dolphin* resort; *Beaches & Cream Soda Shop* at the *Yacht Club* and *Beach Club* resorts; *Sassagoula Floatworks & Food Factory* at *Port Orleans*; *Southern Trace Bakery* at *Dixie Landings*; and *Cinnamon Bay Bakery* at the *Caribbean Beach.*
MAGIC KINGDOM: *Liberty Tree Tavern*, *Tony's Town Square* restaurant, *Plaza Ice Cream Parlor*, *Plaza* restaurant, and *King Stefan's Banquet Hall.*
EPCOT: The ice cream stand at *Sunshine Season Food Fair* in The Land.
DISNEY-MGM STUDIOS: *Dinosaur Gertie's.*
DISNEY VILLAGE MARKETPLACE: *Donald's Dairy Dip.*

ASSORTED SUPER SUNDAES

HOTELS: *Narcoossee's* at the *Grand Floridian* (custard, berries, seven scoops of ice cream, whipped cream, and amaretto); super sundaes at the *Dolphin Fountain* in the *Dolphin* resort; and *Coral Isle Café* at the *Polynesian* resort.
MAGIC KINGDOM: *Plaza Ice Cream Parlor* and the *Plaza* restaurant on Main Street.
PLEASURE ISLAND: Tollhouse Cookie Sundae at the *Fireworks Factory.*
DISNEY-MGM STUDIOS: *50's Prime Time Café* (hot fudge, caramel, marshmallow, or the works); *Sci-Fi Dine-In Theater.*
DISNEY VILLAGE MARKETPLACE: *Donald's Dairy Dip.*

SOFT SERVE

HOTELS: *Captain Cook's Snack and Ice Cream Company* at the *Polynesian* resort; *Food and Fun Center* at the *Contemporary* resort; *Gasparilla Grill and Games* at the *Grand Floridian* resort; *Trail's End Buffet* at the *Fort Wilderness* resort; *Southern Trace Bakery* at Dixie Landings resort; and *Cinnamon Bay Bakery* at the *Caribbean Beach* resort.
MAGIC KINGDOM: *Mrs. Potts' Cupboard*; *Enchanted Grove*; *Aloha Isle*; *Sunshine Tree Terrace*; and *Aunt Polly's Landing.*
EPCOT: *Refreshment Port*; *Refreshment Outpost*; and *Electric Umbrella.*
DISNEY-MGM STUDIOS: *Studio Catering Co.*
DISNEY VILLAGE MARKETPLACE: *Donald's Dairy Dip.*

FROZEN YOGURT

HOTELS: *Intermission* food court at the *All-Star Music* resort; the *End Zone* food court at the *All-Star Sports* resort; *Sassagoula Floatworks & Food Factory* at *Port Orleans.*
MAGIC KINGDOM: *Auntie Gravity's Galactic Goodies*; *Sunshine Tree Terrace.*
EPCOT: *Pure & Simple*; *Sunshine Season Food Fair*; *Beverage Base* in *Electric Umbrella*; *Refreshment Port*; and *Refreshment Outpost.*
DISNEY-MGM STUDIOS: *Min & Bill's Dockside Diner.*
DISNEY VILLAGE MARKETPLACE: *Donald's Dairy Dip.*
PLEASURE ISLAND: *D-Zertz.*

LEMON SHERBET PUNCH

MAGIC KINGDOM: *Liberty Tree Tavern.*

INTERNATIONAL TREATS

EPCOT: Specialties at *L'Originale Alfredo di Roma Ristorante* include Italian concoctions like spumoni and tortoni. For a Mexican treat, visit *San Angel Inn* for *helada con cajeta* (vanilla ice cream with caramel topping).

Lounges

Tambu Lounge: Cozy and clublike, this lounge adjoining the *'Ohana* restaurant is open daily beginning at 2 P.M., and offers a menu of Polynesian-style appetizers. The bartenders have some entertaining tricks up their sleeves. Open from 2 P.M. until midnight.

GRAND FLORIDIAN: The four lounges reflect the Old Florida theme of the hotel.
Garden View Lounge: A view of the lushly landscaped pool and garden area makes this watering hole a pleasant place to relax. Afternoon tea also is served here.
Mizner's Lounge: Named after the eccentric architect who defined much of the flavor of southeastern Florida's Gold Coast, this lounge is on the second floor of the main building.
Summerhouse: This bar serves guests at the pool and beach.
Narcoossee's: An unusual manner of service allows guests to choose from a mug, a half-yard, or a yard of beer. And they mean a yard.

CARIBBEAN BEACH: The tropical theme of the hotel carries through to the lounges here.
Captain's Tavern: Tropical drinks, beer, wine, and cocktails are served at this lounge at Old Port Royale. Chicken, crab legs, and specialty items from the restaurant also are available from 5 P.M. to 10 P.M.
Banana Cabana: Drinks and a variety of snacks are available at this poolside bar.

DISNEY VACATION CLUB: The **Gurgling Suitcase** on the Turtle Krawl boardwalk serves an assortment of Key West specialties along with traditional cocktails, beer, wine, and soft drinks.

N o one ever said the Magic Kingdom's no-liquor policy means that everyone in the World is a teetotaler. Actually, some of WDW's tastiest offerings are liquid (and decidedly alcoholic), and some of its most entertaining places are its bars and lounges.

CONTEMPORARY RESORT: The watering holes here are sleek and offer great views and atmosphere aplenty.
California Grill Lounge: Prime 15th-story digs eye-level to the Magic Kingdom fireworks combine with California wines and other drinks in this spot adjoining the *California Grill*. Open from 5 P.M. to midnight.
Outer Rim Cocktail Lounge: Overlooking Bay Lake, this lounge serves cocktails, appetizers and desserts.

POLYNESIAN: The resort's Polynesian theme has inspired a whole raft of deceptively potent potables like Seven Seas (fruit juice, grenadine, orange curaçao, and rum), Chi Chis (a standard piña colada made with vodka instead of rum), and WDW piña coladas (which include orange juice in addition to rum, pineapple, and coconut cream). There's even a special Polynesian village nonalcoholic treat—the pink Lei-Lani, an orange juice and strawberry mixture.
Barefoot Bar: Adjoining the swimming pool lagoon, serving soda, draft beer, piña coladas, frozen daiquiris, mai tais, and various other mixed drinks. Open from 11 A.M. until 7 P.M. (summer hours extended), weather permitting.

SWAN: A lobby lounge offers pleasant surroundings in which to sip a drink.

Lobby Court Lounge: The winding corridors of the hotel lobby have comfortable couches and chairs, punctuated by pianos where able musicians perform. Drinks as well as specialty coffees are available.

DOLPHIN: The entertaining hotel theme is carried through to its watering holes.

Copa Banana: The wooden tabletops are designed as slices of fruit, and the Caribbean-style appetizers match the surroundings. Deejay music is featured in the evenings.

Harry's Safari Bar: Join the peripatetic "Harry" for a drink and maybe a story or two.

Only's Bar: Partake of the festive atmosphere at *Juan & Only's Cantina*, even if all you want is a drink. Sample rare tequilas and beers from every region of Mexico.

YACHT CLUB: A variety of nautical themes dominate the drinking spots here.

Ale and Compass: Located in the lobby and offering a specialty drink menu including coffee and ale. The bar is open until 11 P.M.

Crew's Cup Lounge: Styled after a New England waterfront pub, this lounge has a masculine feel to it. It's right next door to the *Yachtsman Steakhouse*, has almost 40 beers on hand, and is a choice spot for a drink before dinner.

BEACH CLUB: The two lounges here retain the beachfront feel of the rest of the hotel.

Rip Tide Lounge: This lobby bar features California wines, wine coolers, and frosty drinks that are consistent with the hotel's beachside theme. It also is open until 11 P.M.

Martha's Vineyard Lounge: A light and airy atmosphere prevails at this spot right next to *Ariel's*. Wines from a Martha's Vineyard winery, as well as selections from California, Long Island, and European vineyards, are on the extensive list.

PORT ORLEANS: The hotel's New Orleans theme is reflected in the lounges.

Scat Cat's Club: Traditional offerings from the bar plus light hors d'oeuvres and snacks. There is musical entertainment here five nights a week.

Mardi Grogs: Specialty drinks, popcorn, hot dogs, and hot pretzels are available at this poolside spot.

DIXIE LANDINGS: The two lounges each possess a certain degree of charm.

Cotton Co-Op: Situated in a room designed as a cotton exchange, this lounge features specialty drinks and some light hors d'oeuvres. There is entertainment here five nights a week.

Muddy Rivers: The poolside bar serves snacks and drinks during pool hours.

WILDERNESS LODGE: There is a lounge and a poolside bar located at this rustic resort.

Territory Lounge: Located between *Artist Point* and the *Whispering Canyon Café*, this is a pleasant place to relax with appetizers and drinks. Microbrewed beer and espresso are available.

Trout Pass: This poolside bar serves snacks and your favorite specialty drinks throughout the day.

FORT WILDERNESS: Beer and sangría are served in Pioneer Hall. **Crockett's Tavern** serves cocktails, specialty drinks, appetizers, and full meals. For a change of pace, take a blue-flagged watercraft to the *Contemporary*

shrimp, and seafood marinara are great for a snack, but also substantial enough for a light lunch or dinner.

Village Lounge: This boîte, comfortable as a living room, is one of the World's best-kept secrets. Disney cartoons are shown in the evening to entertain kids while waiting for a table at the adjacent *Chef Mickey's Village Restaurant*.

PLEASURE ISLAND: All the clubs have bars that serve specialty drinks (with and without alcohol), beer, wine, and mixed drinks. The *Fireworks Factory* and the *Portobello Yacht Club* also have pleasant lounges.

EPCOT: All restaurants, including some of the counter-service establishments, offer alcoholic beverages with meals. Restaurants such as *Garden Grill* and the *San Angel Inn* have small lounges at which patrons may wait for tables.

Then there are a few places that specialize in spirituous liquid refreshments:

Rose & Crown Pub & Dining Room: The pub section of this watering hole that's part of the United Kingdom pavilion is a veritable symphony of polished woods, brass, and etched glass. British, Irish, and Scottish beers are available, along with a score of specialty drinks and appetizing snacks imported from the other side of the Atlantic.

Matsu No Ma Lounge: In addition to the exotic sake-based specialty drinks available here, this Japan pavilion establishment offers a fine panoramic view over the whole of Epcot—including the World Showcase Lagoon with Spaceship Earth as a backdrop—one of the best vistas of the property available.

Sommerfest: Just outside the *Biergarten* restaurant in Germany there's a small shaded terrace where soft pretzels, bratwurst, Black Forest cake, steins of Beck's beer, and German wine are available.

resort. Be sure to check the operating hours before boarding so that you don't miss the last trip back. Or, if you have a car, make the short drive to the Disney Village Marketplace or Pleasure Island.

ALL-STAR SPORTS AND ALL-STAR MUSIC RESORTS: These two resorts each have a poolside bar.

Team Spirits Pool Bar: A selection of spirits, wines, and beer is available at this poolside spot.

Singing Spirits Pool Bar: Enjoy your favorite spirits, wines, and beer alongside the pool.

DISNEY-MGM STUDIOS: The settings of the lounges here are their main attraction.

Catwalk Bar: Above the *Soundstage* restaurant is the 90-seat full-service cocktail lounge designed to resemble a movie prop storage area. Appetizers, specialty drinks, beer, and wine are served.

Tune-In Lounge: A sitcom living room setting, with couches, chairs, and fold-up TV dinner tray tables, is found at this lounge adjacent to the *50's Prime Time Café*. Waiters in V-neck sweaters play the roles of sitcom "Dads," and old television sets play scenes from beloved sitcoms. Appetizers, mixed drinks, beer, and wine are served.

DISNEY VILLAGE MARKETPLACE: A couple of Walt Disney World's most enticing lounges are located here.

Cap'n Jack's Oyster Bar: Agleam with copper and right on the water, this bar's specialty is its delicious strawberry margaritas, made with strawberry tequila and fresh strawberries. The nibbles of baked garlic clams, crab claws, Maryland crab cakes,

MORE SPECIAL NIGHTTIME FUN

The Magic Kingdom, open late during several busy periods of the year, takes on additional dazzle after dark. In peak seasons, there's SpectroMagic, a procession so spectacular that it alone is worth the trip to Walt Disney World—even though it's necessary to visit during a busy period in order to see it. Epcot is particularly lovely at night, when the lights sparkle on the lagoon, Spaceship Earth is all aglow, and IllumiNations lights up the sky. The Disney-MGM Studios is home to WDW's best fireworks show, Sorcery in the Sky.

But there are always a dozen or so other special happenings and events going on after dark throughout WDW. Call 824-4321 to find out what's in store during your visit.

FANTASY IN THE SKY: During summer and holidays when the Magic Kingdom is open late, there are fireworks at 10 P.M. nightly. The show lasts five to ten minutes, but packs as much dazzle as those shows many times its length.

SPECTROMAGIC: The Magic Kingdom's biggest extravaganza, this parade makes its way down Main Street twice each night during busy seasons. The advanced technology incorporates holograms, special lighting techniques, and a state-of-the-art sound system.

ILLUMINATIONS: This nightly show is an absolutely spectacular display of music, laser lights, fireworks, and dancing water fountains that can be seen from any point on the World Showcase Promenade at Epcot, usually at closing time. Check at Guest Relations for the exact time.

SORCERY IN THE SKY: Every night during busy seasons, this ten-minute pyrotechnical production outshines the stars over the Disney-MGM Studios' Chinese Theatre. It features music from the silver screen and narration by Vincent Price, and stands out as the best fireworks show on Disney's evening lineup.

CAMPFIRE PROGRAM: This event at *Fort Wilderness*, held nightly near the Meadow Trading Post at the center of the campground, features a sing-along, Disney movies, and cartoons. Open only to Walt Disney World resort guests.

TENNIS: Courts at the *Contemporary*, *Grand Floridian*, *Fort Wilderness*, *Yacht Club* and *Beach Club*, *Disney Vacation Club*, and *The Villas at The Disney Institute* are usually open until 9 P.M. Those at the *Dolphin* and *Swan* are available for play 24 hours a day. (See *Sports*.)

ELECTRICAL WATER PAGEANT: Best seen from the nearest beach on Bay Lake, this sparkling show is composed of a 1,000-foot-long string of illuminated floating creatures. Guest Services or City Hall can tell you when and where it can be seen—usually it's visible at 9 P.M. from the *Polynesian*, 9:20 P.M. from the *Grand Floridian*, 9:35 P.M. from the *Wilderness Lodge*, 9:45 P.M. from *Fort Wilderness*, and 10:05 P.M. from the *Contemporary*.

Index